Unmoored

Unmoored

The Search for Sincerity in Colonial America

Ana Schwartz

PUBLISHED BY THE
Omohundro Institute of Early American History
and Culture, Williamsburg, Virginia,
AND THE
University of North Carolina Press,
Chapel Hill

The Omohundro Institute of Early American History and Culture (OI)
is sponsored by William and Mary. On November 15, 1996,
the OI adopted the present name in honor of a bequest from
Malvern H. Omohundro, Jr., and Elizabeth Omohundro.

Jacket illustrations: *The Royal Reliquary*, by Craig Swan.
Each component 3" × 5" ink and design marker on Moleskine notebook paper, 2015.

Library of Congress Cataloging-in-Publication Data

Names: Schwartz, Ana, author. | Omohundro Institute of Early American History &
Culture, issuing body.
Title: Unmoored : the search for sincerity in colonial America / Ana Schwartz.
Description: Williamsburg, Virginia : The Omohundro Institute of Early American History
and Culture ; Chapel Hill : The University of North Carolina Press, [2023] | Includes
bibliographical references and index.
Identifiers: LCCN 2022024394 | ISBN 9781469671772 (cloth ; alk. paper) |
ISBN 9781469671789 (ebook)
Subjects: LCSH: Puritans—New England—History—17th century. | Puritans—New
England—Social life and customs—17th century. | Sincerity—History—17th century. |
New England—History—Colonial period, ca. 1600–1775. | New England—Social life and
customs—17th century.
Classification: LCC F7 .S35 2023 | DDC 974/.02—dc23/eng/20220601
LC record available at https://lccn.loc.gov/2022024394

FOR MY PARENTS' PARENTS

Acknowledgments

T HE MOTIVATION to write this book began in an observation about friendship, debt, and two strange lists. Two seventeenth-century frontier autobiographers, one an insomniac tobacco-lover, the other an unlucky barrel maker, both concluded their memoirs of misfortune by insisting, against unidentified doubts to the contrary, that they really did have friends. They had so many friends, in fact, that they felt it exigent to identify all of them by name. They doubted because of their debts, this book's fifth chapter proposes. In response to these deep material debts, they began to worry that friendship from a situation of need was not, perhaps, as real as the aphorisms have decreed. The rest of the chapters were researched and written in order to explain the sources of that doubt. As I researched and wrote and then revised them, my own experience of friendship changed. I wouldn't say that I sit now in the center of all beauty, but because of new friendships and new debts, I no longer scramble in the metaphorical schoolyard alone, hiding behind trees and insisting to others that I am an intellectual orphan.

One of my starkest debts is to the School of the Humanities, Arts and Social Sciences at the Massachusetts Institute of Technology, more specifically the Literature Section. I am very grateful for the care and attention of Sandy Alexandre, Eugenie Brinkema, Diana Henderson, and Ruth Perry. I hope the beaver who stars in the second chapter makes the Institute and the Literature faculty proud.

The Diversity Predoctoral Fellowship year at MIT allowed me to synthesize almost three-quarters of a decade of learning from faculty and colleagues at Penn English. I have been grateful in particular for the advising of Max Cavitch and David Kazanjian. It matters to me that they not be displeased with this book. Several very early drafts of these chapters circulated first on either side of Walnut Street: at a Brown Bag workshop at the McNeil Center for Early American Studies and at the AmLit and Theorizing reading groups.

I appreciate the years of work by the respective coordinators of those groups and the responses of my English Department colleagues. Best among these have been the friendship and wisdom of Jazmín Delgado-Shah, Evelyn Soto, and Najnin Islam. Cliff Mak and Grace Lavery continue to be models for the sort of thinking and writing I hope to practice. And of course, I am especially thankful to Kelly Rich and Alice McGrath for teaching me why friendship and sincerity merit critique. Beyond Fisher-Bennett, I have appreciated the vivid insights into intergenerational relations I acquired during the time I spent working at Friends' Central School, the Kelly Writers House, and Riepe College House under the leadership of Marilynne Diggs-Thompson. The book's fourth chapter was one outcome of many challenging conversations I had with various young people there. I am very grateful for Hector Kilgoe and Alli Katz as early companions in developing the insights of that chapter. A little bit before leaving Philadelphia, Gina Patnaik asked me whether I thought Anne Bradstreet thought that she was pretty. This question indirectly catalyzed the argument about shame that is this book's third chapter, which was further helped along by conversations with Devorah Fischler and M. Ty. These friends made a period of great shame bearable by helping me find better ways of thinking about it. Mike McKee, finally, offered me dear opportunities to articulate and revise the critique of Protestant optimism that appears across this book's chapters.

At Montclair State, so many faculty colleagues were encouraging and supportive of this research, most of all Jeffrey Gonzalez and Patricia Matthew. Since then, Texas has introduced me to many more wonderful interlocutors. All my work at UT English has been made possible by the expertise and support of the department staff, Cecilia Smith-Morris, Andrea Golden, Susana Castillo, and especially Jené Gutiérrez. Within the department, my colleagues have been supportive in so many ways, and I am particularly grateful to those who read drafts of different parts of this project and shared written feedback. These colleagues include Martin Kevorkian, Gretchen Murphy, Alison Kafer, Jorie Woods, and especially Heather Houser and Samantha Pinto, without whose friendship, advice, and exemplary scholarship this book would look very different, certainly worse. I found great encouragement and motivation from two writing groups of the Before Times, and I'm very grateful to Alison Kafer and Karma Chavez for organizing them. When in-person writing groups weren't possible anymore, Zoom facilitated wider intellectual networks. I benefited from several groups of collaborators: Xine Yao and Monica Huerta; Mary Grace Albanese and Clare Callahan; John Kuhn and his knowledge of Herbert, Hobbes, and hammocks; Heather Finch, Leila Mansouri, Rachel

Trocchio, and SJ Zhang; Abby Goode, Shelby Johnson, Blevin Shelnutt, Evelyn Soto, and Jessica Taylor; and the seven eighth First Book Institute colleagues brought together by Sean Goudie and Priscilla Wald—Faith Barter, Andrew Belton, David Hollingshead, Renee Hudson, Justin Mann, Paul Nadal, and Danica Savonick. Sarah Rivett and Lisa Brooks generously agreed to do this book's workshop online in a period of great upheaval. And Dustin Stewart and Courtney Weiss Smith continue to provide tremendous intellectual support. Jordan Stein read a full draft of this manuscript and shared incisive, energizing feedback. Along with Jordan, Kirsten Silva Gruesz, Kelly Wisecup, and Jonathan Beecher Field vouched for this project's potential at key thresholds. Marion Rust has, too. Her leadership at *Early American Literature* has coincided with my emergence as a remotely serious scholar, and I have valued all of her guidance and advice, not just for the essay that eventually turned into the first chapter of this book. Of the many conference panels where I've shared parts of this project, I am especially grateful for the encouragement from the 2019 ACLA panel that Andrea Gadberry and Gerard Passannante organized and for my copanelists' advice to be bolder in articulating the proposition about Foucault's career that is now central to the Introduction.

Ajay Batra has listened to me narrate all the turns in this book's journey. He continues to make it possible for me to "think my thoughts," as if, after all this, I could really call them mine anymore. I regret that while revising this project I couldn't think up more jokes to make him laugh.

On the other hand, these revisions might have gone more quickly if I had known what a pleasure it would be to work with the folks at the Omohundro Institute. Cathy Kelly gave me some excellent insights in the last stages of substantial manuscript revision. Kathy Burdette's lessons on prose exposition continue to guide me. And every email Emily Suth sends is a pleasure to read.

Many people in Texas have helped me see new aspects to friendship and selfhood than I could imagine back when I started this project. I hope these brilliant friends are bored at the redundancy of reading my debt to them here: Ashley Farmer, Ade Adamson, Pavithra Vasudevan, Snehal Patel, Mónica Jiménez, Roger Reeves, Nicole Burrowes, Chelsi West, Ashanté Reese, Bedour Alagraa, Traci Wint, Ty Haylies, Jo Hsu, and Aaron Sandel. If not bored, at least not embarrassed.

In my first semester after transferring to UC Berkeley as an undergrad, Kathleen Donegan introduced me to Ann Needham Hett, the elusive figure who is the protagonist of this book's Conclusion and an individual whose misfortune taught me something urgent that I could not easily put into words. The people listed here have made it possible for me explain this, both to myself and hopefully to others. A few months before that encounter, Melissa Kort took me and several community college classmates to the Berkeley Rep to see what was, for many of us, our first professional play. It was a stage adaptation of a Dickens novel, and there was an artfully dodgy twist about a third of the way through that turned me inside out. I wish Professor Kort knew how transformative that experience of art had been. Because she won't be able to read my attempt to approximate it here, I hope some of that delight carries forward to you, whoever you are, holding these words now in your hand.

Contents

List of Illustrations

Unmoored

Great Expectations

The Promise of Sincerity

S INCERITY IS THE protagonist of this book; history, its antagonist. The following five chapters tell a story of the former's struggle to forget the latter. The curtain rises on Anne Eaton, who might have preferred to walk off the stage and watch their contest rather than live their struggle herself. Yes, despite her superlatively comfortable status in her neighborhood, Anne Eaton was unhappy. She lived in the still-very-young American colony that English settlers had named New Haven, and within that colony, she lived richly, in a "magnificent household with seventeen fireplaces, numerous rooms in different colors, and costly furnishings." Eaton shared this household with her second husband, the wealthiest man in New Haven, Theophilus Eaton; even after they separated, she remained materially comfortable because she had inherited, on trust from her first husband, a fortune that would (after investment by her grandson in the slave trade out of Madras) begin Yale University's endowment. Yet her tenacious frustrations rose to such a pitch that, in 1644, rumors of domestic violence obliged the Eatons' next-door neighbor, minister John Davenport, to investigate. In Davenport's eyes, Eaton was deeply dissatisfied with her home life on the frontier between English colonists and their Algonquian neighbors. She disliked Theophilus, who was also governor of the seven-year-old colony, and she disliked her stepchildren, her mother-in-law, her white servants, and the enslaved Native and African captives in her household. But Eaton didn't simply dislike the individuals who surrounded her. She seems also to have loathed a specific quality of the life of the soul that she shared with them. She was hostile toward expectations that she would engage with her unhappy circumstances by talking about them and that she would disclose her experience truthfully—sincerely—to inquiring minds. Eaton did not want her words to be read as raw material for discovering personal truths. This had been the case even before her outbursts of violence. Her piety had already recoiled from the institutions that her church had built to cultivate it. Rather than attend meetings, she "read secretely, and as secretely engaged her spirit." She did not ask her husband for guidance in her reading, "nor did she seek for any light or help from her pastor," nor from "any Member of [the church] body." When asked to explain her hostility, she kept her dissatisfactions vague, claiming an "inability to speak." The magistrates of New Haven reproved her. Yet she was averse to correction and to acknowledging that she had been corrected. After censuring her, New Haven's elders "prayed her speak if she had anything to say," but she "neither would object nor yield to the truth." She rejected discipline, but she also denied that she cared by refusing directly to repudiate it. She "refused to give any private satisfaction." "She sat down and said nothing."[1]

Anne Eaton's silence, her malaise living under the vigilant eyes and ears of her neighbors, foreshadows the quiet siege on sincerity that history wages. Her silence did not reject sincerity directly. It was one plausible response among others to sincerity's reduction to the tiresome task of talking about oneself and to the shared and usually unchallenged premise that this tiresome talk was worth the effort. Less interested in challenging that reduction, Eaton neatly rejected it. The strangeness of her silence, however, pulls that challenge into the center of the stage alongside her. There, her silence is a gauntlet thrown at the feet of the early modern promise, magnified on this frontier, that sincerity could purchase stability, happiness, and fulfillment. Sincerity is often invoked to circumvent or transcend the discovery of historical entanglement. Because of this convention, sincerity may seem an unusual, unwieldy object to subject to historical analysis; the task, a graceless, even suspicious one. This

1. Lilian Handlin, "Dissent in a Small Community," *New England Quarterly*, LVIII (1985), 193–220, esp. 198 ("seventeen fireplaces"); Newman Smyth, "Mrs. Eaton's Trial (in 1644)," *Papers of the New Haven Colony Historical Society*, V (New Haven, Conn., 1894), 133–148, esp. 135 ("secretely," "nor did," "inability"), 136 ("neither would"), 144 ("private satisfaction," "said nothing"); Gauri Viswanathan, "Yale College and the Culture of British Imperialism," *Yale Journal of Criticism*, VII, no. 1 (Spring 1994), 1–30.

awkwardness testifies to sincerity's previous success in claiming a unique, powerful relationship to truth. It does not claim to be the truth itself but, still more subtly, to be the glue that binds individuals to the truth. In its association with truth, sincerity, as an ideal, may seem to indicate the absence of artifice. Irony, a negation of sincerity, appears as paradigmatic artifice, and it thus has occupied literary-historical interest for decades, yielding dynamic returns. By contrast, relatively few studies of sincerity's history exist. Those that do are interested in sincerity as an "artistic standard" and in the representational strategies that writers used to claim persuasively that they were sincere, in situations where both the creator and the reader recognized what sincerity was and valued it as a good. Sincerity named a common-sense relationship to truth to which writers, particularly English and American, have often sought, or claimed to seek, to return. As Lionel Trilling has eloquently put it, sincerity's star has shone brightly, compellingly; it has "stood high in the cultural firmament and had dominion over men's imagination of how they ought to be."[2]

This book concerns itself with that figurative ascent, with the history sincerity claims to have rendered powerless. It explains how sincerity came to seem desirable and possible. Most important, this book explains how sincerity has come to seem to be the special purview of words. A crucial feature of that ascent, however, is its near-invisibility—sincerity's maturation took place through becoming less visible rather than more; less by rising and more by soaking into and saturating the loam of settlers' ideas about what humans were and how their souls moved. Precisely because of that near invisibility, the colonial New England context represents a potent but easy-to-overlook coincidence of many significant factors in this development. New England's settlers were early moderns. They and their contemporaries experienced, both

2. Patricia M. Ball, "Sincerity: The Rise and Fall of a Critical Term," *Modern Language Review,* LIX (1964), 1–11, esp. 1 ("artistic standard"). Lionel Trilling's *Sincerity and Authenticity* remains one of the most well-cited surveys of sincerity but is more concerned with what he takes to be sincerity's waning and its eclipse by authenticity. Before Trilling, Henri Peyre's *Literature and Sincerity* lucidly showed how self-consciously literary writers (for Peyre, French writers) sought sincerity in their uses of artifice. As with the interest in sincerity within studies of Victorian literature, most of Payre's writers see sincerity as a relationship between words and truth that one can and should try to recover—or at least fret about. See Trilling, *Sincerity and Authenticity: The Charles Eliot Norton Lectures, 1969–1970* (Cambridge, Mass., 1972), 12 ("dominion"); Peyre, *Literature and Sincerity* (New Haven, Conn., 1963). See also Ernst van Alphen, Mieke Bal, and Carel Smith, eds., *The Rhetoric of Sincerity* (Stanford, Calif., 2009); Timothy Milnes and Kerry Sinanan, eds., *Romanticism, Sincerity, and Authenticity* (New York, 2010); David Perkins, *Wordsworth and the Poetry of Sincerity* (Cambridge, Mass., 1964).

on the Renaissance stage and in the world that mirrored it, a congealment of psychologically profound yet, they hoped, ultimately knowable interiority. This interiority is the content of sincerity, this book's conceptual "what." The social significance of what they found when they looked inward was increased by the conditions of colonization: the expansion of the worlds they knew and the challenge such expansion posed to previous ontological first principles. This is the context in which sincerity transformed settlers' psychic foundations, its "where" and "when." Through practices of talking, settlers eventually brought into being a relatively new sort of colony—one not interested so much in acquisition or extraction but in re-creating normalcy and a sense of home. These historical individuals produced a great deal of discourse about their experience. They recorded this discourse because talk—specifically, talk about their selves—was vital to achieving normalcy. These practices of speaking were sincerity's methods, its "how." In conditions of extraordinary historical change, the self now appeared as a shimmering foil, the mine from which not only to extract content but, with those materials, to build longed-for stability. This book thus understands these individuals to have been exemplary of a broader shift in European (especially Northern European) self-consciousness, when the wideness of the world, as Georg Lukács lovingly put it, began to lose its feeling of homeliness. Sincerity names the success of the practices that began to locate that home inwardly, over and above the many sources of external turmoil. Because of that power, sincerity, this book argues, is one of modern colonialism's dearest accessories. Sincerity demanded profound individual estrangements even as it heightened desire for the costlier form of social inclusion that it promised.[3]

Sincerity's success was, indeed, costly; those costs invite readers to reflect on sincerity's motivations, its "why." The English colonies in Algonquian lands were not the first or only European colonies abroad, nor were they the first or only Protestant colonies. These settlers were certainly not the first or only group of people who felt lost, confused, awkward, and unmoored. But they were unusual because of their self-conscious, deliberate commitment to the labor of making sense of that unhappiness and because of their desire to integrate that labor into a comprehensive style of living. In contexts of extreme and sometimes self-willed deracination, settlers hoped to use sincerity to make

---

3. Stephen Greenblatt, "Psychoanalysis and Renaissance Culture," in Patricia Parker and David Quint, eds., *Literary Theory / Renaissance Texts* (Baltimore, 1986), 210–224; Trilling, *Sincerity and Authenticity*, 11; Georg Lukács, *The Theory of the Novel*, trans. Anna Bostock (Cambridge, Mass., 1974), 1.

life feel normal. They pursued this commitment in their discourse: they talked a great deal, and they wrote a great deal. As a consequence, the archive they produced comprises more than simply the mine out of which we can extract evidence for their historical importance. The mine comprises a crucial piece of evidence in itself. It reveals the social and political value this society accorded to recruiting all of its members to participate, rigorously and unrelentingly, in the work of turning themselves into both subjects and objects of knowledge. That "arduous effort" wore on individuals, and it did so in a peculiarly frustrating way: how else, besides confession, might one communicate exhaustion with confession? What if no answer to that question ever appeared? Anne Eaton found one way. She communicated dissatisfaction in violent acts toward the people who should have been the most intimate witnesses of her truth. One of her neighbors, Mary Launce, reported that, after Eaton had asked for a kitchen implement—a tap for brewing—Eaton "pinched her," "struck her with the tap in the eye and made it swell, and made it black and pinched her by the arms, and pulled her by the nose, so that she made her nose bleed." Eaton's stepdaughter, Mary, testified that in a dispute about her pace of knitting, Eaton had grown "outrageous, struck her, pinched her, so that the signs appeared upon her, and knocked her head against the dresser, which made her nose bleed much." And Anne's mother-in-law recalled that, while "sitting at dinner," Anne "struck old Mrs. Eaton twice on the face with the back of her hand, which [the elder] Mrs. Eaton saith she felt three days after."[4]

Biopoetics

Anne Eaton's silence calls attention to the curious, but typically unremarkable, intersection of the science of human life and the rationalization of living, on one hand, and on the other, the radiant expressions of human creativity that we often call *poeisis*. Her silence, and the crisis it precipitated, points to this book's "what": the significance of self-knowledge and self-disclosure in the ascent of modern sincerity. Because self-knowledge often takes the form of a narrative, sincerity's maturation is best recovered and told using the methods of literary study, a tool kit that places works of verbal expression in their historical context to reveal their ends and means. Yet the conditions in which early modern settlers researched and composed these stories were unprecedented. These

4. Trilling, *Sincerity and Authenticity*, 6 ("arduous effort"); Smyth, "Mrs. Eaton's Trial," *Papers of the New Haven Colony Historical Society*, V, 138–140, esp. 138 ("pinched," "outrageous," "sitting"), 140 ("struck her with the tap").

conditions infuse the content of their talk—and their silence—with significance beyond their historical place and time. For men like John Davenport, Eaton's silence was a provocation to discover an object of dissatisfaction, and to do so thoroughly and rigorously, with the best epistemological resources they had. Davenport and the men around him wanted sincerity from Eaton. They recognized sincerity best through acts of personal confession. Thus they pressured her to put into words what frustrated her most: her disagreement regarding the age at which an individual could legitimately be conscripted into this small theological community. From Eaton's perspective, however, the theological dispute might have been incidental. Her silence suggests she was dissatisfied less about the argument for or against conscripting infants into this exclusive community before they even knew how to talk, and more about the social and discursive dynamics of the community in which they and she had little choice but to live their lives—and most oppressively of those dynamics, the imperative to translate frustration into words and then communicate it. Eaton preferred not to explain her dissent, and her silence was not external to it. Her obstinate silence *was* the dissent; talking was its critical object. Her refusal to argue according to the theological premises that governed her world, and that govern modern scholarship about her world, invites historians of early American literature and culture to deepen our understanding of the specific epistemology of that theocratic utopia. Still further, and more important, her refusal invites scholars to investigate the delicate relationship that this epistemology cultivated between science and selfhood—that is, how individuals subjected themselves to protoscientific practices and how those practices shaped the desires individuals could recognize and narrate. It's possible to understand this relationship without the keywords that organize the sections that follow: biopoetics (and its counterpart, biopolitics), settler colonialism, subjection, and repression. But these keywords, judiciously engaged, can be instruments in history's hands. They frame a better and more incisive inquiry into sincerity's content, context, method, and motive, respectively. As a bonus, they can help extend the seventeenth century's insights on power and force to illuminate how the contest between sincerity and history continues to shape everyday strategies for achieving something like the good life in the present.

History's hopes for securing recognition from sincerity built on three successive propositions. First, self-knowledge and self-disclosure, the substance of sincerity, were work. They required skill and practice. The seventeenth century saw new and powerful uses for these pursuits, particularly in the colonial setting. Davenport and Theophilus Eaton's New Haven colony, much like its neighbors, was constructed on the premise that introspection was vital to a good society. In various practices of self-examination and self-disclosure, early modern English people worked to build the utopia they believed their deity had commissioned them to create. Second, sincerity's labors participated in an emergent style of experiencing the self that prioritized systematic and rational self-government. The confession Davenport desired would have been one of many instances of colonial volubility on the topic of the self. Colonists kept journals and diaries and sent many letters. They wrote tracts to promote and defend their endeavor and versified their struggles in poems. They met multiple times a week to listen to sermons, and they circulated those sermons in print. They narrated their wars and rumors of wars, and they reflected at length on those wars' conditions and consequences. As this survey of genres suggests, when colonists pursued self-knowledge and practiced what Sarah Rivett has called the "science of the soul," they found templates to be useful research tools. Stories expressed, but they also organized. Templates provided ministers like Davenport easier access to useful data about the soul's contours, and they provided individuals useful vocabulary for aligning themselves better with the ideals their ministers articulated. Discursive templates didn't only disclose sincerity; they molded it, too. The subtlety of this molding is the content of this book's third proposition: although specific historical conditions catalyzed sincerity, making it more effective and efficient as an instrument of self-government, many of those conditions are not visible to the unaided eye. Nor, importantly, are their consequences. Sincerity's maturation took place through a process of deepening, erasing its historical tracks and reappearing onstage as a universal quality, outside of time. Davenport's perplexity is one quiet invitation to look deeper. Anne Eaton's silence disturbed him because, by 1644, such refusals were rare. Self-disclosure was hard work, but most participants in the Protestant colonies seem to have gambled that it was worth the effort. Not everyone did, however. Anne's silence prompts us to reach beyond the immediately evident phenomena to consider the calculations that went into that gamble.[5]

Anne Eaton at first seems to fit neatly within the story Davenport developed to explain her. She occupies the stage as another member of the chorus indicting the gendered double standard of Protestant patriarchy. Unlike other members of that chorus—more-famous women dissidents like Anne Bradstreet or Anne Hutchinson—Eaton refused scripts of gendered expressiveness. She did not refuse the script that guided their expression but, rather, refused

5. Sarah Rivett, *The Science of the Soul in Colonial New England* (Williamsburg, Va., and Chapel Hill, N.C., 2011).

expressiveness as the script itself. She was silent onstage, yet she was still on it, and her silence is part of the talkative history these people lived. More specifically, her silence is a key but largely overlooked (or unheard) part of the history of early modern colonial knowledge production that has preoccupied scholars in the first decades of the twenty-first century, the field's slow and steady epistemological turn. As colonists acquired more reliable knowledge of the world around them, they found themselves always wanting something new and slightly different from knowledge. They wanted certainty. It was, as Toni Morrison has put it, the "pasture they crave[d]." Eaton knew she was one of many objects, including diseases, demographics, and didelphiae, on which early modern researchers like Davenport whetted their beastlike, often thoughtless desire for knowing. The self-representation that he sought, and that she sought to avoid, comprised the triumph of early modern knowledge pursuits over a different, possibly new object: the intimate self. She was to think about what frustrated her and to organize those thoughts into sensible statements for her neighbors. But she didn't want to. Although her violence might have been unusual, her reluctance mostly likely wasn't. Not everyone found knowing so tantalizing. Early modern European science, particularly as it pertained to the self, could be exhausting. On the frontier, its requirements often exceeded the psychic means that most individuals possessed to practice it. That psychic toll could redouble into more frantic claims to certainty, often with violent consequences, as the first chapter below will survey. More broadly, however, that psychic toll expressed itself in the aggressive evangelizing insistence that one's knowledge pursuits, particularly of self-knowledge, could yield certainty, the insistence that sincerity, the possession and circulation of a personal truth, was possible—and desirable—for everyone.[6]

6. Toni Morrison, *A Mercy* (New York, 2011), 128; Lyle Kohler, *A Search for Power: The "Weaker Sex" in Seventeenth Century New England* (Urbana, Ill., 1980); Laurel Thatcher Ulrich, *Good Wives: Image and Reality in the Lives of Women in Northern New England* (New York, 1982); Ivy Schweitzer, *The Work of Self-Representation: Lyric Poetry in Colonial New England, 1650–1750* (Williamsburg, Va., and Chapel Hill, N.C., 1991). Scholarship on the Annes and their motivations is vast. For more recent surveys, see Margaret Olofson Thickstun, "Contextualizing Anne Bradstreet's Literary Remains: Why We Need a New Edition of the Poems," *Early American Literature*, LII (2017), 389–422; Michael W. Kaufmann, "Post-Secular Puritans: Recent Retrials of Anne Hutchinson," ibid., XLV (2010), 31–59. On the epistemological turn, see Joyce E. Chaplin, *Subject Matter: Technology, the Body, and Science on the Anglo-American Frontier, 1500–1676* (Cambridge, Mass., 2001); on didelphiae, see Susan Scott Parrish, *American Curiosity: Cultures of Natural History in the Colonial British Atlantic World* (Williamsburg, Va., and Chapel Hill, N.C., 2005), 134; on diseases, see Cristobal Silva, *Miraculous Plagues: An Epidemiology of Early New England Narrative* (Oxford, 2010). See also Rivett, *Science of the*

Despite her society's insistence on sincerity's transcendental attractions, Eaton disliked the prospect of subjecting herself to systematic scrutiny and discipline. She might have felt like an animal or, worse, a machine. Her aversion sits awkwardly within the stories that scholars of early America have been telling about her society for decades, maybe centuries. Early American intellectual historians have long been familiar with the claim that reform Protestantism, especially the "Puritan" variant developed on the frontier, encouraged rigorous but sensitive introspection, analysis, and self-disclosure. These practices were the foundation for the utopian happiness that these Christians imagined it was their responsibility to bring into existence, however quixotic it might have sounded to their friends and families back in England. These historians have observed the political force these practices had, underwriting the legitimacy of the colonial project. Furthermore, it was through storytelling that individuals who had wandered beyond their society's norms requested access for reintegration. Yet these practices were forceful in yet a more subtle way. The storytelling that settler society required, often guided by Manichean templates lifted from their cult's sacred text, shaped individuals' sense of selfhood, and these stories secured individuals' wills to be responsible and self-disciplining. Every individual was to become, in the words of Sacvan Bercovitch, their "own exegete"—an expert on themselves and the best translator of what was unseen and hidden in the interior for those beyond it. Acquiring self-knowledge, writes Theodore Dwight Bozeman, "was an art." But it wasn't technique for its own sake, much less for aesthetic showmanship. Self-knowledge "was power and ... from it would flow higher grades of skill in self-management." For these intellectual historians, self-knowledge was a technique of mastery. Bercovitch, in the story he proposed about the significance of these practices, saw them

Soul; Sarah Rivett, *Unscripted America: Indigenous Languages and the Origin of a Literary Nation* (Oxford, 2017); Kelly Wisecup, *Medical Encounters: Knowledge and Identity in Early American Literatures* (Amherst, Mass., 2013); Sari Altschuler, *The Medical Imagination: Literature and Health in the Early United States* (Philadelphia, 2018); Molly Farrell, *Counting Bodies: Population in Colonial American Writing* (Oxford, 2016) (on demographics); Pablo F. Gomez, *The Experiential Caribbean: Creating Knowledge and Healing in the Early Modern Atlantic* (Chapel Hill, N.C., 2017); Tita Chico, *The Experimental Imagination: Literary Knowledge and Science in the British Enlightenment* (Stanford, Calif., 2018); Ralph Bauer, *The Alchemy of Conquest: Science, Religion, and the Secrets of the New World* (Charlottesville, Va., 2019); Greta LaFleur, *The Natural History of Sexuality in Early America* (Baltimore, 2018); and recent dissertations, such as Rachel Trocchio, "American Puritanism and the Cognitive Style of Grace" (Ph.D. diss., University of California, Berkeley, 2017); Kimberly Takahata, "Skeletal Testimony: Bony Biopolitics in the Early Atlantic, 1705–1836" (Ph.D. diss., Columbia University, 2020); Ittai Orr, "American Intelligences: Varieties of Mind before I.Q." (Ph.D. diss., Yale University, 2020).

as a precedent for American culture in the centuries to follow, and central to that precedent was the Protestant martial disposition he called "auto-machia," the war against the self to be won through perfecting knowledge about the self. Davenport knew that not everyone would like this war's battles all the time. The practices of self-examination that winning required often made the practitioner lonelier, abandoned with what they knew was worst about themselves. But he believed firmly, obstinately, that the work was a universal duty and that duty would usually prove rewarding.[7]

Bercovitch was one of the earliest intellectual historians to explain the significance of settlers' preoccupation with self-knowledge, but in the 1970s, he wasn't alone in his interest in the important place that projects of self-understanding could have in a social and political context. While Bercovitch was researching and writing *The Puritan Origins of the American Self*, an ocean away, Michel Foucault was developing a more abstract, portable theory to explain how individual self-knowledge could support a more consistent, reliable, and efficient collective life. His first expression of these ideas appears in his lectures at the Collège de France; in 1975, he published his history of prison, and the following year, his history of sexuality. The former, *Discipline and Punish,* explains the dream of social health that spurred modern prison reform—a dream of social life characterized by consistency, predictability, and a statistically defined security, free of abnormalities. The second book explains the practices through which individuals came to believe, confidently, that such scientific reason and discourse could teach them to relate to themselves positively, optimistically, and productively. Through speaking about their desires, Foucault observed, individuals would be convinced of the reality and possible future felicity of what, he claimed, the modern prison had created—the soul. These two texts would become the foundation of biopolitical theory, a name for a diffuse form of political organization that conscripts individual longings for security, health, and fulfillment rather than repressing or denying them. Though different in mood, Foucault's work reaches conclusions that early American settlers, according to their twentieth-century exegetes, would have found congenial, maybe uncannily so. "The panoptic schema" that Foucault described in a book originally titled *Surveiller et punir*—to surveil and

7. Sacvan Bercovitch, *The Puritan Origins of the American Self* (New Haven, Conn., 1975), 19–25, 28; Theodore Dwight Bozeman, *The Precisianist Strain: Disciplinary Religion and Antinomian Backlash in Puritanism to 1638* (Williamsburg, Va., and Chapel Hill, N.C., 2004), 107, 111; Francis J. Bremer, "'To Tell What God Hath Done for Thy Soul': Puritan Spiritual Testimonies as Admission Tests and Means of Edification," *NEQ*, LXXXVII (2014), 625–665; Michael P. Winship, *Godly Republicanism: Puritans, Pilgrims, and a City on a Hill* (Cambridge, Mass., 2012).

punish—"intended to make [power] more economic and more effective ... to strengthen the social forces—to increase production, to develop the economy, spread education, raise the level of public morality." Indeed, "Surveillance of self," Bozeman affirms, "became the 'necessariest lesson in Christianitie' ... because of an almost extravagant trust in its potential to make repentance, and therewith the reform of behavior, more exact and proficient." Bozeman, like John Eliot 360 years earlier, compared this discipline to the neat technology of a screw—penetrating and durable. What a piece of work man might one day be.[8]

One day. In the meantime, what rewards would induce men and women to subject themselves to that often painful, taxing work of screwing themselves? In response to this question, Foucault, or at least the biopolitical theory he has been held responsible for innovating, disconcerts. Biopower's capacity to pervade intimate life lends a pessimistic, paranoid tone to critiques of the past and present that use the term. The concept's impressive breadth and intimate reach paint a bleak picture of human volition and satisfaction. Applied to early American contexts, this pessimism appears to negate the deliberation of Anglo-American history's most famously sincere people. But critics and historians dissatisfied with biopower's pessimism have a sympathetic ally in Foucault himself. In the years before his death, Foucault turned his attention to ambitions for self-betterment such as those that many early reform Protestants cherished as the motive for their penetrating diligence. He began to search out their histories. He busied himself, in his last years, trying to tell a millennia-long story of individuals' attempts to establish fruitful, truth-centered relationships with themselves. In 1980, he expressed weariness with the "worn and hackneyed" topic of biopower, then proposed a new one—or at least, he tried to. The following year, he proposed two candidates, "biopoetics" and "bio-techniques." He clarified: his use of the prefix "bio" denoted more than "the quality of being alive." It pointed to "the way of living this life, the way of leading it, conducting it, the way in which it may be described as happy or

8. Michel Foucault, *Discipline and Punish: The Birth of the Prison*, trans. Alan Sheridan (1977; rpt. New York, 1995), 207, 208; *The Sermons of Master Henry Smith* (London, 1628), 84, quoted in Bozeman, *Precisianist Strain*, 107; [John Eliot], *The Day-Breaking, if Not the Sun-Rising of the Gospell with the Indians in New-England* (1647), rpt. in *Tracts Relating to the Attempts to Convert to Christianity the Indians of New England*, Massachusetts Historical Society, *Collections*, 3d Ser., IV (Cambridge, Mass., 1834), 1–24, esp. 4 ("skrue"); Foucault, *The History of Sexuality*, I, *An Introduction*, trans. Robert Hurley (New York, 1978); Foucault, *The Punitive Society: Lectures at the Collège de France, 1972–1973*, trans. Graham Burchell (New York, 2015).

unhappy"—not simply cheerful, but, as he showed in his last two published books, a life in alignment with contemplatively reached ideals.[9]

"Biopoetics," Foucault admitted, was probably an untenable name. He suspected it was unlikely to stick. He would later turn to a phrase that he liked better: "aesthetics of existence." What he found dissatisfying about "biopoetics," however, makes it a dynamic term to understand sincerity's tumultuous history in general and, more modestly, to understand what was at stake in Eaton's silence, why her reasoning collided so perplexingly with Davenport's in 1644. The term is valuable in at least two ways, maybe three. First, it is derivative, a little formulaic. That can be a good thing. Formulas often expire; words run out of steam. This book, like its protagonists, is skeptical of the durability of signs (say, a freshly coined keyword) to travel far without risking malfunction. Early modern Protestants would have called such malfunction "idolatry." Here, a little less glamorously, it's an inconvenient analytical risk. The farther a term like "biopolitics" travels, the greater the risk it takes of occluding crucial qualities of what its wielder hopes to make clearer. "Biopoetics"—maybe corny, certainly clumsy, and in any case, already variously claimed by researchers in a number of other subfields—seems less vulnerable to that fate.[10]

9. Michel Foucault, *On the Government of the Living: Lectures at the Collège de France, 1979–1980,* trans. Graham Burchell (New York, 2014), 11; Foucault, *Subjectivity and Truth: Lectures at the Collège de France, 1980–1981,* trans. Burchell (New York, 2017), 34; Charles Taylor, "Foucault on Freedom and Truth," *Political Theory,* XII (1984), 152–183; Foucault, *The History of Sexuality,* II, *The Use of Pleasure,* trans. Robert Hurley (New York, 1984); ibid., III, *The Care of the Self* (New York, 1984).

10. Richard White, assessing how far his own most-well-received phrase traveled over its first two decades, expresses good-natured ambivalence toward its resulting dilution: "If the middle ground was everywhere, then it might as well be nowhere at all." See White, *The Middle Ground: Indians, Empires, and Republics in the Great Lakes Region, 1650–1815* (Cambridge, 2011), xiv. For Foucault, see his *Subjectivity and Truth,* trans. Burchell, 34 ("biopoetics"); Michel Foucault, "An Aesthetics of Existence," in Lawrence K. Kritzman, ed., *Politics, Philosophy, Culture: Interviews and Other Writings, 1977–1984* (New York, 1988), 47–53. I call it derivative because several projects of cultural criticism within the past decade seem to have coined the term independent of each other and of Foucault's 1980–1981 lectures. For "biopoetics" as a turn in ecocritical theory, see Brett Cooke, "Literary Biopoetics: An Introduction," *Interdisciplinary Literary Studies,* II, no. 2 (Spring 2001), 1–8; Cooke and Frederick Turner, "Biopoetics: Evolutionary Explorations in the Arts," International Conference of the Unity of the Sciences, Lexington, Ky., 1999. For biopoetics as a poetry-based negotiation with biopower, see Sara Guyer, *Reading with John Clare: Biopoetics, Sovereignty, Romanticism* (New York, 2015). For biopoetics as a strategy of affirmative discourse, see Julieta Yelin, "From Biopolitics to Biopoetics: A Hypothesis on the

Second, and more important, "biopoetics" is a useful heuristic for understanding sincerity and the history it tries to break away from and triumph over. The term likewise depends, at least etymologically, on "biopolitics" and seems unable to break from it. Foucault wrestled with that derivative quality. He tried to claim that his new research agenda differed from his old one, but he kept coming back to the old to explain the new. In his notes for the lecture on January 14, 1981, when he introduced the term, he explained that "biopolitics" named the various ways individuals achieved "normalization," especially how they used self-inquiry and self-disclosure to arrive at rational understandings of themselves. "Biopoetics," by contrast, named "a matter of aesthetic-moral conduct of individual existence." It proposed ways of living that could be approached through highly formal practices of thought, inquiry, and speech. The aim of those practices wasn't necessarily health or self-management. In Foucault's estimation, these practices tried to forge a "relationship of self-to-self" characterized by a commitment to truth—maybe not knowledge. "Biopoetics" named practices that often used subjective inquiry, but not always. Although Foucault tried to develop a theory of biopoetics after proposing his theory of biopolitics, biopoetics, he implied by his turn to the classical past, historically anteceded biopower. The encounter between Eaton and Davenport suggests that the two modes of experiencing the self were not just historically sequential, implicitly exclusive. They coexisted in a tense relationship. "Biopower" describes the burdensome requirement of sincerity as Eaton experienced it; "biopoetics" describes the goals of those required practices as spiritual leaders like Davenport anticipated them. Their etymological similarity and conceptual dependence make them valuable to a study of sincerity's history, and this conceptual intimacy helps clarify how individuals can cherish dreams of wholeness and radiant purity of heart while subjecting themselves and their neighbors to exhausting, self-dividing disciplines, making themselves both machines for truth as well as its fodder.[11]

Biopoetics' cleaved history is a tidy, formal heuristic; its ugliness, apotropaic. But a third, and perhaps the most substantial, value that "biopoetics" brings to a study of sincerity is that the term might have reached its historical apogee in the practices that these specific people (early modern English Protestants) in this specific place (Algonquian territory) developed

---

Relationship between Life and Writing," *CLCWeb: Comparative Literature and Culture,* XX, no. 4 (December 2018), 1–9.

11. Foucault, *Subjectivity and Truth,* trans. Burchell, 34.

in order to feel secure in their claims to really know themselves. Davenport and Eaton's confrontation was not accidental. Foucault was not a historian of early America, but he had friends and collaborators who were. Foucault started to suspect that, at some historical point, the "spirituality of knowledge *(savoir)* and the subject's practice of truth" transformed, slowly and maybe imperceptibly, into "this other apparatus of subjectivity, which is our own and which is, I think, governed by the question of the subject's knowledge *(connaissance)* of himself and of the subject's obedience to the law." What's more, this colony's conditions of possibility bring together themes that preoccupied Foucault across his career. European colonial ventures, he had intimated a decade earlier, had profoundly torqued European knowledge systems, what he called epistemes. The modern "order of things," he had observed, followed the insights of language afforded by the light that "shines … on the frontiers of Western culture." Those frontiers, in turn, became sites for testing and expanding Foucault's hypotheses on knowledge and power. Yet these colonies aren't special to a new story of biopower simply because they were colonies. They are special because they were built by people whose unusual commitment to an old text put them, they thought, at the leading edge of social thought and political philosophy. The Christianity they cherished was the object of Foucault's late work. One of his ends in turning to biopoetics was to reframe Christianity, to put it into a longer history of the practices of the self and those practices' fascination with the idea of truth. In his less formal speculations, Foucault began to notice that a specific variant of Christianity, "Renaissance" Protestantism, had somehow played a key part in the emergence of biopower from biopoetics.[12]

The frontiers of European culture illuminate one reason why self-knowledge might have become so promising an object for investing attention and mental labor in the early modern era, a time of forceful and disturbing world-historical

---

12. Michel Foucault, *The Hermeneutics of the Subject: Lectures at the Collège de France, 1981–1982,* trans. Graham Burchell (New York, 2005), 319; Foucault, *The Order of Things: An Archaeology of the Human Sciences* (New York, 1970), 44; Foucault, *Subjectivity and Truth,* trans. Burchell, 29; William E. Paden, "Theaters of Humility and Suspicion: Desert Saints and New England Puritans," *Technologies of the Self: A Seminar with Michel Foucault* (Amherst, Mass., 1988), 64–79. On the emergence of biopolitical discipline in colonial contexts, see Ann Laura Stoler, *Race and the Education of Desire: Foucault's "History of Sexuality" and the Colonial Order of Things* (Durham, N.C., 1995); Greta LaFleur and Kyla Schuller, eds., "The Emergence of Biopolitics in the Americas," *American Quarterly,* LXXI (2019); LaFleur, *Natural History of Sexuality.*

change. Foucault intuited the mechanism of this attraction late in his career. After turning away from biopower, he thought deeply about why knowledge, especially self-knowledge, should be so successful in recruiting immense reserves of willpower. Imagining himself and his lecture audience as the readers of Seneca's advice in his dialogue *De tranquilitate animi,* Foucault suggested, in a lengthy sequence of rhetorical questions, that self-knowledge's attractions answered an awareness of material vulnerability, the risk that the outside world might transform, even destroy, other potential objects of investigation and love: "Now what object can one freely, absolutely, and always want?" "What object is the will always able to want in any circumstances, without having to alter itself according to the occasion or time?" "What object can one will absolutely, that is to say without relating it to anything else?" Ten years earlier, Foucault had criticized, with verve and eloquence, this very longing. In his polemic essay against hagiographic historiography, he had insisted on the imperative to excavate the historical specificity of "what we tend to feel is without history . . . sentiments, love, conscience, instincts." Over time, however, he felt less pessimistic about the attractions of a love object—in this case, self-knowledge—that historical change could not disturb. Early Americans would have known that disturbance well, and they longed, in response, to love securely. "What *can* we love fervently?" Mitchell Breitwieser asks, taking up the standpoint of their "full heart[s]." The particular full heart that prompts his question about longing for safety from history belongs to Mary Rowlandson, protagonist of this book's fifth chapter and one of the canonical protagonists of American literary history. She wanted answers because life on the frontier had taken away her family, her home, her closest neighbors, her sources of material stability, and, by the time of her writing, her confidence that there was anything or anyone around her, even her deity, that she could love fervently and securely. As with the actors in the first and second chapters, frontier uncertainties whetted her longing for an object that would reliably stay with her. Bereft by the history her fellow English Christians had wrought, Rowlandson turned, with mixed success, to autobiography and the dream of true self-knowledge. She did so because, by 1682, a successful answer had been provided by leaders such as Davenport and taken up widely by her neighbors. The answer that, in Breitwieser's analysis, "attains to ideological allegiance" for Rowlandson and her readers wasn't only the self. It was the sincere self, the notion that a self and its weaknesses could be knowable, disclosed confidently and transparently. By 1682, to Anne Eaton's likely chagrin but probably not her surprise, self-knowledge had become an object of love, and it had become so in response to a slow and subtle mismanagement of the multivalent crises of frontier life.[13]

Settler Colonialism

The single most consequential crisis of frontier life for English people was that, when they got to the lands they wanted to inhabit happily, they could no longer put off confronting the existence of the people already living there. Those people's presence implied the existence of obligations that English people did not wish to recognize. Early in their attempts to establish a political community, these settlers had seen value in remaining a small, distinct, and exclusive polity. But their context—their "when" and "where"—made that isolation impossible. They weren't on the moon. They were unannounced squatters in Algonquian territory. Their introspective documents tend to ignore that context, but not consistently or successfully. When Davenport, for example, visited Eaton to observe her actions, he wasn't the only interested party watching her. In that large and magnificent house, the cloud of witnesses trying to understand Eaton was more numerous and more heterogenous than Davenport's document knew what to do with. He briefly noted, for example, that Eaton's violence toward her family was "done before four Indians, who were then in the Kitchen." These witnesses were probably Pequots taken captive during the 1637 English raid on their Mystic encampment, sixty miles east, and they knew Eaton and Davenport's new home better than their captors did. English settlers sold some captives in the West Indies, but not all of them. These captives, Davenport claimed, were spiritually interesting to him, at least in passing. He asserted that Eaton's violence constituted a "breach of the Sixth Commandment, as it is a just offense to the Indians and so a means of the murder of their souls, and contrary to the rule of the Apostle, 1 Cor. x, 32." He was especially interested in Eaton's eagerness to harm the individuals that her household—like many of the colonial elite, including probably his own next door—kept in slavery. In addition to these Native captives, Eaton was also, Davenport noted, threatening Anthony, an enslaved Black man, for "bewitch[ing] the beer because it would not run when it was mashed." For

13. Foucault, *Hermeneutics of the Subject,* trans. Burchell, 133; Michel Foucault, "Nietzsche, Genealogy, History," in Donald F. Bouchard, ed., *Language, Counter-Memory, Practice: Selected Essays and Interviews* (Ithaca, N.Y., 1977), 139–164, esp. 139–140; Mitchell Robert Breitwieser, *American Puritanism and the Defense of Mourning* (Madison, Wis., 1990), 117.

Davenport, these captives were witnesses but not scientists. They were mostly liabilities, more susceptible, in his mind, to spiritual errancy than Eaton herself. Yet these captives had to think, more rigorously than Eaton or Davenport did, about the conceptual foundations that organized their new worlds. They would have had very different relationships to art, knowledge, power, and the management of the self and others. From the margins of the stage, they probably did not use the same theoretical terms as twentieth- and twenty-first-century scholars in describing what was taking place around them, the goals their captors pursued, and the costs of pursuing them. Nevertheless, these captives' experience on those margins affords insights on sincerity beyond the terms that English settlers used to understand it. And it is especially valuable reframing these newcomers' aversions to broad, expansive obligations—the sorts that motivated their arduous intellectual and discursive work.[14]

These captives knew that the frontier wasn't simply lived as scene after scene of violent conflict. The crises of the frontier were also lived in everyday, vague, and often uncomfortable encounters with difference. Within Davenport's description of the Eaton household, these captives occupied an ambiguous position, but an extraordinarily dynamic one to see and understand what settlers might not have been able to grasp about themselves. When Davenport described these captives, he claimed he wanted to protect them from a harm he thought Eaton posed to them, but these captives also had reason to stay vigilant not only toward Eaton but toward the community she participated in and the climate of stresses that produced her. To our eyes, and to Davenport's, Eaton's actions came most directly and powerfully from her hands and mouth. These captives, however, surrounded as they were by the shouts, smells, and subtleties of white people, might not have distinguished Eaton's actions so clearly from Davenport's. Their assessments of each and both would have used data they had been collecting for years before the 1644 crisis; her fury might have seemed of a piece with the fury that had devastated their homes seven years earlier. Three-quarters of a decade in captivity, these soul scientists probably did understand the vocabulary that English people used to narrate their interiority. Yet they might not have rejected settlers' narrations of their own intentions out of hand as disingenuous or hypocritical, a misfiring of a

14. Smyth, "Mrs. Eaton's Trial," *Papers of the New Haven Colony Historical Society*, V, 139, 142; Alfred A. Cave, *The Pequot War* (Amherst, Mass., 1996); Ann Kibbey, *The Interpretation of Material Shapes in Puritanism: A Study of Rhetoric, Prejudice, and Violence* (Cambridge, 1986); Margaret Ellen Newell, *Brethren by Nature: New England Indians, Colonists, and the Origins of American Slavery* (Ithaca, N.Y., 2015), 43–59; Wendy Warren, *New England Bound: Slavery and Colonization in Early America* (New York, 2016), 83–113.

transcendently good and ultimately felicitous doctrine. Settlers' constant talk about their invisible interior lives would have been part and parcel of the disposition that had dispossessed these captives so spectacularly all those years before. The captives might, eventually, have learned the word "colony" from any English person sensitive to contemporaneous debates on how best, and most neatly, to go about claiming land across the globe. If so, they would have learned such a word from newcomers who saw Algonquian land as a fertile soil to plant crops to sustain themselves, crops like calorie-rich legumes, as Francis Bacon's now-famous essay had proposed. Like Bacon, the newcomers hoped, for convenience's sake, that this soil was "pure" of unwanted neighbors who might get in the way of planting them. The Native captives would also have been very familiar with the colonists' attempts—which sometimes included extermination—to ensure quotidian peace and contentment for themselves. These captives were well acquainted with the violence that English newcomers enacted to satisfy their longing to feel safe, secure, and settled.[15]

"Biopoetics," adjacent to and cleaving to "biopolitics," clarifies the desires that animated these colonists, such as the longing for the peace and confidence, that are sometimes expressed with the word "settle." "Biopoetics" clarifies the ambitions that kept them going despite all of their bungled attempts at happiness. And it clarifies how a framework such as settler colonialism can be applied to their ambitions and to the place of ambitions and intentions. The term "settler colonialism" generally has named a theory that explains a set of actions: how and why strangers from a metropole try to claim a land, live on it, and eventually purport to be natives themselves. To do so, these individuals often attempt to transform the landscape ecologically and, in turn, to dissolve existing relationships between the land and its Indigenous inhabitants. Sometimes, and most dramatically, this means pursuit of genocide, what Patrick Wolfe called the "elimination of the native." Sometimes it means destroying the conditions that make life livable, effecting what William Cronon described as disastrous "changes in the land." Quite often, the form of life with which colonists endeavored to replace those Indigenous relationships with the land is characterized by biopolitical reason and rationality and can inform the subtler, more nefarious acts that express what Jasbir K. Puar has called the "right to maim." Settler colonial theory synthesizes these actions, including mental ones, such as planning and justification. The colonists who settled in New England in the seventeenth century often manage to evade these assessments, however, because the historical study of this people and place has often been

15. Francis Bacon, "Of Plantations," *The Essays* (New York, 1986), 162–164.

a study of intentions, of longings for spiritual fulfillment and satisfaction that resonate with biopoetic dreams rather than biopolitical coercion. The presence of these captives in Eaton's household and in Davenport's account pulls New England back into settler colonial theory's spotlight. These Indigenous captives were survivors of the first attempts by English people in an overseas colony systematically to destroy a people as a people; their lives testify to colonists' imperfect attempts to transform them into objects, exchangeable for other people or things. Their presence and their subjection to Eaton's violence urge a more synthetic reassessment of settler colonialism's means with its ends.[16]

English colonists confessed to many thoughts, deeds, and desires, but they never confessed directly to a desire to inaugurate a settler colony. For historians who, on principle, favor the analytical categories available to historical individuals, this is an inconvenient omission. Most English planters, particularly those animated by a zeal for Protestant reform, risked their former lives because they wanted—with much, if not all, of their hearts—to reproduce a better, more English, more Christian life elsewhere. For the most part, when they did reflect on their desires, they seem to have longed for a "peaceable and quiet resting" in "a place of their owne," as minister John Cotton put it. They craved a "firme and durable possession" from which they would need to "move no more." Settler colonial theory seems to be a bad fit for understanding the history of reformist English settlement because these actors did not often claim to want the violence they wrought. English colonists in nineteenth-century Australia, perhaps the foundational site for studies of settler colonialism, might have been a little franker about their desires for genocidal elimination, but English people in Algonquian territory might not have understood their own desires so baldly. This theory, when it centers genocidal elimination rather

16. Patrick Wolfe, "Settler Colonialism and the Elimination of the Native," *Journal of Genocide Research*, VIII (2006), 387–409; William Cronon, *Changes in the Land: Indians, Colonists, and the Ecology of New England* (New York, 1983); Jasbir K. Puar, *The Right to Maim: Debility, Capacity, Disability* (Durham, N.C., 2017); Jodi A. Byrd, *The Transit of Empire: Indigenous Critiques of Colonialism* (Minneapolis, 2011); J. Kēhaulani Kauanui, "'A Structure, Not an Event': Settler Colonialism and Enduring Indigeneity," *Lateral*, V, no. 1 (Spring 2016), https://csalateral.org/issue/5-1/forum-alt-humanities-settler-colonialism-enduring-indigeneity-kauanui/; Malini Johar Schueller and Edward Watts, eds., *Messy Beginnings: Postcoloniality and Early American Studies* (New Brunswick, N.J., 2003); Lorenzo Veracini, *Settler Colonialism: A Theoretical Overview* (New York, 2010); Veracini, *The Settler Colonial Present* (New York, 2015); Wolfe, *Settler Colonialism and the Transformation of Anthropology* (London, 1999). On the confidence and decisiveness of the "settle" in "settler colonialism," see Jason R. Rudy, "Settled: *Dorrit* Down Under," *Nineteenth-Century Literature*, LXXV (2020), 184–206, esp. 200–201.

than the network of desires in which genocide took place, risks extending the violence that settlers enacted. In stressing the violence of later settlers' policies, historians who apply the theory to early American texts and contexts hazard reproducing the elimination that they claim to be only describing. Settler colonialism may seem casually appropriate, but the past, these historians insist—especially the intentions that guided past actions—is murkier than retroactive, neat labels recognize.[17]

Murkier to us, certainly, through the dark glass of four centuries. Nevertheless, intentions were also, importantly, clouded for historical individuals as they looked at themselves and their neighbors. For many settlers, violence made sense as a response to that opacity—as the first chapter will show, violence was one way to fabricate and confirm sense in a new land, especially a sense of selfhood. Among historians interested in the aptness of the term "settler colonialism," many have already identified sincerity and intention as an opportunity for elaborating and revising settler colonial theory. Intention, they observe, is a trickier, more troublesome historical factor than some students of the past are ready yet to explain. Several leading historians, reflecting together on the use of this critical term, have pointed to intention as a challenge in accounting for the new and strange form of colonization that took place in North America on the cusp of the seventeenth century. Susanah Shaw Romney, for example, notes that, though early modern Dutch colonists knew they were too weak to wage war on neighboring Lenape-Munsees, "many wished they could, making them, at least, aspirational settler colonialists." Michael Witgen observes, of the following century, that although the nascent United States was "locked into a complicated relationship with Native nations," it nevertheless desired *not* to be locked into that relationship—that is, it "aspired to be a settler colonial state." And Jennifer M. Spear proposes a new, more subtle definition for settler colonialism in early America: it comprised "invaders' desire for Indigenous lands and their efforts to deny or eradicate Indigenous sovereignty." Many of these aspirations and efforts would not be described explicitly. Few settlers would tell their neighbors anything so direct as *I want to occupy your land, and I do not want your say about how I pursue my desire to do so.* Biopower can explain some of those pursuits: as Chapter 2 shows, settlers imagined they were smarter and more rational in their lifestyle planning than their new

17. John Cotton, *Gods Promise to His Plantation* (London, 1630), 2; Allan Greer, "Settler Colonialism and Empire in Early America," *William and Mary Quarterly,* 3d Ser., LXXVI (2019), 383–390; Jeffrey Ostler and Nancy Shoemaker, "Settler Colonialism in Early American History: Introduction," ibid., LXXVI (2019), 361–368.

neighbors, and they ignored Native critiques of their plans accordingly; Chapter 3 explains how settlers expressed their commitment to rational technique among themselves. Nonetheless, even biopower has its limits in illuminating how colonial subjects thought about their own longing for deliberation and care and how they responded to the host of circumstances that frustrated their deliberations. Settlers wanted land to live on happily. Crucially, they wanted to choose whom they were beholden to in making those claims. They wanted to be unobligated in their decisions about obligation. Such bonds would have interrupted the happiness they recognized and pursued.[18]

Settler colonialism, in this light, names the hope that conscious intention could step to the front of the stage and speak so authoritatively and persuasively that other voices, obligations, and duties would be forgotten, maybe leave the stage altogether. Davenport refused to contemplate the possibility that the individuals whom Eaton's household had enslaved might have had insights into her violence, far less that he might have a duty to listen to what they had to say about it. Why didn't that thought occur to him? To answer that question requires probing more deeply into settlers' ideas about colonial life—not to discard intention nor to allow it to discard its own historical conditions of possibility. An answer, in other words, requires a more synthetic understanding of English settlers' intentions and the world that shaped those wants. That synthesis isn't easy or obvious. Notwithstanding Jamesonian injunctions to subject everything, "always," to historical materialist analysis, intentions have proved stubbornly resistant. Critics unpracticed in considering desire's artificiality and its subtlety will easily miss evidence of its fabrication as it appears in historical texts. Desire is often elusive. It's not always named directly, in writing or in speech. Sometimes individuals don't know what name to give to a desire. Sometimes they decide against giving it a name because they see misrepresentation or denial to be exigent. Other times, individuals don't articulate their desires because they know or (less consciously) feel other tasks to be more urgent. In some cases, individuals may not realize that they are experiencing desire in the first place. A desire not to be locked into a political relationship, for example, might be experienced as an intellectual conviction of national or ethnic sovereignty. Among early modern Europeans, few would

18. Susanah Shaw Romney, "Settler Colonial Prehistories in Seventeenth-Century North America," *WMQ*, 3d Ser., LXXVI (2019), 375–382, esp. 380; Michael Witgen, "A Nation of Settlers: The Early American Republic and the Colonization of the Northwest Territory," ibid., 391–398, esp. 394; Jennifer M. Spear, "Beyond the Native / Settler Divide in Early California," ibid., 427–434, esp. 428.

have been as sensitive to desire's contingency as these pious Christians should have been. According to the claim of one of their favored ideological exegetes, the culture hero they called Jeremiah, the heart—the seat of the soul—was full of deceit. It was desperate in its vulnerability to imprudent decisions, what English Christians called "wickedness." In its deceitfulness and wickedness, it was also often inscrutable. *Who,* Jeremiah taunted, *can know it?* Jeremiah would be the first in line to affirm that knowledge of such an axiom and a resultant desire for honesty would hardly be sufficient to keep the heart pure from such mendacity.[19]

Early New England, from its Annes to its Anthonys, offers an unusually vivid opportunity to understand settler colonialism as well as its partner in eluding the appearance of crime: sincerity. This site is valuable, but not because it is a neat example of settler colonial theory. Here, on those shining Western frontiers, Europeans began to experiment with policies and practices that would be taken up formally and self-consciously elsewhere. As these early colonists did so, they turned a great deal of attention inward. They reflected on and told themselves stories about the wishes, aspirations, desires, and efforts that they experienced and that they encouraged each other to experience. They did this often and with great intensity. These reformists and utopians experimented with settlement not only early in settler colonialism's history but early in the general history of Protestant settlement. At the leading edge of colonial experiments—in happiness, normalcy, and peaceable resting for some, as well as terror, exploitation, and unrest for others—English people in Algonquian territory produced a remarkable archive about what they wanted to know with certainty about themselves. The evidence of that discourse and, occasionally, of dissatisfaction with it are opportunities to witness the challenges settlers faced in making sense of their own desires and the effects of those challenges on individual and collective happiness. The documents they created indicate that they recognized their unprecedented position. When John Josselyn described a colony as a "sort of people" or when John Cotton described colonies as spiritual grafts, they suggested that colonization also meant being transformed by the work required for survival in a different place. Settler colonization, though they did not have that name for it yet, meant striving not simply to be in a place but, eventually, to be of it, too.[20]

19. Frederic Jameson, *The Political Unconscious: Narrative as a Socially Symbolic Act* (Ithaca, N.Y., 1981), 9; Jeremiah 17:9 (Geneva).

20. John Josselyn, *Colonial Traveler: A Critical Edition of "Two Voyages to New England,"* ed. Paul J. Lindholdt (Hanover, N.H., 1988), 108; Cotton, *Gods Promise,* 14–17.

With biopoetics, settler colonialism is a useful heuristic for reframing the relationship that sincerity sustains with the violence it is often thought to redeem or negate. "Biopoetics" names the longing for earthly happiness that energized Europeans to move far across the surface of the earth, the fantasy of spiritual fulfillment they thought these new worlds would afford them. "Settler colonialism" illuminates the specific frontier challenges they faced in achieving it. Together, these terms can make sense of the dream of utopia that kept settlers going through the dystopian, often apocalyptic consequences they obstinately misrecognized everywhere around them and the strategies their non-English neighbors developed for surviving that apocalypse. Settlers often claimed good intentions when they undertook harmful actions. Together, these terms make it possible to acknowledge good intentions and to push those intentions past their claims to purity, returning them to a network of force and the historical conditions that underwrote it. These words may be anachronisms, but the scope they pursue is not. The enslaved residents of the Eaton household knew other ways of thinking and being, though they had to live within the terms that settlers used to shape their world. Anthony and his fellow captives would have developed their own understandings of the value of veridiction and epistemological innovation, both their ends and their means. There were other ways that talk revealed than simply denoting and other things that talk did than simply reveal.[21]

Subjection

Talk made subjects. Language subjects. These are sentences Anthony might have turned over in his mind as he considered the sort of power his captors exerted over him and what it shared and didn't share with the power that others in the Eaton household experienced. He was likely to have been sensitive to the variety of ways English people used that verb, "to subject," as well as its noun form, "subjection." One reason for this sensitivity was his enslaved status. The verb's primary denotation, "made submissive and dependent," would have applied to him, or at least to the expectations that white people had for him, that they expressed in the words they spoke to him and in the way they treated him. But he would have been sensitive to that word's meaning for a second

---

21. Andrew Delbanco, *The Puritan Ordeal* (Cambridge, Mass., 1991); Ana Schwartz, "Were There Any Immigrants in New England?" *NEQ*, XCIII (2020), 400–413; Gerald Horne, *The Apocalypse of Settler Colonialism: The Roots of Slavery, White Supremacy, and Capitalism in Seventeenth-Century North America and the Caribbean* (New York, 2018).

reason: English might not have been his natal language. Increasing his knowledge of his captors' language increased the efficacy of his will within these circumscribed conditions. Acquiring this language, he would have explored the noun's second, obverse denotation: he could "[exercise] ... control" over certain features of his life. In examining their shared language, the Native captives alongside him were in a comparable position, acquiring new vocabulary with him. All of them would have been sensitive to how English words aligned and did not align with approximate words in their own birth languages, how those words introduced him to new concepts, elided others, and transformed still others. These Native captives might have continued to speak with each other in those birth languages or conversed across Algonquian dialects if not all were Pequots. Anthony might have learned or begun to learn English in the West Indies, possibly alongside some basics of Algonquian languages. Daily, all of them would have confronted conceptual quirks of the language they had to learn, but unlike his Pequot neighbors, Anthony was burdened more heavily to figure out these quirks alone, with his own mental resources in what was, to him, a more alien world. His experience of language crystallizes this book's "how." More silent in this documentary record than even Eaton—who spoke at least enough to charge him with witchcraft—Anthony nevertheless depended on language more sharply and self-consciously than almost everyone else around him and would have recognized more intensely how it operated among them, how it subordinated and isolated them even as it offered them tools for exercising power and pursuing a dream of happiness and inclusion. His enslavers claimed that only their deity was sovereign and that to succumb to the power of substitutes was a serious metaphysical offense. Yet their sensitivity to language gave a deitylike power to this medium of communication and to the hope it offered of fulfilling social integration.[22]

Anthony would have thought deeply about the power of the words, each a social tool, that he possessed. Yet he and the other captives in the Eaton household weren't the only ones doing so. Their captors claimed to find intense motivation in combating what they thought was their countrymen's lazy neglect of the words that the Christian deity had left them in their sacred text. In their plans for a reformed spiritual community, they tried to reenchant words and

---

22. *Oxford English Dictionary*, s.v. "subject," "subjection." In 1644, Anthony lived in New Haven, but the Massachusetts Bay Company had been exchanging Indigenous captives in the West Indies since Captain William Pierce's 1638 trading voyage to Tortuga. See Richard S. Dunn, James P. Savage, and Laetitia Yeandle, eds., *The Journal of John Winthrop, 1630–1649* (Cambridge, Mass., 1994); Newell, *Brethren by Nature;* Warren, *New England Bound.*

their power. In England, when they had talked about their plans for "discipline," their interest in "affection," their desire for "redemption," and their eagerness to "fear" their deity, they knew that most of their closest neighbors recognized those words for their power, would understand their historical and theological subtleties, the minute calibrations that distinguished specialized from quotidian use. They were charged, politically meaningful words. Then these English left England. In a new environment, the presence of strangers pushed their renewal of language further. Some settlers began to learn Native languages. Some, such as colonial missionaries, did so with diligence, leaving the company of their fellow English people. The frontier's estranging effects, however, could take place within English homes, too. As enslaved people, Afrodiasporans and Algonquians, acquired proficiency in English, their enslavers would have become more self-conscious about their own utterances. The conversations exchanged among English family members, between English employers and servants, or among English servants themselves had new listeners. English speech would have been heard by non-English ears, interpreted by non-English minds, using non-English notions. The opportunities for misunderstanding, as well as creative new understandings, were legion. This is a basic characteristic of contact zones, but it carries a quieter, stranger, psychic aspect. Language was, quite often, a source of unease, droning in the background. Few responded to that disquiet with the fury that Eaton showed. Yet the malaise was always there, one of the most persistent yet unappreciated factors in generating settlers' longing for self-knowledge. It shaped the "atmosphere of the land" that, as one twentieth-century social scientist from Massachusetts proposed, is "most essential to any clear conception of the group life taken as a whole." Language, the empowering medium for cultivating relations with self and others, not only exercised a great power over the speaker but, in the colonial context, failed to do that always quietly and unremarkably.[23]

Annoyance and frustration are hard to trace, much harder to quantify. If their absence from most existing histories is to be trusted as evidence of the field's methodological priorities, they are nearly impossible to recruit as historically causal factors. But in at least this historical setting, it's very likely that they were. If the insights of early American studies' epistemological turn are correct—if early modern minds were making so many dynamic discoveries—it's also likely that those minds struggled much more commonly than

23. Anna Brickhouse, *The Unsettlement of America: Translation, Interpretation, and the Story of Don Luis de Velasco, 1560–1945* (Oxford, 2015); Rivett, *Unscripted America;* W. E. B. DuBois, *The Souls of Black Folk* (Boston, 1997), 143.

they succeeded, that they experienced a great deal more errors and dead ends than successful syntheses. In the matter of language, those struggles would have had peculiar stakes. Sometimes, for those on the leading edge of trade and settlement, failure of an initial attempt at communication could lead to "creative misunderstandings," as Richard White put it—improvisations between parties seeking possibly complementary ends. Sometimes, failure could lead to paradigm-changing theological insights. Men like Edward Winslow, Roger Williams, and John Eliot, colleagues of John Davenport (some even friends), thrilled to witness language's failure to fade into the background. The mental acrobatics that study of Algonquian languages required revised their grasp of the foundations of their meaning-making systems. But few in the colonies had undertaken the long, risky, and unpleasant voyage, followed by the more unpleasant and longer-gamble challenges of settlement for the sake of intellectual thrills. Quite the contrary. They had left England to fortify their epistemological commitments, not upend them. For most, any friction in communication was more likely an irritation than an opportunity for scientific innovation. Unlike these transatlantic men of science, most settlers had no access to recognition or acclaim, no clear recompense for their frustrations. Navigating the many opportunities for miscommunication taxed these individuals, and they were already facing serious material and psychic taxations. Against this background, pursuits of sincerity, though frustrating and rocky, offered a tantalizing promise of renewal. One such renewal was the possibility of making something more meaningful and tangible out of these minor, ugly feelings.[24]

Language subjected them. The experience of language wore them down even as it offered the promise of building them back up again. English people were not the first to put themselves through rigorous self-study in order to be happy and feel free; Foucault would insist, at least, that such dreams began millennia earlier. Yet these specific English people might have been the first to experiment with a form of life we now call settler colonialism. As they pursued happiness and peace on that tumultuous frontier, they added to that challenge the obligation to be sensitive wielders of language and insightful storytellers; with these tools, they strove to destroy self-opacity. Their souls, they believed, were at stake. According to their god, they could not decide

---

24. White, *Middle Ground*, xii; Perry Miller, *The New England Mind: The Seventeenth Century* (Cambridge, Mass., 1954); Francis Bremer, *The Puritan Experiment: New England Society from Bradford to Edwards* (Hanover, N.H., 1976), 27; Winship, *Godly Republicanism*; Sianne Ngai, *Ugly Feelings* (Cambridge, Mass., 2005).

the fate of those souls or manipulate him to extend them favor. A good story, a smart synthesis of individual experience with patterns gleaned from their sacred text and expressed with the right vocabulary, however, would be reason to hope that they had been chosen all along. They discerned a good story from a bad one in much the same way we do: not by following a manicule from the sky but by reflecting on the conventions that appeared in the stories of their peers. It became easier to organize evidence and deliver it to neighbors and easier to recognize the value in their own stories in return by listening to, absorbing, and mimicking the patterns one heard day in and day out, in formal and informal settings. Some of this learning was probably conscious and took place deliberately. Many of the features of the famed "morphology of conversion" were apparent to early practitioners of the conversion narrative. For most people who had natal familiarity with English, though, a great deal of this learning was probably more discreet, even unnoticed. To some degree, this is a banal statement about the power of habit and habituation. But social habituation, especially when it organized self-knowledge, had unusual signif-icance in this polity. The expressive and epistemological norms one acquired from neighbors and the approval one obtained through successful language acquisition were, settlers claimed, matters of spiritual life and death. The story might not have been the ticket to heaven, yet individuals learned, consciously and unconsciously, to care deeply about how those stories about themselves appeared to their neighbors. They were concerned about their neighbors' approval more intensely than they could measure.[25]

Self-disclosure had high stakes. Language could be a difficult medium. The decision about what to express was fraught with error. Confession, sincerity's keystone, wasn't simply a matter of externalizing material known in advance. Rather, the self-disclosing utterance was a step in a process of subjecting the self to inquiry, and not only by ministers. Individuals, Calvinist theology demanded, should be practicing soul science on themselves. Yet choosing the words to practice that science could puzzle. Consider a relatively common experience like weariness. Michael Wigglesworth, one of the most famously introspective English colonists of his day, confessed to losing slumber over the

---

25. Patricia Caldwell, *The Puritan Conversion Narrative: The Beginnings of American Expres-sion* (Cambridge, 1983) 163 ("morphology"); Pierre Bourdieu, *Distinction: A Social Critique of the Judgement of Taste,* trans. Richard Nice (Cambridge, Mass., 1984); Michael McGiffert, ed., *God's Plot: Puritan Spirituality in Thomas Shepard's Cambridge,* 2d ed. (Amherst, Mass., 1994); Sandra M. Gustafson, *Eloquence Is Power: Oratory and Performance in Early America* (Williamsburg, Va., and Chapel Hill, N.C., 2000); Jane Kamensky, *Governing the Tongue: The Politics of Speech in Early New England* (Oxford, 1997).

matter of his bedroom arrangements in 1656. To say so, to name that tiredness, could offer him psychic repose; to share a private experience could reintegrate him into a social world. But he would need, first, to have decided that what he felt was indeed exhaustion and not something else. For modern readers, such a decision might seem to come easily. This doesn't mean that those who lived in the past were emotionally stunted. They were some of the most scrupulous, enthusiastic practitioners of self-inquiry. Nevertheless, the imperative to look inward, to consider one's own self-opacities and translate what one found there into shareable knowledge—these activities were not always freely or happily chosen, nor were they easily accomplished. They took place against a social and political backdrop that encouraged individuals to compare their diagnoses with those of their peers and neighbors. Because the stakes were so high, it was, at least in early stages, exigent to second-guess any initial diagnosis of a new feeling. Vague sensations of tiredness or of lacking enthusiasm and energy might, on one hand, have been the result of sleepiness or hunger. They might also have been an experience that their theology considered a vice: sloth. Or perhaps, in the evaluation of more sophisticated soul scientists, these feelings might be a second-order reaction to forestall other, more unpleasant affections, such as anger or lust. There might be other affective experiences without any hitherto-known name. Inversely, it's possible that there had once been a name, but it was now lost to time. If exhaustion were an accurate diagnosis, it might be, at least in part, a consequence of the work of deciding among these and other possibilities against such a live, volatile linguistic background.[26]

Talking, the substance of sincerity, wasn't simply a window onto knowledge; it was an instrument that shaped knowledge. "Self-knowledge" named a successful encounter with language's slippery qualities, since self-knowing individuals would have successfully subjected themselves not only to language's capacity to denote and describe but also to its power to analyze and diagnose. This process, in turn, produced a condition that the English language—according to authorities as diverse as Judith Butler and the *Oxford English Dictionary*—designates with the word "subjectivity," a "condition of being dominated by . . . one's personal feelings, thoughts, concerns, etc." "Subjectivity" names an effect of subjection that often appears to be severed from the circulation of power that shapes it; that is, it appears to be a function of individual personality. Modern and early modern theorists of language have

26. Elaine Scarry, *The Body in Pain: The Making and Unmaking of the World* (Oxford, 1985); Edmund S. Morgan, ed., *The Diary of Michael Wigglesworth, 1653–1657: The Conscience of a Puritan* (Gloucester, Mass., 1970).

already noticed that language's power often exceeds its capacity to denote and to refer. One of the most unsettling objects of that dynamic power might be interiority. Claims about interior experience—thoughts, affections, intentions, memories—can almost never be empirically verified. Their status as factual truth remains elusive, and not only to external parties but to individuals themselves. Certainty itself is one of those unverifiable interior experiences. When applied to personal feelings, certainty is often a species of intuition, not too different in kind from the object it tries to grasp. For these reasons, utterances about the self, though they may claim certainty, are substantially more provisional than we tend to acknowledge, more like the sorts of utterances that produce reality through a provisional illusion rather than describe a content made and known in advance. If so, utterances about the self may also, along the way, be experiments. Statements that claim to disclose interior states more accurately test diagnoses about them. Eventually, these hypotheses land on a description that not only feels right to the individual but also, importantly, conforms to the templates circulating within a community. Understood in this fashion, making a statement about oneself wasn't simply an expression of completed analysis; it was an act of soul science, another episode of wielding, and submitting to language's social power.[27]

27. *Oxford English Dictionary*, s.v. "subjectivity"; Judith Butler, *The Psychic Life of Power: Theories in Subjection* (Stanford, Calif., 1997); Kibbey, *Interpretation of Material Shapes;* Judith H. Anderson, *Translating Investments: Metaphor and the Dynamic of Cultural Change in Tudor-Stuart England* (New York, 2005); J. L. Austin, *How to Do Things with Words* (Cambridge, Mass., 1975). William M. Reddy introduced "emotives" in his 1997 essay, "Against Constructionism." Two years later, he introduced his complementary idea of "emotional regimes" in his essay "Emotional Liberty." Both receive extended treatment in his book two years after that, *The Navigation of Feeling*. Reddy is one of the theoretical foundations that Barbara H. Rosenwein cites in her work on late medieval "emotional communities," work that, in turn, grounds Abram C. Van Engen's work on Calvinist fellow feeling in colonial New England. See Reddy, "Against Constructionism: The Historical Ethnography of Emotions," *Current Anthropology,* XXXVIII (1997), 327–351; Reddy, "Emotional Liberty: Politics and History in the Anthropology of Emotions," *Cultural Anthropology,* XIV (1999), 256–288; Reddy, *The Navigation of Feeling: A Framework for the History of Emotions* (Cambridge, 2001); Rosenwein, *Emotional Communities in the Early Middle Ages* (Ithaca, N.Y., 2006); Van Engen, *Sympathetic Puritans: Calvinist Fellow Feeling in Early New England* (Oxford, 2015). For an application of Reddy's insights to colonial America, see Jerónimo Arellano, "Reading the Affects in the Colonial Americas: The Exteriority of Feeling in Cabeza de Vaca's *Naufragios,*" *Latin American Research Review,* LIII (2018), 548–560. For critiques of Reddy that suggest he exaggerates his difference from what he calls "constructionism," see Chia Longman, "Against Constructionism: Comments," *Current Anthropology,* XXXVIII (1997), 344–345; Catherine Lutz, "Against Constructionism: Comments," ibid., 345–346.

Certainty was prized when it could be claimed, yet it was often a threshold crossed without fanfare or even notice. Like learning a new word, confidence regarding accuracy grew with time and repetition. Choosing a word, a phrase, a sentence, a formula meant not choosing others. It meant renouncing other hypotheses and possibilities without noticing. Moreover, repetition would help shape decisions regarding future diagnoses. Much of this process probably wasn't conscious. Some of it was, but not all of it, and the line between consciousness and unconsciousness, between noticing and forgetting, is necessarily vague. This observation, though basic, transforms any understanding of self-knowledge and its corollary, self-opacity. As experiments that generate confidence over time, statements about interiority carry in-built limitations in their claims to be truth. Individuals become accustomed to certain diagnoses and start to favor them over others. Recognition by peers fortifies that confidence. Eventually, within a given community, certain analyses become more popular and more socially powerful. The popularity of some stories over others shapes how individuals feel about themselves, what they hope will be true about their deepest selves, and what they eagerly anticipate recognizing and discovering. Individuals accustom themselves to the evaluation of outward minds when they look inward. Gradually, some hypotheses, parading as conclusions, come to be "hypercognized," or "overlearned," by individuals and their societies. Others, "hypocognized," or underlearned, recede from view as analytic possibilities. To speak and write about interiority, to try to be certain of its contents, might never be an empirically verifiable task. Statements might have claimed to express truth, but even when they are faking it with the aim of making it, these statements almost always express and answer desire, even if only partially. Yet as the consolations of hoped-for certainty accrue, other descriptions for those experiences, which might acknowledge their crookeder corners, sink back below the threshold of recognition.[28]

What if, as Anthony might have wondered, the relentless work of trying to acquire control of these words proved unsuccessful? What if confident usage never arrived? What Anthony might have wondered, Anne Eaton was supposed to experience, too, in theory. The obligation to know oneself and

28. Alice Isen and Gregory Andrade Diamond, "Affect and Automaticity," in James S. Uleman and John A. Bargh, eds., *Unintended Thought* (New York, 1989), 124–152, esp. 126 ("overlearned"); Robert I. Levy, "On the Nature and Functions of the Emotions: An Anthropological Perspective," *Social Science Information*, XXI (1982), 511–528, esp. 514 ("hypercognized"), 525 ("hypocognized").

to profess oneself sincerely was a uniquely uncomfortable requirement of colonial life in a pious Christian colony. It was different than the cold, hunger, material vulnerability, or longing for distant relations that English people put themselves through. Settlers could hope, one day, to overcome most of those sorts of discomforts. One day they might be warm, sated, materially secure. It could take months or years, but they might one day forget or long less sharply for those they had left behind. Other discomforts had less tangible endpoints. Their potential endlessness was built into settlers' cherished social and theological ideals. That built-in quality was materially and theologically useful in fortifying the insularity of a community, in ensuring that individuals would always care, intimately and perhaps even with an erotic charge, about their esteem in the eyes of their neighbors. This was one of the earliest propositions of religious psychology, as Michael McGiffert noticed half a century ago. He liked to claim that such humiliation could be redeemed by the ecstasies of social recognition. Yes, the exposure that sincerity required could often be humiliating, but, he argued, it was relatively brief. One closed one's eyes, McGiffert's sexualized vocabulary suggests, and thought of England rather than the mortification and exposure at hand. One hoped to be able, on the other side, to look back on that experience of subjection with great satisfaction. And on this side of that fantasy, the fear of never achieving certainty encouraged individuals to submit to and depend on language's social power. Thus templates for self-understanding often became dear objects of love and attachment. These templates generated an optimism about future selfhood that threatened to overshadow, even occlude, the content they claimed to mold in the present. The best colloquial translation that twenty-first-century English has for a clumsy word such as "hypercognition" might be "jargon." The word that Davenport's theology had for it might have been (here, too) "idolatry." Pious Christians were not supposed to take shortcuts in sincerity's introspective labors. They were not supposed to turn these templates into a script, but the unit of the labor of thought was, at least for English people, words. Accordingly, it would be very difficult to notice when a narrative monopoly succeeded mentally, when it transformed from template to apparent truth. Given all the other stressors of this new social world they lived in, the gratifications of certainty probably won over the rigors of iconoclasm quite often, and the success of these triumphs consisted largely of their evading anyone's notice.[29]

29. McGiffert, ed., *God's Plot*, 138, 145.

Language's deitylike power wasn't uniform. For Davenport, language was the medium of soul science. It was the instrument he used to try to master the world, to open it up to his fantasies of intellectual control. For Eaton, language opened her up to the investigations of men like Davenport. This unhappy prospect seems to have informed her silence. She preferred not to take up words as an instrument. She might have avoided speech on principle, as an act of refusal or resistance, but because she never disclosed this of herself, we cannot claim so with certainty. Pursuing that hunch risks aligning her with a template she might not have chosen for herself, on one hand, and, on the other, aligning ourselves with a template for investigation that Davenport and his fellow early modern scientists developed. Anthony's experience of language shared much with Eaton's. Like her, his use of language made him more vulnerable to others' desires to know about him, more vulnerable to their templates for understanding him, and more vulnerable to their tools for achieving sincerity. Anthony would have understood this more intimately than almost any natal English speaker in the colony. More intensely than even his fellow captives, he would have depended on this new language as a lifeline to others, to material well-being, as well as to many other immaterial aspects of wellness that are often difficult to name and difficult, also, to understand. Anthony would have had to learn this social language—not simply its vocabulary but also its idioms, narrative patterns, and evaluative templates. As a consequence, he would have affiliated himself, at least provisionally, with that language's concepts in order to get what he needed, perhaps to get what he wanted, and, throughout, to avoid outcomes that he thought would harm him. As the protagonists of Chapters 3 and 4 intuited, though with varying degrees of awareness, it was probably not possible to escape this dependence. These words were the medium through which alienated individuals repopulated their social world. They might have felt some degree of pride or satisfaction, even though the conditions were not of their own choosing. As one consequence, for Anthony, success in language would have been dearer than for most of his neighbors. From the farthest margins of their exclusive community, Anthony would have been far more conscious of the balance between what he had gained through adopting their language and what it had taken from him along the way—at the very least, time, mental effort, attention, and dignity. For these reasons, Anthony's subjection to speech, the substance of modern sincerity, pushes to the front of the stage a question that few protagonists of early American literary and cultural history have been given space and time to contemplate: how to determine whether their efforts were worth the costs.

Repression

The stage is noisy and crowded. The players are very unhappy, but much of their discontent is muttered and not audible to most spectators. There is a chorus of women troubled about patriarchy. There are also men arguing with them, inviting them to speak more, even as they hope to catch them in error. At least one of these women has wandered away and is beating her children, her servants, and her mother-in law, and there are gossips and good church-men investigating her. Seventeen fireplaces crackle with the sound of burning cords cut from a forest of trees. Uncomfortably warm, several Pequot captives watch, comparing notes with each other about the similarities and differences between this violence and the violence of these women's husbands; there are also evangelists trying to convince these captives that, truly, Christian conver-sion is a good idea. There is at least one enslaved Black man listening to all of this, speculating on his strategy should he be asked to defend himself against charges of being a witch—and keeping a vigilant eye and ear toward the vigi-lant eyes and ears that are following him, searching for evidence. Many of these individuals aren't dreaming, at least immediately, of happiness. Most seem to be trying, in their own ways, to minimize their unhappiness, their stress, and their suffering. At the front of the stage, however, men like John Davenport and his colleagues, rivals, friends, and enemies—John Winthrop, John Cotton, Thomas Shepard, or Richard Mather—are speaking energetically to each other and over each other, all proposing that they know the best formulas for happiness. They know that hearts long to love, and they have answers. They are loud and forceful. They make many positive, prescriptive statements. They have confidence in prescribing because they know themselves. If their hearts are not yet pure, they are, prior critics of this drama assure us, sincere in their desires for purity. They are in touch with who they are, what they want, and what they feel. In their biopoetic striving for satisfaction, they are not telling themselves lies, not even lies of omission. Repression is not a player on this stage. And in their attempts to keep it offstage, critics' most attractive tool has been the vocabulary these loud men at the front kept using: the words they sought to renew so that these words would (successfully, it seems) outlast them. Those words, and their effects, lead to this book's "why." Repression may not be a player, but it has written many of these actors' lines. A prolific playwright, it continues its vibrant cultural work. Although Eaton might not have figured out how to step away from this crowded scene, the remove of several centuries offers modern readers a better perspective than she had to witness repression's skill. Closely examining this sophisticated process, we might be able better to determine, perhaps mitigate, our own conscription onto a similarly unhappy stage.

Christian settlers hated lingering expenses. They didn't mind debt but loathed the prospect of an ambiguous balance sheet, and they expressed that aversion in the sentences they uttered to each other that described their hopes and dreams. Historians tend to favor their priorities as they import settlers' own vocabulary—"holiness," "godliness," "fear," "discipline," and "redemption"—into their own prose with eloquence and ease. Such words, historians' immersive prose suggests, make it possible to imagine and understand an enchantment that the intervening centuries were supposed to have dissolved. But enchantment isn't simply a matter of fairies in the woods or a dove appearing as the heavens part. Enchantment licenses force beyond reason, and these words were attempts to tap into that force. Consider Christian settlers' obsession with the word "redeem" or its noun form, "redemption," a word many seventeenth-century residents of these colonies would have heard and spoken daily. "Redemption" named the transcendent goal, at least ideally, of every action that settlers performed. Theologically, it denoted the benevolent, sovereign nullification of a debt every individual carried against their deity. That nullification took place through a mysterious process whereby the deity counted the value of one mythic event—the torturous execution of his offspring—and transferred the value of that suffering to some of the indebted, wiping clean their individual balance sheet of offenses against him. Selection as one of the lucky ones was beyond anyone's control; but their actions, they hoped, might help them discern that likelihood, so they told each other to think about redemption as the goal of every action they performed, every day.[30]

---

30. Walter Benjamin, "Critique of Violence," in Marcus Bullock and Michael W. Jennings, eds., *Walter Benjamin: Selected Writings*, I, *1913–1926* (Cambridge, Mass., 1996), 236–252; Carl Schmitt, *Political Theology: Four Chapters on the Concept of Sovereignty*, trans. George Schwab (Chicago, 2005). A number of historians, particularly economic historians, have found the polysemy of "redemption" an exciting starting point for research on early modern English settlers, but they tend to be more interested in how spiritual vocabulary shaped economic thought rather than in how spiritual vocabulary, which dovetailed dynamically with economic vocabulary, influenced almost every aspect of settler life, especially psychic life. For exemplary book-length studies, see Stephen Innes, *Creating the Commonwealth: The Economic Culture of Puritan New England* (New York, 1995); Mark A. Peterson, *The Price of Redemption: The Spiritual Economy of Puritan New England* (Stanford, Calif., 1997); Mark Valeri, *Heavenly Merchandize: How Religion Shaped Commerce in Puritan America* (Princeton, N.J., 2010). On staying warm, see Cronon, *Changes in the Land;* Thomas M. Wickman, *Snowshoe Country: An Environmental and Cultural History of Winter in the Early American Northeast* (Cambridge, 2018).

Life is taxing, though. It's difficult even without the labor that settlers assigned themselves: creating a functioning, sustainable utopia from the ground up, when most couldn't even keep themselves warm in the winter. Spiritual redemption was supposed to make this work worthwhile, but in a different register of experience. Its erasure of a spiritual balance sheet was supposed to feel so shatteringly good that it would erase any individual's earthly balance sheet of resentments, dissatisfactions, failed financial investments, failed emotional investments, and the discouragement of the aches and pains of age that returned to the body each morning when one got out of bed. Spiritual salvation was supposed to redeem material suffering. Maybe for some it did. For others—such as the protagonists of this book's fourth and fifth chapters and especially that of the Conclusion—it didn't. Some were more aware of this failure than others. Like Anne Eaton, some perceived and others more inchoately felt the limits of redemption's promises within Davenport's system. Some tried to express their dissatisfaction within that system, but it would be a steep challenge, since it would question the validity of a concept like "redemption" in helping them forget those burdens, struggles, and taxations. It would undermine the promises of happiness that sincerity made in exchange for all those isolating, alienating demands. When a society's entire lexicon for navigating inner life was oriented toward a Polaris like "redemption," it would be difficult to know where and how to begin to express frustration with it.

There are good reasons to stay faithful to settlers' vocabulary and to prioritize it when describing their motivations and actions. Some scholars may be responding to a prior generation of historians who tried to expose settlers' avowals of belief as mystifications of acquisitiveness and a longing to be cruel. Those insights were not worthless—they made it possible to tell new stories, to diverge from the celebratory accounts of colonial settlement that had dominated academic historiography. Yet they often dispatched too quickly with the strangeness of spiritual life. Religion, to them, tended to be only a mystification, and an aggressively bad-faith one at that. Against these reductive explanations of spiritual life, and in tandem with a movement in literary and cultural studies to turn away from harm and toward repair, historians since then have turned to settlers' own explanatory terms as the best, maybe even the only, way to approach the experience of religion with sensitivity and seriousness, to understand how some settlers did, in fact, come to feel that their balance sheets had been wiped clean—at least long enough to write about it. Other historians may wish to avoid straying from settlers' vocabulary because new terms tend to propose that the critic knows more about an individual than they themselves do. This ethical challenge plays out in Eaton and Davenport's confrontation. Eaton did not fit in her society. The reasons perplexed her neighbors and possibly her, too. Davenport saw that ill fit as an opportunity to apply and then refine the principles of his soul science. He believed that he understood Eaton better than she understood herself, and he wasn't hesitant in claiming that superiority. Yet he also believed that he was able to stand outside of what, for her, was an intense struggle with words without being vulnerable to it himself. Davenport fantasized that he was in control of language rather than shaped by it. He did not want to contemplate the possibility that such a fantasy made him, at the same time, more mysterious to himself. Meanwhile, Eaton might eventually have been able, like Anne Hutchinson or Anne Bradstreet, to wrestle her dissatisfactions into words that could circulate and make sense among her neighbors. Her frustrations, which were not theirs, however, required more mental work to explain. They demanded more attention, effort, mental energy. Again, she might have asked herself whether the goal of communication really was so attractive. She might have intuited, skeptically, that the knowledge she forged from self-scrutiny and even more self-narration would not really redeem her previous irritations or erase them from her memory and bring her to the stage's happy front.[31]

Eaton had to make a decision that looks strange only when we make it explicit. Confronted by Davenport, she had to decide whether the work of self-inquiry and self-disclosure was worthwhile. In making that decision, she, along with everyone around her, would have probably considered how powerful, or how weak, her epistemological resources—her words—were. Davenport believed that the "redemption," "godliness," and "discipline" were the best tools for anyone to understand themselves. He might have believed sincerely, but he was wrong. Eaton, and the rest of the cast of the chapters that follow, are evidence of his error. Their various experiences of awkwardness and

---

31. For studies that read religion as mystification, see Richard Slotkin, *Regeneration through Violence: The Mythology of the American Frontier, 1600–1860* (Middletown, Conn., 1973); and Francis Jennings, *The Invasion of America: Indians, Colonialism, and the Cant of Conquest* (Williamsburg, Va., and Chapel Hill, N.C., 1975). On the vulnerability of scholarship of religion to participate in religious epistemology, see Jordan Alexander Stein and Justine S. Murison, "Introduction: Religion and Method," *EAL*, XLV (2010), 1–29. On the turn to repair, see Patricia Stuelke, *The Ruse of Repair: U.S. Neoliberal Empire and the Turn from Critique* (Durham, N.C., 2021). For examples of scholarship that self-consciously commits to settlers' own knowledge of themselves, see Karen Ordahl Kupperman, *Indians and English: Facing off in Early America* (Ithaca, N.Y., 2000), 14; Kristina Bross, *Dry Bones and Indian Sermons: Praying Indians in Colonial America* (Ithaca, N.Y., 2004), 25; Bross, *Future History: Global Fantasies in Seventeenth-Century American and British Writings* (Oxford, 2017), 17.

struggle suggest strongly that any given historical moment may not have apt epistemological resources to explain experiences of enduring dissatisfactions. It may, but it also may not. And when and where those sufficient resources do exist, they might have remained elusive or inaccessible to those who felt themselves responsible for documenting their eras. At the same time, the resources that many colonial settlers did have at hand might have worsened their unhappiness. Anne Eaton had many reasons not to speculate publicly on her sadness. According to one template for explaining the past, she might have been knowingly resisting a coercive pressure to self-disclose. According to a different template—not resistance, but refusal—she might have been striving, a little less deliberately, to evade the climate of humiliation that Davenport's system prescribed. More bleakly, Eaton might not have known what to call that unhappiness, might not have had a vocabulary that would affirm it was real and logical in the first place. Davenport's words weren't likely to grant her much room to consider any connection between her wretchedness and her experience of patriarchy, still less between her wretchedness and her whiteness. Most authorities in her life believed her wretchedness to be an expression of unreason. The ideas that they circulated were not likely to invite her to consider how her unhappiness was, not irrational nor demonic, but within the range of plausible effects of her given circumstances. These ideas were especially unlikely to afford space to think about any unredeemed items on her balance sheet, any accumulation of wretchedness that spiritual redemption failed to erase. When histories of colonists' interiority take up Davenport's vocabulary for soul science, using the words he and his colleagues recited loudly from the front of the stage, they do not leave much room to understand that lexicon's failures. They do not, furthermore, leave much room to account for the political consequences of those failures. This narrowed epistemological experience was part of these men's strategy for pursuing their biopoetic dreams. If plausible alternative reasons for Eaton's unhappiness turned out to exist, then so might reasons to second-guess, as Eaton did, whether redemption's amnesias were worth the work they required, the costs they incurred.[32]

32. On the political consequences of recycling received vocabulary and prose constructions, see James H. Merrell, "Some Thoughts on Colonial Historians and American Indians," *WMQ,* 3d Ser., XLVI (1989), 94–119; Ranajit Guha, "The Prose of Counter-Insurgency," *Selected Subaltern Studies,* ed. Guha and Gayatri Chakravorty Spivak (Oxford, 1988), 45–84; Merrell et al., "Forum: Second Thoughts on Colonial Historians and American Indians," *WMQ,* 3d Ser., LXIX (2012), 451–540; Jordan Alexander Stein, "How to Undo the History of Sexuality: Editing Edward Taylor's Meditations," *American Literature,* XC (2018), 753–784.

Sincerity was the sign under which these men hoped to replace unhappy stories with happy ones and, in that process of replacing, to forget the historically powerful reasons for unhappiness. To be successful, sincerity required work, which was often unpleasant and often added to the balance sheet of discomforts and annoyances. Although critics have insisted that no one on this stage was repressed, the one exception they have found to their claim suggested, when he admitted to his repression, that everyone around him was, too. He saw that the forgetful stories they told themselves about their lives was part of repression's dynamic, if often exhausting, work. This insight from Michael Wigglesworth, one of Davenport's colleagues from all the way around the cape in the settlement of Malden, should not surprise readers who have read the work of the twentieth-century soul scientist most responsible for developing a theory of repression. Almost everyone, Sigmund Freud proposed, represses. Repression is a conventional method for adjusting to the social world. The word names the process whereby the attempts to control antisocial, instinctual responses to the external world's provocations and circumscriptions become habit, how the hard work of socialization falls away from the individual's perception. But Freud isn't necessary to understand this. Early in the diary where Wigglesworth chronicled his nascent career after graduating from Harvard, the Malden minister noted how taxing he found the work of self-scrutiny for the purpose of self-control and self-management: "To repress," he wrote, "costeth me much." For Wigglesworth, repression didn't mean exactly what it would for Freud. Among other differences, the repression that wore out Wigglesworth was conscious. At least, it was initially. It required conscious attempts to know the self, with the aim of better dominating his creaturely body and its uglier dealings. Repression was a basic function of subjection, as he and his fellow ministers proposed it. For Wigglesworth, self-knowledge and the repression it served were very costly. In this, Wigglesworth and the aging Freud agree. Psychic life, for both, followed what the latter called the "economic" principle. That interior life could be described and, Wigglesworth dreamed, managed, just like any other "scarce resources that nature provides." Repression was one vital part of that management; it was not distinct from settlers' attempt to orient their desires "within ordained borders." Obedience to ordained borders was repression's fundamental mechanism. The work of obedience, of subjection, took energy from all the other aspects of living that also demanded Wigglesworth's attention.[33]

33. Morgan, ed., *Diary of Michael Wigglesworth*, v–xv, 22 ("to repress"); Sigmund Freud, "The Unconscious," in James Strachey, ed. and trans., *The Standard Edition of the Complete*

For Wigglesworth, repression found reinforcements in telling and retelling a template. He hoped that the work of self-management would eventually require less conscious thought. Practicing repression, he gambled, would shape his desires over time. He wanted repression to make him a better subject, to help him submit more easily to his deity and to his society's attempts to live happily in service of that deity. He hoped that one day, repression would not be so costly, would not require such conscious energy. He hoped, in other words, that he could forget—that he could repress—the work of repressing. Over the three-year course of his diary, at least, Wigglesworth did not succeed. But many of his neighbors did. Most of them forgot, and their success resulted in the appearance that repression had not been work at all. Successful repression by his neighbors increased his sensitivity to his own failures. Wigglesworth might have envied them, but he did not resign his pursuit of that skill, did not give up his goal to repress in a less costly, more amnesic fashion. In fact, he offered his community a vocabulary and a forum to forget more efficiently, to cognize their lives and their experiences of interiority in a more theologically acceptable and easy fashion. Like Davenport, Wigglesworth undertook that work in public sermons and during private counseling sessions. He listened to his congregation tell their stories and encouraged them to keep practicing. And he found more materially enduring opportunities to shape his community, such as his long poem *The Day of Doom*. This text, an extraordinarily popular verse thriller that modeled forms of thinking about personal fealty and collective justice, enjoyed centuries of popularity, passing

---

Psychological Works of Sigmund Freud, XIV, *On the History of the Psycho-Analytic Movement, Papers on Meta-Psychology and Other Works* (1914–1916) (London, 1957), 161–215, esp. 181 ("economic"); Strother E. Roberts, *Colonial Ecology, Atlantic Economy: Transforming Nature in Early New England* (Philadelphia, 2019), 3 ("scarce resources"); Richard Godbeer, *Sexual Revolution in Early America* (Baltimore, 2002), 55 ("borders"); Edmund S. Morgan, "The Puritans and Sex," *NEQ*, XV (1942), 591–607; Kathleen Verduin, "'Our Cursed Natures': Sexuality and the Puritan Conscience," ibid., LVI (1983), 220–237; Ed Ingebretsen, "Wigglesworth, Mather, Starr: Witch-Hunts and General Wickedness in Public," in Tracy Fessenden, Nicholas F. Radel, and Magdalena J. Zaborowska, eds., *The Puritan Origins of American Sex* (New York, 2001), 21–40; Nicholas Radel, "A Sodom Within: Historicizing Puritan Homoerotics in the Diary of Michael Wigglesworth," ibid., 41–55. One implication of this economic principle is that no bright line exists to cleanly separate the pathological repression that Wigglesworth is often cast to play on our stage from the more apparently healthy work of alignment such as that endorsed by soul scientists like Davenport, Shepard, or McGiffert. Freud would concur. Wigglesworth would want readers to agree, too. See Freud, "Analysis, Terminable and Interminable," in Strachey, ed. and trans., *Works of Sigmund Freud*, XXIII, *Moses and Monotheism: An Outline of Psycho-Analysis and Other Works* (1937–1939), 211–253; and Chapter 3, below.

from one generation to the next. As the fourth chapter below narrates, the poem energetically participated in standardizing the vocabulary that settlers could use to understand themselves. Owing in part to Wigglesworth's sensitive labor, his neighbors learned to repress better and more efficiently. They did not experience this understanding as a loss. But it was. Other, less costly ways to understand themselves faced collective oblivion. This necessarily narrow, sometimes ignorant way of recognizing oneself and one's world would come to seem, at least among settlers, to be common sense.[34]

Sincerity triumphs by forgetting alternatives. In doing so, it forgets the bravery of self-making's labors when the outcome remains uncertain. Sincerity forgets, too, the serious reasons to tremble in the face of failure. Approaching Tiresias, it fumbles the blood. Forgetting, in turn, has had powerful historical consequences. Drew Lopenzina's word for this amnesia is "unwitnessing." The term describes English settlers' tendency, as early as the seventeenth century, to misrecognize the sophistication of Native life and to ignore the consequences of that misrecognition for their own quality of life. Misrecognition probably wasn't deliberate, but it was still important. It buttressed settlers' sense of superiority in the face of so much evidence to the contrary, so much evidence that, in a new environment, they were not as powerful as they had claimed. They were inept, weak, vulnerable morally and materially. In their encounters with other systems of justice, in their violent conflicts with other Europeans over beaver pelts, in their desperate longings to not be unpopular with their neighbors or to have the power their fathers had, and in the disappointments their friends visited on them, they kept stumbling on evidence that they were not the people they had intensely hoped to be. Many refused to accept this evidence. "Unwitnessing" may thus denote more than misrecognition of others. It also implies misrecognition of one's own experiences; it summons fantasies like sincerity for fortification. Lopenzina suggests this when he uses vocabulary from psychoanalysis to describe the limits of settlers' epistemological tools. Colonists, he writes, "behaved much like trauma patients who have 'blocked out' certain memories of the past in order to cope in the present." The traumas they inflicted on others were intricately, but often quietly, connected to the traumas they inflicted on themselves and then insisted on sublimating—on denying by transforming them into stories of success, happiness, and the triumph of their claims to civility. Lopenzina proposes, further, that "historical or cultural amnesia, a willful forgetting

---

34. Mark Rifkin, *Settler Common Sense: Queerness and Everyday Colonialism in the American Renaissance* (Minneapolis, 2014).

of [settlers'] complicity in acts of violence" is a symptomatic manifestation of trauma, poorly managed. A key part of that forgetting was the positive, obstinately sanguine strategy of replacement. Telling stories about what they thought they could know about themselves, assisted by powerful theological vocabulary, allowed them to avoid thinking that they might still be lonely, burdened, deracinated, and longing for approval so powerful and enduring that they might one day be able to forget their former painful struggles.[35]

The claims that the men at the front of the stage made are part of the same story as that lived by the people behind them, whose varieties of unhappiness collided in sometimes spectacular, sometimes banal ways. The men out front have succeeded for centuries in claiming otherwise, and their claims have been shored up by the liberalism that followed, whose amnesias batten on sincerity and the unwitnessing that sincerity has enabled along the way. These amnesias exercise themselves in the cunning political challenge of recognition as critics such as Elizabeth Povinelli, following Karl Marx and G. F. W. Hegel, have described it. "Cunning" doesn't denote malice but rather the frustrating trick of forgetting: liberal society offers individuals the promise of rights-bearing participation and protection as benefits of being recognized as a human, an eligible participant in a political society. But that promise requires an exchange. Liberalism expects individuals to consent to being defined by abstraction rather than particularity, to alienate themselves from the communities and priorities that shaped them. This demand poses a challenge especially to Native peoples, escalating the stakes of assimilation, asking them to forget a history before settler colonialism and then to forget that forgetting ever took place. Liberal subjects often like this forgetting. It flatters their fantasies of benevolence, of democracy's desirability. It is the one thing, Ralph Waldo Emerson asserted, that they seek "with insatiable desire." One reason they came to like it, and with such fervor, is that sincerity—a singular, socially recognized form of self-relation—outshines the terror, misery, or sometimes simply dull and discouraging loneliness of the alternatives, of loitering alone around the quiet rear of the stage, among the rags and the bones, carrying around inchoate feelings that might look like idiosyncrasy or pathology, if they ever found a name at all. Some experiences might never find a name. This was a frightening possibility. Against that fear, socially affirmed self-knowledge, though maybe only partially accurate, could be a relief. The self that feared uncertainty could become an object of knowledge and, perhaps, control—not

35. Drew Lopenzina, *Red Ink: Native Americans Picking up the Pen in the Colonial Period* (Albany, N.Y., 2012), 5–11.

too different an object than the essence and origins of earthly minerals, the motion of a virus's spread and its containment, the size and shape of a population, the local flora and their unexpected uses, or the weird anatomical quirks of the opossum. Knowledge pursuits could be a pleasure, especially when turned inward—or, at least, they could be a temporary balm from pain. This substitute knowledge persuaded individuals to forget alternative ways of living with what they were and to forget the conditions that drew them to one story about that self among others.[36]

The dream those protagonists sent into their future was that of the mind's triumph over matter, a dream gratified by the biopolitical disciplines of the century that followed, that "other apparatus of objectivity," as Foucault described it, that has become "our own." Settlers wanted their inheritors to be happy, but in a narrow, costly way. Their premier strategy for that happiness was to offer templates to persuasively disavow a wide and expansive network of material circumstances that shaped individual selfhood. When John Cotton imagined settlement, he pictured it as a resting place that was both "firme" (unthreatened materially) and "quiet" (unthreatened psychically). This description of settler colonialism should give citizens of a settler society pause. First, this representation of happiness and calm invites historians to reflect on the insights we risk missing when we hasten, as settlers themselves did, to identify major feelings and their meanings rather than ugly, unwieldy, and uncomfortable ones. It invites historians to examine the work that understanding those minor counterparts required, as well as the taxations of that intellectual, intensely personal task. This historically sensitive work participates in what Stephen Best, following Mark Seltzer, calls the "'incrementalist turn.'" These critics would have us find the "accent on the minor" lurking in historical texts. The archive of colonial New England settlement contributes to that turn a dynamic example of how the minor so often and so smoothly pulls itself into the

36. Elizabeth Povinelli, *The Cunning of Recognition: Indigenous Alterities and the Making of Australian Multiculturalism* (Durham, N.C., 2002); Ralph Waldo Emerson, "Circles," in Douglas Crase, ed., *Essays: First and Second Series* (New York, 1991), 171–184; Karl Marx, "'On the Jewish Question,'" in Joseph O'Malley, ed., *Marx: Early Political Writings* (Cambridge, 1994), 28–56; G. F. W. Hegel, *Reason in History: A General Introduction to the Philosophy of History* (New York, 1953), 43–44; Glen Sean Coulthard, *Red Skin, White Masks: Rejecting the Colonial Politics of Recognition* (Minneapolis, 2014); Joanne Barker, *Native Acts: Law, Recognition, and Cultural Authenticity* (Durham, N.C., 2011); Audra Simpson, *Mohawk Interruptus: Political Life across the Borders of Settler States* (Durham, N.C., 2014); Uday Singh Mehta, *The Anxiety of Freedom: Imagination and Individuality in Locke's Political Thought* (Ithaca, N.Y., 1992); Bonnie Honig, *Democracy and the Foreigner* (Princeton, N.J., 2001).

league of the major, how the ugliness of those feelings might impel someone to conscript their unglamorous, itchy unhappiness into a story that can claim sublime beauty, and how the energy-intensive work of learning and retelling those stories ends up producing sublime violence.[37]

Second, Cotton's description of happiness invites readers to consider the happiness we feel as critics and residents of a settler society, the peace and quiet we achieve, especially when that peace and happiness feels most intimate. The goal of such criticism isn't to be unhappy, as if achieving unhappiness would secure moral safety, a distinctly negative, dialectically fugitive sort of peace. That form of study still offers the ego gratifications Michael Warner cautioned against two decades ago. Rather, one goal might be to exercise more thoughtfulness in the stories we tell about the past, the templates that teach us and give us practice in narrating and understanding our present. It is not necessarily pessimistic, "adversarial," or "angr[y]" to undertake more scrupulous accounting of costs. The five chapters that follow do prioritize limits where previous histories have favored freedom and power, but they do so to practice recognizing subjection's quiet cunning and to practice imagining other ways of understanding selfhood, given sincerity's largely successful ascent. The first two chapters show how sincerity's social value required individuals to winnow their ties to robust, if sometimes volatile, social networks and to will increasing alienation. The second, third, and fourth chapters survey how individuals became invested in higher-stakes practices of sincerity to reintegrate themselves into a civic community, how sincerity heightened expectations of individual responsibility and offered them pride and self-satisfaction in return. The fourth and fifth chapters survey the taxations of those practices and their consequences for happiness. Sincerity, the dream engine of Christian utopia in early modernity, eventually limited the happiness settlers could recognize. The book's Conclusion shows how sensitivity to sincerity's struggle with history can have felicitous horizontal effects: it can expand the sorts of happiness we recognize for ourselves and that we make available in the social world we share with others.[38]

37. Foucault, *Hermeneutics of the Subject,* trans. Burchell, 319; Cotton, *Gods Promise,* 2; Stephen Best, *None Like Us: Blackness, Belonging, Aesthetic Life* (Durham, N.C., 2018), 61, 155 n. 108; Mark Seltzer, "The Official World," *Critical Inquiry,* XXXVII (2011), 724–753, esp. 727–728; Ngai, *Ugly Feelings;* Rei Terada, *Looking Away: Phenomenality and Dissatisfaction, Kant to Adorno* (Cambridge, Mass., 2009).

38. Delbanco, *Puritan Ordeal,* 7, 259 n. 9; Michael Warner, "What's Colonial about Colonial America?" in Robert Blair St. George, ed., *Possible Pasts: Becoming Colonial in Early America* (Ithaca, N.Y., 2000), 49–70.

History's agon with sincerity began decades before Anne Eaton's scandalous expression of it, far beyond the walls of her very large home. She found sincerity tiresome because knowledge, especially about the self, had high stakes in a frontier setting, where the presence of different forms of social, political, and moral life threatened the foundations of European knowledge endeavors. This discovery is the topic of the first chapter, "Moral Unmoorings: Fear and the Foundations of Settler Sincerity," which makes this threat apparent in some of the earliest documents recording English settlement, including the rocky attempts by inept, clumsy, and enthusiastically frightened colonists to establish permanent colonies and trading posts at Plymouth, Wessagusset, and Ma-re Mount. In general, most early modern Europeans cherished an ideal of truth as firm, absolute, and universal, and they thrilled at what they saw to be evidence of that moral hierarchy in the world around them. In pursuing knowledge, even intimate knowledge about themselves, however, many early modern English people who left Europe (and not only Christian reformists) ran into a quiet problem. In new lands, they confronted the possibility that the epistemological foundations they used to approach truth might fail them and jeopardize their ability to know themselves as special in their access to goodness. To preserve their knowledge about themselves, they needed threats, so they began to search out evidence to support the deductive proposition that every human, everywhere, shared a fundamentally vengeful, selfish human nature. In short, they amplified their paranoia: the texts that men such as William Bradford, Phinehas Pratt, and Thomas Morton wrote about those early ventures are all fascinated by fear. They differ only in how clearly they could put that fear into words, how well they could tell a story about it. Some, like Bradford, were able to conscript fear into an efficient template that fortified a sense of inner specialness in being Christian, English, and well-born. Other writers, like Morton, used it antithetically, as a reliable plot element to criticize other colonists for their hypocrisy. But still others, like Pratt, seem haunted by an epistemological disturbance, even decades later. Pratt was troubled by the possibility that an entirely different moral universe existed, was valid, and even encompassed his own. These documents of early conflict show how dynamic and dear stories about human nature could be in shoring up their tellers' claims to selfhood. Deducing that neighbors would always behave violently for material benefit, English Christians could repossess confidence that they themselves were always innocent victims to ever-plausible harm. They could be assured that they possessed purity of heart and were capable of transcending what they thought were baser longings in conditions that they thrilled to believe were constantly threatening both their bodies and their souls.

Early colonists believed their fears were real. The stresses of enduring them heightened their hopes for happiness among themselves. These hopes shaped Davenport's misrecognition of Eaton's dissatisfaction: men like him got great satisfaction from listening to the personal stories their neighbors told about themselves, whether happy or sad. He and his colleagues thought this sort of self-disclosure was the substance of sympathetic fellow feeling. Practices of telling and listening to the experiences of others, these men believed, would synthesize affection and reason—but they insisted that synthesis had to take place in service to the goal of social discipline, rationally deduced. The point of sympathy was efficiency, not dissolution into a world of embodiment and flow—a risk that would make them less like the deity they thought humans were made in the image of and more like animals they thought they should control. Chapter 2, "Dreaming on Dry Land: Thoughtfulness beyond Good Intentions," surveys how settlers thought about feelings and felt about thinking and, especially, how their proximity to one nonhuman animal, the American beaver, troubled their confidence that animal affection and human reason were all that distinct in the first place. These doubts appear most vividly in the texts of the first decade of English colonization, when participating in the lucrative pelt trade was still plausible and enticing to English settlers—attracting them with more force than they liked to admit. Responding to those attractions, men like Winthrop used their powers of reason to exhort their neighbors to build and exercise powerful emotional bonds with other humans—and only other humans. Those exhortations, however, took place on a frontier rich with other models of obligation and responsibility, models that crossed the human-animal distinction. Beaver stories beyond the English tradition suggest an alternative to the logic that Winthrop proposed. Rather than sympathy, they solicit thoughtfulness: deliberate attentiveness to the experience of other beings and to the network of dependence that characterizes the material world. Thoughtfulness required realignment of the relationship between feeling and thinking. Rather than dialectical antagonism, thoughtfulness expressed an individual's recognition of shared dependence. Because settlers' visions of moral good required ongoing alienation from a vibrant material world, most English planters declined to pursue such a realignment, even as their commitments to paranoia subjected their neighbors to a perpetual state of fellow feeling toward settlers in order to stay alive. In response to the narrow-mindedness and narrow-heartedness of men like Winthrop, the actions of Massachusetts sachem Chickatawbut show off the possibilities of counter-conversion by manipulating interlocutors' feelings about their earnest claims to be reasonable.

Chickatawbut knew there was wiggle room for negotiation through strategy. He was quick to learn the communicative currency of settler society. Within that society, Anne Eaton had her own methods. She knew that confession would make her life easier, that an autobiographical story could give her qualified power, but to acquire a story to share meant unpleasant work, and putting it into circulation was likewise difficult. The risked alienations surveyed in the first two chapters show, however, that choosing to eschew those conventions was not easy, either. Chapter 3, "Blood, Regret, and Tears: How to Put on Sincerity, and Why," explains some of the reasons individuals worked so strenuously, sometimes mortifyingly, to be able to claim that they knew themselves, as well as some of the ways they managed to preserve themselves from the more humiliating aspects of that sharing. It introduces readers to a number of individuals who, like Anne Eaton, found the prospect of self-disclosure grueling: Michael Wigglesworth, an insecure first-generation college student and eventually leading minister at Malden; Anne Bradstreet, self-conscious trophy wife and aspiring historian at Ipswich; and a cohort of Algonquian converts including Kanoonus, Paumpmunet, Wuttinnaumatuk, Nonqutnumuk, Waompam, William Pease, and Pauchumu, scholars and diplomats at Plymouth. First, Wigglesworth's private inquiries and confessions to his deity show how taxing self-disclosure could be, as well as one advantage they could give him socially—they got ahead of worse humiliations later. Bradstreet's poems offer evidence to confirm this, but they also demonstrate some strategies, such as omission and occlusion, that individuals could take in order to make confession easier. Finally, the Algonquian confessors, especially the Plymouth converts, suggest some powerful reasons individuals gambled that the unpleasantness of confession (and that of strategizing to endure confession) was worthwhile—and it wasn't always for the gratification of the distant Christian deity. All of these converts, especially the ones who weren't English, launched into the work of self-knowledge with zeal, dedication, and sophistication that dulls the bright line between sincerity and duplicity. Their commitment challenges the proposition, often implicit, that sincerity requires singularity of motive. These confessors often entertained more than one motive to carry them through this difficult work. Their multiple possible motives tease out an undernoticed feature of sincerity the previous chapter surveyed: how early modern Christian settlers demanded that individuals winnow, if not sever, their relationships with a lush, fecund, and compromising world in order to pursue purity of heart. But this chapter's observation pushes that feature still further and explains why many confessors would assent to such winnowing: they found themselves often isolated in a world disastrously different from any they would have chosen for themselves. In response to violence that oscillated between clearly intentional and possibly unintentional, Native converts, finally, quietly used sincerity's paradigmatic expression, the confession, to create smaller, more fulfilling communities of mutual beholding.

Rarely was the colonial frontier an ideal setting for exercising choice or agency. Most confessors engaged in self-disclosure in contexts far from those they might have chosen for themselves. Anne Eaton raged in response to this sort of quiet coercion. And she was not alone. With many of her neighbors, she shared a quiet fury about those limitations. Some, however, possessed access to sanctioned outlets for that fury, allowing them yet to reinvest in a system that taxed them severely even as it represented those taxations as the path to true spiritual freedom. Chapter 4, "The Happiest Memories: Duties, Debts, and the Generation of Freedom," identifies resentment as one of the foremost costs of sincerity as settlers exercised it: a longing for suffering's recognition, usually across divisions of age and generation. Settler elders wanted their youth to recognize what they had suffered, so they kept telling stories about those struggles. Some stories were explicit, in the autobiographical mode. They were written and spoken. Other times, these stories were smuggled into a discursive mode such as the jeremiad, a genre whose popularity derived from the low regard it held for the youth next to their elders. These stories acknowledged and tried to vindicate the estrangements and humiliations elders had undergone. Yet the best vindication would be to convince children to undergo suffering and to want it, too. Thus, the jeremiad saturated the literature of the second and third generations of settlement in texts as wide-ranging as Wigglesworth's magnum opus, *The Day of Doom*, and his preppy colleague Increase Mather's prolific sermons. Many of these settler children, when they reached adulthood, did seek to reproduce these desires in their own offspring. Though they experienced success with pleasure, that pleasure wasn't exclusive or consistent. The imperatives their parents passed on to them generated commensurate desires for recognition of their own suffering. These resentments expressed themselves in words and deeds, in patriarchs' morality stories about the 1675–1676 war that engulfed their settlements and in the implicit stories about justice that wrathful mothers and sons expressed through mob violence. Nevertheless, though the pressure to vindicate suffering was powerful, it wasn't ineluctable. Alternatives appear in the sermons of James Allen and in the churchgoing priorities of Dorcas, a formerly enslaved African woman who chose, late in life, to switch church membership in order to attend Allen's sermons. These sermons pay unusual attention to happiness and the value of self-knowledge in achieving it. But they suggest that the content of sincerity, self-knowledge, needn't tie itself permanently to grievance; it can be edited, revised, and perfected over time, possibly interminably. This would mean renouncing certainty of a self shaped by injury—a difficult prospect, since revision would risk exposing the first avowed story, retrospectively, as untruthful and the confessor insincere. Despite such risk, these sermons hint, that inconsistency might prove to be a felicitous, even desirable failure.

If only Anne Eaton had had a network of reliable intimates to commune with rather than living in estrangement from those who expected her to divulge her innermost truths. If only, in other words, Eaton had had friends. But friendship might not have helped her all that much. Friendship in settler society tended to require—and worse, imply the ease and normalcy of—sincere self-knowledge and self-disclosure. Chapter 5, "Friendship, Fair and True: Sincerity Makes a Compromise with History," shows how individuals, not simply communities, may benefit from uncovering what sincerity elides and forgets, yielding a little breathing room from history's heavy and intimate weight. The task of historicizing sincerity seems pessimistic and cheerless, implying that an individual's longing to transcend material determination is doomed form the start. These chapters do suggest that this longing may be doomed, though it needn't be a pessimistic conclusion. It can also be part of a more sensitive understanding of individuality, a step toward alleviating individuality's quiet tolls. This final chapter turns its attention to the effects of sincerity's maturation on a social experience most often associated with happiness, subjective flourishing, and a life worth living—the experience of friendship. It examines four unusual individuals whose intimate lives don't fit within regnant literary-historical analyses of friendship and its value. For them, friendship required a tiresome performance of sincerity: fidelity to a known self. It was difficult for them, and it did not always seem worth the effort. These individuals—Mary Rowlandson, celebrity hostage; Roger Williams, obstinately lonely translator and diplomat; James Quananopohit, civil war double agent; and Anthony Thacher, shipwrecked barrel maker—often didn't know who they really were, and the conditions that produced their doubts were the same conditions that demanded they pretend to know. In order to claim life-sustaining friendships, they had to insist they were robust individuals even as their worlds were being destroyed by individuality's most enthusiastic proponents. Against the grain of virtually all literary-historical scholarship on the experience of friendship, this chapter does not propose that friendship can overcome historical circumstances. For these individuals, it couldn't. Rather, Chapter 5 proposes that friendship is a tense compromise with history, a stopgap and a negotiation with existential challenges specific to circumstances not of an individual's choosing. Friendship was settler sincerity's cold comfort. It blanketed, but only barely, the intense bereavement that settlers have tried to narrate as a triumph of virtue in the wasteland they created for themselves.

Whither sincerity? It may be one vehicle through which Puritanism invented the American self, but the estrangements it responded to and the instruments it used to soothe them were not unique to Protestant settlers in Algonquian territory. These sensitive, often unhappy people nevertheless provide a vivid window into sincerity's disavowed history, its conditions and its consequences. Most dynamic among these consequences, perhaps, is sincerity's power to deny that it has a history; second most dynamic is the near invisibility of sincerity's strategies, many of which now seem universal and normal. Likewise ubiquitous, however, are sincerity's frustrations. This book's Conclusion, "Miserable Comforts: A Dialectical Lyric," proposes one way that those strategies and their frustrations endure. Anne Eaton might have found consolation in knowing and contemplating, if not befriending, her distant neighbor in the Bay Colony town of Hingham, who, like her, expressed frustration with sincerity through acts of violence toward those she was supposed to nurture. Ann Hett heard the Delphic injunction and obeyed it. Yet she did not mistake its pursuit with the discovery of a happy outcome. Hett strove to know herself. Her inquiry, undertaken over at least a decade, yielded nothing but cursedness. But she refused, finally, the promise of redemption, refused the consolations that told her if she would only try harder, for longer, she might one day reach redemptive satisfaction, a joy that would wipe clean the substantial effort it took to achieve. Hett's obstinate pessimism invited her witnesses to wonder why it was so important for them to convince her (and themselves) of sincerity's ultimate worthiness, just as it invites modern readers to reconsider our own enthusiasm for stories of subjective triumph, power, and freedom in the present.

CHAPTER ONE

Moral Unmoorings

Fear and the Foundations of Settler Sincerity

I F PHINEHAS PRATT had been a writer of fiction trying to show rather than tell how he longed for moral and epistemological certainty, he could have done worse than narrate his 1622 journey of warning between his settlement at Wessagusset and that of his neighbors at Plymouth, through the territory of Massachusetts who he thought were likely to attack these English settlements, and during which he got lost in the forest and fell clumsily into a dell. Pratt, of course, wasn't writing fiction when he penned his "Decliration of the Afaires of the Einglish People [That First] Inhabited New Eingland" forty years later. He hoped his readers, the governors of the Plymouth Colony, would receive his relation as fact and respond to its contents with action, since he was writing to request a pension. Given that ambition, there is no immediately evident reason Pratt should have included such vivid sensory detail as he did in his document. To prove his value to the Plymouth governors, he thought it might help to narrate the suffering he had once undergone for their sake—the cold, the disorientation, the risk to life and limb. Something else, however, seemed to motivate him when he recalled, four decades after the fact, what he had seen from the gully. Deciding not to attempt to leave it that night, he found some dry wood, built a fire, and then, in the dusk, looked up beyond the ground that surrounded him and into the sky. There, "the stars began to a pear and I saw Ursa Magor." Between 1623 and 1662, the lightbulb had not yet been invented; Ursa Major was still quite visible to the Plymouth magistrates on cloudless nights. They knew what it was, and so did their fathers, and so had their fathers' fathers an ocean away. Was this some proto-Barthesian "reality effect" meant, in its banality, to convince his readers of the events' truth? Pratt would have been eager to convince his listeners that he was sincere, that he was relating his experience as it had really taken place. He wanted this, first, because of the material benefit—"my subsistance, the remaining time of my life." But he also wanted to succeed because, unlike his audience, Pratt had directly confronted the possibility that the foundations for sharing truth with an interlocutor might have crumbled, that the tools he used to determine truth—and, as a consequence, for claiming to know himself—had quietly stopped working.[1]

Though Pratt was not writing fiction, simply communicating facts caused him great struggle. He rambled, and his audience probably experienced impatience toward his lack of skill. *Why,* they might have wondered, *is this man wasting our time with these details?* Pratt's narrative errancy, though, meant more than he knew. The Great Bear brought Pratt great relief. That relief had material and immaterial qualities, and the material ones are not hard to recover historically. The constellation was probably beautiful to him, but beyond its aesthetic value, it was practical. It oriented him in place after a confusing first day of travel in which, "the sonn being beclouded, I wandered, not knowing my way." These stars didn't simply create an outline of a large quadruped in the sky. Their position also signaled cardinal directions—if one could identify the anatomy of the bear, one could then, perhaps with the help of adjacent Polaris, identify where north was, and then south, east, and west. Knowing that Wessagusset was northwest of Plymouth, Pratt would be able to chart a surer course to Plymouth in the morning. He wanted his audience to know he'd anticipated this; earlier in his testimony, he had recalled the risk of getting lost. "Said I to our Company, 'now is the Time to Run to Plimoth. Is ther any Compas to be found.'" There were none, or at least, "non but them that belong to the ship," and those were unsuitable: "Thay are to Bigg." And so, lacking this instrument, between the white snow underfoot and the white clouds overhead, Pratt got lost. Fortunately, the clouds lifted at nightfall. His

---

1. Phinehas Pratt, *A Declaration of the Affairs of the English People That First Inhabited New England,* ed. Richard Frothingham, Massachusetts Historical Society, *Collections,* 4th Ser., IV (Boston, 1858), 474–487, esp. 484, 487; Roland Barthes, "The Reality Effect," in Richard Howard, trans., *The Rustle of Language* (Berkeley, Calif., 1989), 141–148.

intense relief upon seeing the stars clung with him through the decades. To recall the celestial compass in his writing was to communicate its dearness in a moment of what he thought (and what he imagined Plymouth's elders recognized) to be a moment of great vulnerability and danger. Relief should have been obvious to all English witnesses; so should the background danger that clarified such relief, all of which, he hoped, would bring him a source of material stability before he died. Those were the unhappy conditions that the Great Bear's rising illuminated.[2]

Imagine, however, if Pratt had stumbled into the gully and, as the sunlight waned and the sky darkened, he had looked up to the clearing sky for a renewed sense of direction—yet, rather than Ursa Major, Ursa Minor, or any other of the formerly secure constellations above, he saw chaos without order, patterns of stars and planets he had never seen before, different from the skies that he had seen in England and during the months-long voyage west. As recently as three decades before, this uncertainty had still troubled Europeans, and it now nagged at Pratt's testimony. It comprises the emotional and historical content Pratt smuggled into his text through his seemingly irrelevant attention to detail. That content attached itself to the narrative in a fashion similar to Pratt's account of the fear of getting lost in the white terrain. For Pratt, as he struggled with his limited storytelling skills, it was easier to represent a source of fear (being lost in unfamiliar territory) by relating its consolation and redress (the familiar constellation). This representational strategy may also apply to his exposition of the intellectual terror into which he had stumbled. Pratt might have found it easier to narrate the material threat of ambient hostility, and the reliable heavenly patterns that guided him, than to recount a far more unsettling and fearsome proposition: that his foundations for recognizing threats (unlike the constellation overhead) were not applicable in this new social and political context; that former, guiding moral universals no longer held sway. Christians in Europe had confronted the possibility of moral relativity for more than a century; Pratt wasn't the first to wonder. Nevertheless, Pratt, and the Plymouth elders for whom he wrote, were among the first to try to assimilate that possibility into quotidian life, to make it dull and untaxing to their mental resources. They were among the first for whom survival depended on how they managed a new experience that threatened, in Lionel Trilling's words, to be a "psychic catastrophe," to abolish the moral certainty that Charles Taylor claims is foundational to personal identity. Later English planters, at Plymouth and beyond, would undertake sincerity's rigors

2. Pratt, *A Declaration of the Affairs*, ed. Frothingham, 483.

with dogged enthusiasm, but they felt that effort to be worthwhile because it soothed the dread they felt at the prospect of looking into a moral "firmament" and not recognizing any order to the stars in that sky.[3]

What Pratt feared remained nearly incomprehensible to him. By contrast, many of his English contemporaries tried to understand, or at least claimed they understood, what frightened them. But the fears they could document do not exhaust those they experienced. An unquieted distress still echoes in their documentary archive. The texts of the earliest Plymouth settlement bear this out. They show how early modern English Protestants could barely comprehend the disorienting force of proximity to other ethical systems. To try to make sense of these while keeping their own intact, settlers responded by renewing and expanding their claims about universal human nature. The apotheosis of this response was the paranoia they cherished—better the devil they knew than the possibility of a devil-free world they didn't. Early modern reformists, with more at stake for their sense of selfhood, clung to paranoia more intensely than their less zealous Christian countrymen, but most English people who traveled and engaged with residents of new lands found paranoia useful. They habituated themselves to distrusting the sincerity of others in order to prove to themselves that sincerity was a real quality to claim. The subsequent chapters of this book describe this habit of distrust and the inquiries it energized in settlers' inward-facing social lives, how it shaped the pursuit of happiness among individuals who, by and large, shared epistemological foundations. But before it could reward them, sincerity winnowed. Here, the dream of a happy society, consisting of earnestly self-knowing individuals, required those individuals to sever themselves from obligations to a moral universe larger than their own.

Like Phinehas Pratt, William Bradford was attentive to his environment and often used his reason to make practical sense of it. And like many of their fellow English travelers in the early modern Atlantic, Bradford was curious about his material environment, keen to acquire knowledge of it, and, most of all, enthusiastic to use that knowledge not simply to make practical sense but to propose and strengthen transportable theories about the way the world worked. Bradford struggled with a key step in producing confident knowledge—it was difficult for him to analyze the evidence he collected about his

3. Lionel Trilling, *Sincerity and Authenticity: The Charles Eliot Norton Lectures, 1969–1970* (Cambridge, Mass., 1972), 12, 117; Jose de Acosta, *Natural and Moral History of the Indies,* trans. Frances López-Morillas (Durham, N.C., 2002), 24–26; Charles Taylor, *Sources of the Self: The Making of the Modern Identity* (Cambridge, Mass., 1989).

relationship to his new environment and to make reliable statements about it. And he tried to disguise this struggle with his only slightly less awkward skills in verse composition. Bradford, as longtime governor of the Separatists, was perplexed by the data he had gathered during the early years of settlement. It did not align with the argument he wanted to make. He preserved some of this frustration in his long and long-unpublished poem, "Some Observations of God's Merciful Dealing with Us [the Scrooby Separatists] in This Wilderness [Algonquian homelands]." Over the course of the first three decades of settlement, Bradford had collected observations that he hoped would help him better understand his deity's plans for Bradford's community. But the data disturbed him, particularly regarding his community's relationship with neighbors who were not English and not Christian. Unhappily for Bradford, those relationships were mostly positive. "Hereto, through grace, we have lost no blood, / But rather by them often have found good." English families had arrived in Algonquian homelands without invitation. They had built their forts and fences, consumed Algonquian resources, and acted with hostility and aggression toward their new neighbors, who they imagined were a "people without God, or law." Whatever violence they might have expected in response, however, had apparently not materialized. This worried Bradford. Rather than relinquish three decades of data, Bradford repurposed absence of evidence into evidence of his deity's powerful presence: *Divine providence saved us from bodily harm that our neighbors planned with secrecy so great it looked like peace.* Minimal violence needn't mean a desire for peace. It could also be evidence of great subtlety, which could, in turn, be evidence of that deity's power to discern those plots and to bestow protection.[4]

Bradford's poem is an unusually vivid example of the longing for goodness as it expressed itself in frontier paranoia. And if post-critical self-assessments in literary and cultural studies are correct, Bradford's paranoia was not pathological or even very alien to ways of thinking about enemies in the present. With modern literary critics, Bradford shared the desire to be spared unhappy surprises, and he was skilled in using his deductive reasoning to avoid them. He

4. William Bradford, "Some Observations of God's Merciful Dealing with Us in This Wilderness, and His Gracious Protection over Us These Many Years," in Michael G. Runyan, ed., *William Bradford: The Collected Verse* (St. Paul, Minn., 1974), 200–237, esp. 202, lines 35–36; Susan Scott Parrish, *American Curiosity: Cultures of Natural History in the Colonial British Atlantic World* (Williamsburg, Va., and Chapel Hill, N.C., 2006); Ana Schwartz, "'Mercy as Well as Extremity': Forts, Fences, and Fellow-Feeling in New England Settlement," *Early American Literature,* LIV (2019), 343–379; Andrew Ferris, "'Vile and Clamorous Reports' from New England: The Specter of Indigenous Conspiracy in Early Plymouth," ibid., 381–412.

liked to practice what modern critics call "paranoid," or "suspicious," reading, a model of interpreting actions or representations that features, first, trust in the power of strong theories, like Marxism or psychoanalysis or, here, original sin; second, use of those theories to re-create the logic of an enemy or antagonist; and third, a motivating conviction that, without such application, the systems diagnosed by the strong theories would remain invisible, sometimes deliberately hidden, and be more dangerous. Bradford's skill in this technique—as well as his occasional failures—show the attractions that suspicious reading had for him and may continue to have for historians and literary historians in the present. Bradford liked to practice suspicious speculation because it was one of the most durable tools he had to affirm his proximity to goodness.[5]

Paranoia's relationship to goodness, at least in Bradford's writing, tends to elude detection, however, because his wish to preempt a bad surprise, his fear of bodily harm, and his desire for self-preservation tend to appear as universal, timeless qualities that all humans share. Though desire for self-preservation may turn out to be universal, its rhetorical value for early modern English settlers was formed by specific, local contingencies. The most prominent factor that shaped their fear was their presence in a new environment; but that environment bore other, subtler implications. They were not in a *vacuum domicilium*—an empty, depopulated landscape, as John Winthrop, governor of Plymouth's neighboring English settlement, had theorized it. They were in Algonquian homelands. Their confrontation with novelty wasn't only a collision with new ecological realities but with new political ones, as well, and this conflict implied the possibility of different ideas of the good. Bradford's poem, in its words, claims confidence in the deity that organized settlers' moral cosmology, and it buttressed that confidence in its form: Bradford's recollection of potential harm contains paired lines, ten syllables each, that rhyme with each other—reliable heroic couplets. But in the poem's metrical exposition, a quieter and more fearsome possibility lurks and distresses Bradford's synthesis of data into supporting evidence: when he versifies goodness, he noticeably stumbles: "Hereto, through grace, we have lost no blood, / But rather by them often have found good." These decasyllabic lines resist

5. Eve Kosofsky Sedgwick, "Paranoid Reading and Reparative Reading, or, You're So Paranoid, You Probably Think This Essay Is about You," in Sedgwick, *Touching Feeling: Affect, Pedagogy, Performativity* (Durham, N.C., 2003), 123–152; Paul Ricoeur, *Freud and Philosophy: An Essay on Interpretation,* trans. Denis Savage (New Haven, Conn., 1970); Stephen Best and Sharon Marcus, "Surface Reading: An Introduction," *Representations,* CVIII (2009), 1–21; Heather Love, "Truth and Consequences: On Paranoid Reading and Reparative Reading," *Criticism,* LII (2010), 235–241.

smooth scansion: hardly pentameter, they are still-less iambic. An awkward tetrameter dance of anapests and iambs unfolds until the last six syllables. These align themselves more neatly to heroic conventions. Goodness, reached with gratifying metrical regularity, tries to resolve a line that failed, garishly, to forestall a monumental epistemological shock: What in the literal world did "good" mean?[6]

When Bradford claimed that the Separatists had "found good" through their new neighbors, he meant, broadly speaking, that they had experienced relative safety and the absence of positive harm. But recognizing these states was a more complex mental operation than it may at first appear to be. For early modern planters, the plausibility of harm expressed complex beliefs about reasons for violence as well as enduring expectations regarding the agents and instruments of violence. Among the many tokens of fear, Plymouth settlers were particularly worried about guns—and that their non-Christian neighbors would acquire them. In this, the Pilgrims were probably not unique among European colonists. But the thought did seem to preoccupy them intensely, especially Bradford. The "Symbolic Evil of Gun-Running," as one of Bradford's editors calls it, haunts most of his written recollections of settlement. In a June 1628 letter to Sir Ferdinando Gorges, for example, Bradford surveyed the "desperate state and condition" of the colony. The Separatists, he lamented, expected "daily to be overrun and spoiled by the Savages, who are already abundantly furnished with pieces, powder and shot." How bitterly the threat would have rankled. Early modern technology like firearms had, to English adventurers, been evidence of their own intellectual superiority. Forty years earlier, Thomas Hariot, recollecting the technological encounter, thought of "wildefire woorkes" and "gunnes" just before the "books, writing and reading" and many other "straunge" innovations that "farre exceeded their [the Carolina Algonquians'] capacities to comprehend." And Hariot was fascinated by the Natives' intellectual engagement with European technology, such as when they explained bullets as the form that pathogens took.[7]

6. Bradford, "Some Observations," in Runyan, ed., *Collected Verse,* 202; Christopher Tomlins, *Freedom Bound: Law, Labor, and Civic Identity in Colonizing English America, 1580–1865* (Cambridge, 2010), 148–152.

7. Bradford, "Some Observations," in Runyan, ed., *Collected Verse,* 228; William Bradford, *Governor William Bradford's Letter Book* (Bedford, Mass., 2001), 43; Thomas Hariot, *A Briefe and True Report of the New Found Land of Virginia* (1588), ed. Paul Royster, *Electronic Texts in American Studies,* XX, 39, http://digitalcommons.unl.edu/etas/20; Neal Salisbury, *Manitou and Providence: Indians, Europeans, and the Making of New England, 1500–1643* (New York, 1982), 140, 156–158; Joyce Chaplin, *Subject Matter: Technology, the Body, and Science on the*

For Bradford, however, the thought of Indigenous neighbors' being anything but afraid of guns was distasteful. As he recollected in the year 1628 in his voluminous prose opus *Of Plimoth Plantation*, he thought back to a still-prior time when "the very sight of [a gun] . . . was a terrour unto them." His fear of armed Algonquian neighbors affected his relationships with fellow English people. Consider his rivalry with Thomas Morton, de facto governor of Ma-re Mount after Captain Richard Wollaston fled in 1626. Morton was so ready to engage commercially with Native people and so unconcerned with the possible consequences. So indiscriminately had Morton and his men traded that now, Bradford lamented, "the Indeans are full of peeces all over." Despite the inferiority of guns relative to bows in the hands of Native people and the inferiority of human targets relative to animal ones for Native adopters of firearm technology, his paranoia persisted. Bradford seems to have believed that increased Pokanoket and Massachusett access to firearms meant increased likelihood of Separatist casualties.[8]

Bradford's obsession wasn't exceptional. It exemplifies a pattern that Cassander Smith has observed in early modern English global self-consciousness: for these early adventurers, victimhood was ballast in the belly of moral certainty, lending it weight and stability. Consider the affinity between Bradford's use of deductive reasoning in his fear of Native neighbors and Sir Francis Drake's, half a century before. Drake is remembered for being the first to survive as captain of a voyage around the world, but that survival, a remarkable achievement in its own time, derives value from an appreciation of the risk he saw himself to be undertaking. Some of that risk came from impersonal sources—miscalculating provisions and starving; encountering an unexpected storm and capsizing; or running aground on rocks or sand invisible to the unaided eye. Some of that risk, early modern Europeans believed, came from exposure to other people, especially those who differed in their cosmological

Anglo-American Frontier, 1500–1676 (Cambridge, Mass., 2001), 28–35; Kelly Wisecup, *Medical Encounters: Knowledge and Identity in Early American Literatures* (Amherst, Mass., 2013), 37–65.

8. William Bradford, *Bradford's History "Of Plimoth Plantation": From the Original Manuscript, with a Report of the Proceedings Incident to the Return of the Manuscript to Massachusetts* (Boston, 1898), 283, 287; William Heath, "Thomas Morton: From Merry Old England to New England," *Journal of American Studies,* XLI (2007), 135–168, esp. 140–142; Daniel Walden, "'The Very Hydra of the Time': Morton's *New English Canaan* and Atlantic Trade," *Early American Literature,* XLVIII (2013), 315–336, esp. 319–320; Thomas Cartelli, "Transplanting Disorder: The Construction of Misrule in Morton's *New English Canaan* and Bradford's *Of Plymouth Plantation,*" *English Literary Renaissance,* XXVII (1997), 259–280; Karen Ordahl Kupperman, "Thomas Morton, Historian," *New England Quarterly,* L (1977), 660–664.

first principles. English people valued this latter sort of risk; against that background, Drake's circumnavigation constituted a world tour of potential Protestant victimhood—from the enslaved Africans on the islands of Santiago and Maio to the colonized Guaranís and Charrúas of Brazil and Quechuas of Peru. Like Bradford, Drake saw his Native counterparts as perpetual sources of possible harm, and this evaluation guided his plans, sometimes in the absence of any positive evidence of ill will or aggression. Possible violence, even when it remained imaginary, was useful for English self-fashioning. When Drake, for example, approached Brazil, coastal fires caught his eye. To build a fire, he noted, was a "universall" human practice, but these fires, he speculated deductively, were most likely "ceremonies of conjurations" for protection and revenge in response to the "miserable bondage and slavery" that the Portuguese had brought to the Charrúas. Later, according to his narrative, Quechuas on the Pacific coast mistook his party of well-meaning English adventurers for Iberian colonists because one of his crew used the word "aqua" to ask for water. And before even arriving in the Western Hemisphere, he had glossed the enslaved inhabitants of the Cape Verde islands as bearing a grudge against the Portuguese and anyone who looked like them—a visual similarity that Drake acknowledged. Vigilant to distinguish himself from those Europeans, Drake kept his distance.[9]

Since the early twentieth century, Drake's attitude toward Catholics and non-Christians has had a convenient name—the "Black Legend." It denotes the early modern English conviction that "God is English," and so was his goodness. Early modern Protestants, however, lacked so neat a term for that concept. Antipathy toward Iberians was a vivid, but not exclusive, example of a broader pattern that European Christians, particularly Northern Europeans, used to narrate their better embodiment of cherished ideals. Early modern colonists and their eighteenth-century creole successors often used contrasts to shore up their confidence in their identities and affiliations. That dyadic structure, what Abdul R. JanMohamed has called the "economy of Manichean allegory," appears in Bradford's histories, but with a key modification. For globally conscious early modern English, that allegory drew strength from the presence of a third party—non-Christian supporting actors, whose response to Catholic vice could threaten and confirm English virtue. The early modern English feared the possibility of bad surprises, but their fear of

9. Francis Drake, *The World Encompassed* (London, 1628), 9–10, 14–15, 45–48; Cassander L. Smith, *Black Africans in the British Imagination: English Narratives of the Early Atlantic World* (Baton Rouge, 2016), 59.

the bad became a key part of their process for understanding the good and drawing themselves closer to it.[10]

The Black Legend, as men like Drake and Bradford invoked it, wasn't simply an expression of anti-Catholicism. It was also a theory of human nature that clarified their proximity to goodness. To see and to know that pattern was a dear skill because it helped to narrow the gap between an ideal of goodness and the individual who wanted it. English Protestants, regardless of their zeal for Calvinist theology, liked to imagine themselves as global victims of Catholic cruelty. But in their minds, they were not the only victims. They and their fellow victims were vulnerable to more than violence: English people believed that other victims of previous European oppression were in danger of becoming instruments of violence themselves. For both Drake and Bradford, the memory of prior, worse European colonizers enhanced their own perception of their personal and national goodness—even if the work of sustaining that perception required substantial bodily risk. Like Drake, though less aggressively, Bradford's narration of colonial settlement flirted with mistaken identity, and he found these mistakes exciting opportunities to clarify the piety of English Pilgrims. Plymouth's settlers, for example, learned within the first year of their arrival that the Pokanokets held them in suspicion because, within living memory, an earlier English trader named Hunt had abducted Pokanoket youths and sold them into slavery. Elsewhere in his history, Bradford, like Drake, reflected on Native "cunjurations" against the English. For both Bradford and Drake, the possibility of violence depended on a stable idea of human nature, fixed like the stars in the sky. The two Englishmen imagined that their interlocutors' humanity endowed them with an instinctual enthusiasm for retributive justice, a natural desire, as Drake had put it, to seek "revenge against their oppressors." They were confident that this enthusiasm for retaliation would overwhelm Native peoples' capacity to discern important differences among Europeans. In turn, that confidence made tangible evidence of oppression unnecessary. Drake sailed past the coast

10. Michael Winship, *Godly Republicanism: Puritans, Pilgrims, and a City on a Hill* (Cambridge, Mass., 2012), 14; Abdul R. JanMohamed, "The Economy of Manichean Allegory: The Function of Racial Difference in Colonialist Literature," *Critical Inquiry*, XII (1985), 59–87; William S. Maltby, *The Black Legend in England: The Development of Anti-Spanish Sentiment, 1558–1660* (Durham, N.C., 1971); Shaskan E. Bumas, "The Cannibal Butcher Shop: Protestant Uses of las Casas' *Brevísima relación* in Europe and the American Colonies," *EAL*, XXXV (2000), 107–136; Margaret R. Greer, Walter D. Mignolo, and Maureen Quilligan, eds., *Rereading the Black Legend: The Discourses of Religious and Racial Difference in the Renaissance Empire* (Chicago, 2007).

of Brazil without landing; Bradford frankly admitted that three decades' fears of violence had not materialized.[11]

For Bradford, though, goodness couldn't only be a matter of identifying epistemological distinctions. Goodness also named ideals that organized a political community, and Bradford had to worry about such organization more intensely than Drake because Bradford was stuck with the work of managing a colonial settlement, developing policies that would help his English people build a world for themselves that lasted longer than a two- or three-year circumnavigation. For Bradford, the possibility of non-Christian neighbors' acquiring guns was therefore more valuable rhetorically than distant coastal fires. That possibility didn't just shore up pious victimhood. It also supplemented a claim Bradford sought to make about the moral susceptibilities of fellow English settlers, who, he claimed, refused to be satisfied with their worldly status and longed after material things. This disorder was the reason that the colony was unsafe. In his 1628 letter to Gorges, Bradford explained how the Pokanokets and Massachusetts had acquired those "pieces, powder and shot": they had been "plentifully and publickly sold . . . by our own countrymen." Bradford blamed the "greedy covetousness of the fishermen" for the colony's vulnerability. It had been "the cankered covetousness of these licentious men" that had jeopardized "the safety of ourselves, our wives and innocent children." His nod to "licentious" "fishermen" suggests that, for Bradford, greed originated from beyond the community of Separatists. Yet he was not always so optimistic about the moral commitments of even his fellow reformists. As early as 1626, Bradford lamented that the magistrates who controlled trade with the Separatists' neighbors "begane to be envied" by less wise, more daring and desirous English, who "wente and fild the Indeans with corne, and beat downe the prise, giveing them twise as much as they [the Plymouth elders] had done, and under traded them in other commodities also." Morton was enabling "base covetousness" to prevail in "men that should know better"—among them, Bradford's fellow Separatists.[12]

11. Bradford, *Plimoth*, 119; Drake, *World Encompassed*, 15; Thomas Morton, *New English Canaan; or, New Canaan, Containing the Abstract of New England . . .* (1637), rpt. in Peter Force, coll., *Tracts and Other Papers, Relating Principally to the Origin, Settlement, and Progress of the Colonies in North America, from the Discovery of the Country to the Year 1776*, II (Washington, D.C., 1838), 86–87; "A Voyage Made by Ten of Our Men to the Kingdom of Nauset . . . ," in Dwight B. Heath, ed., *Mourt's Relation: A Journal of the Pilgrims at Plymouth* (1963; rpt. Bedford, Mass., 1986), 70.

12. Bradford, *Letter Book*, 43, 44; Bradford, *Plimoth*, 203, 287.

Decades later, Bradford was still thinking about that arms trade and its risks. In the early years of settlement, he had noted the threat the Native acquisition of weapons posed to Plymouth's investments in the beaver trade. But as time went on, he insisted that settlers' safety was more directly at stake. Thirty years afterward, in his long poem, Bradford expressed this threat most concisely: in one of his couplets, he elided Indigenous people as threats altogether, leaping polemically from avarice among Christians, the content of the first line, to the collective consequences for those Christians in the satisfying fulfillment of the second line: "Base covetousness hath got such sway, / As our own safety we ourselves betray." Bradford presumed the obviousness of Native threat, but it no longer mattered for him to think carefully about its place in the frontier social order. And in *Of Plimoth Plantation,* he renewed the theme. Though the French had begun the arms trade, in time, "Our English fisher-men, led with the like covetoussnes, followed their example, for their owne gaine." Desires for material gain were the catalyst. The perception of treachery, a sustained skepticism toward a vision of safety, was the result.[13]

Universal human nature thus appeared as a timeless constellation that guided Bradford through new, often unnerving epistemological challenges. Its hermeneutic value, in turn, recasts the humanism that some historians have seen in these early colonists. Early modern English people did not exclude their non-Christian neighbors from Christian ideas of fallen humanity. They prided themselves on their fealty to a religion that (theoretically) excluded no one. They believed that all people participated in a condition of species-wide imperfection that could be ameliorated through their understanding of reason. That same idea of imperfection, however, authorized Bradford to misrecognize reason that didn't look like his own and to sort individuals according to the degree to which their reason aligned with his. Bradford presumed that both English settlers and non-Christian Pokanokets and Massachusetts shared similar motivations. According to the Christian myth of Edenic downfall, both shared an innate love of the material world. But their failures to transcend that love were not identical. Bradford reasoned that his non-Christian neighbors threatened English flourishing because apparent lack of laws made them reliably violent; and his Christian neighbors threatened English flourishing because greed for status and property clouded their judgment. Both parties indulged in what seemed to be unreasoned affections, and Bradford's evaluative descriptions manifest the emergence of what Albert O. Hirschman has

13. Bradford, "Some Observations," in Runyan, ed., *Collected Verse,* 229; Bradford, *Plimoth,* 283.

described as "interests" (regularized, disciplined, calculable ambitions) out of "passions" (irregular, unpredictable, vehement pursuits). Bradford proved his rationality by organizing its passionate others into degrees of threat to it. His certainty that he had reasons to fear his Native neighbors underwrote his certainty that English avarice imperiled the collective safety of the settlements. Without that threat, convictions of petty jealousy would remain simply petty. By contrast, confidence about passionate humans beyond the colony's pale—confidence that paranoia was rational and sensible—authorized him, he thought, to organize the passionate humans within it.[14]

But, as Drake's example suggests, it was not only fervent Christians who valued the idea that non-Christians zealously, mechanically pursued justice. So did garden-variety libertines such as Morton, who used this theory of universal vengefulness in his project of endearing himself to the enemies of his enemies: the metropolitan English and Plymouth's Pilgrims, respectively. Throughout his *New English Canaan*, Morton demonstrated that he, too, valued goodness. In chapter after chapter, he busied himself vindicating his desire for goodness relative to the Pilgrims, his favored foils. Unlike his aggressively pious counterparts, Morton rarely claimed sincerity of his own—he is usually remembered, in fact, for his irony. He did enjoy pointing out the duplicity of others around him as a strategy to clarify his goodness. Morton is most famous, of course, for his disagreements with fellow English colonists, especially for his obstinate claim to perceive the "humane" quality or the "humanity" of his Massachusett neighbors in contrast with the relative inhumanity of his English ones. And he is also known for his eventual victimhood to the cruelty at those English neighbors' hands, which he energetically documented: the Plymouth Separatists arrested him and charged him with undermining their colony's attempt to preserve autonomy from England. In 1630, with the help of the freshly arrived Winthrop fleet, they burned his home (and his maypole) at Ma-re Mount down to the ground in front of him, temporarily incarcerated him, and left him to starve on an island. Then they forcibly repatriated him to England. But throughout his narrative, Morton also took for granted his enemies' logic of universal self-interest and enthusiasm for retaliation. His alignment with these premises appears most memorably in an episode of remarkable lawlessness and godlessness that he inserted in the third section

14. Albert O. Hirschman, *The Passions and the Interests: Political Arguments for Capitalism before Its Triumph* (Princeton, N.J., 1997), 32, 48–55; Karen Ordahl Kupperman, "English Perceptions of Treachery, 1583–1640: The Case of the American 'Savages,'" *Historical Journal*, XX (1977), 263–287; Chaplin, *Subject Matter*, 40–41.

of his book: an instance of depravity at Thomas Weston's ultimately failed settlement at Wessagusset, later renamed Weymouth—a strange event that heightened tensions with Algonquian neighbors and that, in Phinehas Pratt's mind, threatened all of the English settlements and convinced him to take his risky, beclouded errand to Plymouth. The episode's extravagance strains belief. Yet it rehearsed a set of conventional premises regarding human nature and used that extravagance to test and affirm them.[15]

In a dispute at Wessagusset over the prudence of defrauding Massachusetts neighbors by hanging an innocent, but conveniently useless, fellow country-man, universally vengeful human nature emerges as the winner. Weston's men, Morton claimed, abandoned almost all rubrics for determining goodness, a departure that has fascinated many of Morton's later readers. In Morton's telling, Weston's men were not only bad planters; they were also bad people. Their badness was the stuff of Shakespearean drama. Sometime between 1622 and 1623, the hungry and desperate men at Wessagusset convened an ad hoc parliament. How, they debated, should they respond to the petitions for justice by their Massachusett neighbors, who alleged that one of Weston's men had stolen food from them? The planters did not try to argue for his innocence. The accusation still disturbed them. One planter observed that, according to the "Lawes of England," theft constituted a felony and deserved to be "punished with death." Could these planters withstand the loss? Specifically, could they survive much longer without the guilty man? Morton explained: the man who had "ranged the woodes" and stolen "a capp full of corne" from "an Indian barne" was unusually strong and "able bodied"—probably because of his unscrupulous behavior. Youth and strength made him "fit for resistance against an enemy, which might come unexpected for any thing they knew." Here, at the frontiers of what English people recognized as civility, universally applicable self-interested reason reigned. As with Bradford, the passion that Weston's men presumed existed beyond the colony's pale underwrote the order they sought to assert within it—even to the point of suspending English laws and charting a new social contract.[16]

15. Morton, *New English Canaan,* rpt. in Force, coll., *Tracts,* II, 15, 20, 40, 77, 87, 97; Richard S. Dunn, James P. Savage, and Laetitia Yeandle, eds., *The Journal of John Winthrop* (Cambridge, Mass., 1994), 39; Cartelli, "Transplanting Disorder," *English Literary Renaissance,* XXVII (1997), 258–280; Heath, "Thomas Morton," *JAS,* XLI (2007), 135–168.

16. Morton, *New English Canaan,* rpt. in Force, coll., *Tracts,* II, 74. For retellings, see William Apess, "Eulogy on King Philip," in Barry O'Connell, ed., *On Our Own Ground: The Complete Writings of William Apess, a Pequot* (Amherst, Mass., 1992), 275–310, esp. 281; Samuel Butler, *Hudibras, Parts I and II and Selected Other Writings,* ed. John Wilders and Hugh de Quehen

Again echoing Bradford's avaricious fishermen, these men's logic depended on certainty that non-Christians knew justice and were eager to enforce it. How, Weston's men wondered, would they satisfy the Massachusetts' perceived "zeale to Justice?" The solution these men developed seems to parody the utilitarian tradition that English philosophers would innovate in centuries to come. In Morton's telling, this proposal followed serious, self-conscious deliberation. One man "conceaved within the compasse of his braine a Embrion, that was of spetiall consequence"—that is, he put his mental powers to use assessing his wondrous new circumstances and suggested his fellow settlers do likewise. Why did it matter, he offered, that they specifically punish the guilty man? Did they think the Massachusetts would care? Did they think the Massachusetts would notice the difference? No, apparently. Given that "you all agree that one must die," he proposed that they take "this young man's cloathes . . . of[f] and put [them] upon one, that is old and impotent, a sickly person that cannot escape death." It is unclear whether they had a specific weak man in mind or whether they planned, like Peters, Parker, Augustus, and Pym aboard Poe's *Grampus*, to draw lots. Did each man think that surely, he could not be the weakest in the colony? Did each man think—once they suspended the spirit of the "Lawes of England" yoking punishment to the wrongdoer—that, in future instances of calculating value on the colonial frontier, any of them would be safe from such a sacrifice? The answer to these speculations seems to have been *yes*—or rather, *Amen:* "Amen sayes one; and so sayes many more."[17]

Morton was probably exaggerating. Like Weston's men, Morton is famous for enhancing the truth with "fantastic garb." Yet even exaggeration can point to truths about settlers' desires and their means of achieving them. Here, Morton's extravagance suggests how closely colonists clung to fictions of universal human desire—even those who lacked any great commitment to Calvinist piety. One such universal was self-interest. Indeed, Morton's success at Ma-re Mount followed a proleptic laissez-faire liberalism that did not distinguish among populations. Similarly, Morton asserted that even unsophisticated men such as the planters at Wessagusset would pursue self-interest above all else. Further, Morton's story depended on English readers' expectations that

(Oxford, 1973); Kathleen Donegan, *Seasons of Misery: Catastrophe and Colonial Settlement in Early America* (Philadelphia, 2014), 140–146; Heath, "Thomas Morton," *JAS,* XLI (2007), 144; Salisbury, *Manitou and Providence,* 126–129.

17. Morton, *New English Canaan,* rpt. in Force, coll., *Tracts,* II, 74; Edgar Allan Poe, *The Narrative of Arthur Gordon Pym of Nantucket* (New York, 1999).

Indigenous people, because they were human, would respond with violence when provoked, even when what provoked them was other parties' pursuits of self-interested survival. Morton's expression of these premises was subtler than Drake's. He did not explicitly endorse the Wessagusset settlers' response to the perceived threat. But he never questioned that response's foundations, even as his protagonists changed their minds on its significance for their decisions.[18]

Certitude of the Massachusetts' "zeale to Justice" and its corollary, a seemingly rational fear, guided Weston's men away from English justice, then back to it. Wessagusset's settlers imagined that they needed to kill someone in order to "pacifie" their neighbors' "complaint." They believed, in other words, that if they did not perform retributive justice, did not make visible their commitment to a putatively universal law of just retribution (a lex talionis), their neighbors would. They worried about the possible reach of that retribution: that their Massachusett neighbors had the power to harm the entire settlement, not only the strongest man in it, and would bring that justice to the rest of the planters. If collective survival was their goal, maybe it would be most strategic—or at least less risky—to give their neighbors what they deduced those neighbors wanted. That fear, guided by deductive reasoning, led to their decision to abandon that plan to defraud their neighbors in hanging an innocent man. They believed, reasonably, that it would be difficult to convince the strong thief to submit to rules that would execute him, difficult to secure "the [guilty] mans good wil" to his own capital punishment. Trusting that this man sought self-preservation as profoundly as they did, they intuited that he had abandoned any scruples that might have prevented him from unearthing Native stores and that such a thief was unlikely to consent to exchange his life as reparation for corn he had appropriated. But their second plan, the spectacular substitution, though resourceful, would be strategically risky. They wondered whether "such deceipts might be a meanes here after to exasperate the minds of the complaininge" neighbors—that is, whether their fraud would "increase the fierceness or violence of" or "embitter, intensify (ill-feeling, passion, wickedness)" in their Massachusett neighbors. Despite their farcical ineptitude, they were still capable, to Morton's mind, of speculating on their antagonists' reasoning and its limits. Stuck between a rock and a hard place—between the likely harm at the hands of their neighbors and the closer harm at the hands of one of their own (a man who "in his wrath,

18. Charles Francis Adams, Jr., *Wessagusset and Weymouth: An Historical Address Delivered by Charles Francis Adams, Jr.* . . . (Weymouth, Mass., 1905), 5–86, esp. 18; Walden, "Very Hydra," *EAL*, XLVIII (2013), 315–336.

did seeme to be a second Sampson, able to beate out their branes with the jawbone of an Asse")—Weston's men revised their charade for a new audience. They jokingly goaded the thief into the noose and then "hanged him up hard by in good earnest." The strong man's biblical enthusiasm to live at all costs punctuated the story of a group of men motivated by the same desires.[19]

As with Bradford, the Wessagusset settlers' material self-interest drew strength from a satisfying certainty that, as Karen Ordahl Kupperman has put it, their non-Christian neighbors "had every reason to want to see the colonies fail." Maybe they did: English colonies very soon demonstrated structural dependence on unsustainable relations with their other-than-human neighbors. But the schadenfreude that Kupperman invokes (*"every* reason") is too hasty. Given the severe mortality in Algonquian territory during the preceding decade, and given the importance of human contributions to that ecology, these new arrivals might have appeared, briefly and circumspectly, to be a source of hope. By contrast, English settlers of all sorts benefited socially and politically from taking that "zeale to Justice" as an epistemological given: Bradford's presumption of vengefulness underwrote his recollected distinctions between virtuous and unvirtuous colonists. Weston's men, if we can provisionally trust this story, depended on that certainty to decide what to do next and to deduce how, more practically, if not more virtuously, to achieve the survival that the unusually robust man had jeopardized in his less wise pursuits. Morton, too (though more subtly), benefited from this premise. The Wessagusset settlers' depraved departures from shared goodness, like Plymouth's cruelty, enhanced Morton's descriptions of his own fairness and intelligence. Morton might not himself have felt as much fear of his neighbors as the settlers at Wessagusset or Plymouth. If he did, he never expressed it. Even so, he found other parties' experiences of fear useful in rehearsing certain ideals of human nature and in shoring up his own goodness. He rarely seemed interested in questioning the contingency of such experiences. These settlers' repeated stories distracted their creators and their readers from other ways of thinking about shared values and of recognizing the good. These repetitions made it harder to perceive what Algonquian peoples might have wanted from their new neighbors.[20]

19. Morton, *New English Canaan*, rpt. in Force, coll., *Tracts*, II, 74–75; *Oxford English Dictionary*, s.v. "exasperate."

20. Kupperman, "Perceptions," *Historical Journal*, XX (1977), 263–287, esp. 278; William Cronon, *Changes in the Land: Indians, Colonists, and the Ecology of New England* (New York, 1983).

Was it possible to know what English settlers' Algonquian neighbors wanted from them besides the failure of their colonies? Men like Bradford clouded their understanding by cleaving to Manichean templates. Modern critics reap the consequences, sifting through the occlusions of their documentary archive for useful evidence of a world beyond. Here and there, however, appear individuals who lacked the material and epistemological resources to misunderstand their neighbors so successfully. Forty years after the attempted fraud, one of Wessagusset's settlers seems still to have been thinking about it. That disturbance prompted him to preserve what is possibly the written archive's most explicit answer to the above question. In 1662, Phinehas Pratt, one of Weston's men, recalled his encounter with a system of ethics, expressed in an idea of justice, rival to his own. Pratt's testimony was itself part of a pursuit of justice that he felt he deserved from the Plymouth Colony: a pension in old age as recompense for what he had suffered on behalf of the English settlements. But what, exactly, had he suffered? Though his testimony's second half features a hazardous journey to relay news of an anticipated plot against the Plymouth Colony, a substantial portion of the document narrates a remarkably detailed, but not immediately relevant, conversation with Pecksuot (or Pexworth), the Massachusett *pniese,* a political adviser. Little in the narrated conversation explicitly recommends Pratt's experience as worthy of recompense or remuneration. During the conversation, he sustained no physical harm. Yet his insistence on recounting it anyway in the petition for redress suggests that to his own mind—and perhaps not his conscious mind—the implications of the verbal exchange demanded attention.

Pratt's text—rhetorically unskilled, digressive, often unclear—was probably hard for his intended audience to grasp, and it remains so for modern readers. It preserves a profound and terrifying epistemological disturbance, yet like most epistemological disturbances, he was not likely to call it that. Readers familiar with practices of suspicious reading might swiftly see his clumsiness as evidence of cognitive distress. Suspicious reading might call that a symptom, the surface expression of a closed, usually harm-producing system that derives at least some of its power from remaining invisible. But symptomatic, or suspicious, reading isn't the only way to make sense of his writing. Recent scholarship in early American studies has suggested that these anomalies may also point to phenomena exogenous to such systems. Anthropologist Neil L. Whitehead has proposed reading them as colonists' recognition of Native cultural norms, unwittingly transcribed. To shift the search for an explanation from the endogenous to the exogenous, Whitehead has suggested the term "texture." And a number of early Americanist scholars have taken it up, deepening the significance of the field's epistemological turn by foregrounding the vast world that existed beyond what Europeans thought they could comprehend. The plain style of these frontier Protestants heightens the significance of moments of texture as modern critics might interpret them. To build a utopian society, these Christians sought to purify their language from representative distractions. Even these writers, however, cherished clarity and forcefulness of exposition; their goals in writing benefited from friction-free prose. Yet time and again, confrontations with Native people seem to have perplexed them, as Bradford's writing on guns shows. Even more forcefully than Bradford, Pratt, who was not especially pious, demonstrates the "narrative fragmentation and formal inconsistencies" that, for readers such as Kelly Wisecup, signal "colonists' transcription of [Indigenous peoples'] knowledge and the influence of that knowledge on colonial writing." Pratt's confused exposition of his season of misery, his failure to summarize a story and tell it straight, points to a feature of Algonquian ethics that ruptured the foundations of English epistemology by suggesting that "humanity" might not be the best name for what settlers and Native people had in common.[21]

Pratt's awkward narration benefits from both models of interpretation, texture and symptom. He struggled in controlling his recollection because its content, a meeting with a Massachusett ambassador, took place where his former closed system of making meaning (the Manichean Christian world) left off, and something else (a different moral firmament) began. Pratt's unskillfulness, that narratively lost quality, is key in this regard. It is bad exposition, but what makes it bad is the evidence of a struggle. It was a losing battle, but one rich with historically useful information nevertheless. First, Pratt floundered because he was likely to have been less educated than a Morton or a Bradford. He could not invoke biblical eloquence or satirical wit. His failure to do so is a historical boon. With fewer instruments in his biopoetic toolkit, he could not easily narrate a path away from mental disturbance and toward peace. Second, he was more vulnerable than his neighbors. All of his English contemporaries faced the possibility of harm and unhappy death on the frontier, sometimes from their English neighbors, sometimes from their own mismanagement, but Pratt, among these three representative colonists, is the only one who

21. Neil L. Whitehead, "The *Discoverie* as Enchanted Text," in Walter Raleigh, *The Discoverie of the Large, Rich, and Bewtiful Empyre of Guiana*, ed. Whitehead (Manchester, U.K., 1998), 35; Wisecup, *Medical Encounters*, 11–15, 197. Other uses of Whitehead's "texture" include Karen Ordahl Kupperman, *Indians and English: Facing off in Early America* (Ithaca, N.Y., 2000), 32; Smith, *Black Africans*, 4–5.

had to confront what he thought was a source of mortal harm with barely any hope for repudiating it materially or, much more frightening, morally. The story Pratt told the Plymouth elders forty years later was of his coming to grips with the possibility that he would be held accountable to a system of justice he barely understood. If his narration looks unskilled, it is because of the enormous intellectual toil it required of him—one that his colleagues were better prepared to neglect altogether.

Pratt's ineloquence illuminates what men like Morton and Bradford longed never to admit to considering: disturbances that were intimately, personally felt but rarely consciously cognized. Whitehead indicates the subtlety of this process when he suggests that texture takes place in an "unconscious way." Expressing disturbances that occur in regions of the mind not often open to direct perception, texture attests not simply to an intellectual encounter but to a deeply psychological one that exceeded, first, an individual's ability to make sense of it and, second, an individual's confidence in his or her episte-mological resources to make sense of the wider world—it was a trauma, as Kathleen Donegan has suggested. Bradford and Morton were pretty good at convincing others and themselves that they had these resources and would not run out of them. The confrontations for which they needed those resources, however, weren't merely encounters with new people and things. They were encounters with new ways of experiencing other people and other things. Because English people, especially reform Protestants, had developed such a robust sense of identity, national and individual, based on the idea that their way of ordering people and things was absolute and universally applicable, these encounters were intensely disturbing. They meant a new experience of the self, of the minds these colonists used to engage with every part of the external world. These experiences were rarely felicitous or welcome, and their impact was unlikely to be immediate. Pratt, decades later, recalling his own confrontation, gathered momentum to try to communicate that impact and what it felt like through small details, such as the comforts of the constellations in the sky. In walking through the forest of his memory, he soon arrived at a more sustained encounter with that different standpoint, and it exhausted the representative resources he had to communicate how afraid he was. This terror is absent from most other English accounts of settlement, even from those that, like Bradford's, make a show of claiming to know reasons to feel fear.[22]

22. Neil L. Whitehead, "The Historical Anthropology of Text: The Interpretation of Ralegh's Discoverie of Guiana," *Current Anthropology*, XXXVI (1995), 53–74, esp. 57; Kathleen Donegan, "'As Dying, Yet Behold, We Live': Catastrophe and Interiority in Bradford's

Unlike Bradford and Morton, Pratt could not forget or suppress the experience of being the object of a neighbor's unhappy reason and judgment and having to negotiate tenuously with that judgment through dialogue. Pratt insisted, even with his limited skills, that his audience witness that very uncomfortable experience. Soon after the Wessagusset men's deliberations on attempting fraud, Pecksuot, pniese of the neighboring Massachusetts, arrived at their door to settle accounts between the two parties. Pratt might have summarized this visit concisely by stating, "Pecksuot arrived. He eventually told us what bothered him." Instead, Pratt spun out into a verbose passage featuring winding dialogue that did little to advance his case for a pension from Plymouth's elders. He described Pecksuot's approach as initially benign: "This Peexworth said, I love you." Pratt returned the greeting: "I said 'I love you.'" Pratt seems to have been capable only of imitation, yet he also wanted his interlocutor to know that he was just mimicking and that his love was contingent: "I said 'I love you as well as you Love me.'" Affection was not the only contingent emotion; so was anger. Pecksuot and his fellow Massachusetts had come armed. When Pratt asked why, Pecksuot answered, "Our Sacham is angry with you." Pratt again delayed direct answer by offering him a conditional proposition: "I said, 'Tell him if he be Angry with us, wee be Angry with him.'" Eventually, Pecksuot responded by turning reciprocity itself into the object of his narration. When Englishmen had first arrived, he recalled, "We gave you gifts and you gave us gifts." Now, he insisted, "Tell me if I or any of my men have don you Rong." Pecksuot implied he knew English ideas of retribution—a wrong for a wrong—but, ostentatiously, he did not admit any actual grievance. Pratt refused to admit fault or perception of fault. He repeated his interlocutor's tentative rhetorical gestures: "First tell us if we have don you Any Rong." This belabored back-and-forth is hard to read. It does not add information directly to the episode it's embedded in. But in its difficulty, Pratt slowly revealed his apprehension, above all, that he wasn't

'Of Plymouth Plantation,'" *EAL*, XXXVII (2002), 9–37. For a more extended reading of trauma and its texturing effects in colonial American literature, see Mitchell Breitwieser, *American Puritanism and the Defense of Mourning: Religion, Grief, and Ethnology in Mary White Rowlandson's Captivity Narrative* (Madison, Wis., 1990). To the reasonable reservation that psychoanalysis, in its conventional preoccupation with sexuality, does not have any direct bearing on the encounter at hand, Jean Laplanche responds, in a lovely essay on psychoanalysis's correspondence with early modern knowledge pursuits, that sexuality names only the most direct mode of apprehending the fullness and intricacy of "the question of the other" (Laplanche, "The Unfinished Copernican Revolution," in Luke Thurston, trans., *Essays on Otherness* [New York, 1999], 65).

only a subject of reason. He was also its object. Another party was observing him, examining him, speculating on his mental workings, and proceeding cautiously based on an analysis to which he had no access. As he and his peers had fretted about the merits of fraud, they had been living under surveillance by people who understood the world differently, in quiet but profound ways. The evening clouds of his mind lifting, Pratt slowly recognized that he and his countrymen had done their neighbors wrong and had thereby entangled themselves into desperate debts. Still more alarming, they did not know the contours of obligation relevant for redress.[23]

More intimately than any of his fellow English settlers, Pratt reached the limits of his first principles in an encounter with another people. He brushed coarsely against novel alterity. But it wasn't any random feature of Algonquian political life that frightened him. He had encountered a quality of Algonquian ethics that cast into doubt the "psychological certitude" that English people found in Christianity. Most English settlers, we have seen, believed that a "zeale to Justice" was part of human nature and that non-Europeans, unrestrained by European manners, would seek retribution with enthusiasm. For these men, justice was easiest to recognize when it was mediated by property—as Hobbes would very soon define it, "the constant will of giving to every man his own." But there may be other ideas of justice, with different consequent ideas of political obligation. Pecksuot's explanation of justice began, not with discrete claims and corollary relations of exclusion, as was characteristic to property, but with relations of fundamental indebtedness. Debt was not a condition to be corrected between two political parties, as has been implied in England's transition from an "economy of obligation" and debt into an economy of credit. Here, instead, debt was the condition of possibility for ongoing relations between polities. Justice expressed itself less in retribution for infringed and supposedly universally salient property claims than in ongoing engagement with a neighboring polity's requests and demands.[24]

For Pecksuot, ineluctable political obligations shaped a polity's internal conduct. These obligations suggest a different understanding of the inside and outside of political life. Pecksuot finally answered Pratt's reversal of his question. The English *had* done the Massachusetts harm. "Some of you steele

23. Pratt, *A Declaration of the Affairs,* ed. Frothingham, 481.

24. Francis J. Bremer, *The Puritan Experiment: New England Society from Bradford to Edwards* (New York, 1976), 28; Thomas Hobbes, *Leviathan: With Selected Variants from the Latin Edition of 1668,* ed. Edwin Curley (Indianapolis, 1994), 89; Craig Muldrew, *The Economy of Obligation: The Culture of Credit and Social Relations in Early Modern England* (London, 1998).

our Corne," he charged. This was not an isolated incident, and it was not so much the theft that disturbed the Massachusetts as the implications of its unrestrained repetition: "I have sent you word times wthout number and yet our Corne is stole." Thus, he and his men had come armed. "I come to see what you will doe." Yet Pratt rejected the demand. Weston's men, he insisted, were not responsible for the theft. They believed that their attempt to punish the thief made them innocent. "Yo[u]r men have seen us whip him divers times, besids other manor of punishments." Pratt tried to pass duty for justice on to the aggrieved themselves: "We give him unto you to doe with him what you please." That was "not just dealeing," however, in Pecksuot's view. "If my men wrong my nabur sacham, or his men, he sends me word and I beat or kill my men, acording to the ofenc." The Massachusetts expected reciprocal discipline from their neighbors. "If his men wrong me or my men, I send him word and he beats or kills his men Acording to the ofence." Pecksuot's description suggests a different ethical principle than that subtending English justice. The Massachusetts did not abandon the guilty to whatever fate existed beyond the pale of their society. There was no juridical bare life wherewith to conveniently abandon someone who had done wrong, no omnipresent external threat to ensure orderly behavior. Just dealing required ongoing communication between parties regarding their mutual satisfaction with each other's behavior, as well as the sometimes-costly work within each party to maintain local peace: "All Sachams," Pecksuot concluded, "do Justis by thayr own men. If not . . . then we ffite."[25]

Pratt may be no more trustworthy than Bradford or Morton. But other documented early encounters with various Algonquian peoples affirm the Native tenets of justice Pratt recalled. In 1624, trader Christopher Levett, who cared, self-consciously, to secure Native people's favor, seems to have understood justice between parties in a similar fashion. One of Levett's men stole a sleeve from members of a Casco trading party, and in response, the Casco sagamore, Cogawesco, visited Levett "with a grievous complaint." Levett did justice by his own men. He searched their possessions himself, in order that "they see my willingnesse to finde the theese out." Later, some of Levett's men beat a party of Penobscot men who, in turn, brought their complaints to Levett. He recalled their desire to "be revenged" on his men, but he mentioned

25. Pratt, A Declaration of the Affairs, ed. Frothingham, 480–482, esp. 482; Salisbury, Manitou and Providence, 128, 187–188; Giorgio Agamben, Homo Sacer: Sovereign Power and Bare Life (Stanford, Calif., 1998), 15–38; Nan Goodman, Banished: Common Law and the Rhetoric of Social Exclusion in Early New England (Philadelphia, 2012), 6–8.

also a strategy that ran contrary to direct punitive justice—the Penobscots said that they planned on "going into *England* to tell King *James* of it." Farther south, Edward Winslow noted a similar convention when a Separatist envoy traveled to Nauset to trade. There, they had "certain Beads, Cissers, and other trifles" stolen from them. Captain Myles Standish enacted English justice when he instructed the sachem to return the items, "or else he would revenge it on them" directly. But the sachem's response reveals a vision of justice with a different emphasis—the expectation that the sachem himself and not a neighboring governor or militia leader was inevitably responsible for meting out discipline. He "delivered the Beads . . . saying, he had much beaten the party for doing it."[26]

Winslow recorded a more vivid instance of cocreated justice soon after the incident involving the stolen "trifles." In January 1622/23, William Bradford traveled to Nemasket and Manomet to get corn for the Separatist settlement. While there, he received "very kindly" treatment from Manomet's sachem Canacum. His favor might have flattered Bradford, given the respect that the sachem received while Bradford was there: a pair of visitors arrived from a neighboring sachem, Manamoick, during his stay. They came seeking advice for a politically distressing situation. "Two of their men," the visitors shared, had fallen into a dispute, and one had killed the other. Troublesomely, the two men's lives seem to have held different values within their polity. One was an unremarkable subject, but the other was a *powah*, "one of special note amongst them." And it was the powah who had killed his counterpart. Manamoick had considered preserving the powah from a death sentence, but special circumstances intervened. "Another people greater than themselves threatened them with war, if they would not put him to death." Faced with a difficult decision on how to proceed, they sent an ambassador to solicit the advice of their esteemed neighbors.[27]

26. Christopher Levett, "My Discovery of Diverse Rivers and Harbours, with Their Names, and Which Are Fit for Plantations, and Which Not," in George Parker Winship, ed., *Sailors Narratives of Voyages along the New England Coast, 1524–1624* (Boston, 1905), 261–292, esp. 272, 277; Edward Winslow, *Good News from New England*, ed. Kelly Wisecup (Amherst, Mass., 2014), 73–74. It's possible that the plan to petition King James is an example of subjection "unto the same king," but 1620 seems a little early for that idea to have been so clearly and explicitly adopted—though, importantly, the principle of justice Pecksuot expressed suggests amenability to such strategic alliance. See Jennifer Hale Pulsipher, *Subjects unto the Same King: Indians, English, and the Contest for Authority in Colonial New England* (Philadelphia, 2007), 18–21.

27. Winslow, *Good News*, ed. Wisecup, 75.

Winslow's anecdote shared qualities with Morton's tale of attempted fraud. Both stories featured the challenge of calculating the value of an individual's life in unusual circumstances. In Morton's narrative, English settlers decided that the individual—any individual, guilty or innocent—was worth less than the collective, and they were willing to follow those laws to serve the vision of greatest happiness for the greatest number. In Winslow's anecdote, the people of Manamoick and Manomet struggled with that decision—as did other, incidental witnesses, like the translator Hobbamock. After listening to advice that Winslow attributed to the translator, the ambassadors from Manamoick decided that the powah was worth less than the Manamoick people: "It was better that one should die than many." Abstract justice was a secondary consideration. Following the quantitative rationale, Winslow added a consideration of guilt: "since he had deserved it, and the rest were innocent." Like Morton, Winslow rehearsed two stories about justice that happened to dovetail in these particulars: first, that thieves and killers deserved death; second, that the happiness of the greatest number of people was key to determining correct political action. In Winslow's telling, there was almost nothing disorienting about these political principles.[28]

But a subtler political principle haunted this story, a lesson that can be easy to miss in the course of the incident's transmission from the messengers to Hobbamock, from Hobbamock to Bradford, from Bradford to Winslow, and from Winslow to his readers. According to Winslow, the Manamoicks found special value in Hobbamock's advice. Despite the admitted fact that "he was but a stranger to them," Hobbamock's superior use of reason, Winslow claimed, had "passed the sentence of death upon [the powah]." Winslow did not report any of the other positions on the matter. He mentioned only that plural others "gave their judgment what they thought best." Their invitation to Hobbamock counterbalanced an important feature of the problem itself: more than the vexing issue of retribution was the challenge of aggressive neighborliness that placed Manamoick's polity in crisis. Although the victim and the aggressor were both Manamoick's subjects and, at least nominally, both the sachem's responsibility, the demand to punish the powah seems to have come from beyond the boundaries of Manamoick's polity—"another people greater than themselves." Neither the calculation of human value nor the vision of retributive justice was necessarily the central problem of the story told that night. Justice was only the quality of the story that was most intelligible, or interesting, to Bradford and Winslow. These men had primed

28. Ibid., 76.

themselves to recognize templates of justice and retribution as the key to conflict at the expense of other political priorities. What the English telling seems not to know how to represent is the challenge of the political decision instigated by an external party.[29]

Manamoick's turn to neighbors for advice might not have been the frame for the story so much as a performance that itself participated in the story, a message for Winslow and Bradford to reflect on. Such didactic techniques would not have been completely foreign or unintelligible to Separatist settlers who knew, for example, that when their deity spoke of fruitless fig trees, camels walking through narrow portals, or women looking for lost coins, the deity was not showing interest in growing fruits, building transportation-efficient cities, or collecting coins. Emblematic representation was a mode in which both parties possessed fluency. Given the brief information that Winslow provided, it's difficult to be certain whether Bradford, serendipitously, had witnessed a real deliberative event or one strategically performed for the instruction of English spectators. The actions of the ambassadors suggest self-conscious strategy. They did not, for example, ever seem to solicit any perspective on justice and right dealings from the English, even as they called on a "stranger," Hobbamock, to weigh in on the matter. Manamoick's ambassadors might or might not have found Hobbamock's advice valuable. In either case, the diplomatic exchange required English listeners to witness a different system of justice, and the difference between ideals of justice, that fitted poorly within the grand, world-spanning formulas the English favored. The Manamoick ambassadors' story invited English witnesses to consider the grounds on which a neighboring polity, even a more powerful one, could make claims to the operations of justice within a political community. The answer was, not that a polity *shouldn't* make such claims, but that there were conventions and procedures to follow in cases where they could.[30]

This difference in ideals of justice would clarify one of the remarkable puzzles of the first treaty between Pokanokets and the Separatist English—why it was that, among the treaty's six articles, the matter of punishment remained unilateral. In the second article, English settlers insisted that "if any of his did hurt to any of ours, he should send the offender, that we might punish him." No corollary agreement exists. If any English harmed any Pokanokets,

29. Ibid., 75–76.

30. Daniel K. Richter, "Intelligibility or Incommensurability?" in Brian P. Owensby and Richard J. Ross, eds., *Justice in a New World: Negotiating Legal Intelligibility in British, Iberian, and Indigenous America* (New York, 2018), 291–306.

no provision guaranteed the Pokanokets a right to punish the offender. It's possible that English settlers, confident in their virtue, could not imagine harming their neighbors. But it's also possible that the Pokanokets, like their Algonquian neighbors, tended to understand justice between two political parties as a matter of mutually indebted responsibility rather than a relation reducible to formula.[31]

If sincerity required that the self be knowable, Pratt's relation, in its vivid texture, suggested that the tools once apt to that task had become obsolete. They were compasses too big and unwieldy to be carried off the ship, perhaps knocked off their magnetic north altogether. Algonquian alternatives to Christian ethics challenged Christian ontology not simply formally but in content, too. Any viable alternative might expose the historical weakness of a system claiming universality. Algonquian ethics might indeed have recognized their own universals. But they seem not to have become the foundation for psychic life so profoundly as the idea of universal human nature had for these early modern English. Algonquian ethics, as Pecksuot articulated them, included provisions for encountering alternatives, a provision that turned English desires for intellectual mastery inside out. Instead of the comforting generalizations about universal depravity that settlers liked to imagine they were discovering in their new neighbors, men like Pratt realized that they were known and understood by those same neighbors, that they were the objects of intellectual activity—yet activity about which they knew very little. English settlers' tenacious paranoia testified to the fright of discovering a new ethical compass, of looking at one's cherished enemies and in those observations, as Bradford put it, finding a new vision of the good. The terrifying irruption of that incommensurate vision into one's sense-making structures would account for the eclipse of old certainties (*we are superior in our moral acuity and thus justified in our violence*) by new ones (*some of us have privileged access to universally salient reason and are thus justified . . .*). Desire for some certainty, moral or epistemological, would guide settlers' more conscious elision of the deceptively familiar conditional "if not . . . then we ffite" into evidence supporting a timeless "zeale to Justice" and, in turn, would whet the convictions of innocent persecution that Bradford held so dear.

Settlers longed to discard those obligations. That longing makes it impossible to read some of their earliest acts of knowledge acquisition in the long-conventional manner, as naive pursuits of curiosity. It is probably true that, in their first encounters with evidence of new people and new social worlds,

---

31. Winslow, *Good News,* ed. Wisecup, 145.

English colonists were "just plain curious." That curiosity, however, led European settlers to act in ways that were far from the innocence that "plain" curiosity implies. Into the twenty-first century, for example, some historians continue to claim that, at the sight of Algonquian graves, English observers like Bradford and Winslow were compelled, naturally, by an urgent desire for knowledge and consequently decided that exhuming them was a worthwhile endeavor. "Curiosity and hunger overcame their better judgment." They were following "fairly straightforward motivations [such] as profit and animosity (and, one might add, curiosity)." For these historians, curiosity exists outside of history, as obvious as hunger and as obviously compelling. The desperate, but sometimes unthought, logic of men like Bradford, Pratt, and the men at Wessagusset, their aversion to unelected obligation, suggests some of that excluded history. One way to make sense of these violations would be as a Freudian parapraxis: such violent activity was a way to provoke a response, possibly also violent, that would reaffirm the sort of proximity to goodness that even men like Drake longed for. A less pessimistic explanation might see their activity as a longing for any sort of response, not necessarily a violent one, to those several first months of settlement, when they were aware they were being watched but knew so little about the parties watching them. Not exclusive to these possibilities, these mortuary violations expressed the settlers' belief, or their desire to believe, that their own ocular knowledge superseded their ethical obligations in value. Acknowledging such responsibilities would put them on the same political grounds as their neighbors rather than allow English people to believe that they could transcend those duties. Grave violation was an act that would affirm in their minds that the moral landscape in which they hoped to settle was clear and empty. The act did not singularly express curiosity; it also allowed these planters to preserve the foundations of their future knowledge-making endeavors, activities in which they did not need to be obliged where they did not want to be.[32]

32. Kupperman, *Indians and English*, 4 ("just plain curious"); Erik R. Seeman, *Death in the New World: Cross-Cultural Encounters, 1492–1800* (Philadelphia, 2011), 146–148, esp. 148 ("overcame their better judgment"); Tom Arne Mitrød, "'Calling for More than Human Vengeance': Desecrating Native Graves in Early America," *Early American Studies*, XVII (2019), 281–314, esp. 284 ("fairly straightforward"); James Strachey, ed. and trans., *The Standard Edition of the Complete Psychological Works of Sigmund Freud*, VI, *The Psychopathology of Everyday Life* (1901) (London, 1960). Throughout *Mourt's Relation*, Winslow and its other authors note evidence that the Plymouth Separatists collected of being watched prior to the first meeting with Ousamequin.

In this longing to control their obligations, settlers were not being insincere: decades of exegesis of their sacred texts primed them to believe that they truly were their deity's favorites and that such status authorized them to use special, earthly powers. In this context, paranoia was a dear comfort. It was a feeling about badness that afforded certainty of goodness. As they examined their thoughts and feelings and practiced sharing what they found with their English neighbors, most settlers absorbed the ambient presence of a fantasy evil within their vision of the prosocial and good. Against this new normal, Pratt's terror revises the methods and moods we bring to this and other objects of historical study. First, Pratt's text illuminates a pursuit of the good that does not depend on contrast but upon communication and cautious collaboration. These alternatives are vital to learn to recognize, particularly in a context where unqueried ideas of goodness often give vent to what Gayatri Chakravorty Spivak has called the "desire to punish," materialized in the penal institutions that settlers would go on to fashion. The first material expression of those institutions was the ad hoc prison that Plymouth settlers built almost immediately after constructing their first homes. In making it, they sacrificed dear caloric energy that they could have spent planting corn. They justified the risk by describing it to themselves as a fort. In calling it that, they were not being evasive. The edifice served both purposes: in using it as a prison, they meant for it to produce fear and for that fear to act as a supplementary fence between themselves and those unlike them. As the next chapter shows, they used the threat of retributive violence to try to habituate and discipline their Indigenous neighbors into being more sympathetic to English desires. But that desire to punish, and the justice that animates it, wasn't always a matter of utility. As they cleaved to a narrow vision of Christian justice, as they sacrificed more and more for it, they found in themselves an intense, sometimes unprofitable, extravagant desire to punish others, as Chapter 4 will explain. Like Pratt, most English planters came to want recognition for the spiritual and epistemological disturbance they had to manage on the frontier; violence became one strategy for getting that recognition. Unlike Pratt, they could rarely admit to having been disturbed in the first place, and their suppression has become all the more difficult to see now.[33]

33. Gayatri Chakravorty Spivak, "Feminism and Deconstruction, Again: Negotiating with Unacknowledged Masculinism," in Teresa Brenan, ed., *Between Feminism and Psychoanalysis* (London, 1989), 214–232, esp. 217; Colin Dayan, "Legal Terrors," *Representations,* XCII (2005), 42–80; Schwartz, "'Mercy as Well as Extremity,'" *EAL,* LIV (2019), 343–379.

Pratt's haunted description of justice is thus, second, an opportunity to think more dynamically about the good intentions that New England studies have for so long privileged. Doing so may complicate many readers' wish for better knowledge of the past as an ethical good in itself—as Eve Tuck and K. Wayne Yang point out when they identify desire for knowledge as one feature of a settler colonial society's pursuit of "innocence." Settlers have often hoped, Tuck and Yang observe, that their personal good intentions nullify their participation in larger structures of impersonal power. On one hand, many historians would probably agree that the early modern reform Protestant colonists had good intentions. On the other, the most memorable accounts of how those intentions yielded violent action tend to read settlers' declarations of intentions as bad-faith mystifications that would prove not only settlers' violence but their deceit, too. Liars *and* killers, they can appear indisputably bad. Bradford's commitment to suspicious reading vividly suggests some reasons why such claims to expose should give modern readers pause. Bradford's commitment to suspicion not only showcases the shelter it afforded him from unhappy surprises; it also shows off the attractions of moral judgment in the treacherous work of modern self-knowledge. It is very hard, Judith Butler has observed, to know oneself fully, to account truthfully, thoroughly, and consistently for what moves one. In the pursuit of self-knowledge, the discovery of internal disorder and inconsistency despite one's best, most earnest intentions might be forestalled, Butler suggests, by turning outward, by unmasking and denouncing what seem to be obvious evils in others. Symptomatic reading, in her account, is a potent instrument for smoothing intractable internal disorder, but it doesn't have to be only that. It can also be valuable for revealing what critics might risk sharing with our objects of critique. It can facilitate better, more historically sensitive accounts of the gratifications of these pursuits and can be one step toward a subtler understanding of good intentions: they are one factor among others, and important, but not in the way that settlers have intended them to be.[34]

34. Eve Tuck and K. Wayne Yang, "Decolonization Is Not a Metaphor," *Decolonization: Indigeneity, Education, Society,* I (2012), 1–40; Richard Slotkin, *Regeneration through Violence: The Mythology of the American Frontier* (Middletown, Conn., 1973); Francis Jennings, *The Invasion of America: Indians, Colonialism, and the Cant of Conquest* (Williamsburg, Va., and Chapel Hill, N.C., 1975); Judith Butler, "Giving an Account of Oneself," *Diacritics,* XXXI (2001), 22–40, esp. 30–31.

CHAPTER TWO

─────────

Dreaming on Dry Land

Thoughtfulness beyond Good Intentions

WHEN THOMAS MORTON championed the humanity of his non-English neighbors, he probably did not have in mind families of seven- or eight-foot-tall occasional bipeds covered in fur, with a flat fifth limb used for building houses, bridges, and barricades out of trees they had cut with their own, very long front teeth. Morton knew about beavers, of course, but he had only ever seen the smaller sort—and even then, not until later into his adulthood. For these reasons, it's unlikely that he contemplated the possibility of sharing much in common with them. But the possibility of partaking in some commonality with beavers—in being something like brothers with them—might have passed through the mind of one of Morton's collaborators, a Massachusetts sachem named Chickatawbut, particularly on a spring morning as the sachem walked through melting drifts of snow to the lands occupied by the newest wave of English people. Chickatawbut had nearly a decade of practice negotiating with these strangely dressed, odd-smelling, and very jittery neighbors. Among his fellow sachems, Chickatawbut might have been most familiar with English desires, both the ones the English were able to communicate directly and the ones they weren't—either because they didn't have the Algonquian words to do so or because Chickatawbut and his fellow Algonquians didn't have the English ones. These negotiations could be tiresome and risky, but the alternative, he suspected, was worse. So, on his way to visit the political leader of these new planters, John Winthrop, on the lands that this new man was already claiming as his own, Chickatawbut thought about the beaver. He knew men like Winthrop wanted beavers, and, more subtly, he had reason to believe that he could speculate about Englishmen's desires by thinking about how beavers themselves pursued desire in their shared world. Though he was outside the charmed walls of the Christians who imagined themselves to be spiritually chosen, Chickatawbut had a unique vantage on the mechanics of selfhood that shaped the happiness these newcomers sought for themselves. He saw the English forgo robust relations with those outside their walls, and he was likely curious regarding what priorities they chose for themselves instead. He also probably noticed that the principles they took to be normal, whatever the consequences for the truth they shared among themselves, further severed them from a broad, shared world—not only from other humans but also from the rich ecosystem of other-than-human actors, including beavers big and small.

Beavers, after all, were the exemplary commodity that engendered relations of "creative misunderstanding" and experimental compromise between settlers and Natives in what Richard White has called the "middle ground." Beaver pelts had turned out to be, in the first years of sustained contact, among the objects that English people most desired in their trade with Algonquian and Haudenosaunee people. Among the English, beaver pelts, warm and water-resistant, emblematized a desirable insulation from that rich but compromising material world. The beaver pelt was one of many objects through which Christians could champion their humanity as they understood it. When English people transformed beavers into garments such as coats and hats, they drew them into a blossoming commodity-based transatlantic market. As animal pelts, furthermore, they were inaugural representations of what Ann Rosalind Jones and Peter Stallybrass have called the "materials of memory." Pelts reminded Christians of the basic relationship between the human and the divine, a relationship in which individuals were required to wear garments to identify their guilty self-consciousness. At first, those garments were animal skins, and they were soon replaced by raiment fabricated by human labor. To adopt the garments of Christians meant to participate in what Europeans imagined was a more advanced relationship with their Creator, a dynamic that ushered them away from a compromising material world. Chickatawbut was likely to be aware of such an interpretation. Within a decade following the meeting between the two men, the Algonquian dialect spoken by Chickatawbut's Narragansett neighbors recognized English people as "waútaconenûaog," that is, "coat-men," or those who wore "cloth coats." Chickatawbut would have recognized that he and his new neighbors shared an interest in the beaver, his people's longtime neighbor. But he would have known, too, that shared interest differed in profoundly important ways.[1]

It was easy for English people to imagine extracting such value from beavers' bodies because English people understood themselves to belong to a category—humanity—that was distinct from the category to which beavers belonged. Chickatawbut and his fellow Algonquians knew beavers differently. They were less objects than agents capable of deliberately engaging with objects in their world. If they were not "humans," they bore striking similarity to culture-making bipeds. Beavers managed their ecological habitats. They organized themselves into polities—so remarkably that English people would sometimes call those collectives "families" and at other times "colonies." Beavers even sometimes accumulated unwisely, disturbing the interspecies balance of their homelands. They were what Margaret M. Bruchac (Abenaki) has called "earthshapers and placemakers." Their capacity to live and build as a collective troubled and disturbed Europeans' claims that they were of a distinct species from beavers and, furthermore, that they were themselves the best example of the reasoning that made their species distinct. In centuries since, European philosophers have begun to reconsider the language they use to understand and categorize the world around them and have revalued the proposition that a bright line separates humans from animals. In developing better phrasing to describe the relationship between agent and action, cause and effect, philosophers like Bruno Latour have suggested a term like "actant," an entity "that acts or to which activity is granted by others." With such language, European thinkers and their inheritors have tried to come closer to a

---

1. Richard White, *The Middle Ground: Indians, Empires, and Republics in the Great Lakes Region, 1650–1815* (Cambridge, 1991); Ann Rosalind Jones and Peter Stallybrass, *Renaissance Clothing and the Materials of Memory* (Cambridge, 2000); Roger Williams, *A Key into the Language of America: The Tomaquag Museum Edition*, ed. Dawn Dove et al. (Yardley, Pa., 2019), 55. Beaver hats, the cherished commodity made from the pelts, were traded widely around the Atlantic world; before the American beaver trade, Northern Europe acquired pelts from Russia. Through the seventeenth and eighteenth centuries, these hats would travel as far abroad as African markets. See Susan Sleeper-Smith, introduction, in Sleeper-Smith, *Rethinking the Fur Trade: Cultures of Exchange in an Atlantic World* (Lincoln, Neb., 2009), xvii–lxii, esp. xxvi–xxvii; Horace T. Martin, *Castorologia; or, The History and Traditions of the Canadian Beaver* (Montreal, Que., 1892), 119–132; Beverly Lemire, *Global Trade and the Transformation of Consumer Cultures: The Material World Remade, c. 1500–1820* (Cambridge, 2018), 30–86; Ann M. Little, "'Shoot That Rogue, for He Hath an Englishman's Coat On!' Cultural Cross-Dressing on the New England Frontier, 1620–1760," *New England Quarterly*, LXXIV (2001), 238–273.

more holistic, sustainable understanding of the human and its place among nonhuman actors.[2]

Twentieth-century European philosophy has, from some perspectives, lagged in this insight. Algonquian people at least as early as the seventeenth century had rich mental resources to consider the various ways that humans might live in their world and bear obligations to it. The Algonquians who met and negotiated with the Europeans who wanted to live on their lands were in an unparalleled position to apply and refine their thinking about these categories. They had to engage with people who invested a great deal of energy in convincing themselves that they were exceptional to the ecologies on which they depended, and they expressed that commitment in activity that often did not make much sense to the minds of their witnesses. But Algonquians had practice making sense—among other neighbors, beavers provoked such mental exercise. Now that there were new human neighbors, Chickatawbut found an opportunity to think about beavers, and other humans, freshly. He would have had his own assessment of the relationship between these parties and the similarities and differences that came into view depending on what human polity one might have been looking at. When he arrived at the residence of his new neighbor, these thoughts shaped his communicative ambitions and the strategies of disclosure and opacity that he used to pursue them. As the two men began to negotiate over the value of beaver and what it could purchase, Chickatawbut's English neighbor might have thought that this Massachusetts sachem was taking steps sympathetic to his own priorities. Chickatawbut, on the other hand, might have been inviting Winthrop to revise his commitment to the bounded, self-knowing individual that enabled his idea of sympathy.

2. Margaret M. Bruchac, "Earthshapers and Placemakers: Algonkian Indian Stories and the Landscape," in Bruchac, Siobhan M. Hart, and H. Martin Wobst, eds., *Indigenous Archaeologies: A Reader on Decolonization* (New York, 2004), 77–99; Bruno Latour, "On Actor-Network Theory: A Few Clarifications," *Soziale Welt*, XLVII (1996), 369–381, esp. 373. See also Jane Bennett, *Vibrant Matter: A Political Ecology of Things* (Durham, N.C., 2010), 8–10. On the belatedness of European philosophers in considering the human as deeply entangled in other-than-human networks, see Vanessa Watts, "Indigenous Place-Thought and Agency amongst Humans and Non-Humans (First Woman and Sky Woman Go on a European World Tour!)," *Decolonization: Indigeneity, Education, and Society*, II, no. 1 (2013), 20–34; Jerry Lee Roziek, Jimmy Snyder, and Scott L. Pratt, "The New Materialisms and Indigenous Theories of Non-Human Agency: Making the Case for Respectful Anti-Colonial Engagement," *Qualitative Inquiry*, XXVI (2020), 331–346.

Alienation, and the sincerity that soothed it, shaped the meeting between Chickatawbut and Winthrop. Alienation and sincerity acted most powerfully in the strategies that Winthrop imagined would facilitate compromise between different parties. For Winthrop, successful compromise required judicious application of sympathy. It required not simply experiencing affection but choosing to experience it as rational agent, a mind not compromised in advance. If exercised properly, reason, Winthrop speculated, could outsmart injudicious affection. Chickatawbut's actions over a decade of engagement with men like Winthrop, however, suggest other ways of understanding reason and affection. They might not be clearly distinct in the first place. On the one hand, reason could try to manipulate and harness affection. On the other hand, reason could be subordinated to the lifelong experience of dependence on others, a life intimately familiar with swampy influences and saturations. Thus, sincerity, the mind's claim to know and its hope to be able to control affection, would have mattered less to Chickatawbut's relations with Winthrop. An individual, human or other-than-human, was not always the most lucid spokesperson for their own desires. This was not because of any particular failing but, more profoundly, because human affection—and human reason—changed and could be changed. Sincerity, confident self-knowledge, might never be possible given the ebbs and flows, damming up and releasing the mutable substance of interior life. One name for this synthetic understanding of subjective experience, of the inextricability of feeling and thinking, mind and matter, may be the deceptively simple term "thoughtfulness."

Thoughtfulness, and its expression, is an illuminating contrast to the antagonism, or at least the quiet tension, between reason and affection as English people saw it. The best expression of that tension appears in one of colonial American literature's canonical texts, John Winthrop's "Modell of Christian Charity." That enduringly charismatic text reveals a desire to transform affection from a liability into an asset. The text proposes what twenty-first-century vocabulary might call a social "hack." The hack would begin with a reassessment of first principles: all humans, Europeans believed, were vulnerable to being affected by the world around them. Their minds and thus their actions were always at risk of influence by movement beyond them, sometimes a consequence of the volition of others, sometimes not. Early moderns like these planters imagined that the body was, as Gail Kern Paster has put it, a "semipermeable, irrigated container" characterized by a "state of internal solubility." There was little solid or safely dry about the bodies in which these souls lived. One's dispositions, as Abram C. Van Engen summarizes, could be transformed. The emotions were not the only party vulnerable to affection, but they were a useful register of the ongoing vulnerability of individuals to be changed, sometimes beyond their will, and early modern philosophers cared deeply about that vulnerability: they often compared it to slavery. To the degree that emotions could be powerful catalysts for action, early modern thinkers watched them with a careful eye. Here was the attractive shortcut of a hack like Winthrop's: vulnerability to outside flows—affectability—threatened to make humans less reasonable, less human. Yet with close observation, that liability could also be useful. Affectability, the "Modell" proposed, could help humans reach reasonable ends more efficiently. Approached strategically, systematically, it could be a feature, not a bug, of the human condition, as men like Winthrop saw it.[3]

But the premise that the best minds were the driest ones was harder to sustain on the colonial frontier, a swampier, more frustrating environment than England. Of the many disturbances to and influences on English minds, perhaps one of the most quietly unsettling was the proximity of one particular nonhuman actant, the American beaver. Both English and Algonquian people recognized that the beaver possessed remarkable qualities: it was social and intelligent, and it contributed to the Algonquian ecosystems—the infrastructure of the Dawnlanders, or the "people of the east," as Algonquians knew themselves. Unlike their English neighbors, however, Algonquian people did not engage in relations with the beaver by imagining these qualities to exist thoughtlessly and instinctually. Rather, they understood beavers to be capable of reflection, if not always virtuously or happily. Beavers showcased the importance of reason in practices of reciprocity, sometimes by forgetting to be thoughtful themselves. Thoughtfulness, as Chickatawbut eventually undertook it at Winthrop's household, at times might look like sympathetic fellow feeling, the meeting of knowable hearts, but it crucially differed from that feeling in its consistent vision of a network of relations rather than the

3. John Winthrop, "A Modell of Christian Charity," in *Winthrop Papers*, II, *1623–1630* (Cambridge, Mass., 1931), 282–295 (hereafter cited as Winthrop, "Modell"); John Patrick Leary, *Keywords: The New Language of Capitalism* (New York, 2019), 85–88; Gail Kern Paster, *The Body Embarrassed: Drama and the Disciplines of Shame in Early Modern England* (Ithaca, N.Y., 1993), 8; Abram C. Van Engen, *Sympathetic Puritans: Calvinist Fellow Feeling in Early New England* (Oxford, 2015), 16; Susan James, *Passion and Action: The Emotions in Seventeenth-Century Philosophy* (Oxford, 1997). "Affectability" has emerged as a term to describe a condition of vulnerability that vexed white eugenicists, particularly in North America, at the end of the nineteenth century and start of the twentieth. In this context, the word names the potential, often inconvenient, to experience affection by an external world. See Kyla Schuller, *The Biopolitics of Feeling: Race, Sex, and Science in the Nineteenth Century* (Durham, N.C., 2018).

narrowed scope of affection that Winthrop's manifesto prescribed. Thought-fulness was a strategic response to earnest but insufficiently rational acts of depletion of a shared world.[4]

Winthrop's claims to purity of heart, desired or real, probably didn't concern Chickatawbut very much on his visit, but the presuppositions that encouraged Winthrop to long for sincerity did matter to Chickatawbut in his negotiation. Notwithstanding discussions on the merits of retiring the poten-tially historically inaccurate epithet "Puritan," the term would have meant little for the Algonquians like Chickatawbut who sustained the most regular contact with those pious English people, and it probably meant just as little to early modern Protestant planters in the cherished stories they told themselves about who they were and why they behaved the way they did. The term evokes a disciplinary commitment that might have been real but was probably super-seded in everyday life by a sense of why such discipline mattered. It mattered because these English people presumed that to be human was to be unend-ingly vulnerable to feelings, unendingly vulnerable to affection, unendingly susceptible and sensitive to the material world. The dream of purity implied a rich and tempting world of influence and the threat of impurity. The ongoing project of vindicating settlers' sensitivity has summoned a great deal of intel-lectual energy in decades past, but even if it hadn't, one could still infer that sensitivity from the same Hawthornian caricature that many twentieth- and twenty-first-century critics have toiled, with great perseverance and energy, to debunk. *The Scarlet Letter*'s infamous Chillingworth, certainly, was a severe man. Yet his severity complements rather than negates the novel's exposition of the richness of feeling that belongs to characters like Dimmesdale, Hester, and Pearl. Severity and strictness showcase and vindicate the existence of deep feeling, and allegiance to rules that would curb some of that richness requires a passionate will to subjection. Conscious suppression is one pos-itive experience of desire and striving in the material world. It is one highly visible token of sincere commitment. Consequently, when the enthusiasm for discipline is understood as a symptom of desire rather than a pure negation of it, Chillingworth and the caricature of severity that he often stands in for emerge as the most passionate of subjects. What colloquially goes by the name of "repression," in other words, requires the existence of deep affective

4. Thomas M. Wickman, *Snowshoe Country: An Environmental and Cultural History of Winter in the Early American Northeast* (Oxford, 2018), 17. See also Siobhan Senier, ed., *Dawnland Voices: An Anthology of Indigenous Writing from New England* (Lincoln, Neb., 2014).

experience as the content one can then repress, and it requires great volition and energy to undertake those rigorous pursuits.[5]

A commitment to rules, however, doesn't simply require energy. It also requires rules to which to commit. Deciding on those rules requires a heightened use of reason, as does the work of explaining to oneself why one commits to those rules. Those reasons claim worthiness through contrast with embodied desire. Because early modern Europeans thought of the body as a permeable membrane between the faculties of thought, on one hand, and almost everything else beyond thought (everything about which one might think), on the other, and because that bodily impressionability threatened thinking and its ambitions, these planters thought of vulnerability to the body's desires as something to overcome, or, as far as possible, to diminish. Yet early modern philosophers often took the body's vulnerability as an opportunity for reason to prove itself. They centered the struggle between reason and affection as the foundation of modern science. Francis Bacon, for example, in his *Novum Organon*, recognized that sense perception was a necessary catalyst to scientific inquiry, but he insisted that cognition should strive to transcend affectability. Such thinking should transform observation and perception—a receptivity to the external world—into reliable propositions about the world, and these could be made less vulnerable to transformation through time. Cognition required insulation. In his *Meditations on First Philosophy*, René Descartes extended the importance of that insulation, asserting that cognition and *only* cognition could be trusted, unlike the suspicious phenomena that cognition honed its acuity in perceiving and observing and from which it would eventually abstract transportable truths. These thinkers did not want to eradicate

5. Nathaniel Hawthorne, *The Scarlet Letter* (1850; rpt. New York, 1983); Michael P. Winship, "Were There Any Puritans in New England?" *NEQ,* LXXIV (2001), 111–138; Norman Pettit, *The Heart Prepared: Grace and Conversion in Puritan Spiritual Life* (New Haven, Conn., 1966); Charles Lloyd Cohen, *God's Caress: The Psychology of Puritan Experience* (Oxford, 1986); Michael McGiffert, ed., *God's Plot: Puritan Spirituality in Thomas Shepard's Cambridge*, 2d ed. (Amherst, Mass., 1994); Charles E. Hambrick-Stowe, *The Practice of Piety: Puritan Devotional Disciplines in Seventeenth-Century New England* (Williamsburg, Va., and Chapel Hill, N.C., 1982); Jeffrey A. Hammond, *Sinful Self, Saintly Self: The Puritan Experience of Poetry* (Athens, Ga., 1993); Amanda Porterfield, *Female Piety in Puritan New England: The Emergence of Religious Humanism* (Oxford, 1992); Patricia Caldwell, *The Puritan Conversion Narrative: The Beginnings of American Expression* (Cambridge, 1983); Andrew Delbanco, *The Puritan Ordeal* (Cambridge, Mass., 1991); Van Engen, *Sympathetic Puritans;* Rachel Trocchio, "Memory's Ends: Thinking as Grace in Thomas Hooker's New England," *American Literature,* XC (2018), 693–722; Judith Butler, *The Psychic Life of Power: Theories in Subjection* (Stanford, Calif., 1997); Sara Ahmed, *The Cultural Politics of Emotion* (New York, 2012), 4.

the affectability of the body completely. Instead, they saw the body as a useful instrument. They recommended vigilance toward the possibility that the body might be overwhelmed by what existed beyond it, compromising the faculties of reason their minds had worked so strenuously to perfect.[6]

Pragmatic, selective vulnerability to affection, literary critics have observed, would go on to be a deliberate strategy for later social theorists in the Anglo-American context. It could be politically valuable in heterogeneous social contexts, substituting for formerly reliable grounds of political community. Mutual affectability—what some historians have called "fellow feeling"—could be, in other words, a useful biopolitical tool. As early as the seventeenth century, susceptibility to affection already seemed to be an attractive and hopeful instrument to prevent disorder and misrule. Consider the strategy proposed in early American literary history's most celebrated theory of affections, the "Modell of Christian Charity," a document some critics have called the "Ur-text of American literature." Despite the uncertainty of its provenance and even of its frontier significance, the text, observes Van Engen, has strongly shaped Anglo-American ideas about who they are and whom they have wanted themselves to be. At the turn of a century that has seen the efflorescence of enthusiasm for the sermon's figure of a hilltop metropolis, the time may be ripe to reassess its dynamic biopolitical potential. The text has been well recognized as a manifesto of utopian ideals, of early modern Protestants' legal, economic, and sentimental priorities, but the text is also an unusually bright example of what John Patrick Leary has called a "hack," a shortcut to flourishing that presages the "bold and arduous Project of arriving at moral Perfection" devised a century later by Benjamin Franklin, who rarely saw a social problem that his more efficient use of reason couldn't solve. The "Modell" identified a clear set of goals and charismatically claimed that individuals could outsmart the major obstacles to reaching them simply by using their hearts. The goals of settlement, the text claimed, were the following: the renewal of an ideal society in decline, the public vindication of the piety that these ideas represented, and, finally, survival in a new land. These, of course, do not exhaust the reasons for removal and settlement, but they were some of the more pressing, higher-stakes goals

6. Francis Bacon, *Novum Organon; or, A True Guide to the Interpretation of Nature* (Oxford, 1855); René Descartes, *Meditations on First Philosophy in Which the Existence of God and the Distinction of the Soul from the Body Are Demonstrated,* trans. Donald A. Cress (Indianapolis, 1993).

and as such were rhetorically useful in justifying the steps that would help the community reach them.[7]

The governor of a reform Protestant utopian polity would have been interested in efficiency as he looked ahead to overseeing his constituents. How, he would likely have asked himself, could he effectively promote, maybe even guarantee, cohesion and coordination among settlers in the face of desires and affections that he suspected were deeply rooted in English hearts? The question would have resonated with special force in a high-stakes environment like a colonial frontier. There, where life-sustaining resources were scarce—to settlers' minds, at least—the biopolitical principle of recruiting willpower to "increase the possible utility of individuals," as Michel Foucault put it (rather than squander that power by suppressing it), would have been crucial for survival. Winthrop approached this task seriously. He drew on personal legal expertise and experience. He had studied law at Trinity College and had

7. Delbanco, *Puritan Ordeal*, 72 ("Ur-text"); Leary, *Keywords*, 85–88; Benjamin Franklin, *The Autobiography and Other Writings* (New York, 1986), 82 ("bold and arduous"); Julia A. Stern, *The Plight of Feeling: Sympathy and Dissent in the Early American Novel* (Chicago, 1997); Elizabeth Barnes, *States of Sympathy: Seduction and Democracy in the American Novel* (New York, 1997); Julie Ellison, *Cato's Tears and the Making of Anglo-American Emotion* (Chicago, 1999); Peter Coviello, "Agonizing Affection: Affect and Nation in Early America," *Early American Literature,* XXXVII (2002), 439–468; Michel Foucault, *Discipline and Punish: The Birth of the Prison,* trans. Alan Sheridan (New York, 1995). Some scholars have provocatively suggested that John Winthrop might not have been the author of this text. Yet these scrupulous textual historians nevertheless suggest Winthrop was a thoughtful and sensitive man who likely could have written the text, given the overlap between its ideology and his own position. See Hugh J. Dawson, "John Winthrop's Rite of Passage: The Origins of the 'Christian Charitie' Discourse," *EAL,* XXVI (1991), 219–231; Abram C. Van Engen, "Origins and Last Farewells: Bible Wars, Textual Form, and the Making of American History," *NEQ,* LXXXVI (2013), 543–592. For representative readings of the text, see Dawson, "John Winthrop's Rite," 219–231; Scott Michaelsen, "John Winthrop's 'Modell' Covenant and the Company Way," ibid., XXVII (1992), 85–100; Ivy Schweitzer, "John Winthrop's 'Model' of American Affiliation," ibid., XL (2005), 441–469; Mark Valeri, "Religious Discipline and the Market: Puritans and the Issue of Usury," *William and Mary Quarterly,* 3d Ser., LIV (1997), 747–768. On renewal of an ancient, declining society, see Theodore Dwight Bozeman, *To Live Ancient Lives: The Primitivist Dimension in American Puritanism* (Williamsburg, Va., and Chapel Hill, N.C., 1988). For enduring vindications of optimism in that piety, see Van Engen, *City on a Hill: A History of American Exceptionalism* (New Haven, Conn., 2020); and Daniel T. Rodgers, *As a City on a Hill: The Story of America's Most Famous Lay Sermon* (Princeton, N.J., 2018). For a discussion of the seriousness of this desire for exemplariness, see Bozeman, "The Puritans' 'Errand into the Wilderness' Reconsidered," *NEQ,* LIX (1986), 231–251. On the serious challenges of surviving, see Kathleen Donegan, *Seasons of Misery: Catastrophe and Colonial Settlement in Early America* (Philadelphia, 2014).

administered it working as a commission of the peace at Suffolk between 1615 and 1629, specializing in the administration of inheritances. Before leaving the Winthrop estate at Groton for a distant colony, he also presided as that estate's lord, governing a community of laborers. If practicing property law had not already shown him how troublesome adjudication of justice could be when it intersected with personal claims, he soon learned from the litigious liquidation of his family estate during his transatlantic move. He likely drew on these experiences in considering the consequences of personally felt ideas of justice and merit in the colony. Property, justice, and merit were culturally specific ideas, yet ones that many early modern English people imagined to be universal and undergirded by transcendently applicable reason. They could just as easily be obstacles to collective flourishing as conditions for it. Given his theological commitments to an idea of untrustworthy, or "fallen," human nature, Winthrop did not imagine that any society, even one that he governed, would be free of obstacles like these, but his task as a governor would have been to ensure that these obstacles did not undermine the success of the overall endeavor. As he looked ahead to settlement, he probably spent some time coming up with ways to make his administration as smooth and efficacious as possible.[8]

The de facto opening statement of the "Modell" shows some of his grounding presumptions. Foremost is the rightness of property. The "Modell" asserted that some people were always going to be rich and others always poor. The Christian deity, Winthrop claimed, did not want a world of material equals. To more modern readers for whom the great chain of being has waned in explanatory power, Winthrop's assertion can seem shockingly illiberal. Many modern scholars have sought to blunt the edge of so alarming a proposition by explaining the historical conventionality of inequality—at least, its conventionality in the minds of early modern property owners. Winthrop, they propose, was only rehearsing an early modern English belief in a cosmology wherein everyone had their proper place and role to play in a vertically organized hierarchy, and where the wealthy were closer to God—more responsible and therefore more authoritative in earthly affairs. The "Modell" rehearsed this trope by narrowing

8. Michel Foucault, *Discipline and Punish: The Birth of the Prison,* trans. Alan Sheridan (New York, 1977), 210; Francis J. Bremer, *John Winthrop: America's Forgotten Founding Father* (Oxford, 2003), 25 ("fallen"), 78–83, 105–123, 168–169, 427–430; Edmund S. Morgan, *Visible Saints: The History of a Puritan Idea* (Ithaca, N.Y., 1963); Bremer, *The Puritan Experiment: New England Society from Bradford to Edwards* (Hanover, N.H., 1976); Bozeman, *To Live Ancient Lives;* Michael P. Winship, *Godly Republicanism: Puritans, Pilgrims, and a City on a Hill* (Cambridge, Mass., 2012).

it severely, from a landscape of several degrees of social power to a neat dyad. In 1577 William Harrison, surveying English society, wrote that there were at least four strata to ideal human society. But in New England, Winthrop reduced details. Here, there would only be two, differentiated clearly. On one hand were the dependent, the "meane and in subjeccion"—or, more simply, the "poor." On the other were the autonomous, relatively independent persons "such as are able to live comfortably by theire owne meanes duely improved," whom Winthrop called the "rich." There were, in other words, those who were "competent" and those who were not. Using these simplified categories, Winthrop offered his most famous solution for cohesive, flourishing social life. He recommended that individuals on either side be "knitt more nearly together"—that they self-consciously attune themselves toward each other, creating a community wherein perception of someone else's emotional state translated directly onto one's own emotional state. This, in turn, would more naturally—"natively"—produce prosocial cooperation.[9]

For Winthrop, "native" cause and effect seemed to be the most reliable and potent answer to what he speculated would be a significant administrative challenge. It was not enough to explain why mercy should be desirable; Winthrop sought a more solid strategy to ensure the triumph of that desire. An occasional exhortation could be useful, but, Winthrop worried, it might not be trustworthy in the long term: "The way to drawe men to the workes of mercy is not by force of Argument from the goodnes or necessity of the worke." There were limits even to his own rhetoric. His discourse might be able to "enforce a rationall minde to some present Act of mercy," but what would happen in weeks or months, when the glow of the rallying sermonic experience had faded? These moments could not "worke such a habit in a Soule as shall make it prompt upon occasions to produce the same effect." Consciously coordinated will, Winthrop observed, drawing subtly on contemporary conventions regarding the weakness of the mind in relation to the

9. Winthrop, "Modell," 282, 283, 288; Arthur O. Lovejoy, *The Great Chain of Being: A Study of the History of an Idea* (Cambridge, Mass., 1964); Frederick J. Furnivall, ed., *Harrison's Description of England in Shakespere's* [sic] *Youth* (London, 1877), 105, quoted in Keith Wrightson, *English Society, 1580–1680* (London, 1982), 4. For sanguine readings that argue for more clemency toward what might otherwise seem to be a reactionary desire for domination by the wealthy, see Dawson, "John Winthrop's Rite," *EAL*, XXVI (1991), 219–231; Valeri, "Religious Discipline," *WMQ*, 3d Ser., LIV (1997), 747–768; and Van Engen, "Origins and Last Farewells," *NEQ*, LXXXVI (2013). See also David Cressy, "Describing the Social Order of Elizabethan and Stuart England," *Literature and History*, III (1976), 29–44; Daniel Vickers, "Competency and Competition: Economic Culture in Early America," *WMQ*, 3d Ser., XLVII (1990), 3–29.

body, might occasionally obey the "force" of an argument, especially a strong and rational one. But social cohesion was a marathon, not a sprint. Affections, Winthrop noticed, were stronger and more robust, their persistence more reliable. It might be possible to harness them to ensure the efficient business of being fitter, happier, and more productive participants in their utopia.[10]

Winthrop was frank about his strategy to hack social will. He turned to affection because he thought it could be a powerful master of the body's activity and "sett all the faculties on worke." This phrase, "set on work," though unobtrusive in the rhetoric of the "Modell," was a powerful commonplace of early modern English social policy. To "set on work" denoted forcefully regulating production to banish the idleness that many comfortable English believed was ruining their society. The *Oxford English Dictionary*'s cited examples for this discrete phrase, "to put (also *set*) on work," demonstrate this political cliché, foregrounding the moral virtues of industry in contrast to the vices of idleness and featuring an irresistible, often coercive power doing the putting or the setting. By the end of the seventeenth century, John Locke brought the phrase home, literally. Locke used it to describe one of the ideal means of shaping a child into a responsible political subject. In his 1693 *Thoughts concerning Education*, Locke instructed parents that *"Reward* and *Punishment,* are the only Motives to a rational Creature; these are the Spur and the Reins whereby all Mankind are set on work." Winthrop likewise hoped affection would be useful. Like a clock's gears and springs, affection, he dreamed, could be disciplined. His sermon compared the individual to a clock in order to convey affection's power to ensure reasonable, efficient regularity: "When wee bid one make the clocke strike he doth not lay hand on the hammer which is the immediate instrument of the sound . . . which hee intends." That would make the innovation of the mechanical clock irrelevant. Rather, Winthrop claimed, affection should be mechanized. Affection, subordinated to reason, could be harnessed and made automatic, "as any cause doth produce the effect."[11]

10. Winthrop, "Modell," 288.

11. Ibid. On early modern English antipathy to apparent idleness, see Brian Vickers, "Leisure and Idleness in the Renaissance: The Ambivalence of Otium," *Renaissance Studies,* IV (1990), 1–37; Keith Thomas, "Health and Morality in Early Modern England," in Allan M. Brandt and Paul Rozin, eds., *Morality and Health* (New York, 1997), 15–34; David Rollison, "Discourse and Class Struggle: The Politics of Industry in Early Modern England," *Social History,* XXVI (2001), 166–189; and Patricia Fumerton, *Unsettled: The Culture of Mobility and the Working Poor in Early Modern England* (Chicago, 2006). See also *Oxford English Dictionary,* s.v. "work." Christopher Tomlins, noting the ubiquity of the phrase "set on worke" and the coincidence between work and virtue that it suggests, used that phrase "Setteynge many on Worke" as the

The "Modell" claimed affection could be rationally useful. This document was not advocating a total disenchantment of psychic life. Focusing exclusively on this paragraph at the center of the sermon can make it seem to be a neat summary of Max Weber's critique of early modern reform Protestantism's unfolding, particularly in America. Other paragraphs counterbalance this aspect of Winthrop's argument and preserve it from too bleak a vision of human manipulability. For example, Winthrop described the relationship between individuals and their deity as a "Covenant"—that is, a "[clause] of an agreement contained in a deed." Yet the divine party in this covenant, for reform Protestants, was notoriously unpredictable, and the affections themselves were not always easy to control. Affection was an ambiguous experience, and one might not always feel what one wanted to feel when one wanted to feel it. The instability of affection testified to an unsystematizable aspect of Winthrop's prescription, at least in theory. Nevertheless, in thinking about these aspects of social life, Winthrop hoped that they could be made useful—and he staked a great deal on these hopes. He described failure as a metaphorical "shipwracke." Winthrop hoped to harness the affection that, according to contemporary conventions, exceeded reason and threatened to overwhelm and sink it. Masterful, innovative reason, he proposed, could preempt this fate.[12]

Winthrop's prescription that all settlers cultivate affection in order to forgive each other—with mechanical regularity—sounds plausible and even pragmatic. It is hard to disagree with the proposition that people who like each other and work to imagine each other's lives are more amenable to forgiveness and cooperation. Yet as a prescription for social practice, the "Modell" built on epistemological premises that were not only not definitive but also had powerful consequences for political life. First, despite centuries of arguments by defenders of private property that the best way for a society to express solidarity with the poor was to put wealth in the hands of the rich, the option did exist for a governor like Winthrop to develop and propose policies that

title to his chapter on the attraction of the American colonies as sites for ensuring that the idle did not overrun England. See Tomlins, *Freedom Bound: Law, Labor, and Civic Identity in Colonizing English America, 1580–1865* (Cambridge, 2010); John Locke, *Some Thoughts concerning Education,* ed. John W. Yolton and Jean S. Yolton (Oxford, 1989), 115. On the mechanical clock's impact on modernity, see David S. Landes, *Revolution in Time: Clocks and the Making of the Modern World* (Cambridge, Mass., 1983).

12. Winthrop, "Modell," 294–295; Tomlins, *Freedom Bound,* 32n; Max Weber, *The Protestant Ethic and the "Spirit" of Capitalism and Other Writings,* trans. Peter Baehr and Gordon C. Wells (New York, 2002).

aspired to destroy rather than naturalize the gap between the two. Second, and more significant for an understanding of sincerity, the "Modell," in explicitly prescribing affectability as a rational strategy, presented reason as the ideal master of affections, something that maybe possessed the power but definitely the responsibility to make the affections work.[13]

For Winthrop, the best and most virtuous use of reason required drawing away from the things of the world, even if that useful reason proved its value in applying itself to that world. Aboard the *Arbella,* surrounded by the cry of pulleys and the swell of canvas sails, bedsheets, and blouses in the wind, Winthrop believed that duty required him and his fellows to be part of the world—a world that was often wet, slippery, and overwhelming and would continue to be so even after reaching land. Piety required men like him to engage in that worldliness with their reason and to do it diligently. This was the heavy burden, Christians thought, of being made in the image of their deity and being made unique as a species. Though reason risked being overpowered by affection, that overpowering could be harnessed rationally, in a dialectic of triumphant overcoming. For the "Modell," reason could and should have the last say in its encounter with affection. It was not that affection, feeling, or emotionality should not exist. Rather, good Christians expressed their duty and their virtue in using affection skillfully and rationally toward goals reached through personal reason, the faculty that Christians thought distinguished them from other creatures. This deliberation was useful for individual self-management as well as the governance of a potentially fractious community.

Yet affection, the experience of subjective boundaries' erosion, enhanced individuals' sense that there was an interior self to be known and shared and that it was an entity distinct from that world. Winthrop conveyed this individuality, and its necessary boundedness, in a metaphorical register that many of his listeners would have understood. A piously fellow-feeling community was one that understood itself to be "knitt . . . together"—as the *OED* clarifies, "knotted, tied, fastened," or "contracted together." More actively, to "knit" means "to tie in or with a knot," "to knot string in open meshes so as to form (a net)," or "to interlock, interlace, intertwine." As any sailor or fabric worker would have known—and among the Protestants who left England in the early seventeenth century, there were many fabric workers—in order to be able to knit or to knot, one's fibers should not be entangled. Early modern English people were attuned to the tenors of such vehicles. Sensitive listeners might

13. Bernard Bailyn, ed., *The Apologia of Robert Keayne* (New York, 1964), 20–21; Valeri, "Religious Discipline," *WMQ,* 3d Ser., LIV (1997), 747–768.

have noticed that not being tangled is the condition for being made into a knot, even though knotting's final product has place- and relation-fixing effects remarkably like that of a tangle. Affection, Winthrop implied, depended on an a priori disentangled people—as Herman Melville's Ahab reflected two centuries later, "uninterpenetrat[ed]" subjects. Only if they recognized personal responsibility and discrete mastery could they summon affection as an efficient means to a desirable end.[14]

Histories of early modern and Enlightenment thought have long acknowledged the lurking threat of affection in the development of modern reason. "No intellectual passions are stronger than those involved in achieving precision, standards and conventions," writes Barbara Solow, citing Steven Shapin's work on the emergence of empiricism in the British seventeenth century. More recently, new materialist scholars have pointed out how modern humanistic reason has depended dearly on imagining a clear and firm boundary between the faculties of reason on one hand, and on the other, the unthinking world impinging on it; between a "calculable natural world," as Diana Coole and Samantha Frost put it, and the "sense of mastery bequeathed to the thinking subject . . . as ontologically other than matter." That mastery wasn't simply a metaphor for epistemological apprehension. Denise Ferreira da Silva has observed the effect of this dialectical contest on Western thought's aggressive claims to be certain of racial difference. Post-Christian European reason, exemplified in Cartesian thought, desired to be the only occupant of the "Transcendental I," a form of personhood capable of thinking through every problem or inconvenience. European philosophers thought they could achieve this unique status by using their powers of reason to confirm their suspicion that there existed other parties *too* vulnerable to affectability, what Silva calls "outer determination." Eventually, desires to preserve their selves from that vulnerability led them to invest intellectually and psychically in the idea of racial difference and the idea that coercively subordinating racial others, through slavery and colonization, was in the best interest of everyone involved. What they saw as biopoetic ambition for happiness in their own lives turned into biopolitical regimes, coercively enforced, in the lives of others. Reason,

---

14. Winthrop, "Modell," 283; *Oxford English Dictionary,* s.v. "knit"; Herman Melville, *Moby-Dick; or, The Whale,* ed. Hershel Parker and Harrison Hayford, 2d ed. (New York, 2002), 360; George C. Homans, "The Puritans and the Clothing Industry in England," *NEQ,* XIII (1940), 519–529. Early Americanist literary critics have pointed out early colonial sensitivity to such textile polysemy. See Robert Blair St. George, *Conversing by Signs: Poetics of Implication in Colonial New England Culture* (Williamsburg, Va., and Chapel Hill, N.C., 1998); Michelle Burnham, *Folded Selves: Colonial New England Writing in the World System* (Hanover, N.H., 2007).

in other words, cherished affection. Reason required affection as a vivifying counterpart.[15]

This dependence played out on the frontier in ways that Europeans did not always predict. English people, historians have argued, did not imagine their Indigenous counterparts to be less than human. Rather, they saw themselves sharing a basic humanity with their Native neighbors. This meant that these English people applied culture-specific notions of what humanity consisted of to their non-English neighbors. Even "the human," as Sylvia Wynter has argued, was fraught with opportunities to exercise prejudice and pave the way to violence, but not all the thinking agents that settlers encountered in America were of a species with Europeans. They discovered this, awkwardly, when they encountered the beaver, one of the most intellectually powerful and disturbing actants in Algonquian territory. Beavers were powerful not only in what they brought to Europeans and the various Algonquian polities with whom Europeans traded. Beavers were also powerful in how they provoked European thought in conscious and unconscious ways—how, in other words, beavers affected Europeans. Yet for those with different founding statements regarding species distinction—for those who did not claim that their proximity to the divine entailed domination over the other-than-human world—beavers held a differently ambiguous yet instructive status in social and ecological life. Beavers, for Algonquian peoples, demonstrated the value and the challenge of thoughtfulness as a mode for sustainable relations within one's immediate and most definitive community—and beyond it, too.[16]

Winthrop developed his theories of Christian sympathy as he looked ahead, anticipating an environment of looming affective engulfment that threatened to demote English settlers from their elevated species status in the great chain of being. Once he was in that environment, a different sort of threat emerged. Rivals to humans' elevated place might have lived there, but that conflict recedes in the documentary archive behind those rivals' material value. To English adventurers, merchants, traders, and settlers, beavers were primarily

15. Steven Shapin, review of Alan H. Cook, *Edmond Halley: Charting the Heavens and the Seas* (Oxford, 1998), in *London Review of Books,* XX (July 2, 1998), 12, cited in Barbara Solow, "The Transatlantic Slave Trade: A New Consensus," *WMQ,* 3d Ser., LVIII (2001), 9–16, esp. 9; Diana Coole and Samantha Frost, "Introducing the New Materialisms," *New Materialisms: Ontology, Agency, and Politics* (Durham, N.C., 2010), 8; Denise Ferreira da Silva, *Toward a Global Idea of Race* (Minneapolis, 2007), 28.

16. Sylvia Wynter, "Unsettling the Coloniality of Being / Power / Truth / Freedom: Towards the Human, after Man, Its Overrepresentation—An Argument," *New Centennial Review,* III (2003), 257–337.

a commodity. Yet they were not simply one among many. Beavers were one of the most sought-after products of the northern parts of the Western Hemisphere. They do not appear in Thomas Hariot's 1588 description of America as a list of discrete, rhetorically deracinated, extractable objects. Hariot did identify both fur and musk as prized goods that America had in abundance. In Algonquian territory, Hariot had witnessed animals like otters, deer, and possibly lynx, and he had speculated about the profits that their pelts promised. He noted evidence of "civet cattes," who possessed glands desirable for their perfume, much like beavers' castoreum. In territories farther north, however, beavers were an exciting European prospect for profit. They were among the key commodities, along with fish and whale oil, that Europeans extracted from distant lands and waters. French traders and adventurers were at the leading edge of this extractive economy, but English colonists in northern Algonquian territory also recognized the unusual profit to be gained in the beaver trade. They often staked some of their ambitions for survival and solvency on that creature. Two decades after the fact, for example, William Bradford recalled the Separatists' discovery of beaver and the profit it yielded: "At first, being alltogeather unprovided for trade; neither was ther any amongst them that ever saw a beaver skin till they came hear, and were informed by Squanto. The fraight [*sic*] was estimated to be worth near 500[£]." John Winthrop likewise noted the beaver's presence and its value, enthusiastically. On August 6, 1633, he noted Mr. Graves's success in acquiring "between 5: and 6000 weight of Beaver" and, later that year, anticipated a yearly yield of "1000: skins"—if only the English could secure control of trading posts along the Kwinitekw River that had, for some time, been controlled by the Dutch. And it wasn't only the well-off who noticed and monitored these possibilities. Nearly starving Bay Colony servant John Pond despaired as he noted what he perceived to be the recalcitrance of some sachems to trade with the English: "Whareas," he wrote, "we ded expect gret stor of bever her is littell or non to be had." Nor would he stop despairing. He concluded his letter to his father by remarking again, "Her whare we live her is no bever."[17]

17. Thomas Hariot, *A Brief and True Report of the New Found Land of Virginia* (1588), ed. Paul Royster, *Electronic Texts in American Studies*, 20, http://digitalcommons.unl.edu/etas/20, 12–13; William Bradford, *Bradford's History "Of Plimoth Plantation": From the Original Manuscript, with a Report of the Proceedings Incident to the Return of the Manuscript to Massachusetts* (Boston, 1898), 130; Richard S. Dunn, James P. Savage, and Laetitia Yeandle, eds., *The Journal of John Winthrop, 1630–1649* (Cambridge, Mass., 1994), 93, 99; John Pond to William Pond, Mar. 15, 1631, *Winthrop Papers*, III, *1631–1637* (Cambridge, Mass., 1943), 17–19, esp. 17, 18; Virginia

Beavers were useful to the English materially, but they had also, for some time, been useful to the English emblematically. As animals, beavers possessed a particular place in the Christian hierarchy of divinely created nature. Accordingly, the actions attributable to them had figurative, edifying value. Within the English animal imaginary, and building on classical sources, beavers were fabled for their industry. They worked together, in remarkable cooperation, building complex structures such as dams and lodges with intricate roofs and strategically difficult entryways. They were not the only animals who worked together; early English surveyor William Wood compared the collective labor of beavers to that of ants. Yet beavers' cooperation engaged with the landscape in a manner uncannily similar to English ideas of improvement.[18]

Wood went on: they built dams and lodges "of wood and clay" up to "three stories high." Beavers were, in Wood's assessment, "almost . . . a reasonable creature." Strother E. Roberts notes that they were just as invested in changing the land as humans were; beavers "apply their labor to the natural resources around them" and "profoundly reshape the physical world." Together, beavers undertook large-scale waterworks projects reminiscent of the projects that were captivating European engineers across the globe, from Dutch lowlands to the mountains of Mexico City. Dry land, to Europeans, meant mastery. It meant productivity and economic power. It promised greater safety from permeation and from vulnerability to other actants, both visible and—depending on the water's opacity—invisible. English people dreamed of being able to control where was wet and where was dry, and they discovered, in these marshes and swamps, that there was at least one other creature who might be dreaming the same dreams.[19]

Beavers had "wisdom and understanding," "Art and Industry," Wood continued. They had families that appeared to be structured by monogamous,

DeJohn Anderson, *Creatures of Empire: How Domestic Animals Transformed Early America* (Oxford, 2004); Sleeper-Smith, introduction, in Sleeper-Smith, *Rethinking the Fur Trade,* xviii.

18. William Wood, *New Englands Prospect: A True, Lively, and Experimentall Description of That Part of America, Commonly Called New England . . .* (London, 1634), 25.

19. Ibid.; Strother E. Roberts, *Colonial Ecology, Atlantic Economy: Transforming Nature in Early New England* (Philadelphia, 2019), 25; Erica Fudge, *Brutal Reasoning: Animals, Rationality, and Humanity in Early Modern England* (Ithaca, N.Y., 2006); Patricia Seed, *Ceremonies of Possession in Europe's Conquest of the New World, 1492–1640* (Cambridge, 1995), 16–40; Monique Allewaert, *Ariel's Ecology: Plantations, Personhood, and Colonialism in the American Tropics* (Minneapolis, 2013); Vera S. Candiani, *Dreaming of Dry Land: Environmental Transformation in Colonial Mexico City* (Stanford, Calif., 2014); Johan van Veen, *Dredge, Drain, Reclaim: The Art of a Nation* (The Hague, 1952).

lifelong partnerships. In Wood's account, they even took captives of other beaver families. Perhaps Wood was seeking confirmation of their militancy, drawing on an older English tradition regarding beaver character as approaching political capacity. In making nationalist political associations from observations of the natural world, Wood was following precedent. In 1612, Michael Drayton had described the European beaver, by then extinct in England and, very likely, in much of the rest of Europe. Similar to the American beaver, the European beaver not only built castles and made use of sleds but also forts such as those Drayton described on the Welsh river the Tivy (Teifi). These forts were so magnificent that it might seem, Drayton fancied, that English people "from this Beast to fortifie had learn'd." In examples like these, the innate skill of the animal was presumed and continued to be until at least as late as 1868, when Lewis H. Morgan turned his attention to the matter to clarify the intellect of the species over and above its instinct. Beavers, like ants, built homes, fortified them, and distinguished between those they recognized as kin and those they did not. These were, in English eyes, instinctual actions, inclinations developed within a natural set of cognitive limitations.[20]

Beavers were lucrative objects in European markets, but many of the animal's market-irrelevant qualities also disturbed Europeans. As settlers arrived in a supposedly new land, they saw a creature that their recent ancestors had made scarce and, in some places, extinct. Now they observed this fabled creature with their own eyes, but like the opossum, the beaver's anatomy unnerved these Europeans. Consider, for example, the frenzied assortment of creatures that the otherwise erudite and sophisticated prose stylist Adriaen van der Donck turned to in order best to describe the North American beaver in 1655: "The shape of the beaver suggests a cucumber with a flat stalk at one end." Then he corrected himself. Rather, it was "like a duck minus the neck and the head." That didn't satisfyingly describe what he was seeing, either. No, it was more "like an elongated and somewhat flat ball of yarn"—but not just any ball of yarn. He was thinking of a ball of yarn that "may also be thicker than it is long." Yet there were still other remarkable but perplexing qualities. The beaver was also "like a hog, whose sides run fairly straight from the back to the belly." The last and most satisfying comparison he could come up with

20. Wood, *New Englands Prospect*, 25–26; Michael Drayton, *Poly-Olbion: A Chorographicall Description of Great Britain* (London, 1889), 108–109; Gillian Feeley-Harnik, "Lewis Henry Morgan: American Beavers and Their Works," *Ethnos*, LXXXVI (2021), 21–43; Richard Helgerson, *Forms of Nationhood: The Elizabethan Writing of England* (Chicago, 1992); Lewis H. Morgan, *The American Beaver and His Works* (Philadelphia, 1868); Roberts, *Colonial Ecology, Atlantic Economy*, 31.

FIGURE 1. "[Animals of North America]." In Arnoldus Montanus, *De Nieuwe en onbekende Weereld: of Beschryving van America en 't zuid-land . . . (The New and Known World; or, Description of America and the Southland . . .)* (Amsterdam, 1671). This seventeenth-century representation of the beaver believed the creature to be wondrous enough to include it alongside similarly astonishing animals such as the unicorn and the moose. Courtesy of the John Carter Brown Library

required him to turn to the subterranean, exhumed and made visible, then posthumously destroyed: "The beaver resembles a dead mole that has been trod on but not entirely flattened." For van der Donck, the sight of the beaver produced an itch for accuracy that no single association or simile satisfyingly scratched. This Dutchman's itch provoked him to turn, in his description, not only to death but also to postmortem violence. The beaver's bizarre aspect, alongside its crucial commodity status, catalyzed an aversive, hostile reaction in this reflective, scientifically proficient observer.[21]

Beavers' ubiquity, intelligence, and dynamic effects on the environment challenged Europeans' vision of a divinely ordered creation where humanity presided near the very top. Conveniently, however, success and solvency in the colonial setting required settlers to hunt out and destroy evidence of this extravagant potential outlier to the great chain of being. Desire for control over the beaver trade had been one of Bradford's anxieties when he turned to paranoid logic to criticize the apparent imprudence of the less wealthy, more vulnerable—those Winthrop would call, frankly, "poore"—in selling firearms to their Algonquian neighbors. Even the poor mistrusted these Indigenous neighbors: John Pond, for example, expressed his suspicions that Wonohaquaham, a Massachusetts sachem, had been cheating the English in trading with them. But beavers not only destabilized relations between settlers and their Indigenous neighbors or relations within a given settler colony. Beavers also challenged peaceful relations between different English plantations, even Christian ones. In the early years of arrival, Winthrop recalled one such dispute between Plymouth colonists and one of Sir Ferdinando Gorges's agents. Disagreement about which party could claim to control trade along the Kennebec River resulted in a tense standoff, followed by the murder of one English planter by another. In his diary, Winthrop expressed regret about this derangement, lamenting that Englishmen had come to be "cutting one anothers throats for Beaver."[22]

The desire for beaver pelts—more than, say, desire for corn or cod, in these Englishmen's eyes—was responsible for settlers' temporary loss of reason and, in some cases, loss of life. Morton saw this effect with unusual acuity and interest. Indeed, from the perspective of objects, the protagonist of *New*

21. Adriaen van der Donck, *A Description of New Netherland*, trans. Diederik Willem Goedhuys (Lincoln, Neb., 2008), 121; James Edmund Harting, *British Animals Extinct within Historic Times* (Boston, 1880), 33–60; Susan Scott Parrish, "The Female Opossum and the Nature of the New World," *WMQ*, 3d Ser., LIV (1997), 475–514.

22. Winthrop, "Modell," 282; John Pond to William Pond, Mar. 15, 1631, *Winthrop Papers*, III, 17; Dunn, Savage, and Yeandle, eds., *Journal of John Winthrop*, 115.

English Canaan is not the libertine first-person protagonist's "host" but the beaver pelt. In anecdote after anecdote, Morton described the promise of beaver disturbing human reason—"such," Morton wrote, "is the thrist [*sic*] after beaver." Beavers provoked somatic, urgent desires in settlers; they were dear to English bodies like water. Beavers reminded them, if not always consciously, of those bodily desires. The prospect of the beaver being a "reasonable creature" and not simply "*almost* . . . a reasonable creature"—even as humans (English, Christian humans, at that) were losing their rationality to desire and to affection—would have been perhaps too uncanny for these settlers to contemplate. That similarity edged close to the "*menace*" that, as theorists of the colonial psyche have observed, haunted European colonial prospects.[23]

There were other ways to engage with the other-than-human world, other foundations for understanding and acting on animal-human relations. Among Algonquian peoples, beavers had a special place. Many animals populated Algonquian stories; each had a particular role sustaining these homelands. But beavers seem to have provoked specific reflections on political relations. Farther north, among the Mi'kmaq, French missionary Chrestien Le Clercq recalled pleasure in observing the "natural industry" of the beaver. That "natural" industriousness, Le Clercq elaborated, "transcends the imagination of those who have never seen the surprising evidences thereof." To describe it fully, he turned to the estimation of those who had been witnesses to those "evidences thereof" for much longer. According to Le Clercq, "the Indians say that the Beavers have sense," and not only sense, but political cohesion: they "form a separate nation." The Mi'kmaq were eager that the beavers should "speak, howsoever little, in order that they might learn whether the Beavers are among their friends or their enemies." Morton, among the Massachusetts, recalled a description that might have struck his English readers as perhaps even more uncanny, even more frightening: "Wee supposed, when they spake of Beasts thereabouts as high as men, they have made report of men all over hairy like Beavers, in so much as we questioned them, whether they eate of the Beavers, to which they replyed Matta, (noe) saying they were almost Beavers Brothers." Here, the Massachusetts shared historical memories of the giant beaver, the species identified by later American zoologists as *Castoroides*

23. Thomas Morton, *New English Canaan; or, New Canaan, Containing an Abstract of New England . . .* (1637), rpt. in Peter Force, coll., *Tracts and Other Papers, Relating Principally to the Origin, Settlement, and Progress of the Colonies in North America, from the Discovery of the Country to the Year 1776* (Washington, D.C., 1838), II, 93; Wood, *New Englands Prospect*, 26 ("*almost*" [emphasis added]); Homi Bhabha, "Of Mimicry and Man: The Ambivalence of Colonial Discourse," *October*, no. 28 (1984), 125–133, esp. 132 ("*menace*").

The Cataract of NIAGARA, some make
this Water-Fall to be half a League while
others reckon it no more than
a hundred Fathom.

FIGURE 2. Detail of Herman Moll, *A New and Exact Map of the Dominions of the King of Great Britain on the Continent of North America* . . . (London, 1715). Moll's eighteenth-century survey of the Eastern littoral, nicknamed the Beaver Map, features an exaggerated depiction of the social coordination among beavers as they created their lodges and dams. Courtesy of the John Carter Brown Library

FIGURE 3. Veremondo Rossi, "La caccia dei castori" ("The Beaver Hunt"), in Marco Coltinelli, *Il gazzettiere americano contenente un distinto ragguaglio di tutte le parti del Nuovo Mondo . . .* , I (Livorno, 1763). This eighteenth-century illustration of a beaver lodge features a cutaway revealing the interior structural complexity that amazed Europeans. Courtesy of the John Carter Brown Library

ohioensis, a species of megafauna that could measure up to nine feet long without the tail, and whose size might heighten the significance of fraternity with an other-than-human creature.[24]

Just as beavers were both materially and emblematically important to English people, they were materially and emblematically vital for Algonquian people. The history that Algonquians and beavers shared, however, differed from the history that English people knew and that they thought made them distinct as a species. Rather, humans and actants like beavers were together creators of a vital world. Lisa Brooks notes that beavers "participated productively, along with humans, in the continuation of this abundant dish"—the deliberate ecosystem of the Kwinitekw River valley and Algonquian homelands more generally. The figure of the dish designated a shared space of reciprocity, like a village. The dish could be flexible in scale, and it was characterized by a space of sustainable mutual concern, from which participants could "eat together"—derive cooperative nourishment. Beavers participated in that dish and that nourishment, but in the stories Algonquian peoples told about the beaver, it was not an unthinking, instinctual creature. Brooks troubles early modern European ideas about human-animal relations, about species difference, and about the monopoly over reason, that have been grounding principles for historiographic methods. Citing Abenaki poet Cheryl Savageau, Brooks retells the stories of Ktsi Amiskw, the Great Beaver, namesake of the mountain that shapes the bowl of the Kwinitekw River valley. Savageau's poem "At Sugarloaf, 1996" narrates Ktsi Amiskw engaging in behavior special, even unique to beavers—swimming, building dams—and in misbehavior too. The Creator notices. The Creator responds in a fashion that Christians familiar with the deity of the Old Testament might consider familiar—he transformed,

24. Chrestien Le Clercq, "On the Hunting of the Gaspesians," in Le Clercq, *New Relation of Gaspesia: With the Customs and Religion of the Gaspesian Indians,* trans. William F. Ganong, Publications of the Champlain Society, V (Toronto, Ont., 1910), 276–277; Morton, *New English Canaan,* rpt. in Force, coll., *Tracts,* II, 66. Adriaen van der Donck observed that although Mohicans and perhaps, farther north, the Mohawks along the Muhhekunnutuk River (renamed the Noort Rivier and later the Hudson) *did* eat beaver, they held it in an elevated status and refused to let their dogs eat from the beaver's bones. See van der Donck, *Description,* trans. Goedhuys, 130. See also Bruchac, "Earthshapers," in Bruchac, Hart, and Wobst, eds., *Indigenous Archaeologies,* 77–99; Jane C. Beck, "The Giant Beaver: A Prehistoric Memory?" *Ethnohistory,* XIX (1972), 109–122, esp. 110.

maybe demoted, the animate creation into less animate form: Lot's unnamed wife into a pillar of salt; Ktsi Amiskw into the stone mountain.[25]

Whereas the total salinification of Lot's wife is the end of her story, petrification is not the end of Ktsi Amiskw's. Though stone, Ktsi Amiskw retains consciousness. He "lies still," but he also has nightmares: "a world without beavers." Savageau's telling, staging the dreaming after the petrification, suggests, for a time, that these difficult dreams come to Ktsi Amiskw passively. Yet by the end of her narration, in turning to transitive use of the verb "to dream," Savageau suggests that mental, psychic life can have a dynamic relation to action, can have effects in the shared world: "he dreams the rivers back, young mothers building, secure in their skins, and a pond full of the slapping tails of children." For Savageau, and for the cosmology that Savageau articulates, even stones act in a subtle but powerful way on human and other-than-human affairs. Throughout, a host of other-than-human actors, from stones to beavers, possesses the capacity for reflection and transformation. Thoughtfulness, a witnessing of and reflection on the consequences of one's actions, is not a capacity exclusive to humans.[26]

Like the older Algonquian stories that Savageau updates, this poem wrestles to make sense of activity that may seem alien to reason: given the exchange necessary for shared flourishing, why would the beaver hoard? Stories like Savageau's express an epistemology different from the humanism that early modern English understood to be normal rational thought. This difference usefully alienates English reason, which wanted to claim universality, from readers in the present, who may share certain elements of early settlers' logic, such as the idea of self-interest's ubiquity and the consequent idea that hoarding possessions is a safe strategy for survival. Yet there were, and are, other ways of experiencing the world, its other actors and actants, and the relationship that one shares with them. Savageau's story is most vital in this regard. It presents hoarding as an unusual and strange activity rather than an obviously rational intuition, unnecessary to investigate or historicize. Here, Ktsi Amiskw's opaque motivations are an opportunity to re-create

25. Lisa Brooks, *The Common Pot: The Recovery of Native Space in the Northeast* (Minneapolis, 2008), 20, 50–64; Cheryl Savageau, "At Sugarloaf, 1996," *Mother / Land* (Cambridge, Mass., 2006); Bruchac, "Earthshapers," in Bruchac, Hart, and Wobst, eds., *Indigenous Archaeologies,* 77–99; Margaret Bruchac, "The Geology and Cultural History of the Beaver Hill Story," *Raid on Deerfield: The Many Stories of 1704,* https://repository.upenn.edu/anthro_papers/144 (Philadelphia, 2005); Katharine M. Abbott, *Old Paths and Legends of the New England Border: Connecticut, Deerfield, Berkshire* (New York, 1907), 164.

26. Savageau, "At Sugarloaf," *Mother / Land.*

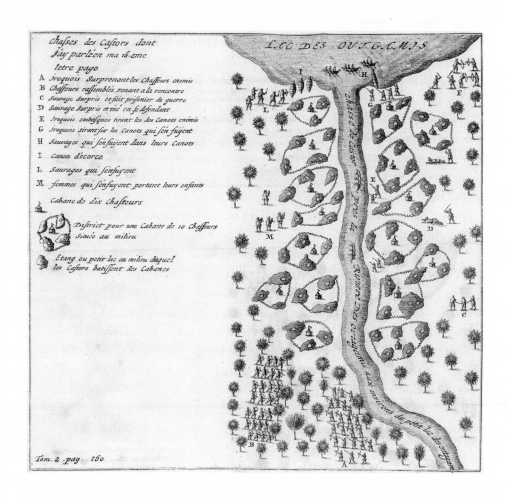

FIGURE 4. "Chasses des castors . . ." ("Beaver Hunts"), in Louis Armand de Lom d'Arce, *Nouveaux voyages de Mr. le baron de Lahontan dans l'Amérique septentrionale . . .*, II (The Hague, 1703). This illustration by an eighteenth-century French naturalist who participated in beaver hunting himself emphasizes the collaboration among humans that this endeavor required. Courtesy of the John Carter Brown Library

another being's logic. To get closer to the beaver's reason requires close reading of actions and their consequences. Savageau does not summarize Ktsi Amiskw's actions into a neat, critiquable quality, though she comes close. She describes his actions clearly: "He has built a dam. The water in his pond grows deeper. He patrols the edges, chasing everyone away. This is all mine, he says. The people and animals grow thirsty." These actions do not begin with morally reprehensible intent. In fact, they do not begin with any indication of motive or intention. Yet as they progress, and as Ktsi Amiskw's relationship to his own material world progresses, the impact of his actions becomes more evident. Immediately before her description of these actions' effect on people and animals—a more literal thirst than Morton's— Savageau represents Beaver's (Ktsi Amiskw) interiority discursively: "This is all mine, he says." Is this greed? That would seem to be a straightforward gloss of Savageau's description of Beaver's claims to possession, along with the actions that precede it.[27]

If so, Beaver's actions exemplify the classic description of property that William Cronon borrowed from Huntington Cairns to describe of the effects of settlers on the dish that the beavers shared with English and Algonquian peoples. Like English property claims, Beaver's relation to his dam and its captives was triadic, one of exclusion: "'A owns B against C,' where C represents all other individuals." Ktsi Amiskw imagines himself to have a claim to the water and its inhabitants, against anyone else who would approach them. Yet Savageau does not name this relationship as "Eurocentric property ideals," nor does she qualify Ktsi Amiskw's desires as greed. Ktsi Amiskw is not moved by instinct but, rather, is susceptible to desire and to noticing desire's consequences. For Savageau, this longing is best analyzed as a series of actions and their outcomes, not a quality of character. Individuals, human or not, can change their behavior. The possibility of change, rather than the enduring quality of

27. Ibid. The turn to contemporary literary and cultural work, particularly by members of Native communities, as a key to understanding the past is one of a number of strategies proposed by recent scholars of early American literature in response to the need to "complete the turn" to more respectful methods in research pursuits. Lisa Brooks models this strategy in both *The Common Pot* and in *Our Beloved Kin: A New History of King Philip's War* (New Haven, Conn., 2018). For more on the turn's completion, see Alyssa Mt. Pleasant, Caroline Wigginton, and Kelly Wisecup, eds., "Materials and Methods in Native American and Indigenous Studies" special issue of *EAL*, LIII (2018), 407–444; and Mt. Pleasant, Wigginton, and Wisecup, eds., "Materials and Methods in Native American and Indigenous Studies," *WMQ*, 3d Ser., LXXV (2018), 207–236.

personality, an inner character to be discovered and known, is the theme and the lesson of this beaver episode.[28]

Brooks extends the significance of Savageau's demurral: Ktsi Amiskw's actions caused great harm among the participants of the dish, but the results were not permanent, and neither was the unidentified motive that catalyzed Ktsi Amiskw's actions: "For living out of balance," writes Savageau, he remains incapable of preventing the harm brought by the "fur-lust from across the sea." Though he remains immobile, "his descendants are trapped in every stream, caught in every river . . . their pelts buy blankets, cloth, weapons, knives." These are the conditions in which Ktsi Amiskw dreams the possibility of "a world without beavers." Yet Brooks explicates the relationship between Ktsi Amiskw and his descendants to highlight the possibility of overturning that imbalance—though the overturning, or even its possibility, would be costly: "Ktsi Amiskw's children became vehicles for the reconstruction of human networks disrupted by disease and warfare." Participation in what eventually was a destructively extractive fur trade, Brooks suggests, was undertaken as an experiment in trying to sustain life in their shared dish. This reconstruction came at a dear cost and was not a clear-cut good. Wampum and furs, Brooks points out, could be used as "conduits for condolence and reparation," but in a fashion that often seemed to exacerbate rather than de-escalate "further cycles of war." Together, Savageau and Brooks work through the consequences of imprudent actions and improper relations, and these consequences, like the relations themselves, are never static. They bear some of the resources for restoration. Though he builds dams, Ktsi Amiskw, for Savageau's story, is not an inherently or instinctually greedy creature. Although his capacity to build dams is unique to him, his pursuit of a certain relation toward what he builds does not seem to emerge from any innate qualities of his species. His actions, like anyone else's, can err as a result of limits in his thinking, but they can also be opportunities for reflection and self-correction, unconnected to traits of personality or idiosyncrasy. Thoughtful reflection is a condition for the restoration of balance.[29]

28. Huntington Cairns, *Law and the Social Sciences* (New York, 1935), 58–59; William Cronon, *Changes in the Land: Indians, Colonists, and the Ecology of New England* (New York, 1983), 58; Savageau, "At Sugarloaf," *Mother/Land*. Beck's survey of Northeastern Algonquian beaver stories likewise suggests that beaver-human relations, or at least beaver-Gluskap relations, aren't determined by the characters of either party. Sometimes it's "just that Gluskap dislikes him and that he is where he shouldn't be." See Beck, "Giant Beaver," *Ethnohistory*, XIX (1972), 114–115.

29. Savageau, "At Sugarloaf," *Mother/Land*, quoted in Brooks, *Common Pot*, 20–21.

These were some of the reasons that Chickatawbut might have been thinking about the beaver on his way to negotiate with yet one more of these aggressive new traders. There is also perhaps one more reason. Readers are not the
only witnesses of this sequence of events—Ktsi Amiskw himself also watches.
Savageau's story implies this, but Brooks teases out this shared experience of
beholding. "For living out of balance, Ktsi Amiskw lies still," Savageau writes,
suggesting an implicit relationship between, on one hand, that stillness and
inability to intervene materially and, on the other, the dreams he has while
immobilized. Brooks's reading explains further: "Ktsi Amiskw sat above the
wôlhana, watching as the women planted and men fished." And again: "Ktsi
Amiskw watched as John Pynchon built a trading post downstream." "Ktsi
Amiskw watched as unfamiliar sicknesses spread through family networks and
tore them apart." Here, anaphora heightens attention to Ktsi Amiskw's process
of becoming conscious of accretive, intensifying harm, but the anaphora also
heightens the shared process of learning among parties through time, from
Ktsi Amiskw himself to Algonquian listeners; perhaps to some of the settlers
they engaged with during the seventeenth and eighteenth centuries, when this
story emerged; and most recently, though not finally, to readers of Savageau's
poem and *The Common Pot.* For Savageau and more explicitly for Brooks, the
possibility of Beaver's witnessing and learning from his former thoughtless
actions is the narrative condition of possibility for humans also to learn from
these events and their effects. Ktsi Amiskw's capacity for thought and reflection, in other words, facilitates human capacity for change, self-reflection,
and restorative action.[30]

The story differs in its details through time and among different Algonquian
communities; yet Savageau's account of Ktsi Amiskw's actions and reflection
suggests a key difference between settler and Native understandings of entanglement in a rich landscape of human and other-than-human relations. These
stories invite readers to exercise thinking about other actors' thoughts. Gillian
Feeley-Harnik has suggested it's not impossible that beavers do possess what
she calls "semantic structures of communication beyond human speech"
and that they might, in fact, apprehend their own entanglement within their
homelands. Beavers' similarities with humans might tempt some to recruit
them into a commensurate intelligence. But as Joyce E. Chaplin warns, they,
along with other nonhuman animals, remain alien to human reason as European thought has organized it. Beavers, like humans, were capable of building
things and organizing politically and were vulnerable to impulsive, thoughtless

30. Ibid.

action. The occasional appearance of irrational behavior was an opportunity, though, an invitation for the actor and any witnesses to notice, reflect on, and learn from the contingent circumstances that affected and guided the actor's decisions.[31]

That possibility, in turn, has consequences for an understanding of the human and its authority and obligations. For English settlers, the notion that beavers were incapable of thoughtful reflection qualified that creature to be dominated. When they looked to the beaver for edification, they found confirmation of an existing set of human priorities (fortification's value, say) in the animal's "instinctual" actions. For Algonquian peoples, by contrast, the beaver was not incapable of thoughtful reflection. Beavers' actions, though they might not have been initiated thoughtfully and though they might occasionally be "heedless," could still appear as opportunities to witness and theorize, to behold and more closely apprehend a set of relations that one might otherwise neglect. Taking this opportunity (as well as neglecting it) would have serious consequences for oneself and one's acknowledged and unacknowledged relations. Here, thoughtfulness emerges, not as the antithesis to affection, but as a recognition of the possibility of easily overlooked entanglement, affective and material.[32]

These were the various beaver qualities that Chickatawbut might have been considering as he traveled to Winthrop's on that April afternoon. Beaver was a significant object of trade, but Beaver was also an actant who provoked useful ways of thinking about relationships between other traders and the objects traded as well as the effects of those relationships with the shared world. Beavers could be cautionary tales as well as a thought experiment to consider what moved sometimes-opaque other parties, despite their best intentions to know themselves and to share what they knew with the world. Like the human-size beavers who had historically shared Algonquian homelands, English colonists sometimes—often—behaved in ways that puzzled Native people, and because of their size and technological innovations, that behavior could have powerful, not-always-desirable effects on other humans and their other-than-human counterparts. Regardless of species similarity or difference, Chickatawbut knew it would be a good idea to practice reasoning thoughtfully about these materially powerful counterparts. It would be

31. Ibid.; Feeley-Harnik, "Lewis Henry Morgan," *Ethnos,* LXXXVI (2021), 38; Joyce E. Chaplin, "Can the Nonhuman Speak? Breaking the Chain of Being in the Anthropocene," *Journal of the History of Ideas,* LXXVIII (2017), 509–529.

32. Roberts, *Colonial Ecology, Atlantic Economy,* 42.

A SACHEM of the ABENAKEE Nation, reſcuing an ENGLISH Officer from the Indians

FIGURE 5. "A Sachem of the Abenakee Nation, Rescuing an English Officer from the Indians," in [Benjamin West], *Bickerstaff's Boston Almanack, for the Year of Our Lord 1769* (Boston, 1768). This illustration is meant for white readers' consumption. Foregrounding sympathy across difference, the image and its caption efface the material conflict that white settlement generated, yet not entirely successfully, given that Ktsi Amiskw may be the mountain in the background. Courtesy, American Antiquarian Society imperative to use one's faculties of induction, deduction, and speculation to come closer to understanding what their motives were, what their consciousness of their motives were, and where there might have been a gap between the two. Familiarity with the opacity of other-than-human actors, like beavers, was practice in the sensitivity required to negotiate with these new neighbors, who, though they would later extend the promise of Christian brotherhood, might have seemed far less like brothers, far less logical or predictable than more familiar castors.

For Chickatawbut, reason and affection had less discrete careers. One reasoned because one was affected by material conditions, but the goal was not to outsmart those conditions, to engineer an outcome that could preserve the self and its chosen community from unchosen vulnerability. Rather, the goal was to use reason to shore up sustainable relations between affected parties. Sometimes, however, such thoughtfulness required not simply reason but strategy, especially when trying to negotiate with individuals who longed to use their reason to disoblige themselves and liked to avoid the affections that, for the purposes surveyed in the previous chapter, disturbed their ideas of the good. Consider the example of Polin, an Algonquian diplomat trying to negotiate with an English governor a century after Chickatawbut. Like beavers, both English and Algonquian people found value in occasionally damming up waterways. Algonquian people and beavers had long experimented with the most efficient ways to engage with the power of these waterways, but English people tended to be shortsighted in their interventions. In 1739, Polin, concerned with English colonists' setting up unsustainable dams along the Presumpscot River, traveled to meet with Massachusetts governor Jonathan Belcher to try to convince him to reconsider his thoughtless, or at least insufficiently foresightful, plan. Polin's negotiations, according to Lisa T. Brooks and Cassandra M. Brooks, required him to imaginatively re-create the emotional and intellectual experience of his interlocutor in order to decide how to act: he "knew he had to speak carefully so that he would encourage those people to learn from their mistakes, and release the trapped fish, rather than make them turn away in anger or shame." This activity does share some similarities with Winthrop's idea of fellow feeling but differed from it in at least three key aspects. First, Polin's actions didn't depend on sharing the experience of affection. One needn't feel shame oneself, for example, to see value in trying to avoid shaming another party. Second, Polin's strategy extended the scope of sympathy as English people idealized it. The goal of sympathy was to accommodate individuals to unpleasant structures within their societies, whereas the goal of strategic thoughtfulness was to achieve cooperation in changing a system that affected many parties adversely. Finally, strategies like Polin's built on a different understanding of the category of the human. Here, the human was not the embodiment of divine potentiality; it was one agent using its unique qualities to engage responsibly within a condition of entanglement with other agents—other humans, rivers, and their diverse inhabitants.[33]

Beavers, in addition to their function as a guide through abstract thought, became the unhappy catalyst for more urgent and strategic thoughtfulness among English colonists and many Native polities. In an earlier decade of colonization, English pursuit of beaver had led to scene after scene of conflict, circumstances where Ktsi Amiskw's example might have been instructive. Because of that thirst for beaver, Chickatawbut's relations with English people were characterized by the unrelenting risk of *not* engaging thoughtfully with English feelings. Thomas Morton memorialized one such threat in his anecdote about the misadventures of Master Bubble and of his guides. Innovative plans for acquiring beaver, a bold "new device," drove Master Bubble from his fellows in the Plymouth settlement into an environment whose risks he was not ready to confront, at least not alone. In order to pass through the forest, Bubble hired two Indigenous guides, since his idea, in addition to being "beyond Imagination," was also beyond his actual skill. Bubble, however, let himself be carried away by that extravagant brain. He misinterpreted, or was "misapplying," his guides' gestures and, succumbing to conventional paranoia that used European first principles to try to re-create the interior lives of his neighbors, deduced that his guides were plotting to harm him. Master Bubble departed from their company under the cover of night, leaving behind his shoes and "all his other implements."[34]

Sympathy isn't necessary to understand the gravity of Bubble's decision from the guides' standpoints. To wake and see the absence of a man who was not capable of guiding himself through the forest was bad news, especially when his safety had been their responsibility. That discovery produced a situation where it was imperative for these guides to re-create another party's interiority—not simply Bubble's but the thoughts and feelings of the English to whom he had fled. One of the guides had spent considerable time among the English and knew their preoccupation with the possibility of being harmed. Morton noted their apprehension; they were "feerfull what to doe," fearful about "what

---

33. Lisa T. Brooks and Cassandra M. Brooks, "The Reciprocity Principle and Traditional Ecological Knowledge: Understanding the Significance of Indigenous Protest on the Presumpscot River," *International Journal of Critical Indigenous Studies*, III (2010), 11–28, esp. 17.

34. Morton, *New English Canaan,* rpt. in Force, coll., *Tracts,* II, 85–86.

FIGURE 6. *Sugar Loaf Mountain, Deerfield.* 1833. By Orra White Hitchcock. This nineteenth-century lithograph emphasizes the height of Ktsi Amiskw by composing a contrast with a small settler homestead at its base. Boston Athenaeum

FIGURE 7. *Sugarloaf from Meadows*. Ca. 1909–1911. By Mary Electa Allen. After the drainage and clearing of the swamps that beaver dams produced, settlers found they needed to work even harder to keep the soil productive—as in this photograph from the turn of the twentieth century, carting fertilizer to the fields themselves. The bare fields clarify the silhouette of the beaver in the mountain behind. Courtesy Pocumtuck Valley Memorial Association's Memorial Hall Museum, Deerfield, MA

would be conceaved [by] the English" regarding what "was become of this mazed man." The two guides discussed how best to move forward considering their counterparts' feelings, and they decided to present a "relation of the truth" to defend themselves—at least, until they noticed that Bubble had left his shoes behind, and "it was thought hee would not have departed without his shoes." English settlers were relatively eager, inductive, detail-oriented detectives when it came to their own countrymen's interiority. By contrast, toward those not of their kind, deductive, generalized extrapolation was sufficient.[35]

Given the dense communicative networks that Algonquian people had developed, if Morton knew about such an event, Chickatawbut probably knew, too, and knew first. The actions and reactions that comprised the episode could be a useful source of information by which Chickatawbut (then known as Obtakiest) might better understand his new, often reckless neighbors. Along with their readiness to feel fear, Obtakiest was likely to have noticed and reflected on English people's fondness for ultimatums—for confrontationally proposing binary decisions with high stakes, decisions that often feature demands for their interlocutors to take their professions of sincerity with utmost seriousness. After determining that Master Bubble's guides were responsible for his disappearance, for example, English colonists "straightly chardged" those guides to "finde him out againe," or "else their wifes and children should be destroyed." It wasn't the first or the last time settlers made demands so aggressively. They had already practiced making more forceful, and complicated, demands of their neighbors' imaginations. In some of their earliest forays beyond their settlements, the Separatists had accused their Massachusett neighbors at Nemasket of being insensitive to their goodwill, spurring the settlers' aggression. When Plymouth settlers were worried that the sachem Conbitant was plotting against them, they attacked a Nemasket home where they thought he had hidden among the women and children taking shelter there. English people described that attack as logical and necessary, and they insisted that their interlocutors should be smarter and more rational in response to it: if Conbitant continued to act in a fashion they perceived to be a threat, "there was no place [that] should secure him" from their violence. English planters required that their neighbors should be constantly wondering what counted as a perceived threat in English minds, and these English newcomers insisted that their new neighbors' insensitivity to English people's feelings was a failure of sympathy, a failure to discern their sincerity. They had, Edward Winslow recalled his countrymen reminding the

35. Ibid., 85–86.

Wampanoags, "kindly entertained him [Conbitant]" and "never intended evil towards him."[36]

Obtakiest would have also been one of the intended witnesses of these stories, in addition to hearing about them through the Algonquian information network. When Myles Standish and the Plymouth militia publicly executed Massachusetts pniese Wituwamat—part of their response to the news of a possible attack that Phinehas Pratt had brought to Plymouth—they paired their violence with a staged act of sympathy: they released a captive they thought was affiliated with Obtakiest, and they implied that they could have killed him if they wanted but held back "that we might shew mercy as well as extremity." They wanted Obtakiest to see that show. They sent the captive away so "he might carry a message to *Obtakiest* his master." As with the assault at Nemasket, these ultimatums centered on the sincerity of English actors, and their sincerity demanded their interlocutors reason with their own assessment of their innocence. Just as they hadn't intended evil at Nemasket, here, too, they wanted Obtakiest to know that they were pure of heart: "It never entered into our hearts to take such a course with them, till their own treachery enforced us thereunto." It's possible they meant this avowal sincerely; as the previous chapter has shown, when settlers made claims to goodness, they probably did not mean to be disingenuous—and that was exactly the danger and the power these claims harbored. Settlers might have been sincere in making them, even as the fuller story exceeded the account they told of it. For Native interlocutors like Obtakiest, assessments of hypocrisy were not very useful. If settlers were earnest in those claims, the sachem would have to engage with that earnestness and the opacities that made it work. The challenges might have been new, but he drew on old strategies to engage them.[37]

Obtakiest was a thoughtful leader. He had developed sensitivity in engaging with what others knew and didn't know about their relations to the world beyond them. He honed this sensitivity from where he lived at the literal crossroads that connected two, and in some cases three, different, often mutually antagonistic parties of English settlers: Weston's men at Wessagusset, the small but active traders assembled under Morton's leadership at Ma-re Mount, and the Separatists at Plymouth who spoke only—or at least answered only—to

36. Ibid., 86–87; "A Journey to the Kingdom of Nemasket . . . ," in Dwight B. Heath, ed., *Mourt's Relation: A Journal of the Pilgrims at Plymouth* (1963; rpt. Bedford, Mass., 1986), 76.

37. Edward Winslow, *"Good News from New England,"* ed. Kelly Wisecup (Amherst, Mass., 2014), 97; Ana Schwartz, "'Mercy as Well as Extremity': Forts, Fences, and Fellow Feeling in New England Settlement," *EAL*, LIV (2019), 343–379.

God. Obtakiest was adept in making that sensitivity politically useful, and that skill impressed Morton, who wrote about him in detail. Thoughtfulness was a resource that Obtakiest used in awkward, risky situations, such as when he confronted the task of stewarding his homelands from incursions by multiple outside parties. Like many Algonquian sachems in the era of early contact with Europeans, Obtakiest had to deal with challenges beyond the strange rationality that English people brought with them. He also struggled in response to the first wide-scale mortality crisis his people experienced during the epidemic of 1616–1617, which, by some accounts, reduced his population to around sixty people—a drop of 90 percent. That loss was uneven across the people of the Dawnland. Obtakiest's neighbors to the southwest, the Narragansetts, remained largely untouched. By 1630, the Narragansetts could spare a party of "100. persons" to winter in Massachusetts territory, which they did, and meanwhile began to deplete its resources: "a Turkie could hardly escape them: Deare they killed up in great abundance, and feasted their bodies very plentifully: Beavers they killed by no allowance: the skinnes of those they traded away . . . my neighbores had a wonderfull great benefit by their being in those parts." Here, Morton seems to have come close to apprehending one reason for the near-total depletion of beavers and the perplexing participation of Native people in it: "Not harvesting as many pelts as possible," Roberts observes, "became tantamount to handing them over to the enemy; an enemy who would exchange their poached beaver for new weapons that might be turned against one's own community."[38]

This situation troubled Obtakiest, but he developed a calculated response. "Not being of power to resist," at least materially, Obtakiest drew on what he knew of English paranoia and of the Narragansetts' own understanding of English paranoia and its potentially disastrous consequences. He pitted these two against each other in order to reclaim stewardship of his land. Obtakiest told the English that the Narragansetts wanted proximity not simply for better trade but for strategic, potentially aggressive power. Massachusetts territory afforded them proximity to English people and better insight into their weaknesses. English people knew better than to attack the robust Narragansetts directly yet made a show of their willingness to do so. The immediate effect of that show tickled Morton: the English arrived at negotiations with the Narragansetts in their elaborate European armor, "look[ing] like lobsters,

---

38. Morton, *New English Canaan,* rpt. in Force, coll., *Tracts,* II, 31; Roberts, *Colonial Ecology, Atlantic Economy,* 41; Kathleen Bragdon, *Native People of Southern New England, 1500–1650* (Norman, Okla., 1996), 26.

all cladd in harnesse." The longer-term effect was that both parties, fearful of each other and doubting the sincerity of the other party's professed interests in trading, evacuated Massachusetts territory. The Narragansetts "lost the best trade of beaver that ever they had." Obtakiest was unusually well poised to practice the keen, speculative intersubjectivity that Morton, because he shared foundational ideas of "the human" with Winthrop, excluded from the concept of "sympathy." From his standpoint, Obtakiest had little choice but to be attuned to and affected by his neighbors' depths of feeling.[39]

Beavers were ambiguous brothers, even before they had been dear, ocean-crossing commodities. Now they made brotherly relations among humans trickier. That ambiguity was among the many contextual conditions that Obtakiest—by now taking the new name Chickatawbut—contemplated as he made his way to meet these new coat-men a few years later, in that spring snowmelt. Maybe his mind turned to beavers and their cocreation of that shared space, building dams that shaped rivers and streams, creating ponds and marshes, and transforming wetlands into dry ones and back again. Now that these beavers were fewer in number, the land was drier, harder, barer, and more exposed. There was more land, but it was less fecund and fertile, less hospitable to the older networks of life. Maybe these landscapes occasioned reflection on Chickatawbut's part regarding the visible and invisible, the active ecologies that lay beneath seemingly placid surfaces and the invisibility that made such diverse life possible. Sometimes, working diligently to bring what was submerged to the surface could be valuable, but not always. In time, and according to schedules that sometimes outlasted the life of the individual, even the murkiest marshes might be drained, made accessible to instrumental reason—this, famously, had been Sigmund Freud's fantasy as he looked out on the centuries-long project of draining van der Donck's sometimes-dangerous Zuider Zee. Chickatawbut, in his own way, would have thought about the sedimentations of history. As he traversed his homelands on his way to meet these new neighbors, he might have reflected on their former inhabitation by his kinspeople, whose various styles of engaging with a shared world had become familiar to him over the course of his lifetime—and many of whom, by 1631, had died very suddenly. He knew he had to take up again the labor of re-creating that formerly shared world.[40]

39. Morton, *New English Canaan*, rpt. in Force, coll., *Tracts*, II, 32–33.

40. Roberts, *Colonial Ecology, Atlantic Economy*, 30; James Strachey, ed. and trans., *The Standard Edition of the Complete Psychological Works of Sigmund Freud*, XXII, *New Introductory Lectures on Psycho-Analysis and Other Works* (1932–1936) (London, 1965), 3–192, esp. 80.

Chickatawbut's reflections about beaver might have included devising ways to use beaver as an invitation to think more expansively about a shared world—an invitation to be more thoughtful. More immediately, however, he might have been thinking about beaver because he had brought two beaver pelts to Winthrop's three days earlier, in exchange for an English coat. Presenting Winthrop with the pelts meant Chickatawbut was inviting his English counterpart to slow down and think more expansively about his own wants, his affectability, the new entanglements that bound him to this newer world. Winthrop confessed that the encounter had bothered him: in his recollection of their first meeting, Winthrop had to clarify for Chickatawbut some of the social conventions that mattered to him as they began a relationship. When Chickatawbut brought forward the pelts and requested an English coat, Winthrop inferred that Chickatawbut was proposing to buy a coat from him. Winthrop disliked what this implied about him: that he was a merchant. Such an implication didn't align with the prestige Winthrop wanted to claim for himself; being a merchant would have meant closer dependence on the vagaries of the market, less distance from dependency on others, which, according to his "Modell," characterized the poor. He was among the propertied elite, and in his *Journal* he noted telling this to his visitor: "The Governor tould him, that Englishe Sagamores did not use to trucke." He preferred to begin his relationship with Chickatawbut by presenting himself as a sovereign gift giver and host.[41]

Nevertheless, Chickatawbut insisted on participating in an exchange with Winthrop. Although Winthrop recorded the transaction as if Chickatawbut were making an ignorant error, the Massachusetts sachem would not have been as naive as Winthrop imagined. Chickatawbut had his reasons for entering into that relationship, and some were probably pragmatic according to priorities that made easy sense to English people. He might have led with his gift giving because he wanted a strategic alliance with Winthrop and was signaling his willingness to trade with the new settlement in the future. In the early years of the transatlantic beaver trade, Susan Sleeper-Smith observes, Native people drove the exchanges with their pursuits of European goods. Even if that were the primary reason for Chickatawbut's forthrightness, however, it wouldn't preclude other, related ambitions. Chickatawbut had

41. Winthrop, "Modell," 283; Dunn, Savage, and Yeandle, eds., *Journal of John Winthrop*, 50; Michelle Burnham, "Anne Hutchinson and the Economics of Antinomian Selfhood in Colonial New England," *Criticism*, XXXIX (1997), 337–358; Little, "'Shoot That Rogue,'" *NEQ*, LXXIV (2001), 238–273; Felicity Heal, *Hospitality in Early Modern England* (Oxford, 1990).

extensive experience with English surveyors, colonists, and traders. Many of these encounters were less than happy, from his perspective. English surveyors had desecrated his mother's burial site, stealing the pelts with which he'd honored it. Colonists had sent him aggressive ultimatums, threatening violent action if he did not support them and sensitively, continually consider their vulnerability to fear. Along with the Narragansetts, English people had been on the verge of transforming his homelands into a quarry for extracting other-than-human life. If he considered forging an alliance with these new English neighbors, he might have been trying to shape his trading partners' attitudes or at least provoke them to think of the world they shared in a less thoughtless manner.[42]

And so, when he requested the coat from Winthrop, Chickatawbut might have understood already, before Winthrop clarified, that his request would disturb this governor. Chickatawbut had witnessed at least three English settlements: one that had practiced, at least for a while, collective use of resources; one whose members independently and directly engaged in trade with Native people and white merchants; and one whose inhabitants' total incapacity to take care of themselves made them ready to serve as bondsmen, to submit to the will of others in order to access the resources they needed to survive. Chickatawbut did not need William Harrison to point out a hierarchy among these new arrivals or to hypothesize about the logic they used to explain it. He would have witnessed, too, that Winthrop commanded the wills of others, and this knowledge heightens the significance of his request to exchange the pelts for a coat. Winthrop's thirst for beaver meant that he could be bought or at least influenced by the promise of material goods, despite his protestations that he was not a merchant. His longing for that commodity meant that he was willing to sell objects that had the potential, over time and habituation, to make Englishmen English.

In the three days between receiving the pelts and giving Chickatawbut his coat, those pelts sat in Winthrop's house—in 1631, mostly likely still a small dwelling—taking up space with their scent. During these days of debt, Winthrop might have wondered whether Chickatawbut saw him as a bondsman, imagined him to be vulnerable to manipulation by his desires. Long after he sent those pelts away to England to be transformed from pelt to fur, fur to felt, felt to hat, Winthrop could expect to be reminded of that momentary vulnerability in any encounter with Chickatawbut where the

42. Morton, *New English Canaan*, rpt. in Force, coll., *Tracts*, II, 35–36, 72–73; Winslow, "*Good News*," ed. Wisecup, 97–99.

sachem donned these materials of memory he had acquired in exchange. Chickatawbut did not invite Winthrop to put himself in the coat and shoes of another. This was an adventure that English people, given their ideals of sartorial self-fashioning, were unlikely to take. Instead, Chickatawbut reversed the direction of the investiture. He presented Winthrop with the opportunity to reconsider his entanglement with his environment and the relations he would need to cultivate, with and beyond the human, in order to achieve his goals there.[43]

What Chickatawbut probably didn't realize was that his new trading partner would become famous for his theory of speculative intersubjective knowing. If the sachem could have foreseen Winthrop's fame, he might have changed his strategy for inviting Winthrop to think more expansively, but probably not by much. Sympathy made sense in a world populated by thoughtless beavers: sympathy liked to imagine that it could tear down walls, rebuild them, and tear them down again, but in these powers, sympathy willed itself to be in control of those walls. Sympathy balked at the prospect of walls' irrelevance. Sympathy abhorred a swamp. Chickatawbut, knowledgeable about the effects of the sorts of walls that beavers (for one) built, was probably not against all walls everywhere, but these English people were recklessly eager to build them, and therefore it might be useful, in their future relations, if English people took time to contemplate that eagerness, pondered other ways of being in this shared world. For neighbors like Chickatawbut, walls were material expressions of settlers' convictions of sincerity. They proceeded from a belief that one could be confident in one's knowledge of oneself, distinct from one's relations with the world. English people, however, held on tightly to their ideals. Even the more liberal of these planters seem to have been able to understand Algonquian difference only through their Christian ideas of universality. Roger Williams, for example, celebrated Narragansetts for their apparent alignment with Christian ideals, in a move of inclusion that anticipates the political cunning of recognition illuminated by twentieth- and early-twenty-first-century critics of settler-Indigenous relations. Yet, as Lisa Brooks remarks, Algonquian practices of reciprocity were not an "altruistic ideal but a practice that was necessary to human survival." The urgency of this practice reframes the strategies that Indigenous people undertook. Rather than serving as attempts at conversion for the sake of an otherworldly reward,

43. Shoes are the single instance that Ann Little finds of English people donning Native clothing. See Little, "'Shoot That Rogue,'" *NEQ,* LXXIV (2001), 251–252.

these early communicative exchanges sought to transform English ways of seeing in this world.[44]

Thoughtfulness and sympathy may share similar expressions, but they are substantially different in their essence. Sympathy among settlers appears, on its face, to be a felicitous thing. A polity full of individuals who cherish one another would be more likely to survive, and maybe, from some angles, flourish, than a polity riven by antagonism. But at what cost? As Sara Ahmed has observed, love is often an exclusive style of relation: love among a people defines itself through exclusion of those whom one does not love; and love is given value by the exercise of violence in the name of protecting those one does love from those one does not. Reform Protestant settlers' own lifestyle manual asked Christians to reflect on at least part of this process of exclusion: "For if ye love them which love you," the Christian deity challenged his acolytes, "what thank shall ye have? for even the sinners love those that love them." What would colonial intersubjectivity have looked like if it deprioritized the search for moral affirmation through affective experience? It might instead have drawn on its capacities of observation and extrapolation—of thoughtfulness—to search out and observe ever-wider networks of material affectability. The outcome need not have been mastery, and more reliable control, rather than a more prudent and sustainable shared world. Settlers might have discovered that the capacities that, they imagined, made them exemplarily human were not so unique after all.[45]

44. Brooks, Common Pot, 5; Van Engen, Sympathetic Puritans, 197; Schwartz, "Mercy as Well as Extremity," EAL, LIV (2019), 343–379, esp. 360–361; Williams, Key into the Language; Elizabeth A. Povinelli, The Cunning of Recognition: Indigenous Alterities and the Making of Australian Multiculturalism (Durham, N.C., 2002); Glen Sean Coulthard, Red Skin, White Masks: Rejecting the Colonial Politics of Recognition (Minneapolis, 2014).

45. Luke 6:32 (Geneva); Ahmed, Cultural Politics of Emotion, 62–81, 122–143.

CHAPTER THREE

Blood, Regret, and Tears

How to Put on Sincerity, and Why

S OMETIMES, the most enthusiastic spokespeople for the happy rewards of fellow feeling could be a little rude.

This was the experience of one Plymouth proselyte on the July afternoon in 1666 when he presented himself to his congregation for an evaluation of his spiritual sincerity. Prior to that meeting, they had informed him that he had offended their moral standards, as well as their deity's. However, they were also interested in witnessing his regret, forgiving him, and bringing him into spiritual and material happiness. But revealing sincere regret was a task fraught with peril. Many were the opportunities for shame. This was already supposed to be the one of the most high-stakes, frightening moments of his life. If he succeeded in showing his sincerity, he could join a community of happy spiritual kin who had already undergone that experience. To navigate the risks, this proselyte would have studied examples, listened to previous confessors, and thought about the words they had chosen to openly express parts of their interior lives they were least proud of, those things they had done or not done that they wished they could forget about. He would have studied their compositions, then tentatively applied some of their phrases and narrative strategies to those of his own memories he wanted to forget. His goal was to communicate his specific mortifications honestly, but in a fashion that did not draw too much scrutiny to himself and those nearly unbearable recollections. After the hopeful proselytes had undergone months, maybe years, of self-study, the Plymouth congregation, led by John Eliot, assembled that July day to listen to seven confessions. Halfway into the second one, however, Plymouth's elders interrupted the confessor and told him that he was taking too long. They did not have all day. It would be wise for him to hurry along his exposition.[1]

Eliot and his colleagues were probably not being malicious. They were likely being thoughtless, inconsiderate to the experience of this vulnerable individual. Their colleague John Winthrop, after all, had never proposed a rubric for measuring the accuracy of intersubjective speculation. Long after the sting of the interruption had faded, after the shame of performing incorrectly in an unexpected way burned less hotly, this confessor might have reached such a conclusion. In the moment, the intrusion would have felt cataclysmic, an intensification of the shame and the loneliness he had already been trying to rein in. What would he do next? With the eyes and the ears of the congregation directed toward him, he would have to improvise a response. He would have to think on his feet about the most important takeaways from his prior self-inquiry without being able to call a friend for help. Interrupted thus, he would have felt sincerity's essential structure with extraordinary sharpness. The promise of happiness shone at him from what he hoped was the very near future. But to get there, he had to spend time reflecting intensely on his own responsibility, his own selfhood, what he and only he had done to offend the people he hoped would forgive him. On the other side was a community of individuals similarly trained to love their individuality and responsibility dearly. They promised him that crossing over was ineffably happy. But he didn't know such happiness when he began to study. In this moment of disruption, he would have feared the shame of telling wrongs and of telling them wrongly. That he kept going anyway suggests there was something else he feared worse.

By the time of the interruption, this proselyte had probably asked himself many times, *Is this worth it?* Conversion meant many opportunities, anticipated and unanticipated, for public humiliation. And it was supposed to. Shame was a feature, not a bug; a central and dynamic feature of settlers' social and spiritual lives. It was the guarantee of a biopolitical practice's orientation toward real biopoetic fulfillment, a litmus test of whether the deity

---

1. J. Patrick Cesarini, "John Eliot's 'A Brief History of the Mashepog Indians,' 1666," *William and Mary Quarterly*, 3d Ser., LXV (2008), 101–134; Patricia Caldwell, *The Puritan Conversion Narrative: The Beginnings of American Expression* (Cambridge, 1983).

had opened the inner eyes of the individual to see the right sort of knowledge for true felicity. Thus, shame was less an obstacle to longed-for happiness than an essential, if complicated, technique in the art of achieving it. Accordingly, one key element of that shame's unpleasantness, the presence of witnesses, is vital to answering this question of worth. It doesn't directly answer it—a goal that most scholars of colonial confessions have prioritized in their studies and a concern that tends to dispose them to answering affirmatively—*Yes, their distress, in conclusion, was worth it.* Far less scholarship has explained how individuals went about answering that question and how their rubrics for evaluation might have varied. One reason for this neglect is that the archive that documents these ambitions for fulfillment is preoccupied, understandably, with positive answers, or at least hope for a future positive answer, which amounts to a provisionally positive answer. Yet occasionally in this archive, individuals appear who couldn't quiet that question, and this smaller record of dissatisfaction is hidden, somewhat ostentatiously, in plain sight: in the poems of critics like Michael Wigglesworth and Anne Bradstreet. The record of tenacious unhappiness isn't the only thing hidden in plain sight. Some of these poems, particularly Bradstreet's, disclose the affordances of poetry in providing a hiding place within high-visibility confessional practices, within the prized expositions of deep interiority. Bradstreet was especially skilled at such hiding. This is at least in part because of her location within the domestic sphere, where she experienced narrower channels for community witnessing, but there are still other perspectives on the discomforts of being a spectacle. The colony's Native converts—confessors like Kanoonus, interrupted at Plymouth in 1666, or his six companions, Paumpmunet, Wuttinnaumatuk, Nonqutnumuk, Waompam, William Pease, and Pauchumu, along with hundreds of their fellow Algonquians—show still other conditions that made shame tolerable. Despite being told to hurry his story along, Kanoonus still willed himself through that doubly humiliating ordeal. This was because performances of shame, these unpleasant professions of sincerity, re-created communities of witnessing in the face of broader, uneven social depletions. Kanoonus willed sincerity, despite shame, in response to the social and material dispossessions that settler colonialism had visited on him.[2]

Wigglesworth's self-loathing is an excellent example of shame's attractions. Despite his enduring status as poster boy of Puritan repression—a man more dour than Dimmesdale—Wigglesworth longed deeply to be liked. He wanted

2. John Demos, "Shame and Guilt in Early New England," in Carol Z. Stearns and Peter N. Stearns, eds., *Emotion and Social Change* (New York, 1988), 69–86.

affirmative companions. "One of the main things I desire upon earth at present," he confessed, as Walt Whitman might have two centuries later, was that "any of them I love most should be near me." The diaries in which he recorded this wish remain some of the most fastidious documents of interiority in the early modern English colonies. Faithfully, unpleasantly, they preserve his wish to be beheld by his community. They record his want not only to be beheld but to be beheld favorably. This want is the second most consistent theme of his diurnalistic writing. He noted, for example, that he longed for appreciation and respect from the young men he taught at Harvard, some of whom had been, only a few years before, his schoolmates. After securing a position as minister at Malden, as he made plans for his marriage to his cousin and for his mother to move in with them, he noted that he wanted his neighbors not to think of him poorly for his domestic arrangements. Later in life, at the age of thirty-two, he sailed to Bermuda for the sake of his health, to overcome "that old Malady that annoys me." Although the trip was not successful in that regard, he meditated on the way back that it might have had other benefits. His absence might have made his congregation's hearts grow fonder: "Finally it may be the Lord carried me to Bermuda for a Time that he might make me more welcome here to his people at my return." His corporeal health continued to suffer, but his social health might have improved. "And indeed," he wrote, "I have found more love from the people generally (both Church and Town) since my return then I did before."[3]

Wigglesworth's modern biographers and critics tend to miss this quality of his character because the first, most consistent theme in his diurnalistic writing is his scrupulosity in documenting all the evidence he found that he was not likable. Wigglesworth despised himself. Or at least he frequently claimed he did, especially in private, when he believed no one but his deity was paying attention. Virtually all explanations of his self-loathing derive exclusively from the now-published diary that he kept for around three years (1653–1657) of his seventy-four-year life (1631–1705). These years witnessed Wigglesworth passing through important thresholds in his life and career: his transition from work as a teacher to his vocation as a minister; moving from Cambridge to Malden five miles north and integrating himself with new

3. Edmund S. Morgan, ed., *The Diary of Michael Wigglesworth: The Conscience of a Puritan* (Gloucester, Mass., 1970), 3, 6–7, 21, 26–27, 30, 36, 39, 49, 52, 55, 69, 86, 94; John Ward Dean, *Memoir of Rev. Michael Wigglesworth: Author of the Day of Doom* (Albany, N.Y., 1871), 75, 76; see also Richard Crowder, *No Featherbed to Heaven: A Biography of Michael Wigglesworth, 1631–1705* (East Lansing, Mich., 1962).

neighbors and congregants; and marrying and setting up a new household. His sense of his own unlikability during this time was acute. In his diary, he recorded example after example of his inability to be the self-disciplined leader that he believed his communities expected him to be. With occasional interruptions to very briefly describe events taking place in the world around him, the diary relentlessly confesses to personal failings. He was particularly sensitive to his body's desires, to his inability to control those desires, and to the divine plenitude against which his lack of control was so horrible an offense. "I loath my self," he reported dutifully and frankly in 1653, "and could even take vengeance of myself for these abominations." This is not an extreme example of his self-loathing, but it isn't pathological, either. Rather, it expressed his unconventional commitment to a conventional desire. His earnest labor of chronicling his unlikability was one step in a larger strategy of catching his own faults before they were caught by those he liked and hoped would like him back. In this regard, Wigglesworth was hardly an exception within his society. He was simply more explicit about, and more faithful to, the unhappy liabilities of self-knowledge that sincerity required and that most of his neighbors found it convenient to forget.[4]

Wigglesworth found it worthwhile to review what he felt was shameful about himself. He saw that review as a useful tactic to mitigate public shame further into the future. Self-inquiry was one feature of the responsibility he felt for being liked, a burden he experienced more keenly than most. The responsibility itself, in its essence, was quite typical for his time and place. His theology's notions of responsible personhood actively, aggressively encouraged individuals to become as well acquainted as they could with their own shameful qualities. Yet this knowledge was Janus-faced. To be a good person required that one know one's deity's priorities for lived conduct. Early modern reform Protestants tended to believe that this knowledge wasn't impossible to acquire. It was accessible through relatively straightforward work, such as reading sacred documents. When disputes about the meaning of those texts surfaced, rituals such as weekly meetings could help communities reach consensus. Knowledge about those principles, however, was supposed to beget pursuit of knowledge about one's relationship to them, too. These principles were patently severe—everyone, they asserted, would fail at living up to them. And, like Leo Tolstoy's families, failure could be unhappy in a variety of different ways. That failure was often easier to detect in others than in oneself. Still, it was an individual's obligation to try to understand his or her

4. Morgan, ed., *Diary of Michael Wigglesworth*, 5.

own unique failings. In a society that was relatively small, that limited sources of public entertainment, and that understood peers to be robust resources in the attempt to fail less, the possibility of having one's peers discover one's failings was omnipresent. Better, then, to acquire knowledge of one's own faults before they did.

Preemption required practice. Sometimes that practice took place privately; other times it had a public component. Diaries were one site for private practice, and Wigglesworth's is an excellent example. But it was not exceptional. In Cambridge, his colleague Thomas Shepard rehearsed knowledge of his own shortcomings with similar intensity. "On Saturday night I felt nothing but death, darkness in me," he observed in February 1643. The feeling of darkness, death, and nothing else was useful. It alerted him to the true essence of his actions: "All my actions were works of darkness and dead works like the principle whence they came." In England, Calvinist ministers had encouraged Christians to consider themselves what Arthur Dent had called a "stie of filthinesse," and in America, Calvinist ministers tried to ensure that their congregants wouldn't forget the filthiness they had carried over. Shepard, for example, encouraged his congregants to view with similar horror the distance between the divine ideal and their actual behavior. He recorded these performances of their self-knowledge with just as much zeal as he recorded his own, frequently slipping from his third-person narration to first-person transcription, sometimes in the same sentence. Listen to Cambridge congregant Edward Hall, who avowed that "the Lord had made him loathe himself." This condition of cursed self-loathing metastasized. Hall detested himself a second time for being someone that his deity hated. Another congregant, George Willows, "lay under the anger of God and . . . so saw nothing but hell due to him." More horrors from congregant John Sill: "I saw my vileness." Joanna Sill, his wife, said nearly the same thing: she "saw her nature, how vile it [was]." John Stansby announced: "I know I came in the world a child of hell, and if ever any child of the devil, I."[5]

Wigglesworth learned from these examples. In the same notebook he used to keep his diary, he recorded some of the confessions from Shepard's Cambridge congregation, such as that of John Greene, who testified to "being in a

5. Thomas Shepard, "The Journal," in Michael McGiffert, ed., *God's Plot: Puritan Spirituality in Thomas Shepard's Cambridge,* 2d ed. (Amherst, Mass., 1994), 124 ("works of darkness"), 140 ("Saturday night"), 150 ("loathe himself"), 154 ("nothing but hell"), 160 ("my vileness," "her nature, how vile"), 180 ("child of the devil"); Arthur Dent, *The Plaine Man's Path-Way to Heaven: Wherein Every Man May Clearly See whether He Shall Be Saved or Damned* . . . (London, 1607), 86.

miserable sickness" wherein "the Lord was pleased much to awaken me to it and to let me see that I was a miserable creature." Shepard would eventually become the shining example of this spiritual skill. For Shepard, discovery of reasons to hate oneself was one vital step toward ecstatic spiritual redemption. He believed that shamefully disclosing experiences of self-loathing helped him achieve an experience of unity with the deity. This outcome, he claimed, was so pleasurable that only metaphors of sexual experience would capture it. Wigglesworth probably also desired that pleasure. Although direct gratifications of the spiritual sort seem consistently to have eluded him, confession possessed its own consolations. Confessions in his diary could assist him in awakening, and staying awake, to his knowledge of wretchedness and unlikability before any of his neighbors could.[6]

Wigglesworth's elusive desire to be liked hides in the lacuna of his highly visible knowledge of his unlikability. How come? One important reason is that the physical body that presented him to his neighbors—those he hoped would like him—wouldn't let him forget his unlikable dependence on it. Wigglesworth could not easily control his body, although he dearly wanted to. Like most men he knew, he desired to use his reason to master affection, as Winthrop's sermon in the previous chapter illustrated. Wigglesworth, spongily, desired to absorb affection and esteem from his neighbors. But he also, to his great distress, leaked. The "Malady" that "annoyed" him did so "most at night"—when he wasn't conscious to control it. He could never witness his failure, either, which made mastering it close to impossible. All he could witness were the results of his failure. He frequently woke up to the unpleasant discovery that he had ejaculated in his sleep. He deduced that he had succumbed to his desires while he had had little to no conscious knowledge of this temptation in the first place: *"Friday night it came again without any dream that I know of."* Alone in bed, Wigglesworth could also not escape early modern ideas of gender, shored up by the most advanced European ideas about the human body. Like most of his peers, Wigglesworth believed that,

6. Morgan, ed., *Diary of Michael Wigglesworth*, 114. See also Philip Greven, *The Protestant Temperament: Patterns of Child-Rearing, Religious Experience, and the Self in Early America* (New York, 1977), 65–68. On confession's pleasures, see McGiffert, "The People Speak: Confessions of Lay Men and Women," in McGiffert, ed., *God's Plot*, esp. 144–145; and Amanda Porterfield, "Female Piety in the Lives of Thomas Hooker, Thomas Shepard, and John Cotton," in Porterfield, *Female Piety in Puritan New England: The Emergence of Religious Humanism* (Oxford, 1992), 40–79, esp. 43–44, 56, 72–79. For a critique of the gendered slant of those gratifications, see Ivy Schweitzer, *The Work of Self-Representation: Lyric Poetry in Colonial New England* (Chapel Hill, N.C., 1991).

because of the identity of his genitals, his relationship with his body should be one characterized by control. The human body, early modern European anatomy had proposed, was like a sponge. Some bodies, mostly women's, were thought to be spongier than others—more susceptible to permeation and to seeping. Both permeation and leaking were difficult to control. The stakes, however, differed between men and women. To leak as a woman was thought to be conventional—to succeed in fulfilling men's expectations that women failed to control the boundaries of their human bodies. To leak as a man was to fail to be a man. Thus, Wigglesworth wasn't worried only about unhappy awakenings. He was also worried about others discovering them. Exhaustingly, he worried about being perceived as having secrets that could be exposed. Early modern English individuals derived pleasure from deriding other people's failures. Wigglesworth was committed to sincerity's task of self-knowledge because the threat of having his society share that knowledge was, to him, unusually burdensome.[7]

Wigglesworth's fears weren't simply abstract or hypothetical. They made it very difficult for him to move forward into his adulthood and to claim the house, home, and, hopefully, family that would have confirmed his social manhood. These concerns hounded him, for example, as he contemplated his reasons for and against leaving his teaching position at Harvard for more stable employment as the minister at Malden and his reasons for and against marriage. These were not unambiguously positive prospects. He worried about accidentally exposing his body's failure to avoid gendered sponginess. At Malden, where he would set up household with his new fiancée, he would be able to give shelter to his mother after his father's recent death. But at Malden, he would only have one bed, and *"we must lay together constantly which I can't bare* [sic]*."* Within a neighborly society composed of what Helena M. Wall has called "voluntary spies," Wigglesworth anticipated that his neighbors would eventually learn of his sleeping arrangements and, still worse, learn of what he saw to be his bodily derangements. This kept him up at night: *"We can't lay severally without obloquy and reproach neither can we lay together without exposing me to the return of grievous disease."* That exposure, in turn, made the prospect of marriage a terror. When he learned that his suit to his cousin Mary

7. Dean, *Memoir of Rev. Michael Wigglesworth*, 76 ("Malady"); Morgan, ed., *Diary of Michael Wigglesworth*, 75, 80 *("Friday night")*, 86; Elizabeth Maddock Dillon, "Nursing Father and Brides of Christ: The Feminized Body of the Puritan Convert," in Janet Moore Lindman and Michele Lise Tarter, eds., *A Centre of Wonders: The Body in Early America* (Ithaca, N.Y., 2001), 129–144; Gail Kern Paster, *The Body Embarrassed: Drama and the Disciplines of Shame in Early Modern England* (Ithaca, N.Y., 1993).

Reyner had been successful, the news did not make him happy. Far from it. The news filled "my spirit suddenly with marvellous sorrow and perplexity more then I wel knew how to bear." This horror extended his use of the language of being filled, overwhelmed, engulfed: "I am laden with a body of death"; "I ly down in my shame"; "I sink in discouragement"; "my spirit so drown'd in my studys"; "I find such a bottomless gulf of vilness in my heart"; "I feel such an Ocean of deadly poyson in my heart." Aggravating these experiences would have been the suspicion that, as Sacvan Bercovitch memorably put it, "God *wanted* [him] to experience the slime."[8]

Confessions like these have titillated historians and literary historians for decades. Their prurient interest, however, tends to depend on forgetting the ordinary desire that underwrote them: Wigglesworth's need to be liked and the hope that his body would not get in the way. These confessions are thus valuable because they are frank in explaining that challenge, a challenge that those with more masterful, less beastly relations with their bodies usually forgot. One reason it was possible for them to forget was because the Christian vocabulary they used to describe their ideals inverted conventional understandings of what consciousness consisted of. This vocabulary tried to consign bodily existence to forgettable, unconscious experience, the world of sleep and dreams. Consider one final idiosyncrasy of Wigglesworth's unhappiness—the close connection between his lack of corporeal and spiritual control and his vulnerability to the vicissitudes of history: specifically, childhood poverty that endured into his adulthood.

Wigglesworth probably wasn't the only one to associate the limits he felt in controlling his body with the limits of his material power in the world, but Wigglesworth experienced the entwinement of the two with rare intimacy and frustration. On one hand, Wigglesworth's use of water figures to represent spiritual overwhelming was a conventional, maybe even banal, trope in early modern colonial conversation about conversion. On the other, helpless exposure to water was a particularly intimate and uncomfortable memory for Wigglesworth, an experience whose literal overwhelming would have been difficult to forget. His parents had brought him from England to the Massachusetts

8. Morgan, ed., *Diary of Michael Wigglesworth*, 8 ("body of death"), 14 ("ly down"), 32 ("Ocean of deadly poyson"), 47 ("sink in discouragement"), 49 ("drown'd in my studys"), 50 (engagement), 62 ("gulf of vilness"), 75 ("sorrow and perplexity"), 92 *("grievous disease")*, 94 *("we must lay together")*; Helena M. Wall, *Fierce Communion: Family and Community in Early America* (Cambridge, Mass., 1990), 13; Sacvan Bercovitch, *The Puritan Origins of the American Self* (New Haven, Conn., 1975), 14–15; Ann M. Little, *Abraham in Arms: War and Gender in Colonial New England* (Philadelphia, 2007).

Bay Colony in early childhood. Like many colonists, and especially children, he would have been unpleasantly affected by the crowded, confined, rarely wholly dry experience of transatlantic crossing. But that was not the last of his opportunities to be drenched. When Wigglesworth was six years old, within months of disembarking on dry ground, the covered pit at Rowley in which he and his family lived was compromised by heavy rains. The walls caved in. His residence and shelter, the boundary that should have protected him from the external world, flooded, and he awoke to a literally overwhelming wetness. To a spongy early modern body, a child's body, no less, this sudden trauma would have imprinted itself deeply. As with his nighttime ejaculations, as with the nosiness of his neighbors, as with the cold of the American winters, as with his existence in America in the first place, this event greeted his body at the limits of his ability to control it. Wetness, for Wigglesworth, was the somatic memory of historical helplessness. He risked recalling it every time he lay down to sleep.[9]

Being awake might seem to be a solution. It was, but it generated problems of its own. Wigglesworth's enthusiasm for being awake is another one of the utterly conventional features of his diary. His specific attraction to being awake retrieves and dusts off a less obvious, but very important, feature of the search for self-knowledge that was sincerity's substance. Wakefulness wasn't a repudiation of the sexuality that lurked at night; it was a more concentrated, masterful engagement with it. Like his Christian neighbors, Wigglesworth favored the term "awaken[ed]" to describe the effects of the deity on his consciousness and apprehension. For Wigglesworth, figurative awakening generally took place in the morning, around the time of literal awakening. The word denoted a return to a realm of greater control over bodily desire, or at least over exposure to that desire. But not total control. The figurative use of the word—"to rouse into activity, to stir up, excite; to kindle (desire, anxiety, interest, attention, etc.)"—denoted, not less sponginess, but narrower, more focused, and heightened sensitivity to the world beyond one's bodily borders. These denotations, according to the *Oxford English Dictionary*, were fresh and vivid in the 1650s, a novelty that can be easy to overlook from the other side of the Great Awakening of the eighteenth century. To be awakened from sleep did not mean the negation of vulnerability to what Wigglesworth called

9. On spiritual overwhelming, see Caldwell, *Puritan Conversion Narrative*. On the experience of crossing, see David Cressy, *Coming Over: Migration and Communication between England and New England in the Seventeenth Century* (Cambridge, 1987). On the flooding of the Wigglesworth household, see Crowder, *No Featherbed*, 8.

"the creature's" desires. It meant the transferal of desire from the body to the mind—less a repudiation of sexuality than, as historians of sexuality in early America have pointed out, an intensification of it. Wigglesworth's figurative use of the word "awaken[ed]" might have been motivated by features of his biography, but it would not have diverged from contemporaneous usage. Rather, it more zealously conformed to and drew from it. By contrast, the vicissitudes of the body that he tried to control during the long days raged tumultuously in the land of sleep, a shadowy world that one eventually, for the most part, forgets.[10]

Wigglesworth probably favored waking consciousness to sleep. Yet being awake meant being responsible for those desires, for properly expressing them, and for how his expression might get in the way of his desire to be liked. And so, being awake, too, was often unhappy for Wigglesworth. He felt burdened by wakefulness. His acute consciousness of how his neighbors perceived him nagged at him and wearied him. This weariness, in turn, made it nearly impossible for him to claim sincerity in his relations with his neighbors. One final instance exemplifies the demand the body made on sincerity's achievement. Consider his prolonged meditation on how to be a good, likable neighbor to his colleague Jonathan Mitchell. In his diary, he confessed that he was "much distressed in conscience" because he had seen "a stable dore of Mr Mitchels beat to and fro with the wind." He was troubled because he was not sure what to *do* about this sight, "whither, I should out of duty shut it or not." And he reflected about what he saw to be the personal failings that made that sight so upsetting: "No temptations perplex me so sorely as such like, when I am not clear concerning my duty." Neighbors were a duty, certainly, but what that duty consisted of eluded him. Three weeks later, he was still thinking about his duty and his neighbor's door:

> The wise god who knoweth how to tame and take down proud and wanton hearts, suffereth me to be sorely buffeted with the like temptation as formerly about seeing some dores blow to and fro with the

10. Morgan, ed., *Diary of Michael Wigglesworth*, esp. 13, 33, 51, 52, 60, 61, 62, 65 ("awaken," "awaking"); *Oxford English Dictionary*, s.v. "awaken"; Christopher Looby, "Sexuality and American Literary Studies," in Caroline F. Levander and Robert S. Levine, eds., *A Companion to American Literary Studies* (Malden, Mass., 2011), 422–436; Jordan Alexander Stein, "How to Undo the History of Sexuality: Editing Edward Taylor's 'Meditations,'" *American Literature*, XC (2018), 753–784; Greta LaFleur, *The Natural History of Sexuality in Early America* (Baltimore, 2018); Ann Marie Plane, *Dreams and the Invisible World in Colonial New England: Indians, Colonists, and the Seventeenth Century* (Philadelphia, 2014).

wind in some danger to break, as I think; I cannot tel whether it were my duty to give them some hint that owe them. When I think 'tis a common thing, and that 'tis impossible but that the owners should have oft seen them in that case, and heard them blow to and fro, and that it is but a trivial matter, and that I have given a hint to the one that dwels in the hous, and he maketh light of it; and that it would rather be a seeming to check others mindlesness of their own affairs, and lastly that there may be special reasons for it that I know not; why the case seemeth clear that 'tis not my duty.

Wigglesworth wanted to "obey with chearfulness all gods will." Unfortunately, regarding his will on the matter of stable doors, Wigglesworth's deity remained silent. Wigglesworth's relentless introspection did not change this.[11]

Lacking direction from his god, Wigglesworth shouldered the vagaries of his desire for satisfying, piety-affirming company. His gloom in that task shows how taxing and unrewarding a studious commitment to self-knowledge could be. Wigglesworth cared about being a good neighbor, but, as he put himself into the imagined perspective of his neighbor, he worried that Mitchell would recognize how deeply he cared, how deeply his desire for his neighbor's esteem permeated him. As Wigglesworth recalled the sight of Mitchell's stable door, he re-created the ways this recognition might unfold. The unhinged door, he acknowledged, might not have been that unusual to begin with: "'tis a common thing." It was conceivable that Mitchell had already noticed it and not cared: "Tis impossible but that the owners should have oft seen them in that case, and heard them." Would the implication that Mitchell *should* care be offensive? Maybe "it would rather be a seeming to check others mindlesness of their own affairs." Maybe Mitchell had already noticed and left it thus on purpose. "There may be special reasons for it that I know not." Wigglesworth was sensitive to the possible insult of implying that he thought he knew better. Throughout, he was awake to the danger that mentioning it would reveal that he was thinking about it at all, was too affected by what should have been a "trivial matter." Indeed, he had already "given a hint to one that dwels in the house"—probably not Mitchell himself, but someone whose esteem he cared about less keenly. But Wigglesworth had been rebuffed, even teased for caring: "He maketh light of it."[12]

11. Morgan, ed., *Diary of Michael Wigglesworth*, 69–71.
12. Ibid., 71.

Like the specter of being exposed as incontinent, exposure of Wigglesworth's desire to be liked terrified him. The two are not, however, as distinct as Wigglesworth's critics have thought or have wanted to think. Wigglesworth's uncertainty registered formally in his recollection of oscillating movement: "to and fro"; should he "shut it or not"; how he was "sorely buffeted"; "seeing some dores blow to and fro"; and how he "heard them blow to and fro." These penetrating details have rendered the passage psychoanalytically interesting: poor Wigglesworth—his erotic desire was so repressed! Those readings have not necessarily been wrong. And their attempts to make psychoanalytic methods legible in the field of early American studies have been valuable. Yet their ambition to implicitly pathologize and then diagnose his struggles misses what's unexceptional about them: Wigglesworth grappled with the same task of self-knowledge as most of his neighbors, or at least those who documented their interiorities. Yet these neighbors were much more successful in ignoring and forgetting it. Like a Muybridge photograph, Wigglesworth's uncertainty captures stages on the course of sympathetic speculation that often go unnoticed. His imaginative re-creation of Mitchell's many possible responses obeyed the ethos articulated most clearly in Winthrop's sermon, and his fealty to that ethos meant staying awake to the possibility of his own error, his own overreach. It also meant confronting the prospect that Mitchell would recognize the concentration and focus he exerted in being such a good neighbor, in being helpful, pious, and likable.[13]

Wigglesworth longed to be certain that his contemporaries would not misunderstand him, and he spent great mental energy trying to attain that certainty. Yet despite his worries and their taxations and costs, Wigglesworth liked company and camaraderie. It was "company drew me on," he explained when reflecting on his initial reluctance to attend his colleague Zechariah Symmes's preaching at Watertown, five miles west. And in his poetry, Wigglesworth could be clear about his desires. His poem "In Solitude Good Company," the sixth "Riddle Unriddled" of his "Meat out of the Eater," listed some of these desires: timeless constancy, care during sickness, company during perambulation, true pity and active support during times of misery, comfort and cheer, and even impromptu visitation. Yet probably more intensely than most

13. Ibid., 70–71. For exemplary readings of Wigglesworth's buffeting, see Eva Cherniavsky, "Night Pollution and the Floods of Confession in Michael Wigglesworth's Diary," *Arizona Quarterly*, XLV (1989), 15–33; and Nicholas F. Radel, "A Sodom Within: Historicizing Puritan Homoerotics in the Diary of Michael Wigglesworth," in Tracy Fessenden, Radel, and Magdalena J. Zaborowska, eds., *The Puritan Origins of American Sex* (New York, 2001), 41–55.

of his colleagues, he knew how unlikely those gratifications were: he knew how costly sincerity could be and how thoughtless his fellows could be to the work of understanding it. As a result, he turned to the divine as a source for comfort throughout his duty-bound pursuit of potential humiliations. The deity, he claimed, could be a source of "abiding friend[ship]" that proved itself in fruits like the feeling of safety and security—particularly in corporeally volatile times, such as when he found himself lying prone and even ill in bed. Reflecting on those desires, he disclosed at least one open secret about settler sociability: that most people didn't like it.

> To be alone sometimes
> And want no Company
> Whilst men are Musing; this you'l say
> Is no great Rarity.

Yet he didn't give up on the possibility of horizontal love. His versified, ear-gratifying representation of nominally pessimistic content, especially his solicitation of an affirmative reply ("this you'l say"), suggests that he intuited there might be others in his society who experienced sociability with similar dissatisfaction.[14]

Unfortunately for the literary historian, those less likely to forget the body's spongy weight were also less likely to have written their experiences down. However, of the few who both couldn't forget and did write, at least one wrote eloquently about what she did with that pressing, unhappy consciousness. Like Wigglesworth, Anne Bradstreet spent time thinking about water and the sometimes unpredictable flows of other liquid substances. Also like Wigglesworth, she probably spent more time thinking about those flows than she would have liked. In 1630, among the many thoughts she had aboard the ship *Arbella* as it approached what looked like a convenient harbor of a new continent, one of her more visceral feelings might have been relief at returning to a stable ground on which to manage her body's effluences. This isn't to say that she wanted "privacy" as many twenty-first-century readers probably understand it. Early modern English people, especially women, lived in a social world

---

14. Morgan, ed., *Diary of Michael Wigglesworth,* 48 ("company"), 100 ("abiding friend[ship]"); Michael Wigglesworth, "Meat out of the Eater," in Ronald A. Bosco, ed., *The Poems of Michael Wigglesworth* (Lanham, Md., 1989), 223 ("To be alone"), 225–227, 229, 230; Adrian Chastain Weimer, "From Human Suffering to Divine Friendship: 'Meat out of the Eater' and Devotional Reading in Early New England," *Early American Literature,* LI (2016), 3–39.

characterized by greater proximity to others and with a wider network of intimates than many modern readers experience in daily life. Whatever those norms were in Bradstreet's land-bound life, they were narrowed further on board a ship. While at sea, bodies cried, coughed, and sneezed, drank and ate, urinated and defecated, seeped, copulated and ejaculated, vomited, sweated, menstruated, gave birth, and otherwise bled closer to others' bodies than they would have on land, and there was a smaller perimeter for moving away from those other bodies. Moreover, given the boat's rocking, it was likely that any of your neighbor's bodily fluids might find their way to you, might soak and seep through your clothes such that even after you dried or, days or weeks later, found the opportunity to wash, the memory of that contact might be preserved on your clothes as a stain.[15]

Bradstreet, along with all the other passengers on the *Arbella*, probably got used to it, though that didn't mean they liked it. So when the ship sailed closer to the freshly visible land, Bradstreet might have looked out at the solid ground with relief. On land, she'd be better able to control the reach of those fluids and the sight of her own body's fluids in the perception of others. For women, these ebbs and flows could be an ostentatious factor in their claims to sincerity. Absence of one fluid, for example, might attest to a woman's penetration by another, and depending on her lane along the highways of what Gayle Rubin has called the "traffic in women," these absent or present fluids could disclose her virtue to her neighbors. Bradstreet thought a great deal about this visibility. Her longing for control over that appearance emerges in her poems. Like Wigglesworth, Bradstreet recognized that social fulfillment, the like and esteem of her neighbors, depended on her ability to seem in control of her body's many liquid substances. Unlike Wigglesworth, Bradstreet was a little more accustomed to having public attention directed toward her fluids. In response to her society's disgusted fascination with unmanaged fluids, Bradstreet didn't try to pretend she didn't have any. She knew that some leaks could afford her limited, but useful, rhetorical power. What made shame worthwhile to her was showing off what looked like a sincere struggle to keep those fluids in.[16]

15. Laura Gowing, *Common Bodies: Women, Touch, and Power in Seventeenth-Century England* (New Haven, Conn., 2003); Cressy, *Coming Over*; Kathleen M. Brown, *Foul Bodies: Cleanliness in Early America* (New Haven, Conn., 2011).

16. Gayle Rubin, "The Traffic in Women: Notes on the 'Political Economy' of Sex," in Rayna R. Reiter, ed., *Toward an Anthropology of Women* (New York, 1975), 157–210.

Bradstreet developed this strategy at least in part through her considerable scientific knowledge. Like many of her male contemporaries, she was fascinated with science, with the natural world, and with humans' activity through time in engaging with it. She was not especially interested, at least in her longer poems, in applying the pursuit of knowledge to herself. As she grew older and accumulated experiences, she came to find value in examining her interiority and in recording the outcomes of her research, at times circulating them among her companions and neighbors. She most likely did a significant amount of this sharing in everyday life, in direct conversation with her peers. Yet in her early poems, she favored other topics to represent and rhyme, to subordinate scientifically and metrically. By 1654, an overwhelming majority of those lines were about the external world. Line for line, most of the manuscript volume that her brother-in-law took to England and published as *The Tenth Muse Lately Sprung up in America* discussed environmental science and classical history. As Bradstreet's literary historians have shown, she thrilled to contemplate the intersection of past history and present politics, and she sought opportunities to present these topics in a fashion that would illuminate and embody the ideals her theology proposed. She was aware, for example, of the Crusades and the unattained goal of Christian supremacy they represented. That history informed her sense of the stakes of popular anti-Stuart factionalism in England, and she was energetic in turning to the literary output of English writers like Sir Walter Ralegh in examining the course of world history that had produced the events of her time. She was also interested, a little less obviously, in power as it worked intimately. Though she recognized the effects of gender on her life, especially on her status as a poet, she intuited that the world of wars and kings she wrote about wasn't entirely inaccessible to her as a woman. Her status as an object of spectacular disgust—the knowledge that others claimed to have of her sincerity through recourse to the sight of her bodily emissions—showed her that women could approach power, even wield it themselves, if they could control the visibility of those fluids, especially blood, as it flowed through them.[17]

Gender organized much of her scientific writing, and women's experience shaped how she wrote about the natural world and what existed beyond it. Whereas "The Four Monarchies" is her longest poem, the "Quaternions" may be her most ambitious. Anthologies of early colonial writing or American women's writing frequently pass over these long poems in favor of her shorter,

17. James Egan, *Oriental Shadows: The Presence of the East in Early American Literature* (Columbus, Ohio, 2011); Jane D. Eberwein, "Civil War and Bradstreet's 'Monarchies,'" *EAL,* XXVI (1991), 119–144.

later poems about domestic desires, yet these two works constitute the bulk of her poetic oeuvre. Of these two, the "Quaternions" is probably her most complex. It was the third poem in her manuscript, and it made a forceful claim to intellectual ambitions. The root of its title, *quater*, points, first, to four categories of the natural world—elements, humors, ages, seasons. These four categories are, collectively, the topics of 1,800 lines of heroic couplets. Each of these categories, in turn, unfolds in four parts. Elaborating that complex structure, Bradstreet identified and described correspondences across the categories. The humor of Choler, for example, corresponded to the element Fire, the age of adulthood, and, finally, the season of Summer—and in case readers forgot which personified element matched which personified age or humor by the time they reached the final set, Bradstreet, who was sensitive to the loss of mental energy across long intellectual projects, signposted her progress to remind them. Seventeen hundred lines in, for example, she introduced Summer by recalling its resemblance to "choler, fire and middle-age; / As Spring did aire, blood, youth in's equipage." Bradstreet heightened the gratifications of those correspondences through contrast, highlighted harmony by beginning with dissonance. In the first half of the "Quaternions," the first two categories, the elements and the humors, are not organized by time, as the ages of man and the season are. Unorganized, they fight, or at least, they try to pick fights. Women's experience was useful for her in the exposition of that conflict. Her first two sets of sisters are angry, aggressive, and through it all, acerbic. These aren't by any means exclusively women's emotional states, but one effect of her exposition through feminized mouthpieces is that these women show the ability to exercise reason—and wit—despite heated antipathy. In these confrontations, motivated by an aggressive desire to be correct, she showed off what she knew about each party's special qualities—an elaborate rock paper scissors game that explained the relationships that organized the world around her.[18]

As Bradstreet concluded her treatment of the four humors, however, she suggested one relationship that might have interested her especially: the relationship between Phlegm and Blood that showcased what she saw to be the power of well-regulated bodily fluids. The four humors, in the order she presented them, were Choler, Blood, Melancholy, and Phlegm. As had their four predecessors, Fire, Earth, Water, and Air, they proceeded to insult each other and parried the invectives they received by insisting on the supremacy of this or that quality, usually an aggressive, belligerent one. But Phlegm did something

18. Joseph R. McElrath, Jr., and Allan P. Robb, eds., *The Complete Works of Anne Bradstreet* (Boston, 1981), 48–49.

different, an act characterized by peculiar self-consciousness. Phlegm refused to will her way to theoretical domination. She wasn't like other girls. She accepted her accommodating, un-aggressive personality and then pointed to proof of its superior power. In contrast with Blood, she had aesthetics on her side. And Bradstreet knew that aesthetics could be quite powerful. The mixture of phlegm and blood—a blush—aroused men. In the pursuit of possessing the compelling aesthetic qualities that aroused them, they were ready to go to war. That, Bradstreet observed, had been the triumph of Homer's Helen. Her appearance at the end of Bradstreet's "Quaternions" suggests that, in Bradstreet's assessment, Phlegm won (perhaps allowing Blood to share in her triumph).

Bradstreet understood, as she composed this long and potentially quite boring poem, that dissent within a category could heighten the excitement and gratification of noticing correspondences across them. For the most part, the dissent within each category was a matter of claiming brute force. Yet other forms of power, Bradstreet knew, were possible. Embodied aesthetics, in particular, fascinated her, a form of power that required two conditions in order to be effective, and neither could be taken for granted on the colonial frontier. First, to exercise this distinct power, one would need to be outwardly, epidermally phlegmatic—she would need to have white skin. Bradstreet pointed to this requirement twice: when she described Phlegm as "Lilly white" and when she described her "Ivory face." Second, to access the power that white skin afforded, one would need to have absorbed the set of morals that made shame and its expression instinctual—she would need to modulate Blood's visibility and blush in a conventionally attractive fashion. It wouldn't have done for Menelaus or Paris to see Helen's blood directly in order to be ready to spill others'. As Molly Farrell has argued, the sight of women's blood would more likely have disgusted Bradstreet's male contemporaries, as well as the kings who lived in her mind and on her page. But Phlegm's value existed in qualifying that appearance, in transforming it into an object of desire by muting its intensity. Bradstreet might have drawn on personal longings for beauty in writing this passage—personal appearance quietly preoccupied her. Here, Phlegm suggests at least one reason why: the partial control over Blood's visibility that whiteness enabled in turn brought pellucid women like Bradstreet closer to men's exercise of power.[19]

19. Ibid., 32; Ana Schwartz, "Anne Bradstreet, Arsonist?" *New Literary History*, LII (2021), 119–143; Molly Farrell, "Disgusting Affects from the Antinomian Controversy to the Anti-abortion Movement," *American Literature*, XC (2018), 785–813; Anne G. Myles, "Queerly Lamenting Anne Bradstreet," *Women's Studies*, XLIII (2014), 346–362.

Why would she want that? One basic reason is that she lived in a community where men made most of the explicit rules. It was men who decided when to declare war or launch ships. More quietly, it was men who determined positive law and many of the rules that governed daily life. Most subtly, it was men who decided when to prosecute those laws and when to suspend them. The existence of patriarchy doesn't mean that Bradstreet or women like her were looking for opportunities to rebel or even that they recognized any feelings of great unhappiness. It did mean, more prosaically, that she had to organize her life around men and men's rules, even when what she might have been pursuing at any given moment had nothing to do directly with men. Let us say she wanted to have friends and companions and to be recognized as a meaningful participant in her community. The actions she took would have to align with patterns of behavior that men didn't consider suspicious or worthy of censure. Like most women, she probably habituated herself to those rules and over time stopped thinking about them. But Bradstreet, similarly to Phlegm, wasn't like most women. She presumably wanted to be liked, but she also wanted to write poems. She got pleasure from organizing syllables into lines in ways that could affect and revise their meaning. This desire, powerful men knew, could have unpredictable social effects, so she had to be careful and self-conscious in how she pursued it. She found ways to create objects of aesthetic value that men appreciated. Her strategy, by and large, seems to have been to align her writing with reproducing the Bay Colony's ideals. She wrote poems that were didactically useful—both in general and specifically for young women. In selecting topics, she took cues from her father, and she acknowledged his influence in the dedicatory poem to *The Tenth Muse,* the book of poems that her brother-in-law arranged to be published without, it seems, her consent. She also claimed inspiration from Protestant writers like Ralegh and Guillaume du Bartas, presenting herself as wise in her selection of male figures by whom to be spongily affected. She even conceded that too much publicity could be a bad thing, as in her poem on the abduction and publication of her poems. If her verses were to circulate "out of door," she would make a show of staying, by contrast, within the parameters of the domestic. She made a show, too, of knowing how important it was to present oneself as aesthetically attractive when beyond that boundary: mended clothes, clean face, not unevenly limbed.[20]

20. McElrath and Robb, eds., *Complete Works of Anne Bradstreet,* 177–178; Lyle Koehler, *A Search for Power: The 'Weaker Sex' in Seventeenth-Century New England* (Urbana, Ill., 1980);

Verse sophistication, proposed that poem ("The Author to Her Book"), was one way to mediate one's appearance to the world. Bradstreet reflected on that affordance and exploited it, too. Consider the exceptional moments of confessional self-scrutiny in her longer, typically un-self-reflective poems. Although she had proposed to discuss epic themes of war and kings, it turned out to be a more difficult task than she ultimately thought was worth the effort. On completing the third of the four ancient empires, Greece, she gave up. She eventually tried to write the fourth and final monarchy, Rome, but then gave up again after fewer than two hundred lines. As she contemplated quitting altogether, she seems to have recognized what later scholars, such as Ivy Schweitzer and Farrell, have explained—her social world, especially the men in it, wanted to claim access to women's interiority, especially when they (women) suffered. And so, as she navigated her failure, she versified her decision. She produced a confession that was deliberately self-conscious of a readership, and in that spectacle, she showed off what her body felt: "No more I'le do," she wrote at the end of her Roman monarchy, "sith I have suffer'd wrack." When it came to her feelings, to her emotional experience of regret and shame, however, she gave her readers significantly less than her lines, initially, seem to be offering. At the break that concluded her third monarchy, she admitted: "For what is past I blush, excuse to make / But humbly stand, some grave reproof to take: / Pardon to crave, for errours, is but vaine." A conventional paraphrase might yield the following: *I am embarrassed, and my blushing should excuse me; I am preparing for correction with humility; I desire forgiveness for my serious mistakes.* A slower reading of the first and third quoted lines, and in particular, attention to their use of infinitive verbs, reveals far less abjection: *I would blush if I were making excuses for what I have composed. I am humbly confronting serious correction from someone. Asking forgiveness for mistakes is only a performance.* On the heels of her admission that the "taske befits not women, like to men," this passage acknowledges that men claimed superior intellectual status. Yet the passage may not claim either shame or apology. It indicates only that she knew men expected affective subordination—and maybe an intuition that men valued white skin for the blood that circulated beneath it and the opportunities it offered to expose white women to shame.[21]

Elizabeth Ferszt, "Transatlantic Dame School: The Early Poems of Anne Bradstreet as Pedagogy," *Women's Studies,* XLIII (2014), 305–317.

21. McElrath and Robb, eds., *Complete Works of Anne Bradstreet,* 135 ("taske"), 136 ("For what is past"), 140 ("suffer'd wrack"); Schweitzer, *Work of Self-Representation;* Farrell, "Disgusting Affects," *American Literature,* XC (2018), 785–813.

More than pain or sincere regret, this passage shows off Bradstreet's knowledge of what her world wanted from her, and not only what men wanted but also many of the women who by and large had ceased thinking about the rules that men had made. Her neighbors wanted to know her interiority. They wanted her to know they felt a claim to that knowledge. Her performance of sincerity paid lip service, at least, to that claim. And her body wasn't always on her side. Even knowing that gender wasn't really indicative of an inferior brain, or that being a woman didn't fit her for a needle at the cost of a pen, wouldn't be enough to make writing verse easy. Such knowledge wouldn't buy her time to think, write, and revise nor to suspend the gendered obligations that claimed the hours of her day, and simply understanding that her brain wasn't inferior to men's would not shield whatever she wrote from the interventions of those men reading it. But grasping that gender consisted substantially in a set of expectations for social presentation rather than a set of bodily limitations did make it easier for her to perform gender in a fashion that allowed her some leeway for living with the abjection those expectations required. Along with that leeway, knowledge that gender didn't make her any less intelligent could buy her distance from patriarchy's more severe, at times cruel, expressions of power. Representing blood at a distance, she knew, afforded her that degree of self-determination. She did so adroitly. It was not a skill she developed in circumstances of her own choosing, yet with greater knowledge of the circumstances that hemmed her in, she could exercise some degree of power over her life.

Years of exercising that skill would have taken a toll. Tiredness may be one way to explain her turn, later in life, to less abstract, intellectual themes and toward the introspection for which the lyric tradition and American literary history remember her. After the 1650 publication of her manuscript without her consent, she did not write another poem about anything other than her deity and the cares of her domestic life. There is one poem in which she compares the disconcerting experience of publication to an embarrassingly ugly child, a handful of poems about the pursuit of piety, a poem to her "Dear and loving Husband," then "Another," and then "Another," and elegy after elegy for family members who died. Among the poems of hers that exist in her son Simon's handwriting are a few on the challenges of living piously in a body that failed her, another handful on the presence, distance, or healthfulness of her family members, and one poem about a house fire that consumed three and a half decades of homemaking labor in one night. The longest of these poems reaches 264 lines; most stay under 50. Because they are short, relatively easy to read, and often describe personal feelings like desire, frustration, and sadness, these poems align felicitously with the lyric sensibilities that nine-teenth- and twentieth-century theorists of poetry would prioritize. On the strength of this alignment, Bradstreet has come to be a "pioneer" of American literary creativity. Indeed, next to the caricature of repression in which her colleague Wigglesworth would eventually be cast, these writings do look like a triumph of subjective expression. It is possible that she really did find, late in life, something more real, more fulfilling in making claims about her true and sincere feelings and then rearranging those words into rhymes. Nevertheless, that appearance comes at the cost of recognizing the history of disappoint-ment to which these poems likely responded and the relentless imperative she would have felt to disclose these disappointments, sometimes to those responsible for them.[22]

Regarding her sincerity in these later poems, it is probably impossible to be certain, though she would have known that the men in her life loved to consider that question about women like her. A subtler testament to her tired-ness, though, appears in her prose recollections of the end of the transatlantic voyage that closed off her life in England, the memories she shared with her children for their moral benefit at the end of her life on earth. In prose, not troubling herself with verse, Bradstreet briefly admitted that her arrival in what she called a "new World" might have initially been a loathsome prospect: "After a short time I . . . came into this Country, where I found a new World and new manners at which my heart rose, But after I was convinced it was the way of God, I submitted to it and joined to the ch[urch], at Boston." This disclosure has long fascinated Bradstreet's readers and critics. It is directly autobiograph-ical and looks frankly confessional, unmanipulated by verse's conventions. To many readers, it also looks to be confessing a shred of subversive, or at least recalcitrant, spirit against the optimism of settler leaders such as her husband, her father, or her father's famous colleague, John Winthrop. These readers' arguments lean heavily, but not unpersuasively, on the antithetical conjunction "but." What they miss, however, is the exhausted triumph her biographical fragment preserves. They miss her ultimate concession to those circumstances beyond her own choosing. She wanted her children to know that, in the struggle to subordinate her will to the rules of the world around her, she had won. Whatever rebellion she had felt, she quelled it. Or had she?

22. Louisa Hall, "The Influence of Anne Bradstreet's Innovative Errors," *EAL*, XLVIII (2013), 1–27, esp. 27 ("pioneer"); Patricia Caldwell, "Why Our First Poet Was a Woman: Bradstreet and the Birth of an American Poetic Voice," *Prospects*, XIII (1988), 1–35; Virginia Jackson, *Dickinson's Misery: A Theory of Lyric Reading* (Princeton, N.J., 2005).

So fascinated by what her heart's rising might figuratively represent, we have overlooked the plain fact that Bradstreet decided not to say what feeling, literally, the heart rising denoted; we have also overlooked that any blood flushing rebelliously through her was hidden in its cardiac home, wherever that home was moving next.[23]

Bradstreet and Wigglesworth faced shame strategically. For Wigglesworth, shame exercised sincerity through self-inquiry. It was a tactic to preempt the dislike of his neighbors. For Bradstreet, shame was tolerable because of the skill she developed to limit her exposure to criticism and ridicule. (That both this man and woman were worried about ridicule from neighbors who considered themselves exemplarily sympathetic is one reason to not take those neighbors' claims to possess unusual proximity to the good as the last word on their goodness.) Neither appears to have set out deliberately to subvert society's conventional hunger for shame. They probably didn't like it, and maybe they had critiques of it, but more prosaically, they were seeking to live a more robust life within those social conventions. Unlike, say, Anne Eaton at New Haven, Bradstreet seems to have concluded that being a welcome member of her community was, though costly, worthwhile. Yet Bradstreet's skill in managing expressive conventions was, if not unique, unusual. Experimenting with these conventions was a risk, but her odds in succeeding, relative to those of most other women, were in her favor, given her social standing and the education that reflected and reproduced it. The presence of risk is valuable, however, in revising one of the pressing questions about shame within a society that had institutionalized sincere self-disclosure: *Is this shame sincere?* It's a question that preoccupied settlers themselves, but it's not the only question that Bradstreet's performances prompt. One might also ask: *Given the risk of failing to satisfy known conventions, what desire does the will to undertake that risk in performing shame represent?* Bradstreet desired to write poems, to be a meaningful part of her social world, and to not have one come at the expense of the other. The principle of those desires, to some degree, but with distinct differences, applies to Native converts like those at

23. McElrath and Robb, eds., *Complete Works of Anne Bradstreet,* 216; Elizabeth Wade White, "The Tenth Muse—A Tercentenary Appraisal of Anne Bradstreet," *WMQ,* 3d Ser., VIII (1951), 355–357, 360; Perry Miller, "Errand into the Wilderness," ibid., X (1953), 3–32, esp. 9; Ann Stanford, "Anne Bradstreet: Dogmatist and Rebel," *New England Quarterly,* XXXIX (1966), 373–389, esp. 374; Rosemarie M. Laughlin, "Anne Bradstreet: Poet in Search of Form," *American Literature,* XLII (1970), 1–17, esp. 1. Charlotte Gordon, in *Mistress Bradstreet: The Untold Life of America's First Poet* (New York, 2007), confidently claims that the heart's rising indicates nausea (5).

Plymouth in 1666 who similarly confronted the injunction to disclose their shame. These converts might have been furthest from the biopoetic dream of individual fulfillment, but their will to confess anyway directs attention to the historical circumstances that sincerity sought to forget. These converts might have endured humiliation for the sake of what settlers called the "glory" of their deity, but the converts also undertook those performances to renew social attachments in the face of great obstacles: not so much Wigglesworth's fear of ridicule or Bradstreet's intuition of objectification but a historically unprecedented loneliness that severely taxed Native peoples' familiar ways of flourishing together.

Risking shame was a crucial step in the process of what English people called conversion, and, for Native Algonquians, it was one experiment in a process of moving forward through a moment of great crisis. Recognized as essential to that process, shame, in turn, moves our understanding of this period in Algonquian history away from the gothic tropes that often appear in the existing literature documenting it. Two epidemics had taken place in the years just before and after the English began to settle with intentions of permanence in Algonquian territory. The first, probably plague, took place between 1616 and 1618; the second, probably smallpox, occurred in 1633 and 1634. Conventional narratives of Algonquian conversion often attempt to convey the severity of those events by turning to the sublime or grotesque, reviving an earlier representational strategy. In his *New English Canaan,* Thomas Morton implied that the severe and widespread mortality reminded him of the story his religion told of the torture and execution of the Christian deity. Perversely extending the European convention of naming an American location by describing it as a newer version of an old, known site, Morton called it a "new found Golgotha," a newer version of the site of the Christian deity's spectacular suffering, and many historians of early contact favor this evocative phrase in their own descriptions.[24] But most Native survivors would not have

---

24. On causes of mortality, see Erik R. Seeman, *Death in the New World: Cross-Cultural Encounters, 1492–1800* (Philadelphia, 2011), 143–184; Kenneth M. Morrison, *The Embattled Northeast: The Elusive Ideal of Alliance in Abenaki-Euramerican Relations* (Berkeley, Calif., 1984), 203 n. 9; Thomas Morton, *New English Canaan; or, New Canaan, Containing an Abstract of New England . . .* (1637), rpt. in Peter Force, coll., *Tracts and Other Papers, Relating Principally to the Origin, Settlement, and Progress of the Colonies in North America, from the Discovery of the Country to the Year 1776* (Washington, D.C., 1838), II, no. 5, 19. For examples of that convention's attractions, see Kristina Bross, *Dry Bones and Indian Sermons: Praying Indians in Colonial America* (Ithaca, N.Y., 2004), 37; Robert James Naeher, "Dialogue in the Wilderness: John Eliot and the Indian Exploration of Puritanism as a Source of Meaning, Comfort, and Ethnic

understood those losses according to so gruesome a cultural reference point. They would have had to think more intimately about its social consequences—not only how to keep living materially but how to re-create and sustain a shared sense of peoplehood. When settlers arrived in large numbers, a few years after the first major mortality crisis, they did not immediately seek out mutually upbuilding contact with those Native survivors. Their first actions, as we have seen, often had very unhappy outcomes for Native people; so when English settlers eventually did send out cultural diplomats, many Native people bore suspicions and rejected their offerings. Still, a significant number of Native people professed interest in what diplomats like Eliot shared with them. Again and again during the 1650s, as Eliot pursued donations from the English metropole, the stories he told to get that money often featured optimism, and central to that optimism was an application of soul science that English spectators would have thrilled to read. However, the words and actions that he attributed to these potential converts tell a story that veers in another direction. Maybe they truly performed shame, or something like it, in order to join men like Eliot in an English heaven with an English deity that, to the settlers, everyone on the globe should long for. But if they did have those ambitions, the performance of shame also promised them more earthly, intensely local compensations.

Cultural diplomats like Eliot and Thomas Mayhew probably misrecognized this because they were so eager to witness sincere understanding of existential abjection. Tears, to Eliot and Mayhew, indicated "mourning" and "holy fear of God" that was the orthodox response to recognizing such self-disgust. The tears they witnessed might have been sincere, but they were not necessarily representing that specific knowledge. These tears might have also responded to profound sadness regarding the loss of loved ones. As Wigglesworth had confessed, too, these converts testified that friendships were significant parts of their lives, yet this significance was narrated in its sudden loss: "I having many friends who loved me, and I loved them," recalled Totherswamp, "I thought it enough if they loved me." It is possible that proselytes pursued conversion because men like Eliot were successful in presenting Christianity as an investment against future losses. The English deity, he claimed, was like a physician. And it is possible that, for the sake of that protection, these

<hr />

Survival," *NEQ*, LXII (1989), 346–368, esp. 352; Seeman, *Death in the New World*, 154; Craig White, "The Praying Indians' Speeches as Texts of Massachusett Oral Culture," *EAL*, XXXVIII (2003), 437–467, esp. 438. On the variety of approaches to widespread illness and death, see Cristobal Silva, *Miraculous Plagues: An Epidemiology of Early New England* (Oxford, 2001).

proselytes submitted to the humiliations of expositing their tears according to these diplomats' conventions. More immediately, however, presentations of tears might have expressed longing not simply for friends they had loved but for the love those friends had cherished for them in return, as Totherswamp's attention to mutual, reciprocated love suggests. "I [had] many friends that loved me," he recalled, before noting that "few of them"—and fewer sources of feeling loved—were left. Along with recollections of dead family members, these testimonies of lost sources of love stand as many individual sources of grief, many reasons one might be brought to tears. Given their attention to being formerly beheld with love, it's possible that, in the wake of these losses, converts hypothesized, even hoped, that conversion would help them rebuild.[25]

Conversion thus didn't consist merely of high-stakes exercises in abasement. Converts expressed interest in recovering a sense of dignity for their loved ones who had passed. Consider converts' fascination with the story of Sodom, a tale that intrigued settlers and Indigenous people, but for distinct reasons. Sodom, as Michael Warner has memorably shown, obsessed settlers as a case study for immoderate affection, and that negative preoccupation was one reason that Wigglesworth's nights haunted him so miserably during the daytime. Cultural diplomats who were very concerned with Native sexuality, such as Eliot, were likely to have told that story often to their Native audiences in an attempt to stretch their values into a plausible sense of meaning that would cover Native experiences of loss and grief. Native converts turned to that story frequently, too, but their preoccupation seems to have been less with finding reasons to feel shame than to relieve it. *"How many good people were in* Sodome *when it was burnt?"* they asked Eliot, communicating their interest in the failure of Abraham's attempt to bargain with his deity for the city's protection. Because God destroyed Sodom, it can be easy to forget the possibility that there were, in fact, good people in the city—though perhaps fewer than Abraham had expected—who died along with those who had angered the deity. This question brought those innocent, possibly virtuous dead back into the story of Sodom's citizens' demise. It would be impossible

25. [John Eliot], *The Day-Breaking, if Not the Sun-Rising of the Gospell with the Indians in New-England* (1647), rpt. in *Tracts Relating to the Attempts to Convert to Christianity the Indians of New England*, Massachusetts Historical Society, *Collections*, 3d Ser., IV (Cambridge, Mass., 1834) (hereafter cited as *Tracts*), 1–24, esp. 8 ("mourning"); Eliot, *Tears of Repentance; or, A Further Narrative of the Progress of the Gospel amongst the Indians in New-England* (1653), ibid., 197–260, esp. 223 ("holy fear"), 229 ("I having many friends," "few"), 230 ("I thought it enough").

to know who they were, however, and this made blanket condemnations of those citizens, as well as of the more recent dead, less forceful. Their own beloved relations might have been among those virtuous and innocent, despite evangelists' attempts to blame them for their own deaths.[26]

Engaging with settler diplomats' stories about spiritual meaning, Native people experimented with new ways of understanding unprecedented trauma. They also speculated on conversion's value as a way to draw closer to these freshly interested neighbors. Questions like the challenge to Sodom's total sinfulness, scholars have shown, were part of a repertoire of Native sociability.[27] They also might have been testing and extending the scope of community beyond its former perimeter. Such an expansion may illuminate one perplexing comment that Eliot recorded in his second promotional tract. He wrote that the proselytes expressed desires "to come into the *English* fashions, and live after their manner" and that they "thought that in 40. yeers more, some *Indians* would be all one *English,* and in an hundred yeers, all *Indians* here about, would so bee." As with most of what Eliot wrote, he might have been making it up, exaggerating, or revising details to suit the interests of prospective donors, but the content of this statement seems not to have been part of Eliot's vision for English-Algonquian relations. Though Christianity, he claimed, was universally accessible, the distinctions of Englishness were dear. He responded by conceding that successfully taking up English norms might one day make Indians "all one with *English* men," using a preposition ("with") indicating his hope that Englishness would remain adjacent to and distinct from Native people, even those who converted. The fantasy of being the same population was not Eliot's fantasy—far less a fantasy of his readers in England. Twenty-five years earlier, Robert Cushman tried to recruit planters to Plymouth by reminding them of their obligation to evangelize the Indigenous peoples and proposing that it would be more convenient to go there rather

26. John Eliot, *The Glorious Progress of the Gospel, amongst the Indians in New-England* . . . (1649), rpt. in *Tracts,* 69–99, esp. 84; Michael Warner, "New English Sodom," *American Literature,* LXIV (1992), 19–47; Daniel K. Richter, *Facing East from Indian Country: A Native History of Early America* (Cambridge, Mass., 2001), 124–125; James P. Ronda, "The Bible and Early American Indian Missions," in Ernest R. Sandeen, ed., *The Bible and Social Reform* (Philadelphia, 1982), 9–30, esp. 14–15; White, "Praying Indians' Speeches," *EAL,* XXXVIII (2003), 437–467; Gen. 18:16–33 (Geneva).

27. David Silverman, "Indians, Missionaries, and Religious Translation: Creating Wampanoag Christianity in Seventeenth-Century Martha's Vineyard," *WMQ,* 3d Ser., LXII (2005), 141–174, esp. 143. See also Jean M. O'Brien, *Dispossession by Degrees: Indian Land and Identity in Natick, Massachusetts, 1650–1790* (Cambridge, 1997), 58–60.

than bring others onto their "full" island. Yet if English people were more vigilant about whom they let into their proximity, there were reasons Native people might have considered expanding theirs, even their identity categories. These reasons ranged from the emotional (the loss of loved ones) to more strictly material (the loss of human participants in their complex ecological networks). Their will to acquire the conversational conventions of their new neighbors showed thoughtful amenability to compromise that could be useful to decades-, even century-long plans for social renewal.[28]

So there were reasons to experiment with these diplomats' suggestion that they try on shame and see how it would shape their lives. Sometimes these prescriptions were part of explicit rules for discourse. Converts should recognize that, according to Christian philosophy, they were possessed of natures they should try to hide; and in a clumsy performative chiasmus, they should show off their knowledge of that possession. If this was tricky, there were other, less paradoxical prescriptions as they figured out those expressive requirements. They could, for example, build new houses in the English style, as those converts who assembled at Natick did. These houses had "partitions in them for husbands and wives together, and their children and servants in their places also, who formerly were never private." Eliot hoped these material transformations would slowly habituate converts to recognize more instinctively "what nature is ashamed of." He was thinking, primarily, of procreative sex. He hoped that these practices and norms would educate desire and then habituate Native people more generally to the rules of gender that Englishmen thought were best. Eliot was therefore eager to record the effects of those disciplines. Though he had encouraged women not to ask their theological questions directly but to communicate them through "their Husbands, or the Interpreter privately therewith," he also seemed enthusiastic to report women disclosing their experiences of seemingly newfound Christian bashfulness, as he did a few pages later when a woman asked *"Whether she might not go*

28. "The Letter of Mr. Eliot to T. S. concerning the Late Work of God among the Indians," in Thomas Shepard, *The Clear Sun-Shine of the Gospel Breaking Forth upon the Indians in New-England . . .* (1648), rpt. in *Tracts*, 25–68, esp. 50; [Robert Cushman], "Reasons and Considerations," in Dwight B. Heath, ed., *Mourt's Relation: A Journal of the Pilgrims at Plymouth* (1963; rpt. Bedford, Mass., 1986), 88–96, esp. 91; Harold W. Van Lonkhuyzen, "A Reappraisal of the Praying Indians: Acculturation, Conversion, and Identity at Natick, Massachusetts, 1646–1730," *NEQ*, LXIII (1990), 396–428, esp. 414; David J. Silverman, *Red Brethren: The Brothertown and Stockbridge Indians and the Problem of Race in Early America* (Ithaca, N.Y., 2010), 11–29.

and pray in some private place in the woods, when her husband was not at home, because she was ashamed to pray in the Wigwam before company."[29]

Fluency in the conventions for publicizing shame was a deliberate goal of Native converts as they experimented with English social disciplines. Eliot's sixth tract, *Tears of Repentance*, shows off their acquisition of this fluency. As Wigglesworth had witnessed at Cambridge and as Bradstreet had practiced in her composition, in Eliot's writing, these converts showed great facility in making visible their knowledge of a self they should want to hide: "I was ashamed to pray," claimed Totherswamp, "and if I eat and did not pray, I was ashamed of that also"; "I am ashamed of all my sins," he responded to Reverend [Thomas] Allen's inquiry into his heart's disposition toward repentance. "I am ashamed of all I do," declared Waban; Ponampam described being "ashamed of my sins." Some recalled awkward visibility: Antony reflected on the deity's seeing him, both in the future (*"we must shortly appear before Jesus Christ"*) and in the present ("I know God seeth [me]"). Knowledge of being watched strengthened his own critical self-surveillance: "I did dayly see my sins," he concluded. John Speen described his heart being "greatly abased." In another idiom, Nishohkou preferred to speak less of shame and more of humility: "my heart is humbled, and then I pray"; "my heart is humbled, and then I repent"; "sometimes my heart is humbled, and I desire to fear God."[30]

For Algonquians who sought to develop relations with these English diplomats, the ability to perform shame was an achievement. They didn't simply point to the presence of shame; they showed that they grasped its quiet workings. They understood that shame could be proved in unexpected places, such as in the discovery that one did not feel it sincerely yet. Ponampam admitted, "Sometimes my heart was ashamed." Specifically, he confessed shame that he could not feel shame when he wanted to, and he made sure to show that this was not a permanent condition: his "sometimes" indicated that, at other times, he did feel it and knew how to recognize it. Likewise, Nishohkou avowed, "Yet again I think I cannot be ashamed of sin; but now I am ashamed of all my sins, and my heart is broken." Other confessions show Natives' understanding that

29. Shepard, *Clear Sun-Shine,* rpt. in *Tracts,* 41 ("their Husbands"), 47 (*"Whether she might not go and pray"*), 62 ("partitions," "what nature"); Ronda, "The Bible," in Sandeen, ed., *Bible and Social Reform,* 9–30, esp. 15; Van Lonkhuyzen, "Reappraisal," *NEQ,* LXIII (1990), 414–415; Ann Stoler, *Race and the Education of Desire: Foucault's "History of Sexuality" and the Colonial Order of Things* (Durham, N.C., 1995).

30. Eliot, *Tears,* rpt. in *Tracts,* 229 ("ashamed to pray"), 232 ("ashamed of all I do"), 242, 243 ("ashamed of my sins"), 246 ("greatly abased"), 250–251 ("my heart is humbled"), 257 (*"shortly appear,"* "God seeth"), 258 ("I did dayly").

sources of shame, like pride, could appear in unexpected places: Monequassun narrated discovering that he should feel shame not simply about his outward appearance but in his attachments to his appearance: "I heard that Word, That it is a shame for a man to wear long hair . . . at first I thought I loved not long hair, but I did and found it very hard to cut off; and then I prayed to God to pardon that sin also." Affection could catch you by surprise, Monequassun observed, and he filed away that discovery as useful discursive content. As with Bradstreet, knowledge of confession's conventions was a skill to cultivate, and these converts worked diligently to acquire it. Charles L. Cohen has suggested that Native converts' confessions do not show quite the "magnificent self-disgust" that English testimonies do, but he is wrong. Native people were just as capable of perfecting these conventions as Shepard's congregants. And their reasons for acquiring those skills were just as important.[31]

Professing knowledge of shame required familiarity with conventions, not simply for successful persuasion but to avoid more intense humiliation. This is one reason that tears were so significant: it was not that tears, or conversion's other nonverbal components, were immune to fraud. Winthrop, for example, recorded his suspicions of fake conversions, such as that of John Underhill. Underhill was adept in persuasive rhetoric. He had been banished, among other reasons, for seducing married women by persuading them to join him in special prayer sessions. In his second attempt to apologize and convince elders to revoke his exile from the Massachusetts Bay Colony, he presented himself before the Boston church "with many deep sighs and an abundance of tears," "a spectacle which caused many weeping eyes," but Winthrop noted that his performance, which earlier had lacked sufficient "sincerity," still seemed to be "standing upon a form." From the standpoint of English Christians, the form could be faked. Dissembling would require great confidence, a result of great familiarity. But from the standpoint of new converts, tearfulness was one more risky liability—all the riskier if, as Harold W. Van Lonkhuyzen observes, public weeping had been "strongly discouraged" within the social codes of Algonquian peoples in the Northeast. As part of the sincerely willed performance of conversion, the strategy of crying required still more study, still more practice of and habituation to other people's expressive norms.[32]

31. Ibid., 239 ("I heard"), 241 ("sometimes"), 251 ("yet again"); Charles L. Cohen, "Conversion among Puritans and Amerindians: A Theological and Cultural Perspective," in Francis Bremer, ed., *Puritanism: Transatlantic Perspectives on a Seventeenth-Century Anglo-American Faith* (Boston, 1993), 233–254, esp. 251.

32. Richard S. Dunn, James P. Savage, and Laetitia Yeandle, eds., *The Journal of John Winthrop, 1630–1649* (Cambridge, Mass., 1994), 262–264, 319 ("sincerity"), 334 ("with many deep

The course of renewal on which Native converts gambled was a rigorous one. There were many opportunities to fail. Study and rehearsal, as the 1666 Plymouth converts learned, was no guarantee that the confession of shame and the narration of Christian doctrine's transformation would be successful. The first two confessors, Paumpmunet and Wuttinnaumatuk, were best positioned to show off that they knew what shame was proficiently enough to apply it to their lives. But because the English elders who presided over the event failed to anticipate delays produced by the required translation, they felt they had to interrupt, and the confessors that came after now felt greater pressure. "The time being far spent, he [Kanoonus] and those that follow were called upon to contract themselves," Eliot wrote, "and that is the reason," he explained in advance, "of the shortnesses of the following Confessions." The converts complied with the new instructions, but they shortened their testimonies in revealing ways. These elisions expose, most importantly, an experience of humiliation that was probably quite real—so intense that it would not be named directly.[33]

Unlike Paumpmunet and Wuttinnaumatuk, Kanoonus, who went third, did not share any details that explicitly referred to his unique life. He cited key passages from the sacred text, and he shared an orthodox exegesis of these texts, yet he did not share details of his personal experience to exemplify these teachings. Similarly, Nonqutnumuk adhered very closely to his knowledge of sacred texts, sharing which ones he thought most relevant to conversion and why. The only explicit detail he shared about his life was his swift and efficient admission that his belief was weak and that he had, at one point, "loved murther, Adultery, fighting, cousening." Waompam, the fifth convert to speak, condensed his personal testimony even more than Nonqutnumuk and Kanoonus. He included conventional, if vague, sins like "Adultery and filthynesse" and a brief and haunting memory of the "thought of my Father that his Gods could not deliver him from death, but this God could." His testimony lasted seven sentences. The two remaining converts testified the next morning, in private conference rather than in public, and shared more details about their lives. Yet the severe contraction of the third, fourth, and fifth testimonies, which almost completely elide any personal details, suggest a sudden, intensified self-consciousness toward exposing those aspects of their lives that these new teachings openly told them they should want to hide.

sighs," "spectacle"), 335 ("standing"); Van Lonkhuyzen, "Reappraisal," *NEQ*, LXIII (1990), 396–428, esp. 418.

33. Cesarini, "Eliot's 'A Brief History,'" *WMQ*, 3d Ser., LXV (2008), 129.

After an interruption so contrary to one of their society's foundational social customs—respectful attention to public oratory—these men had palpable, direct reason to think that those aspects of their personal failures ought not to be publicized, and they acted on this belief.[34]

According to Eliot's record of the events, it seemed everyone in attendance expected that the confessions would take one sitting and that all seven proselytes (out of ten who were considered for the ceremony) were expected to testify at that single event. Eliot had encountered this requirement eight years earlier; this would not have been the first such surprise. At Natick, he had interrupted Monequassun's confession because he—"being slow of speech" in the eyes of impatient English missionaries—was producing a "great confusion." There is little evidence, for example, in the Shepard corpus, that an English confessor was similarly interrupted or told to condense his or her confession for the sake of impatient elders, though there is evidence of ongoing controversy (among ministers rather than laypeople) over how much talking was too much. Maybe Eliot, too, thought only English people deserved to be recognized for their "magnificent," or at least prolix, self-disgust. Or maybe he deprioritized these converts' inauguration into a spiritual community, caring more about other plans in his busy schedule. The consequences of that error, regardless of its cause, suggest how myopic the question of converts' sincere humiliation has been. These initiates wanted conversion deeply enough to reorganize much of their lives and to estrange themselves from many of their kin for it. Even when they thought they had acquired sufficient aptitude in the requisite conventions, they would still be vulnerable enough to unanticipated exposure that at least three of these seven men seem to have responded to with even more shame. They went forward anyway. Exposure, at the very least, would mean witnesses, and witnesses would mean—however provisional or thoughtless—a new social world, a life with new possibilities.[35]

For Native converts, confession's artifice required extraordinary intellectual labor. These converts probably recognized, especially in settings such as the Plymouth meetinghouse, that their English witnesses might have been more pleased to judge their fluency in that artifice than to learn of the transformations they used that skill to narrate. But those conventions could be a source of horizontal pleasure, too, a pleasure that might have been all the

34. Ibid., 131; Kathleen Bragdon, "Gender as a Social Category in Native Southern New England," *Ethnohistory*, XLIII (1996), 573–592, esp. 585.

35. Eliot, *Tears*, rpt. in *Tracts*, 238; Charles Cohen, *God's Caress: The Psychology of Puritan Experience* (Oxford, 1986), 137–140.

more gratifying for eluding English witnesses. On December 19, 1649, Eliot stumbled on a scene of mutual recognition that, disconcertingly, had little to do with his judgment:

> There had been at that time some strange Indians among them which came to see them who prayed to God, as one from *Martin's Vineyard,* who is helpful to Mr. *Mahu* to tell him words, etc. and I think some others, *when those strangers came,* and they perceived them to *affect Religion,* and had mutual conference about the same, there was very great *gladnesse of heart* among them, and they made these strangers exceeding welcome; Hereupon did the Question arise, namely what is the reason, that when a strange Indian comes among us whom we never saw before, *yet if he pray unto God, we do exceedingly love him: But if my own Brother, dwelling a great way off, come unto us, he not praying to God, though we love him, yet nothing so as we love that other stranger who doth pray unto God.*

In the seven tracts he wrote between 1648 and 1655, Eliot narrated only a few sustained scenes of horizontal sociability among converts and across convert communities, but it probably took place quite often beyond Eliot's notice. The Natick and Noepe converts labored seasonally in English society and were likely to meet in transit. Recalling this encounter, Eliot told a story of successful transmission of soul science. Converts identified the gestures of true conversion (these strangers "prayed to God") and Eliot noted that they seemed "to *affect Religion"*—that is, they exercised their familiarity with conventions in beholding each other and discussed those conventions together, having "mutual conference about the same."[36]

Eliot seemed pleased to note their enthusiasm to talk about the Christian principles that he had introduced to at least half of them. He recorded a "Question aris[ing]" from someone—why should love for fellow Christians supersede affiliations organized by birth? The question, in Eliot's mind, longed to be turned into a teachable moment. Eliot claimed that their unexpected affection exemplified "that which the Scripture calleth *love of the Brethren."* Unbeknown to them, Eliot insisted, they had embodied Christian ideals, a claim that has remained attractive to some modern historians. They might

36. John Eliot, *The Light Appearing More and More towards the Perfect Day,* rpt. in *Tracts,* 100–148, esp. 125; Margaret Ellen Newell, *Brethren by Nature: New England Indians, Colonists, and the Origins of American Slavery* (Ithaca, N.Y., 2015), 121.

have. But Eliot wanted more. He tried to insist to these converts that he knew what they were feeling better than they did. He told them that the love they felt when they discovered these strangers was the same love felt by distant English Christians whose benevolence they were enjoying and should hope to continue to enjoy—in no small part because of his eagerness to publicize their shame. And then Eliot asked them a question that departed from the catechistic style. He asked them to improvise. Could they use their reason to extend the principles of community that he thought he had given them? Could they imagine brotherhood with those distant English in return?[37]

Improvising collectively, they disappointed him: "They answered no." Maybe Eliot was capitulating to a familiar, favored caricature of Native converts as childish or naive. Maybe their "no" was a criticism of English self-aggrandizement—*"Doe not Englishmen spoile their soules, to say a thing cost them more then* [sic] *it did?"*—or of English settlers' ease in treating converts with considerably less affection. Or maybe they were simply far less interested in the regard not only of strange Englishmen whom they had never seen before but of those whom they would probably never see, who never had to undergo the mournful introduction to shame that they had or the rigorous intellectual obstacle course of confession. Here was a horizontal love that was not universal. It answered grief in a fashion that was made stronger by shame and that, in turn, made shame bearable. Although discovery of that love was new to Eliot, it might not have been new to its participants. Eliot turned to "others of them" later, narrating that unexpected encounter. He asked them whether they had been affected in the same manner and "how they found it in their hearts." They affirmed: yes, "they all found it so in their hearts." Though they had not been present at the chance encounter with Noepe converts, they had already been discussing, without his guidance, the sort of community they found most nourishing and vital. For an unknown period of time before, and unwitnessed by Eliot's eager surveilling eye, the opportunities for love and mutual beholding "had been a matter of discourse among themselves."[38]

37. Eliot, *Light Appearing*, rpt. in *Tracts*, 126; Abram C. Van Engen, *Sympathetic Puritans: Calvinist Fellow Feeling in Early New England* (Oxford, 2015), 144–172.

38. Eliot, *Light Appearing*, rpt. in *Tracts*, 126 ("no"); Eliot, *Glorious Progress*, ibid., 85 ("*spoile their soules*").

CHAPTER FOUR

The Happiest Memories

Duties, Debts, and the Generation of Freedom

I F INCREASE MATHER had gone from his own congregation at Boston's Second Church to visit his colleague James Allen's congregation at the First Church in the years after the violent martial conflict that profoundly disoriented the entire colony, he might have been surprised to see one of its communicants there in the meetinghouse. In 1677, the First Church approved for membership a woman named Dorcas. Her presence there would have taken Mather aback because Dorcas had been a celebrated, even cherished, member of a different congregation for much of the first half of Mather's life. But not in Boston; rather, in Dorchester. Thirty-six years earlier, in 1641, Dorcas had been the first Black member to join the spiritual community of the reform Protestant settlements. Her induction was unusual enough that John Winthrop, who didn't attend her church or even live in her town, wrote about it in his journal. To be inducted required the sort of unpleasant self-exposure contemplated by Michael Wigglesworth, Anne Bradstreet, and the Native converts in Plymouth. It also required approval by one's fellow congregants. Though it was too much for them collectively to do away with the institution of lifelong bondage, those same congregants, twelve years later, drew on their sovereign fellow feeling and purchased her manumission from her enslaver, Elizabeth Stoughton, widow of Israel Stoughton. It is nearly impossible for Mather not to have known about her membership at Dorchester and her eventual manumission. And the reasons for this likelihood might also have produced an unpleasant feeling for Mather: resentment. Born two years before her induction, he knew Dorcas well because he had grown up in the same congregation; she had been a presence in the spiritual community that shaped his early life. His father, Richard Mather, had baptized her and presided over her manumission. Though she was legally free in 1677, Increase might have wondered, was she free from her obligations to his family?[1]

Dorcas's possible debt turns Increase Mather's fantasy of spiritual autonomy on its head. As the previous three chapters have shown, sincerity represented the subjection of the self to a pious, loquacious society through practices of self-inquiry and self-disclosure, a form of subjection that required unrelenting vigilance to distractions, obligations, and injudicious affectability. But one could go too far in heightening the significance of personal responsibility. Estranged from a wide network of obligation, an individual might come to doubt the worthiness of the task. Sincerity had required individuals to reject a host of obligations, with the result that it was not always clear which relationships were worth honoring and how rigorously one might be expected to work to honor them. Within this network of ambiguity, Dorcas, and her commitment to piety, flattered English settlers' longings to believe that their values transcended the material circumstances that reminded them of the contingency of their virtues. She gratified their longing to believe that their vision of goodness—a vision for which they had suffered intensely—was truly universal, and her performance of self-knowledge and self-disclosure positively affirmed their longing to believe that they were sympathetic and that sincerity's rigors were worthwhile. Although Dorcas went through the motions of self-disclosure, however, she preserved some self-opacity for her spiritual life. She seems to have noticed that what sincerity gave with one hand, it already had taken with two, and she sought to restore the satisfactions of a stolen world in ways that Mather could barely have comprehended. She sought to keep her social world broad, expansive, and rich to better manage not only what the good life had cost her but also to whom she owed it.

1. Richard S. Dunn, James Savage, and Laetitia Yeandle, eds., *The Journal of John Winthrop* (Cambridge, Mass., 1996), 347.

Formal freedom widened the world of obligation, reciprocity, and debt in which Dorcas could now circulate. Before moving to Boston, Dorcas had traveled widely already, from the West Indies to Dorchester and perhaps even farther. Those earlier removes had been coerced; she had been obliged by the threat of violence. Yet her move from Dorchester to Boston, no longer forced, did not mean abandoning the links that connected her with her neighbors. Her travels, and their impact on those who witnessed them, illustrate the effects of the external, social, and political world on those parts of interior experience that often feel most true and permanent—one's sense of justice, one's attachment to family, one's desire for freedom. For many settlers, debt, during this period, began to feel like one limit to freedom and happiness. As anthropologists from Marcel Mauss to David Graeber have observed, debt need not be an undesirable condition. In many societies, including those in which many readers themselves participate, debt quietly guides harmonious life. Networked indebtedness can moderate social behavior and fortify relationships that sustain life and help it flourish. In the early modern English colonies, debt was also desirable. Recent historians have shown this. Yet the apparent need to point out the debt's desirability reflects a curious feature of this documentary archive: the most popular, enduring texts that circulated among early English settlers were obsessed with debt, particularly intergenerational debt, but they tended to present it as oppressive, something that individuals would hope to transcend. That historians have had to make a case for more subtle ways of understanding debt suggests that colonial parents' strategies might have worked. These texts produced quiet resentment and longing for recognition, particularly among children, who did not, after all, cease to be children once they reached adulthood. Children's contributions to family life tended to fall off the public balance sheet, and one of the most powerful strategies to restore those contributions to visibility was for children, once grown, to claim that they were profoundly owed, too. These debt-obsessed texts also hastened planters to a crucial threshold in sincerity's development. Many white settlers probably noticed sincerity's costly demands, and it's possible some thought it wise to begin counting those costs. If they had undertaken that work of second-guessing the value of redemption's costs, they might, in turn, have softened their stance on the universal necessity of working toward their doctrine's specific vision of earthly happiness. Maybe some did, and maybe some eventually acquired distance from the intense desire to persuade their children to vindicate their own, severe decisions. The literature they wrote in the second and third generation of settlement, however, suggests that most did not. In fact, most doubled down: they energetically advocated for more taxations, demanding them from their own inheritors in a fashion that fortified the power of distinctions of race and blood.[2]

In this process, sincerity was one of the most crucial levers of authority and power, particularly its ultimate inscrutability: the gap between the plausibly sincere, visible saints and the real, invisible ones. "Visible saints," of course, is Edmund S. Morgan's concise description of the elusiveness of reform Protestant sincerity. Because the truth of one's status as divinely favored was mysterious and unknowable, early moderns did the best they could with the evidence they had in the realm of the "visible"—though, as Wigglesworth's best-selling poem *The Day of Doom* shows, humans always risked reasoning wrong. One of the more reliable sources of evidence of divine favor, at least for early English settlers, was their status as settlers in the first place, the willingness to commit to an ideology and to leave behind an entire way of life to pursue it. But the trustworthiness of that evidence waned. Over time, those who hadn't chosen to be part of that community comprised more and more of the population. The crisis that ensued has been narrated many times, but sincerity opens a new and vivid window onto it. As the evidentiary power of simple presence in the settlements waned, where would authority in determining fitness for community participation lie? The jeremiad stepped in to answer this uncertainty: it proposed that elders who had suffered to prove their sincerity could claim authority to judge the sincerity of youth—not only their own children but all children of the settler community. Some children, English boys, would eventually be able to access that authority, but to access it meant risking lifelong resentments with disastrous consequences for settlers' neighbors, as the preoccupations with faithful English blood during King Philip's War shows. Dorcas's life, as it intersected with Mather's, illuminates this process in at least two respects. Her presence in Boston as a "visible saint" reminded settlers of sincerity's ultimate uncertainty and testified to the doctrinal source of their filial resentments, and her absence from Mather's congregation suggests some alternatives to that doctrine.[3]

2. For monograph-length studies of debts to elders, see Perry Miller, *Errand into the Wilderness* (Cambridge, Mass., 1956); Sacvan Bercovitch, *The American Jeremiad* (Madison, Wis., 1978); and Michael W. Kaufmann, *Institutional Individualism: Conversion, Exile, and Nostalgia in Puritan New England* (Hanover, N.H., 1998); Marcel Mauss, *The Gift: The Form and the Reason for Exchange in Archaic Societies,* trans. W. D. Halls (London, 2002); David Graeber, *Debt: The First 5,000 Years* (New York, 2011). See also Craig Muldrew, *The Economy of Obligation: The Culture of Credit and Social Relations in Early Modern England* (London, 1998).

3. Edmund S. Morgan, *Visible Saints: The History of a Puritan Idea* (Ithaca, N.Y., 1963).

If Dorcas had attended Increase Mather's congregation, she would have witnessed one of reform Protestantism's exceptionally prolix theorists of Christianity's disturbing first principle: eternal life wasn't, or at least wasn't only, a promise. Eternal life was also a threat. That menace was the background to all social exchanges in the reform Protestant colony, and it could have many moods. Michael Wigglesworth, for example, recorded that threat and its social consequences in his poem *The Day of Doom* with great buoyancy. The poem narrates what Christians called the "day of judgment," a point in the unknown future when the deity, no longer interested in human drama, would decide to end human life on earth and then sort those to whom he had extended his arbitrary favor from everyone else. The former, the deity would admit into heaven. The latter, he wouldn't. But first, interestingly, the latter would have to discover that they were not worthy and, furthermore, that they had been wrong in thinking they were. Wigglesworth saw the potential for making their collective anagnorisis fun, at least for readers, and exploited that promise by writing internally rhyming eight-line stanzas with a metrical scheme that modern readers may recognize from the nursery rhyme "Jack and Jill Went up the Hill." He continued those stanzas for nearly eight thousand lines, during which he tried to make other people's doom delightful. He seems to have succeeded. Between finishing the poem in 1662 and the earthly chapter of his life in 1705, Wigglesworth saw his poem undergo between six and nine printings on both sides of the Atlantic. Perry Miller praised Wigglesworth's skill in appealing to readers of all ages, especially children: "They loved it." It wasn't only skilled prosody that made the poem so compelling. His poem emotionally exploited one of the most frightening features of the Christian cosmology: the premise that a discrete consciousness, once conceived and brought into the world, would never cease to exist.[4]

In general, Christians believed it was important to work to discern the status and fate of the soul because their deity saw that status to be unhappy and loathsome by default. If unchanged, this status would, after one's death, lead to an eternity of almost unimaginable suffering. Calvinist theology, at the leading edge of early modern reform Protestantism, refined this theory. It proposed, first, that little could be done to alter one's status. Labors of self-knowledge, Protestants thought, were about as much as an individual could do to change it. Yet they also saw willingness to undertake that work as a useful sign of the

4. Michael Wigglesworth, "The Day of Doom," in Ronald A. Bosco, ed., *The Poems of Michael Wigglesworth* (Lanham, Md., 1989), 11–66; Bosco, "Introduction," ibid., vii–xliii, esp. x; Miller, *Errand*, 218.

deity's favor and maybe even his intervention to change that status. Importantly, however, they claimed that this research, the work of knowing the self and testing that knowledge through practices of self-disclosure—as we have seen, the work of sincerity—was completely unshareable. You had to, in the words of the Christian exegete Paul, "work out your own salvation with fear and trembling." One of the reasons Wigglesworth's poem was so successful was that it exploited this fear and trembling and made it a shareable aesthetic experience.[5]

Wigglesworth's poem was also successful because it had a finger on the pulse of the lived, social experience of that fear and trembling as elders hoped to communicate it to their children. Settlers on the colonial frontier lived the Christian philosophy of individual spiritual responsibility in a fashion unique to their historical circumstances. They claimed to be faithful to that doctrine, but their practices were not so clearly obedient to it, especially in family life. Elders had suffered materially and emotionally for it, and they longed to bring their offspring into a community that would uphold it. So reform Protestants argued intensely over whether and to what degree a community could effectively determine an individual soul's fate. Most Protestants who had left England agreed that external help, in practices like symbolically washing an infant, wouldn't directly affect the status of a child. But, some argued, those practices weren't useless. Symbolic washing could express the status of the parent. In that regard, it could convey the greater sociological likelihood that an infant would later discover him- or herself to be one of the special few. Even though responsibility was an unshareable burden, in activities like these, parents often insisted on intervening, drawing their own offspring into that fearful and quaking condition. Their success in doing so wasn't measured simply by a child's nominally independent decision to share the elders' ideology. Success was measured by a child's desire to draw their own progeny into it, in the child's sincere persuasion that their own metaphysical alienation was the wellspring of truest earthly meaning.

The outcome might have been happy, but the process wasn't. Wigglesworth's poem gratified readers not only in its buoyant rhymes. It also acknowledged the unhappiness of that process and turned it into a science fiction scenario. *The Day of Doom* depicted an apocalyptic scene that ruptured ordinary senses of time. It aligned the life trajectories of every person at the moment of their death—when their will ceased to matter. Every individual who had ever lived was now poised on a volatile brink, and beyond this

5. Phil. 2:12 (Geneva).

threshold, they would experience the consequences of their presumably willed behavior while their wills still had efficacy. Most thought they had been using their wills wisely—this confidence in the efficacy of good intentions is one of sincerity's enduring risks. Reform Protestantism, through the mechanism of predestination, fine-tuned Christianity's internal safeguard against such foolishness. And indeed, in Wigglesworth's poem, almost everyone turns out to have been wrong about what they sincerely believed was true about their souls. They had used their reason and their will unwisely. Five stanzas into Wigglesworth's poem, it was too late to do anything. One life, however—that of the reader—remained outside this alignment. That person's will was still efficacious, their day of doom not yet at hand. In example after example of bad reasoning and decision making, the reader could take sober pleasure in recognizing his or her own will's present efficacy. Like waking from a bad dream to realize that circumstances are not as dire as they had seemed, the poem's severities intensified the desirability of escaping them.

Schadenfreude complemented relief. Doom could be enjoyable when it was someone else's. That pleasure wasn't simply a result of the reader's capacity to avoid it. At a position of relative distance from damnation, readers could think about the rationality of the deity's judgment and, depending on their mastery of Christian doctrine, partake in the satisfaction of being smarter than the parties he was condemning, one after the next. It was fun to be right. *The Day of Doom,* like a pop quiz, presented at least ten opportunities to know the answers correctly when others didn't. The poem depicted ten distinct parties protesting their damnation. And the deity, in even meter and regular rhyme, answered each. Wigglesworth, like an earnest scholar, cited his sources: each response from the deity featured marginal annotations pointing to relevant passages from the shared sacred texts. The deity's answers were not esoteric or mystical. They were not guesswork, a matter of darts in the dark. They were patently available for anyone who could read. Children who had learned their spiritual lessons well would already have known the answers to each protestation. Precocious children would have known the sources for those answers from the shared source text that they believed their deity had given them. The protestations varied in sophistication. The first seven parties who tried to argue with him received efficient, swift responses. Few of those lasted more than four stanzas. Their errors had been theoretically straightforward, consisting typically in a misapplication of the sacred text, or ignorance about the details of their own lives—individuals who could be easily unmasked as insincere. Readers who knew the sacred text well could then claim to understand better the pitfalls of hypocrisy, to be more sensitive to disingenuousness—and, through the process of contrast surveyed in the first chapter, they could understand themselves to be sincerer and more skilled at the labor of self-knowledge than the doomed, of which there were many.[6]

The final three parties, however, presented very different arguments: relative to the first seven, they were aggressively, disturbingly sincere. They were clear-eyed about the limitations of identifying the deity's favor, and they did not try to claim good intentions. The pleasures of knowing how to answer these protests were likewise more emotionally complex. The eighth party didn't actually protest. This group of doomed individuals didn't insist they deserved any mercy. Instead, they admitted frankly that they weren't perfect. The poem called these the "impudenter sort" because they observed that trying to live without offending the deity would have been useless, since he "ordains . . . endless pain" for some and not for others. They knew, they claimed, that there was nothing to be done to change that. A ninth party of *"Heathen men"* followed, a party that colonial readers might quickly associate with Indigenous people prior to the evangelizing efforts of men like Roger Williams, Thomas Mayhew, or John Eliot. These people claimed innocence because they had lacked access to Christianity in the first place: "We did not know a Christ till now." Their use of an indefinite article ("a Christ") suggests surprise in discovering the salvific figure that precocious English readers would have recognized easily. A tenth party of *"Reprobate Infants"* concluded. They had died before they could even actively offend their deity. For the sake of the poem's rhetorical conceit, Wigglesworth gave them language, intellect, and a robust sense of justice. Thus endowed by their creator, they were able

---

6. First, there were the hypocrites—individuals who claimed to have been real Christians but who were revealed, in the final judgment, to have been pretending. Second were well-intentioned individuals whose good intentions turned out not to be good enough. Third came those who claimed they had the good intentions to eventually undergo full conversion but whose intentions had been foreclosed by death's unexpectedly swift arrival. If they'd had the time to pursue pleasure, the deity responded, they had time to pursue religion. A fourth party claimed lack of guidance, but the written word, the deity insisted, was guidance enough. Still, a fifth party insisted, what about those who had read the sacred text but hadn't understood its complexity? It wasn't that complicated, the deity replied. A sixth party claimed that they had been afraid of suffering loneliness and persecution. Well, they should have feared eternal suffering more. But wasn't the Christian god a *loving* deity, a seventh party claimed? How could such a deity *want* to see his creation suffer? The prospect of what we might call a sadistic, or at least vindictive, deity—one who took pleasure in producing suffering—seems to have unsettled Wigglesworth. His response, which went on for nine stanzas, insisted that the deity did not take pleasure in others' suffering and had already offered opportunities to take advantage of divine mercy.

to protest: "Not we, but he, ate of the Tree." They insisted that the offensive fruit-eating of the first man, Adam, had no bearing on their souls' status: "How is his sin our[s]?" These infants concisely expressed the criticism they shared with the prior two parties: "How could we sin . . . without consent . . . we never had a pow'r."[7]

The judging deity would not be stumped. He had answers. For each, as with the first seven, Wigglesworth's poem cited and quoted authorized sources, then versified the explanation derived from them. The deity's retorts increased in length, and they also increased in vehemence. During these responses, the divine judge let slip that he might have been emotionally invested in damning these dead, despite claiming that he was impartial, that he was simply following the rules his own father had given him. In response to the "impudenter sort," he made a show of insisting on this. These were not his rules, he argued. His father-deity had made them. "God did ordain Sinners to pain / and I to hell send none." The line is explicit, going out of its way to clarify who wanted this damnation in the first place. And in going out of its way, it stumbled: of the poem's nearly eighteen thousand lines of generally regular iambs, this one trips. Readers who anticipated the midline trochee "Sinners" as they scan and plan ahead would be more likely (particularly in repeated readings) to transform the line's first two syllables into trochees as well in order to restore balance to the line: "*God* did ordain *Sin*ners to pain." The filial judge insisted he was just doing his job.[8]

But *was* he just doing his job? Elsewhere, his responses suggest that he might have had skin in the game. He began his answer to the impudenter sort by showing his readiness to damn them, invoking the damning directly. J. L. Austin, lecturing three hundred years later to the successors of Wigglesworth's colleagues and students, would categorize "I damn you" as a "performative utterance," a statement that doesn't make a proposition that can be evaluated for its truth content so much as it does something in the world—or in this case, in the next world. Performative utterances tend to be direct. This one brought the second person and the first person together as the judge used language to act directly on his interlocutor. He sustained that direct second-person address, too, using the second person frequently in the rest of the eighth response. The

7. Wigglesworth, "Day of Doom," in Bosco, ed., *Poems*, 46 ("impudenter sort," line 1146), 47 ("ordains to endless pain," line 1153), 50 (*"Heathen men,"* line 1249, "We did not know," line 1273), 52 (*"Reprobate Infants,"* line 1321, "Not we," line 1336, "How is," line 1341, "had a pow'r," lines 1340–1343).

8. Ibid., 48, line 1193.

words "you," "your," and "yourselves" pepper its conclusion. They comprise a full quarter of the syllables of the stanza's last four lines:

> You have your selves, you and none else,
>   your selves have done to dy.
> You chose the way to your decay,
>   and perisht wilfully.

Between the start and the end of the deity's answer to these objectors, his emphasis shifted from his own powers of damnation to the activity of the damned in bringing about their own fate. Responsibility for damnation could not be much clearer than in this concluding statement. Why, then, invoke the first person, and with such force, at the start of the passage? What did it add?[9]

Theologically, not much. But emotionally, quite a lot. The "I" brought to the poem a sense of grievance. The "I" who damned was an "I" who had suffered. Furthermore, he had suffered without adequate attention and recognition. The judge eventually admitted that recognition of his actions mattered to him. In the penultimate stanza of this response, the judge again used the first person, but he wasn't indicating present tense actions ("I send," "I damn"). Instead, the judge recalled action in the past. He described having suffered, and repeatedly: "I often stood tend'ring my Blood," he claimed. He had bled many times. And if those impudenter sorts had been paying attention, they would know that he, singularly among all people, had not deserved it. What recompense had he received for his generous suffering? The first seven protesters had let his benevolence go to waste, but at least they had all recognized it. These final three despairing people, however, refused even to acknowledge that the deity's suffering had mattered. That was their impudence. They refused a gift, rejected the obligation that the gift proposed—an offense that early modern English people, who possessed a keen sensitivity to relations of gift and obligation, would have noticed as particularly insulting.[10]

The Christian deity may or may not be a resentful figure, but Wigglesworth wasn't writing sacred history; he was writing a fiction inspired by events gleaned and extrapolated from a shared lifestyle manual. Resentment and moral indignation heightened the emotional climax of his retelling, and if

---

9. Ibid., 47 ("I damn you," line 1170), 49 ("You have," lines 1237–1240); J. L. Austin, *How to Do Things with Words* (Cambridge, Mass., 1975).

10. Wigglesworth, "Day of Doom," in Bosco, ed., *Poems,* 47 ("I damn"), 48 ("I . . . send," line 1194), 49 ("I often stood," line 1225); Muldrew, *Economy of Obligation.*

the publication history is an index of his success, those qualities seem to have resonated with readers. Those readers, however, were not very likely to have been the younger children who Miller had suggested were the poem's biggest fans. Given modernist lyric sensibilities that associate prosodic regularity with childish verse, as well as Miller's language describing these children ("terrified," being driven "crazy"), it may be easy to presume that this poem's greatest enthusiasts were non-adult children. This minor observation clarifies the poem's gratifications—specifically, whose ears and memories it delighted. Maybe younger readers did see themselves in a position analogous to the judge. Maybe they did feel themselves suspended between parents who made severe moral demands on one hand and weaker, dependent individuals on the other, from whom they desired recognition, if not gratitude (to say nothing of recompense). But that unhappy in-between state better describes children who had grown up and become parents themselves and yet who continued to feel obliged to requite the decades of care and attention from their own parents. Infants and young children, after all, were not likely to be the buyers driving sales of the poem.[11]

Colonial parents, who continued to be their own parents' children after having children themselves, carried the memory of their childhood into adulthood, into their longings to transmit their visions of justice to the "precious and immortal soules of their inheritors." The poem assuaged these longings when it transformed a descriptive proposition (*I inherited debt*) into a prescriptive one (*inherited debt is ineluctable*). The latter proposition was the thesis that concluded the parade of protestations. In the conversation between the infant and the judge, the last and the longest in the poem, the deity explained the logic of these damnations: the doctrine of original sin. Culpability, the judge explained, transcended an individual's experience of will. "But what you call old *Adam's* Fall . . . both his and yours it was." The tendency to offend the deity's purity was so reliable that these babies' wills—all babies' wills—would, had their places been switched with Adam, always have led them to choose to break the divine rules. Furthermore, the poem argued that the burden of "original sin" was an inheritance. It wasn't simply like the freedom to choose that distinguished all humans from animals; it was logically inseparable from it. Though these infants protested that they had not consented to that inheritance, the judge observed that they had not protested their inheritance of the "welfare" and "so much good" that they likewise enjoyed as humans. These

11. Miller, *Errand*, 218; Meredith Martin, *The Rise and Fall of Meter: Poetry and English National Culture, 1860–1930* (Princeton, N.J., 2012).

were gifts received at birth. If one received "good" from one's parents—alphabetic literacy, a book of poems, the freedom to choose piety—one was also indebted to choose correctly. As with eternal life, birth to Christian parents was both a promise and a threat.[12]

The Day of Doom did not invent the resentment of the adult child. It only expressed it in a vivid, narrative fashion. For most early modern English people, saturated in the vocabulary and the meaning-making templates of Christian doctrine since their earliest days, most of this emotional landscape would have felt intuitively familiar. But it didn't have to be this way—adult proselytes, such as Dorcas and the 1666 Plymouth converts, knew this and probably noticed settlers' attachments to injury more astutely than their white counterparts did. They would have noticed more explicitly Christianity's foundation in scenes of gift and injury, and, in turn, they would have understood the obligation to recompense, especially through the Christian values of personal renunciation, even suffering. Christian piety on the colonial frontier required even more renunciations for the sake of piety's success. It also required individuals to absorb those renunciations, along with other injuries of life's journey, as very important, maybe essential, to their sense of selfhood, and to identify virtue as the meaning of their suffering. Wigglesworth's poem articulated that experience of suffering and affirmed its reality to members of families that had lived through struggle for at least one, sometimes two generations. Hot on the heels of the poem's debut, a complementary expression of unsatisfied debt emerged: the jeremiad and its litany of intergenerational dissatisfaction. The jeremiad gratified many of the same desires for recognition as Wigglesworth's long poem had. Early settlers might have noticed this affinity, but they didn't need to notice for it to work, as it powerfully shored up their sense of justice. This story intensified resentment's conditions: it fell on the ears of aggrieved parents and their offspring, reminding those children, week after week, of their burdensome debts. The jeremiad emphasized the obligations of birth. In doing so, it intensified allegiance to a version of personhood organized by race in its earliest manifestations. These sermons, extending the doctrine of Wigglesworth's poem, heightened longings for recognition that expressed themselves in very costly ways.[13]

12. Richard Mather, *A Farewel Exhortation to the Church and People of Dorchester in New England* (Cambridge, Mass., 1657), 10 ("precious"); Wigglesworth, "Day of Doom," in Bosco, ed., *Poems,* 53 ("old *Adam's* Fall," lines 1365, 1368), 54 ("welfare," line 1393).

13. Karen Halttunen, "Humanitarianism and the Pornography of Pain in Anglo-American Culture," *American Historical Review,* C (1995), 303–334.

Most men found satisfying recognition soon enough, in their quiet transformations from debtors to creditors. Increase Mather, as he circulated among the ministerial elite in Boston (such as William Stoughton or James Allen), knew himself to be indebted for his profession and his social standing to his father, Richard Mather. Like most men around him, however, he eventually came to feel empowered to claim the status of creditor as part of that inheritance from his father. Most adults who were creditors were debtors, though the debts of adults, particularly adult men, tend to evade visibility. Few adult inheritors liked to recall debt for its own sake, and those numbers were even smaller among those who had the time and the social standing to write texts that their own inheritors would preserve. Adult inheritors preferred to claim the social power of credit. Early modern English people, even those on a frontier distant from England, shared what Craig Muldrew has called an "economy of obligation," and in colonial New England, it was happier to inhabit this economy from the position of the creditor than the debtor. This had been so from very early on in the plantation's history. In one of the most memorable passages in his *Of Plimoth Plantation,* for example, William Bradford presumed this preference on the part of his subjects. Individual Separatists, he wrote in narrating the end of the "Common Course" in 1623, preferred not to be materially obliged to each other. They "deemd it a kind of slaverie." Here, Bradford didn't mean individuals; he meant households. He turned directly to the case of Plymouth's "yong-men that were most able and fitte for labour and service [who] did repine that they should spend their time and streingth to worke for other mens wives and children, without any recompence." These exemplary young men rejected communal labor because they could presume that labor for their own wives and children generated satisfying recompense. No one needed to make this explicit. Young men knew they could reasonably expect that their labor for their households would produce returns, and not only material ones.[14]

Increase Mather's most powerful cultural artifact, the jeremiad, drew momentum from the fact that the family already was, as Lionel Trilling has observed, a "narrative institution." The jeremiad made sense because, in the stories early modern English people told themselves about good, happy social development, the family was the place where sensible men might reliably look for one particular return. These men could look forward, the jeremiad

14. Muldrew, *Economy of Obligation;* William Bradford, *Bradford's History "Of Plimoth Plantation": From the Original Manuscript, with a Report of the Proceedings Incident to the Return of the Manuscript to Massachusetts* (Boston, 1898), 163.

promised, to becoming masterful arbiters of sincerity, to wielding authority over the young: moral authority that translated into social and political authority. Social historians have shown that matters between parents and children were often quite loving, that "mutual dependence" characterized quotidian life, particularly between generations. Yet one of the most popular genres of cultural expression in the colony rarely depicted that dependence as a two-way street. And the texts that document that relationship as it was lived suggest parents were often ambivalent about this mutuality and might not have wanted their children to understand it so. Parents tried to tip representations of mutuality in their favor. This wasn't a strategy of deliberate duplicity. They weren't trying to ruin their children's emotional lives—far from it. They had reasons to believe they knew what was best for those youth. But what they knew about their children wasn't the whole story—the story of their sincere desires for their children can obscure the limits these parents faced in understanding themselves and especially in understanding the consequences of their own experiences of childhood. When they manipulated the scales of mutual dependence, these parents were often responding, with a significant degree of self-opacity, to their own experience of being deeply, unhappily obliged.[15]

Some of those debts can seem obvious, but in appearing so, they easily slip off the account books. Children's dependence on parents, for one, can seem simple. Most children required protection for survival, especially on the colonial frontier. Settler elders encouraged fear of non-Christian enemies implicitly and explicitly, and patriarchs imagined themselves to be unique sources of protection from cherished threats. Children also depended on parents for access to "competence," or relative independence. For many young men, competence meant helming a household; for many young women, it meant supporting the man at the helm. At the end of parents' earthly lives, children were, still further, indebted to them for bequeathed property. Unlike in England or the Chesapeake colonies, New England families sought to distribute inheritances widely rather than narrowly. Frontier English parents would go as far as transplanting to a new town and becoming members in a new church in order to ensure access to land to claim and bequeath. Children weren't inert recipients of all this work; after the age of roughly seven or eight,

15. Lionel Trilling, *Sincerity and Authenticity: The Charles Eliot Norton Lectures, 1969–1970* (Cambridge, Mass., 1972), 139; Miller, *Errand*; Bercovitch, *American Jeremiad*; Anne S. Lombard, *Making Manhood: Growing up Male in Colonial New England* (Cambridge, Mass., 2003), 47. See also Holly Brewer, *By Birth or Consent: Children, Law, and the Anglo-American Revolution in Authority* (Williamsburg, Va., and Chapel Hill, N.C., 2005); and Helena M. Wall, *Fierce Communion: Family and Community in Early America* (Cambridge, Mass., 1990).

they could contribute to the household's labor. This was particularly the case during the first decades of settlement, since, as Anne S. Lombard points out, most of the first English settlers in America had to take up manual farming labor, whether or not they had been farmers in England. Sometimes, children were sent out to neighbors' and friends' households. The motives for this practice varied—from wishing for the individual child's moral development, to preventing the high rates of adolescent vagrancy that the first planters had experienced in England, to securing economic benefits for their birth families—but it seems to have been a conventional feature of New England settlers' shared lives. Children were also parents' hopes for support in their eventual old age, when they would no longer be able to care for themselves.[16]

Mutual dependence characterized spiritual relations, too, though in a fashion that was much less self-evident. Parenting was hard, complicated work. It wasn't enough to provide materially for one's future inheritors. Richard Mather observed in 1657 that any parent on earth could do that, even the enemies of good Christians—he identified "Turks and Indians." Christian parents also had to manage the household's spiritual condition. They thought they had great power and therefore great responsibility when it came to their children's souls, and this was particularly keen among the Calvinists. Best practices in soul care were the topic of heated disputes across generations, among parents who had once been the objects of such fretting themselves. Parents wanted to perfect techniques to maximize the likelihood that their children would enjoy a felicitous eternity rather than a tormented one. They tried direct pedagogy and indirect influence, using didactic literature like Wigglesworth's *Day of Doom*, James Janeway's *Token for Children*, or John Cotton's *Spiritual Milk for Boston Babes*. They also tried baptism, church attendance, and discipline of varying

16. Lombard, *Making Manhood*, 6–7, esp. 7 ("competence"); Thomas Morton, *New English Canaan; or, New Canaan, Containing an Abstract of New England* ... (1637), rpt. in Peter Force, coll., *Tracts and Other Papers, Relating Principally to the Origin, Settlement, and Progress of the Colonies in North America, from the Discovery of the Country to the Year 1776* (Washington, D.C., 1838), II, no. 5, 77; Ann M. Little, *Abraham in Arms: War and Gender in Colonial New England* (Philadelphia, 2007), 22–25; Daniel Vickers, "Competency and Competition: Economic Culture in Early America," *William and Mary Quarterly*, 3d Ser., XLVII (1990), 3–29; Brewer, *By Birth or Consent*, 37–39; Anne S. Brown and David D. Hall, "Family Strategies and Religious Practice: Baptism and the Lord's Supper in Early New England," in Hall, ed., *Lived Religion in America: Toward a History of Practice* (Princeton, N.J., 1997), 41–68; Carole Shammas, Marylynn Salmon, and Michel Dahlin, *Inheritance in America: From Colonial Times to the Present* (New Brunswick, N.J., 1987), 11; Edmund S. Morgan, *The Puritan Family: Religion and Domestic Relations in Seventeenth-Century New England* (New York, 1966); Susan Brigden, "Youth and the English Reformation," *Past and Present*, no. 95 (1982), 37–67.

degrees of emotional vehemence, which included efforts by parents never to disagree with each other about that discipline. No single act, parents agreed, would determine a happy eternity for one's offspring. And it was possible, at the end of the day, that this labor wasn't even necessary—according to the contract-like agreement between their deity and their figurative biblical predecessor Abraham, these actions might have been redundant because English children might have inherited favor simply by being born to good Christians. It wasn't certain, but parents deeply hoped it was, so keenly that, by the 1670s, it had become a cliché to propose that a child's exemption from eternal torment might not depend on early modern helicopter parenting but on what "ran through" the organs that lived between his mother's and father's legs. It was, in short, very tricky, maybe impossible, to know whether the immense work that parents put into parenting was worthwhile.[17]

But even in their spiritual relationships with parents, children weren't inert recipients, draining resources with abandon. They were the sources of important immaterial goods. Anne S. Brown and David D. Hall suggest this when they observe that New England's adults didn't simply find children useful. Rather, they "craved" them—that is, they desired them on a level that exceeded conscious reason. Adults depended on children to sustain their wills after their death, as Richard Mather intimated when he reminded parents, "You know your selves must not live alwayes." And thoughts of death hinted at more terrifying forms of dependence: children had the power to pull the rug out from under parents' confidence in their own claims to sincerity. A parent might possess rigorous personal morality and a persuasive conviction of their divinely favored status, but a child's behavior and disposition could suggest otherwise. According to the idea of genital transmission that Increase Mather had expressed, an impious child indicated that the parent had never been among the favored in the first place—and as the characters in Wigglesworth's poems saw, this outcome could be a very unhappy surprise. Richard Mather put the matter directly: if children were to be "plagued and damned in Hell for their sin," then "Parents also shall be in the same condition." Finally, men nearing adulthood especially craved children because paternity meant access

17. Richard Mather, *A Farewel Exhortation to the Church and People of Dorchester in New England* (Cambridge, Mass., 1657), 10 ("Turks and Indians"); Increase Mather, *Pray for the Rising Generation* (Cambridge, Mass., 1678), 12 ("ran through"); Lombard, *Making Manhood*, 23; Philip Greven, *The Protestant Temperament: Patterns in Child-Rearing, Religious Experience, and the Self in Early America* (New York, 1977), 34; Wall, *Fierce Communion*, 10–11.

to widely recognized social credit. They could then exercise moral authority both within their household—and beyond it toward their neighbors.[18]

Historians see mutual dependence clearly. Colonial children might have, too. But if parents also saw this reciprocity, some wanted to prevent their children from understanding it. It could make parents vulnerable to something like extortion, as Helena M. Wall has sensitively suggested in the example of a child in Essex County who wrote to his or her mother from what was probably an apprenticeship to request more money. The child cast money as an investment in the mother's own future: "I pray bee not [bac]kward for my preferment for I hope to bee a comfort to you in your old age." The thought of such leverage was unpleasant to some parents, who recommended keeping dependence a secret and speculated on how to misrepresent it. Such were the plans of Cotton Mather, son of Increase, grandson of Richard. Cotton developed psychologically sophisticated punishments for his children, and he described those punishments in precise detail. He wanted his children to imagine that they mattered little to him, and therefore they should not take for granted any attention from or intimacy with their parents: "To be chased for a while out of *my Presence* I would make to be look'd upon, as the sorest Punishment in the family." The rich documentation of parental affection doesn't nullify moments like these. They complement each other. Moments of chilled affection underscored the sovereignty of the parent, whose capacity to withhold intimacy was also capacity to control intimacy's value. Children grew into adulthood constantly reminded that their parents' labors for the good of the household outweighed their own.[19]

Cotton Mather didn't develop these ideas alone. Almost everyone in the reform Protestant colony already held these attitudes by the time Cotton was born because his father had popularized them, particularly in the jeremiad sermon that he caused to flourish in the third and fourth decades of English colonial settlement. Increase Mather wasn't the first to use the template, but he did begin publishing them aggressively, catalyzing the colony's printing industry. The jeremiad expressed anxiety about the future and wounded disappointment about the sufferings of the past, and it was named after the biblical teacher and prophet who, in settlers' sacred stories, had warned the

18. Brown and Hall, "Family Strategies," in Hall, ed., *Lived Religion in America*, 43 ("craved"); Lombard, *Making Manhood*; Mather, *Farewel*, 9 ("You know"), 10 ("plagued and damned").

19. Wall, *Fierce Communion*, 120 ("I pray"); *Diary of Cotton Mather, 1681–1724*, Massachusetts Historical Society, *Collections*, 7th Ser., VII–VIII (Boston, 1911–1912), VII, 536 ("To be chased"); Greven, *Protestant Temperament*, 50–54; Mitchell Robert Breitwieser, *Cotton Mather and Benjamin Franklin: The Price of Representative Personality* (Cambridge, 1984), 35–45.

chosen political community of the risks they ran in their insufficiently sincere comportment toward their deity. The young, the jeremiad claimed, were not working as arduously for the flourishing of the community as their parents had. Their actions were hollow, their hearts duplicitous. They were overdrawing their credit. Thus the community could expect severe retribution for the chil-. dren's negligence—if not from parents, from the deity himself. Their paranoia toward non-English neighbors made this template extraordinarily durable.[20]

The jeremiad gratified parents' wish to control the terms of debt, to moderate their expression of "craving." This wish energized a renewal of old debates about baptism's value. Whereas the question had once been, *What did baptism retroactively signify?* its tenor changed: *What did baptism's absence portend for the future?* Children who were not baptized and who did not choose to undergo the rigorous work of proving their sincerity (or who thought it prudent to proceed more slowly and cautiously with their spiritual lives) were excluded from civic enfranchisement. Deferral didn't always mean impiety. It could also mean, as several critics have observed, a sense of the gravity of the endeavor, a sense of *"seriousness"* regarding "the demands of the fathers," as Sacvan Bercovitch puts it. Nevertheless, the timing did confront the legitimacy of congregational governance awkwardly—what if there came to be no plausibly true congregation to legitimize political life? In response, many parents, extrapolating their deductions that divine favor might have been inherited, sought to make baptism easier. If the practice was only ever provisional, it couldn't hurt. Or could it? On one hand, a decision to decline or even delay adult baptism might suggest the artificiality of the colony's legitimacy. On the other, baptism's expansion was also risky. As Holly Brewer has observed, the clearer the certainty that children had of their inheritances, the harder they were to control. In response to that risk, the jeremiad was a provisional stopgap: its emphasis on defaulted debts gratified parents seeking to preserve at least the emotional aspect of that control.[21]

Not all ministers turned to the theme of filial debt as consistently and emphatically as Increase Mather. Most invoked it eclectically, as one technique among many. Some ministers even cautioned against overapplying it. William Hubbard, pastor at Ipswich and, in some accounts, Increase's rival,

20. Michael G. Hall, *The Last American Puritan: The Life of Increase Mather, 1639–1723* (Middletown, Conn., 1988), 135.

21. Ibid., 87, 140–146; Sacvan Bercovitch, *The Puritan Origins of the American Self* (New Haven, Conn., 1975), 97; Brewer, *By Birth or Consent,* 37–39, 45–86. See also Katherine Gerbner, "Beyond the 'Halfway Covenant': Church Membership, Extended Baptism, and Outreach in Cambridge, Massachusetts, 1656–1667," *New England Quarterly,* LXXXV (2012), 281–301.

openly criticized overapplication.[22] At the 1676 Election Day sermon—one of the most public forums for colonial polemic, during one of the most volatile years of the colony's history—Hubbard observed the popularity of ministers' "complain[ing] of the present age wherein they live." James Allen, teacher at Boston's First Church, suggested something similar, though less aggressively, in his own election sermon three years later. It might seem logical to "charge the positive and meritorious evil upon the times"—that is, to understand material struggles as a consequence of the spiritual failings of the present, but, he argued, that was too facile an engagement with history. It preempted a nuanced understanding of the deity's power. Ministers like Allen and Hubbard resisted the jeremiad's clichés. Yet they felt the need to make their departure from the jeremiad's conventions explicit, particularly in those high-stakes colonial forums, the yearly election sermons. Their expressions of hesitation suggest how common those clichés had become, how attractive the later Mathers and other ministers knew that rhetoric to be.[23]

The jeremiad's logic was ubiquitous. It went beyond sermons. In general, Christian ideas of personhood cherished the proposition that existence meant a priori debt, and, as Wigglesworth's poem suggested, childhood was an acute experience of debt. The theme of childhood debt especially pleased adults who didn't like to think about the intensity of their own debtor status. The jeremiad didn't so much offer these elders a way out of the debt as it did a diminution of debt's felt intensity. Those men who had access to documentation, who wrote and whose writing endures, often wielded the most social credit. They were also, necessarily, some of the most obliged. They owed both the deity and their parents, whose social standing afforded them the distinction and eminence that, in turn, afforded them access to what would become archival longevity. The devotional literature of settlement emphasized this debt. In 1646, the man who would become Increase Mather's father-in-law, John Cotton, published *Spiritual Milk for Boston Babes* (1646), a catechism that parents used to teach their children the basics of the spiritual principles that they hoped to bequeath. It articulates childhood indebtedness with remarkable clarity. The text invited children to perform their knowledge of the deity's rules and taught them how to apply those rules to their lives. The fifth of those rules required

22. On the rivalry, see Anne Kusener Nelsen, "King Philip's War and the Hubbard-Mather Rivalry," *WMQ*, 3d Ser., XXVII (1970), 615–629; Hall, *Last American Puritan*, 112–126.

23. William Hubbard, *The Happiness of a People in the Wisdom of Their Rulers* (Boston, 1676), 51; James Allen, *New-Englands Choicest Blessing and the Mercy Most to Be Desired by All That Wish Well to This People* (Boston, 1679), 6.

them to "Honour thy Father and thy Mother . . . that thy dayes may be long in the land, which the Lord thy God giveth thee." Then, the text prompted children to elaborate. Of what did "the honor due unto [parents]" consist? "[Reverence], Obedience, and (when I am able), Recompense." Maturity was defined by children's capacity to repay their debts to parents, to answer satisfyingly the investment that Bradford's exemplary young men saw as the happier alternative to slavery. Parents encouraged children to understand themselves as perpetually owing, regardless of their contributions to their parents' households during minority.[24]

Adulthood didn't mean debt's nullification, however, much less its abolition. Adulthood meant only greater command over debt. Although the jeremiads weren't exceptional in their message about owing, they did help to reinforce the authority of the fathers as the perpetually owed. The jeremiad might have exaggerated the dependence and debt of children, occluding the rich world of mutual dependence between generations, but within the jeremiad, the emphasis on that debt has not been exaggerated, and those public sermons expressed and intensified an emotional reality. As they were rehearsed time and again in public forums, the genre fortified parents' claims that children should never consider themselves free from debt. The theme of unchosen debt appears consistently across these texts. In 1657, the year of Dorcas's manumission, Richard Mather expressed the theme of unchosen debt in broad, very abstract strokes: the deity had "sen[t] his Christ *into the world to save sinners,*" yet, he observed, "sinners . . . neglect to come to this Christ or to accept of him, as if they had no need of him, or could do well enough without him." Neglecting to acknowledge receipt of a gift was a very grave offense, Mather insisted: it would "doubtless be the damnation, the great and deep damnation of a world of men at the last day."[25]

That conditional relationship (*if* special gifts, *then* special debts) obsessed colonial elders for decades. "Hast thou Estate which the Lord hath blessed thee with[?]" asked Jonathan Mitchell ten years later, in 1667. It would be your responsibility not only to *"do no hurt,*" but according to your place and opportunity do *good* to *Israel.*" Ten years later, in 1677, Samuel Hooker sounded that theme in a series of rhetorical questions: "Is this the Nation that I gathered out of the midst of a Nation, with a mighty hand, and a stretched out arm? Is this the people for whose sake I rebuked the Heathen?" Were these the same beneficiaries who also failed to "[call] the Sabbath honourable . . . do you say,

24. John Cotton, *Spiritual Milk for Boston Babes* (1646; rpt. Boston, 1684), 4.
25. Mather, *Farewel,* 23–24.

what a weariness is it?" Hooker's rhetorical questions invited congregants to evaluate what obstacles made a swift "yes"—a swift self-identification as the indebted—difficult. If Hooker's prosopopoeia, evoking Wigglesworth's aggrieved, bleeding judge, did not convey the matter's urgency convincingly, he could put it still more bluntly: "Believe it sirs; tis a dangerous, a very dangerous thing to forsake the wayes of truth and holiness." Another ten years later, in 1687, James Allen observed that the *"People of God,"* whom the deity had blessed with the possibility of sovereign favor, had a greater debt to that deity for right behavior. They were *"more fearfully under the guilt of"* returning to their former idolatries. Ten years after that, in 1697, Increase Mather—grown and no longer in Dorchester but in Boston, a few miles away from James Allen's congregation—was still sounding the theme. He compared the degeneracy of the present generation with those who had returned from Babylonian captivity by the special care of their deity. Both were guilty of a "neglect of Divine Institutions and Worldliness" despite receiving great material favor. For children in the present, such disregard was that generation's "special Sins."[26]

Voracious were the credit columns of the elder generation. Even the books that passed these teachings on were counted as debts. When Samuel Greene and Marmaduke Johnson published "NEW ENGLANDS True Interest NOT TO LIE"—the sermon that William Stoughton, teacher alongside Richard Mather at Dorchester, delivered at Boston's Election Day in 1668—they appended a preface by a "J. S.," who instructed "the Christian Reader" not to take for granted the added ease they found in the printed text. It was an "advantage" to be able to "stay and dwell upon what we have first a minde to . . . without depriving our selves of opportunity of doing the like, with any other part of it afterward." That advantage came at a cost. "God, whose Providence hath brought this to thy hands, expecteth a sutable improvement." Books, and alphabetic literacy to read them, were gifts. They demanded commensurate, reciprocal piety. When Increase Mather published a biography of his father, Richard, he used his father's authority to rehearse that message. In the biography's conclusion, the younger Mather quoted his father's will. The document included specific provisions for his immediate offspring and, more generally, an itemized list of the gifts that his father, along with other elders, had given the colony's youth: "Their Father which begat them, and their Mother which

26. Jonathan Mitchel, *Nehemiah on the Wall in Troublesom Times* (Cambridge, Mass., 1671), 25; Samuel Hooker, *Righteousness Rained from Heaven* (Cambridge, Mass., 1677), 17–18; James Allen, *Neglect of Supporting and Maintaining the Pure Worship of God* (Boston, 1687), 10–11; Increase Mather, *David Serving His Generation* (Boston, 1698), 18.

bare them, with all the Prayers which they have made, and Tears which they have shed for them, their Example, their Admonitions and Exhortations which they have administered to them." Ventriloquizing his father, Increase explained why those gifts mattered: "All these will rise up against them as so many Testimonies for their Condemnation at the last day." According to the jeremiad's logic, nearly everything constituted a binding debt to one's elders: from the pamphlet in hand to one's memory of childhood punishments. For all these, children were expected at least to express gratitude in performances of sincerity. The future of the colony, parents said, depended on that obligation.[27]

For more than half a century, intimate and public discourse insisted on this debt. Ministers knew it was a popular theme. The sensitive among them knew that parents wanted recognition of their own lifelong faithfulness intensely, especially because so little of their parenting work could be definitely identified as worthwhile. Ministers counseled these parents, and many were parents themselves. Children, dependent as they were materially, were a captive audience for those litanies of debt. Although many children, on reaching adulthood, would be able to lower the volume on these litanies, they still had consequences. Anne S. Lombard has suggested some of these costs in reviewing strange outbursts of adolescent violence. Young men in the colony felt "resentment" and "anger toward the fathers and masters who had so much power over them." Resentment, however, outpaces anger; it isn't a neat synonym. More tenaciously than anger, resentment binds the aggrieved to the offender in a relationship that clings to a sense of justice, as Friedrich Nietzsche would assert in his *Genealogy of Morality*. It's not necessary to go as far as Nietzsche's theory of *ressentiment*, however, to observe resentment's "existential depth and emotional complexity." Even garden-variety resentment can illuminate some sources of an individual's commitment to their vision of fairness and justice. When, as Lombard begins to observe, these children burst with irrepressible violence, they expressed a sense of the unfairness of the accounting sheets their parents manipulated. They carried this intuition into adulthood when they became the parents of their parents' children's children. Those outbursts reveal sources of injustice, but they also point to the structures that preserved them. These adult children by and large did not reject the principles to which they'd been subjected. Rather, they expressed

27. William Stoughton, *New-Englands True Interest: Not to Lie* (Boston, 1670), 3; Increase Mather, *The Life and Death of That Reverend Man of God, Mr. Richard Mather, Teacher of the Church in Dorchester in New England* (Cambridge, 1670), 37 ("their Father," "all these").

renewed fealty to them, revised through an alignment with emerging regimes of race and blood.[28]

Why, English youth on a remote frontier would have wondered, did sincerity have to be such thankless work? For elders, the answer was, "Because God said so." The answer to youth was some version of "because the elders said so." Recompense would come, for some, later. The elders who said so were the same leaders who kept insisting—week after week, in sermons, in print, and probably in conversation—that in such hard work, the youth were ever derelict in their duties, and youth depended on recognition from their elders to move fruitfully into their own adulthoods. For early modern reform Protestants, in general, successfully claiming identities required great labor, even great suffering, in pursuit of the requisite social recognition. If one had a body that looked male, success consisted in acquiring property and parenthood, and it brought authority to assess others' claims to spiritual sincerity. Yet that success wouldn't come quickly. For others, it wouldn't come at all. Within a community that placed historically novel importance on the spiritual meaning of everyday life, to be told, week after week, year in, year out, that these efforts weren't sufficiently sincere would likely exacerbate unhappiness. This "state of injury," as Wendy Brown has described it, tends to "[produce] an affect (rage, righteousness) that overwhelms the hurt" of unrecognized suffering. This would be an especially powerful desire in contexts characterized by unprecedented contact with global difference and by heightened emphasis on personal responsibility—contexts very much like the early modern frontier, as the first and second chapters showed. In turn, Brown notes, that affect seeks "to inflict hurt as the sufferer has hurt." Such an observation would lead us to expect to see settlers who longed for recognition engaging in seemingly irrational, even cruel, violence. They did. In this longing, settlers undertook acts of populist violence that made visible their otherwise-unacknowledged travails and that afforded them some of the authority that would, they felt, aptly recompense the unending labor of producing a community of pure hearts.[29]

Disappointment, unhappiness, and unease stalked generations of colonists. Certainly not everyone was bitter every moment of every day. It's likely

28. Lombard, *Making Manhood*, 138 ("anger"), 169 ("resentment"); Ashraf H. A. Rushdy, *After Injury: A Historical Anatomy of Forgiveness, Resentment, and Apology* (Oxford, 2018), 158 ("existential depth"); Friedrich Nietzsche, *On the Genealogy of Morality*, trans. Carol Diethe (Cambridge, 1997).

29. Wendy Brown, *States of Injury: Power and Freedom in Late Modernity* (Princeton, N.J., 1995), 52–77, esp. 68; Michael Zuckerman, "The Fabrication of Identity in Early America," *WMQ*, 3d Ser., XXXIV (1977), 183–214.

that most quotidian interactions weren't particularly morose or aggressive. Still, if settlers had instead found ways to name their dissatisfactions with their shared lives, if they had learned to describe more directly the structures that made them unhappy beyond their familiar, hypercognized templates for shame, if they had chosen not to accept repression's scripts for their lives, their individual triumphs might have been less collectively costly. Forgoing over-familiarized scripts for self-recognition might have averted the vehemence of the war that broke out in the 1670s among the children and the grandchildren of the first planters, might have surprised chroniclers a little less. English violence startled settler historians, sometimes caught them off guard. Historian Daniel Gookin was especially sensitive to it. In his *Historical Account of the Doings and Sufferings of the Christian Indians in New England, in the Years 1675, 1676, 1677* (1836), he noted the "great . . . rage and unreasonable prejudice" of the English militia, their "causeless rage and cruelty." He recalled the "fury of the people" and their eagerness to "[wreak] their rage." Gookin's perception may not surprise modern historians—first, because rage during war may seem banal to twenty-first-century readers; second, because Gookin was a well-known sympathizer with the Native converts who were at the heart of the martial dispute and who were most often the recipients of that rage. Yet he wasn't the only one to notice. Rhode Island deputy governor John Easton, in his *Relation of the Indian War,* noted settlers' anger, how its intensity rebounded against them in foiling the possibility for alliance and strategic compromise. He recalled, for example, how Weetamoo, *saunkskwa* of the Pocassets, had sought to negotiate peace with her neighbors at Plymouth colony, but "some of our English also in fury against all Indians, would not consent that she should be received to our Island." Settlers' wrath got in the way of treaties for peace. Nathaniel Saltonstall, in one of the tracts that comprised his pamphlet collection, *The Present State of New-England* (1675), observed that fury and noted its popularity. Narrating a mob that broke into a Boston prison in an attempt to hang Algonquian converts suspected of being insincere in their fidelity to the English, Saltonstall even gave that fury a name. He called it "the People's Rage."[30]

---

30. Daniel Gookin, *An Historical Account of the Doings and Sufferings of the Christian Indians in New England in the Years 1675, 1676, 1677,* American Antiquarian Society, *Transactions and Collections,* II (Cambridge, 1836), 423–524, esp. 453 ("great . . . rage and unreasonable prejudice"), 454 ("causeless rage and cruelty"), 485 ("fury of"), 494 ("[wreak] their rage"); John Easton, *A Relation of the Indian War, by Mr. Easton, of Rhode Island, 1675,* ed. Paul Royster, *Faculty Publications, UNL Libraries,* 33 (2006), 8 ("some of our English"); N[athaniel] S[altonstall],

Fury and violence gratified English people who had been on the receiving end of a lifetime's worth of accusations of insincerity. Young men were among the most visibly angry. Sometimes civic and martial leaders sanctioned their rage, but often they didn't. Youthful rage at times expressed itself in unseating and replacing these elders and leaders. That temper, Jenny Hale Pulsipher observes, wasn't unique to them as men, however. During this time, "neither gender nor class was a barrier to anti-Indian attacks, but the violence does seem to have had a generational slant." Colonial chroniclers noticed this, too. Gookin, again, was one of the more sensitive witnesses. Narrating the mob that tried to break into the Boston prison, Gookin clarified who these rage-filled English were. The "disorderly rout in Boston," as Gookin recalled it, consisted of "about thirty boys and young fellows." Though the captives were from Natick, though they had performed sincere conversion, though they were "not accused of any crime," they still infuriated these young men, who sought to "kill them, lest they should be released." These acts of violence frustrated plans for strategic affiliation with Native converts, who men like Gookin and Eliot had hoped would side with the English in the event of a frontier war. In 1675, when an English-Algonquian party under the leadership of James Richardson passed through the town of Woburn, a "young fellow, a soldier named Knight, discharged his musket and killed one of the Indians stone dead, being very near him." Such episodes troubled Gookin. Near the end of his manuscript, he tried to assemble an account of these conflicts and their causes and to derive an explanation. "I cannot deny," he wrote, "but that many of them, especially the younger sort" were particularly vulnerable to the spirit of rage.[31]

"Boys will be boys" is one answer to Gookin's puzzlement. But it's a satisfying answer only when the category "boy," a condition of violent naivete, exists outside of history. Colonial settlers certainly didn't invent the "boy," but the experience of boyhood in these settlements was shaped by priorities specific to that context. Here, boyhood meant the promise of gendered empowerment, a promise that was limited, for an indeterminate period, by the disempowerment of youth. As historians of the colonial family like Lombard and Wall have pointed out, this was an unhappy condition, not

The Present State of New-England with Respect to the Indian War . . . , in Samuel G. Drake, ed., *The Old Indian Chronicle: Being a Collection of Exceeding Rare Tracts* (Boston, 1867), 153.

31. Jenny Hale Pulsipher, "Massacre at Hurtleberry Hill: Christian Indians and English Authority in Metacom's War," *WMQ*, 3d Ser., LIII (1996), 459–486, esp. 466, 477; Gookin, *Historical Account of the Doings and Sufferings*, 466 ("rout"), 475 ("young fellow"), 515 ("younger sort"); S[altonstall], *Present State*, in Drake, ed., *Old Indian Chronicle*, 150–154.

least because it seemed inescapable. It was not easy for these young people to consider, even to imagine, challenging the socially organizing norms of gender and age in seventeenth-century English society. Settlers' biopoetic practices—the stories they told themselves and each other about happiness and fulfillment—rehearsed the same scripts for recognizing the self and the returns on suffering. Alternatives would have been extraordinarily difficult to imagine, much less to propose in place of the genocidal outcomes that settlers wanted to believe—desperately and sincerely—were divine will. Yet the near-impossibility of thinking beyond those structures does not mean that gender and age as social values were innocent and undamaging. These values were costly for settlers; their bungled attempts at alliances show this. These values were costly, too, for their neighbors. Because settlers did not want to consider that boyhood's defining social values were fabricated rather than divinely granted, they needed to believe that the rage of English youth was unpreventable. Their attempt to fix these violent circumstances made the lives of their Native allies more vulnerable and dispossessed them further, exiling them to Deer Island and recruiting double agents among those who wanted to save their families from starvation. Contemporary scholarship on racial innocence affirms this harmful, if unintended, effect.[32]

These men were sincere in their longing for recognition. They deeply wanted their elders to affirm that they were good. The effects of that desire, however, constitute one of the most profound challenges to the idea that what settlers knew about themselves is a sufficient resource to explain their actions. In their commitment to organizing their lives around English ideals of gender and maturity, they were probably as sincere as any society ever has been. Occasionally, they also noticed that youthful rage wasn't necessarily natural or innate. Almost four decades earlier, this degree of aggression caught settlers off-guard. It called for explanation. John Underhill, one of the more enthusiastic killers of the colonial period, knew that his readers would want him to explain his ruthlessness. "It may bee demanded, Why should you be so furious (as some have said) should not Christians have more mercy and compassion?" His passive subjunctive "it may be demanded" wasn't hypothetical. He had specific witnesses and their perplexity in mind when he proposed this question. It was younger fellow soldiers who were shocked by his actions. "Great and dolefull was the bloudy sight to the view of young souldiers that never had beene in Warre." During the first decades of colonization, when

32. Robin Bernstein, *Racial Innocence: Performing American Childhood from Slavery to Civil Rights* (New York, 2011).

most settlers old enough to participate in violence would have been born in England, youthful aggression could not be taken for granted. The rancor that late-seventeenth-century chroniclers noted was itself very new. The violent young men of the 1670s were dissatisfied with their distance from authority, but they did not often express interest in replacing age and gender as organizing categories in the world they inhabited. Their anger was a testament to how dearly they cherished those categories.[33]

And it was not only men who felt those attachments so deeply. Consider the rage expressed by those who could not expect one day to achieve such powerful authority as recompense. Recall how "neither gender nor class" was the greatest indicator of someone's propensity to anti-Indigenous violence. Rather, it was categorical distance to the authority that male elders, specifically, held. Boys and childless young men were separated from that authority by their age and non-paternity. Women were separated from that authority by their gender. Relative to young men, women do not often appear as angry in the documents of colonial chroniclers. Yet when they do, their words and actions suggest how deep and widespread was the wish for one's suffering to be recognized. Young men experienced powerlessness as a feminization that they yearned to transcend, but women did not always enjoy the condescending experience of feminization, either. Most men found their way out of that powerlessness eventually. They got married, reproduced, and became patriarchs in their own right. Most women did not. Rather, they found ways to assert power within the worlds they could access. Colonial Englishwomen accustomed themselves to the power and its ensuing responsibility to "perpetuate the race." That work was primarily reproductive. But women's race-perpetuation also expressed itself in an enthusiasm for destruction and violence. Five decades into colonization, Mary Rowlandson expressed this memorably. She knew that that race—a vision of inheritable English Christendom heightened through contrast with ethnic and epidermal difference—was at stake in the war that led to the raid on her town of Lancaster and the destruction of the world she had loved. When she recalled the "primal scene" of that morning's attack, Rowlandson could name that the substance of race—the blood of English people, the blood of Christians. And she did so with memorable intensity:

33. John Underhill, *Newes from America* (London, 1638), 39–40; Kristina Bross, *Future History: Global Fantasies in Seventeenth-Century American and British Writings* (Oxford, 2017), 123–146.

"Thus we were butchered by those merciless Heathen, standing amazed, with the blood running down to our heels."[34]

In this remarkable opening scene, Rowlandson invited her readers to visualize women's labor and proposed that women knew why they were being asked to do it. Rowlandson, of course, wasn't butchered. She lived long enough at least to tell the tale, but her sister did actually die, as did some of her children, her sister's children, and most of her neighbors. Though they had been dead for almost ten years when she wrote it down, the blood with which she began her story vividly materialized what English people thought they shared with each other, both biologically and spiritually, the substance that bound Mary to her sister Sarah, to their unnamed neighbors, and to pious readers. More than that: blood made visible the coincidence of the biological and the spiritual that these invisible saints hoped distinguished them. Rowlandson knew what elders claimed was under attack during that war, and she made sure her readers knew she knew. She also, importantly, proposed that she shared a special relationship to that blood, a relationship specific to her status as a woman and mother and characterized by close to half a lifetime of bodily suffering. By early 1676, Rowlandson had given birth at least four times. At least half of her readership would have been able to recall lurid scenes of childbirth, too. And anyone present at a birthing—a percentage of the population that would have far exceeded half—would have memories of a human body covered in its mother's blood from head to foot. Rowlandson's representation of the attack on Englishness, on English blood, centered a motif that recalled her labor producing that precious shared substance. It recalled for her readers what "ran through the loins" of godly parents. In addition to what, it recalled how. And it recalled these from the perspective of someone for whom such loin-running was full of pain and only the start of decades of intimate, embodied labor. For this labor, she could not expect the recompense, social standing, esteem, and authority that her children's father would.[35]

---

34. Pulsipher, "Massacre," *WMQ,* 3d Ser., LIII (1996), 477; Laurel Thatcher Ulrich, *Good Wives: Image and Reality in the Lives of Women in Northern New England, 1650–1750* (New York, 1982), 9 ("race"); Bridget Bennett, "The Crisis of Restoration: Mary Rowlandson's Lost Home," *Early American Literature,* XLIX (2014), 327–356, esp. 338 ("primal scene"); Neal Salisbury, ed., *The Sovereignty and Goodness of God, by Mary Rowlandson, with Related Documents,* Bedford Series in History and Culture (Boston, 1997), 69 ("Thus we were butchered"); Lombard, *Making Manhood;* Ana Schwartz, "Anne Bradstreet, Arsonist?" *New Literary History,* LII (2021), 119–143.

35. Mather, *Pray,* 12 ("ran through the loins"); Gil Anidjar, *Blood: A Critique of Christianity* (New York, 2014).

Rowlandson wasn't alone in her longing to have her world see and affirm that she had labored strenuously on that world's behalf, in activities as everyday as "buying the groceries" or "getting the laundry done," as Perry Miller has put it, to those as risky as birthing more humans, generating more Christian blood. Other women occasionally wrought violence, too, and because men became alarmed to notice that *women* could be so furious, they sometimes went through the trouble of recording how women accounted for it. On the northern frontier of the war, for example, a year after the conflict was supposed to have ended, the spirit of the populist mob formed again. It awoke in a group of Marblehead women waiting at the docks when an English ship approached their harbor carrying several captive Algonquian men. When the boat reached land, these women seized the captives and killed them gruesomely on the spot. These women volunteered their reasons, and readily. According to the deposition preserved by Robert Roules, "They cried out and said, if the Indians had been carried to Boston, that would have been the end of it, and they would have been set at liberty; but said they, if there had been forty of the best Indians in the country here, they would have killed them all, though they should be hanged for it."[36]

Why, these women (like young men) asked, did reproducing a sincere, saintlike community have to be such thankless work? When would their suffering receive recognition? And who was slowing the line down ahead of them? James Axtell has called these women "vengeful." The word's evocative quality is apt. With it, Axtell points to the intensity of their feeling to correct a wrong, an intensity that took them beyond, perhaps even put them in conflict with, the official lines for redress. It is difficult to name their sense of wrong explicitly, though, because the women themselves didn't. Yet their words do point to the contours of their justice and the sources of their commitment to it. Resentment, as Wendy Brown suggested, preserves righteous rage in response to an aggrieved ideal. Vengeance expresses it. These women had a clear sense of the righteousness of their rage. They claimed that they would cling to it, despite possible harm at the hands of a larger, more powerful assembly of their victims ("If there had been forty") or their own juridical system ("though they should be hanged for it"). They had labored, in multiple senses of the word, on an uncomfortable frontier to reproduce Englishness. They were deeply invested in their birthright and the prominence of their place in determining the rights attendant to birth. In their vision of justice,

36. Miller, *Errand,* 14; James Axtell, "The Vengeful Women of Marblehead: Robert Roules's Deposition of 1677," *WMQ,* 3d Ser., XXXI (1974), 647–652, esp. 652.

non-English people—those not birthed to English women—did not deserve access to the due process essential to that birthright. These women's violence tried to prevent the captives from reaching Boston, where the courts would, at least nominally, listen to these non-English captives' case. If, as Natalie Zemon Davis suggests, mobs engage in violence as a form of lay preaching, these women's retribution, like Saltonstall's lynch mob, delivered their own sermon on their ideas of justice: a world organized by distinctions of birth. In this vision, Christian status ("the *best* Indians in the country") was irrelevant next to non-English status. Political recognition was due only to those born to English parents, who had been baptized in blood as they passed through the loins of their white Christian mothers. As these women pursued what they thought was justice, they sought to be recognized as arbiters of authenticity, the best judges of saintliness's conventional invisibility.[37]

Boys' violence spoke similarly, but because it was easier for boys eventually to access the role of arbiter, their rage, though shocking in degree, was not shocking in kind. It was an easier story for colonial historians to tell. These writers liked to narrate examples of what they called bravery, a readiness to commit violence in battle—especially a son's readiness on behalf of his father or a father's on behalf of his son, or the ideals that bound fathers to their sons and vice versa. Increase Mather, William Hubbard, and Thomas Wheeler himself all enthusiastically reviewed the story of Thomas Wheeler, Senior and Junior. Mather narrated the son's "willingly hazarding his own life to save the life of his Father." Hubbard praised the son's "undaunting courage" and his stoicism through being wounded. Thomas Senior narrated his son's behavior as piety: "Whereupon he endeavoured to *Rescue me,* shewing himself therein a *loving and dutiful Son."* Thomas Junior proved himself to be the sort of child who knew his duty to recompense, when he was able. In Gookin's narration of the ambiguously motivated murder by the young Knight at Woburn, his pious lineage softened the possibility of being charged with homicide. By contrast, English writers did not recognize Native neighbors' fealty, obedience, or respect for their elders, a misrecognition, or unwitnessing, that justified English violence toward their enemies.[38]

37. Axtell, "Vengeful Women of Marblehead," *WMQ,* 3d Ser., XXXI (1974), 652; Natalie Zemon Davis, "The Rites of Violence: Religious Riot in Sixteenth-Century France," *Past and Present,* no. 59 (1973), 51–91, esp. 55.

38. Increase Mather, *A Brief History of the Warr with the Indians in New-England* (1676), rpt. in Richard Slotkin and James K. Folsom, eds., *So Dreadfull a Judgment: Puritan Responses to King Philip's War, 1676–1677* (Middletown, Conn., 1978), 79–163, esp. 91 ("willingly"), 99 ("undaunting courage"); Thomas Wheeler, *A Thankeful Remembrance of Gods Mercy to Several*

When English women, along with the youth they nurtured, acted so violently, they expressed the untallied costs of the reformed church's celebrated invisibility as it shaped everyday English family values. Consider one justification for English settlers' sweeping acts of violence, from the lynch mob at Boston to the internment of Native allies and converts at Deer Island. Gookin, reflecting on "causeless" English rage, conceded that English paranoia made sense to him. He understood his fellow settlers' blanket misrecognitions: he, too, thought it was "very difficult, unless upon long knowledge" to distinguish between Christian and non-Christian Natives. In this, he was of like mind with his political antagonists, such as Saltonstall. The latter insisted that even well-intentioned English soldiers "cannot know a Heathen from a Christian by his Visage, nor Apparel," but that line of reasoning wasn't new. It was the same principle that organized reform Protestant settler society internally. It was the same principle that animated debates on intergenerational relations, that made arguments about baptism's value so perplexing: divine favor couldn't be rationalized and neither could the sincerity that was that favor's special mark. No child could depend on visible signs for certainty of their salvation, and neither could their parents.[39]

It had always been impossible for parents to know whether their material descendants were spiritual inheritors. Visage, the embodied similarities that children shared with parents, was not sufficient. Neither was apparel, an emblem for those actions, including the habits of English culture, that might represent desired status. By the same token, it would be impossible for children to affirm with certainty that they were themselves spiritual inheritors by pointing to how much they looked or acted like their parents. Even if a young man—say, someone like a young Increase Mather—received positive affirmation and recognition from his parents, he would have grown up in a social and cultural climate that was eager to negate his confidence in that possibility. His social world encouraged him to worry about how best to make that divine favor, or at least, a sincere desire for that divine favor, visible. It wasn't an impossible task. Even those who seemed not to have English parents were, theoretically, capable of performing those gestures. Evidence of that theorized universal accessibility was everywhere on the colonial frontier. If Mather had not been paying attention to the efforts of men like Gookin and

---

Persons at Quabaug or Brookfield (1676), rpt. ibid., 237–257, esp. 245; S[altonstall], Present State, in Drake, ed., Old Indian Chronicle, 149–150.

39. Gookin, Historical Account of the Doings and Sufferings, 454; S[altonstall], Present State, in Drake, ed., Old Indian Chronicle, 136.

Eliot, his childhood in the congregation at Dorchester, attending meetings with Dorcas several times each week, offered one more data point. When he became an elder himself, he launched into the project of ensuring that youth knew they were expected to undergo the same rigors.

Week after week, year in, year out, Mather returned to the theme of generational debt. His templates were popular. They offered congregants gratifying stories to tell themselves, guidelines for understanding their emotional and material lives. Those attractions encouraged listeners and readers to forget about other templates for experiencing cultural continuity, other stories to tell oneself about meaningful participation in one's world. The templates that did circulate were powerful because material conditions reinforced them. By the time Increase Mather and his peers reached maturity, they would have learned from their parents' lives what they could expect for their own. Most of these parents had appropriated land and labor and thereby prospered. They had achieved lives whose material trappings were attractive. Why should their children go looking for alternatives? First, they stood to inherit materially. Second, if earthly treasures weren't enough, intellectual gratifications were available. Though Mather's sermons produced a climate of conscious and unconscious emotional discomfort, they also, efficiently, offered avenues for making good on that discomfort. Knowledge—here, specifically, a claim to understand the ends of suffering—meant that unhappiness could eventually take a better form: socially valuable experience. Witnessing, reflecting on, and even producing suffering for others, as Mather endorsed doing in his sermons and his war chronicles, could draw individuals more firmly into a consoling relationship with the ideas that their community nominally shared. For these reasons, it might have been incomprehensible to Mather—a disturbance to his confident knowledge—when he discovered that Dorcas, now freer than she had been in decades, perhaps in her life, was not interested in recompensing obligations to the Mather lineage as he represented it. Alienated from paternity's obligations, Dorcas might have understood justice and memory in a fashion that, by 1677, Mather was very unlikely to have recognized.

To Mather's credit, that difference is still difficult to recognize. One reason for its elusiveness is that parents' desire to produce obligations in their inheritors has come to seem normal, intuitive, and beyond historical reckoning. Black women like Dorcas were not the only external sources shoring up English people's confidence that their way of life was desirable. Sometimes, English people cast Algonquian women to fulfill that task. Take, for example, John Eliot's narration of an unnamed woman's last words to her offspring:

"She called her children to her, especially two up-grown daughters," and instructed them,

> I shall now dye, and when I am dead, your Grand-Father and Grand-
> mother, and Uncles, etc. will send for you to come live amongst them,
> and promise you great matters, and tell you what pleasant living it is
> among them; But doe not beleeve them, and I charge you never hearken
> unto them, nor live amongst them; for they pray not to God, keep not
> the Sabbath, commit all manner of sinnes and are not punished for it:
> but I charge you live here, for here they pray unto God, the word of God
> is taught, sins are suppressed and punished by Lawes; And therefore I
> charge you here live all your dayes.

Eliot's fantasy tacitly follows the conventions that English people cherished for themselves. It echoes the emotional pressure of Richard Mather's own deathbed litany, his list of "the prayers which [parents] have made, and the Tears which they have shed, their Example, their Admonitions and Exhortations which they have administered." It's possible that this Natick woman, as early as 1649, had in fact aligned herself with the spirit of the jeremiad, that she understood the best redemption for her labors to lie in her hopes for her offspring. It's likewise possible that the desire to redeem one's sufferings through reproducing them for future generations really is universal. It seems more likely that this was Eliot's exaggeration, given its alignment with the priorities that would blossom explicitly in the jeremiad in the coming decades, yet the fantasy of parental credit translated and bequeathed as debt is so powerful that it continues to structure explanations for parenting strategy beyond the community of pious English.[40]

One reason that parents often succeeded was because most English children, adult and otherwise, would have known that other forms of coercive obligation existed. English ideas of inherited debt benefited from contrast nearby. When William Stoughton exhorted English children "to be an upright Generation" and to "stand *feelingly* under the *weight* of all those Engagements that lye upon us," he did not mean to crush the children who heard his words.

40. John Eliot, "The Glorious Progress of the Gospel, amongst the Indians in New England" (1649), rpt. in *Tracts Relating to the Attempts to Convert to Christianity the Indians of New England*, Massachusetts Historical Society, *Collections*, 3d Ser., IV (Cambridge, Mass., 1834), 69–99, esp. 80; Mather, *Farewell*, 37; Ana Schwartz, "Were There Any Immigrants in New England?" *NEQ*, XCIII (2020), 400–413. For a recent example of a parent's desire to redeem their sufferings by passing on their values to their children, see Bross, *Future History*, 122.

That weight was bearable for at least two reasons; Stoughton would have known both intimately. The *"weight* of all those Engagements" came with a material inheritance. His parents, Israel and Elizabeth Stoughton, had prospered during the first decades of settlement in America, and he, William, would continue to benefit, but Stoughton was also familiar with his father's means of procuring that prosperity. He knew that more intense, less rewarding forms of obligation existed because he had seen them firsthand. He had grown up in a household that prospered by exploiting the labor of enslaved people, including Dorcas. When Dorcas had joined the church, William had been ten years old, yet he was forty-six when that church voted to free her from the condition of enslavement to his father's widow, Elizabeth. A third of a century had passed, during which time he become a father himself. He knew better than almost anyone in the colony that, for all of reform Protestantism's denunciations of parental power, biological descent mattered a great deal to one's material outcomes.[41]

And Dorcas knew better than William. Intergenerational continuity was probably a significant factor that attracted her to Christianity. But it might not have been the most important factor, given that her experience of Christianity wasn't static and probably changed over the next four decades of her life. Church participation, as Wendy Warren has observed, offered relationships that would have compensated for slavery's characteristic genealogical deracination, what Orlando Patterson famously called "natal alienation." Dorcas knew this alienation and estrangement personally. From her place in the Stoughton household, she would have been able to contrast her own perception of that alienation with the intense forms of obligation, individuality, and the corollary resentments that settlers cultivated. Dorcas had probably been in the colony for several months or years before her conversion, and during this time she perhaps noticed, and began to speculate on, the marked absence of elders among white Christians. During the large westward movement of English people to America, an entire generation of elders had been left behind. In America, Dorcas might also have witnessed settlers' curious enthusiasm to loosen themselves from their elders in the colony, their readiness to winnow material ties with parents and to start new households and claim new land, sometimes moving to new towns if necessary. She had probably overheard or even read Wigglesworth's long and lilting poem and reflected on its message, on how her enslavers believed that a disciplined terror of life's eternity was an apt strategy for producing a community of fellow feelers. She observed that, for

41. Stoughton, *New-Englands True Interest,* 29.

these enslavers, Christian doctrine was one strategy for shaping filial fidelity. Maybe she considered it as a useful strategy for her own life.[42]

But children, and an intense bond with them, might not have been Dorcas's ambition in converting to Christianity, pursuing manumission, or moving to Boston. English people might have craved children. It's likely that Dorcas gave birth to several of her own. She would have looked at that future with a different perspective, however, than her white counterparts. Enslaved women knew that their reproductive capacities could be exploited and manipulated by settler patriarchs to ensure debts in their own inheritors. In 1645, Emmanuel Downing had calculated that an enslaved person would be twenty times more profitable than an indentured white servant, and he was not referring only to the cheaper labor from more direct coercion. He also had in mind the turning of enslaved women into reproductive labor. The power to coerce reproductive labor, Downing saw, meant an increased capacity to manipulate wages and, in turn, mold the desires of poor whites in the colony. Downing was clear on this matter. Yet it wasn't necessary, Jennifer Morgan points out, explicitly to "[articulate] a position on the logic of 'breeding' the enslaved." It was an "inherent supposition," and it had been a reality in New England at least as early as 1638, when Samuel Maverick had tried to order the rape of an enslaved woman to systematically increase his estate.[43]

42. Orlando Patterson, *Slavery and Social Death: A Comparative Study* (Cambridge, Mass., 1982); Deborah Colleen McNally, "To Secure Her Freedom: 'Dorcas the Blackmore,' Race, Redemption, and the Dorchester First Church," *NEQ,* LXXXIX (2016), 533–555; Wendy Warren, *New England Bound: Slavery and Colonization in Early America* (New York, 2014), 139–142; John Demos, "Oedipus and America: Historical Perspectives on the Reception of Psychoanalysis in the United States," *Annual of Psychoanalysis,* VI (1978), 23–39; Greven, *Protestant Temperament,* 25. Alison Games has offered substantial quantitative detail regarding the ages of the first waves of planters in New England. Her figures cluster people aged twenty-five to fifty-nine and prompt still further questions about the distinctions within this category. Of the 4,870 subjects departing England for its colonies in the year 1636, those above the age of sixty comprised .2 percent of the population. If *all* .2 percent were headed for the New England colonies, this would mean about ten people. See Games, *Migration and the Origins of the English Atlantic World* (Cambridge, Mass., 1999), 25.

43. Jennifer L. Morgan, *Laboring Women: Reproduction and Gender in New World Slavery* (Philadelphia, 2004), 128; McNally, "To Secure Her Freedom," *NEQ,* LXXXIX (2016); Schwartz, "Were There Any Immigrants?" ibid., XCIII (2020), 400–413; John Josselyn, *An Account of Two Voyages to New England,* ed. Paul J. Lindholdt (Hanover, N.H., 1988), 24; Wendy Anne Warren, "'The Cause of Her Grief': The Rape of a Slave in Early New England," *Journal of American History,* XCIII (2007), 1031–1049.

Dorcas had unusual insight on features of New England cultural reproduction that most of New England's planters preferred not to write about, perhaps even think about. Seven miles separated Maverick's Noddles Island estate from Israel Stoughton's at Dorchester. Within so densely communicative a settlement as New England, Dorcas likely knew what was going on there—she could have communicated with that enslaved woman directly: Maverick had personal connections with Dorchester, since his father, Reverend John Maverick, had been the teacher there. John Maverick continued in that position after John Davenport and many from his congregation moved to New Haven along with the Eatons, and Richard Mather replaced him as pastor. The elder Maverick died in 1636, the year before the first slaving voyage New England chartered to the West Indies. But his son Samuel would likely have maintained connections in the town, and it's possible that the people he enslaved accompanied him on visits. Dorcas might already have known about these practices from previous exposure to English colonists in the Americas, evident in her skill in testimony. Admission to membership, overseen by so well-regarded a minister as Richard Mather, was not available to simply anyone. Mather's first controversy in New England was precisely on the matter of leniency in church membership. Since New England's participation in the slave trade had begun only four years earlier, her skill in performing alignment with Christian principles might have built on established knowledge of that language and religion, on exposure to English colonists before her arrival in New England—probably in Barbados, where she would also have witnessed the forms of exploitation that Downing proposed and that Maverick enacted. The existence of a legacy for white settlers to bequeath and the foreclosure of both legacy and lineage for Black captives complemented each other; Black women's coerced reproduction made this possible. Dorcas was in a unique position to notice this correlation. One result of this perspective, Jennifer Morgan points out, was a different emotional response to the prospect of children. Rather than "craving" children and the material, social, and emotional benefits they conferred, enslaved women, and women with the memory of enslavement, would have considered children with what Morgan describes as a "mixture of tenderness and trepidation."[44]

44. Morgan, *Laboring Women*, 112; Josselyn, *An Account*, ed. Lindholdt, 175; Dunn, Savage, and Yeandle, eds., *Journal of John Winthrop*, 36; "January Meeting, 1885," Massachusetts Historical Society, *Proceedings*, 2d Ser., I (1884), 360–373; Robert Middlekauff, *The Mathers: Three Generations of Puritan Intellectuals, 1596–1728* (Berkeley, Calif., 1999), 48–51; John A. Albro, *The Life of Thomas Shepard* (Boston, 1847), 210–222; Marisa J. Fuentes, *Dispossessed Lives: Enslaved Women, Violence, and the Archive* (Philadelphia, 2016).

Thus, Dorcas's interest in the Boston church wasn't simply motivated by desires for sounder vertical relations. It might have responded to desires for horizontal ones, for relations with others who shared her memories and experiences. Thirty-six years after approval at Dorchester and eighteen years after that congregation purchased her freedom from Israel Stoughton's widow, Dorcas applied successfully for membership at the First Church in Boston. Rather than move outward from the colonial centers and away from congregational communities so she might claim land to bequeath to children, Dorcas moved to the center, and this direction suggests that she was cultivating a wide, horizontal network rather than a narrow, genealogical one. Membership in the Boston church would have supplemented the network of relations she had sustained during her first three and a half decades in these colonies. Not all of these neighbors were white Christians. Residence in Boston, or at least a regular reason to travel there, meant more reliable occasions to engage with many other enslaved and formerly enslaved Africans in the colony, in relations that Stephanie E. Smallwood has described as the "situational linkages of fictive kinship," with people like Zipora, Angola, Grace, and Richard, who all lived in Boston at least as early as 1653; or with Memeno, who lived there as late as 1673; or perhaps even with Jack, Maria, Chefaleer, and Coffee, who appear in the Boston archives in 1681—her "countrywomen" and "countrymen." Dorcas's move was part of a different sort of "family strategy," all the more urgent for enslaved and formerly enslaved Africans in New England as they increased in age.[45]

If Dorcas's relocation was motivated by what she remembered and who else remembered it, that decision might also have been informed by a concern for how she remembered. Women like Dorcas and her kinswoman at Noddles Island, Morgan has observed, "occupied a crucial conceptual position in the unfolding of racial slavery in the Americas"—dear for reproductive capacities, but a dearness determined by their negative participation in inheritance, according to shifting, yet increasingly calcified, structures. From that position, Morgan insists, they were also some of the earliest theorists of the category of the human as Europeans variously and sometimes unpredictably applied it in their colonial endeavors. Women like Dorcas "themselves generated an intellectual and political response" to their often-confusing environments. Thus, alongside its genealogical and social affordances, Boston offered her

---

45. Stephanie E. Smallwood, *Saltwater Slavery: A Middle Passage from Africa to American Diaspora* (Cambridge, Mass., 2007), 114; Warren, *New England Bound*, 137–139, 199–200, 202–203.

more choices in caring for the mind that engaged in this theoretical work, more choices in caring for her spiritual life. The First Church was one of three in that city. If her goal had simply been to strengthen her networks of neighbors, she could have chosen Boston's Second Church, given that she had known the pastor there since his infancy: for at least four years before her move, the Second Church's pastor had been Increase Mather, the son of the Dorchester minister who had approved her for membership. But Dorcas might have chosen otherwise according to a very conventional motive in the New England colonies. She might have liked the theology taught in one church better than another. If her move had been based on a commitment to the tenets of the Halfway Covenant that Richard Mather had famously endorsed, she might have moved to the Third Church, whose reason for coming into existence in 1669 was its disputes with the First Church over that issue.[46]

Nevertheless, Dorcas chose the First Church, helmed by James Allen. Relative to colleagues like Davenport, Stoughton, or the men of the Mather lineage, Allen was a literally unremarkable figure. Given his standing in Boston—he "lived in a handsome stone house, and was possessed of a large estate"—he might have enslaved people himself. He showed little interest in pursuing fame as Increase Mather had. Literary historians have followed his lead. Like Dorcas's life, Allen's theology must be gleaned from relatively sparse records. Only seven sermons preserve his ideas about harmonious relations between humans and the divine. Across these sermons, however, certain priorities are clear. Above all, Allen was concerned for his congregation's happiness,

46. Jennifer L. Morgan, *Reckoning with Slavery: Gender, Kinship, and Capitalism in the Early Black Atlantic* (Durham, N.C., 2021), 10 ("intellectual"), 24 ("occupied"). If Dorcas had wanted simply to preserve connections between Dorchester and Boston, she might have applied years earlier, when John Davenport had triumphantly, if somewhat controversially, returned from New Haven to Massachusetts to assume a ministry there. Before his inquiries into Anne Eaton's spiritual distress, before his fascination with her relationship with Anthony, the Black man her household enslaved, or the Pequot captives whose soul security he thought she threatened, Davenport had been the minister at Dorchester. If Dorcas had been brought to New England before the spring of 1638, before Davenport left Dorchester to help found the colony of New Haven, he would, very briefly, have been her introduction to reform Protestant theology. In 1670, Davenport died. John Oxenbridge—a man who, before arriving in New England the previous year, had counted among his friends in England the poet Andrew Marvell—replaced him. Three years after his appointment, Oxenbridge died "suddenly of apoplexy," leaving James Allen the lone pastor for almost ten years. See Arthur B. Ellis, *History of the First Church in Boston, 1630–1880* (Boston, 1881), 129–130; Richard C. Simmons, "The Founding of the Third Church in Boston," *WMQ*, 3d Ser., XXVI (1969), 241–252; Mark A. Peterson, *The Price of Redemption: The Spiritual Economy of Puritan New England* (Stanford, Calif., 1997), 25–30.

and he was sensitive to the place of thoughtful self-reflection in achieving that happiness. An interest in aesthetic pleasure echoes through his sermons, from his attention to piety's *"delight"* to the "flower and sweetness" of divine benevolence that, when found in a "Needful season," could be a source of "beauty." For Allen, harmony between the human and the divine grew out of reckoning seriously with the dependent's capacity for reason. Allen's sermons rarely depict the deity as a parentlike sovereign. He was not beyond comprehension or eager to prove that even sincere humans had misapplied their reason, as Wigglesworth's deity had been. Rather, Allen's deity was a "rational Agent aiming at a spetial mark in the Deliverances he gives." Allen cautioned his congregants that the deity "sometimes useth Soveraignty"—that is, he sometimes acted with little recourse to rule or principle, but usually, he engaged with humans in a reliable fashion, and he did so to encourage and to affirm the efficacy of their reflection. To enhance that reflection, Allen encouraged his readers to second-guess their first impressions, to view "a thing on every side, and round about it." Certainly, he wasn't unique among reform Protestants in encouraging introspection, yet Allen emphasized the gratifications to be had along the way—"every side, and round about"—rather than the far side of humiliation and pain. Allen expressed his soul science in a different key. Its pleasures seem less attuned to the mastery that knowledge afforded than to the quality of the time spent contemplating, when the deity "reveals what is good, and his way to his Happiness."[47]

Most consistently, Allen's sermons lack passion. Or, at least, they lack the intensity of the passionate conviction that has been recovered by decades of American religious historians. Colonial sermons, they've shown, were not doom and gloom ubiquitously. But there are a variety of ways to not be a caricature of terrorizing coercion, and distinctions within this variety would matter to a woman like Dorcas as she considered the spiritual mood of the community with whom she hoped to spend the later years of her life. Ministers like John Cotton have long been held up as examples of the pleasures that the Christian deity could offer. Cotton has exemplified a strain of Protestantism obsessed with passion, fascinated with representing the ideal Christian as a woman eager to be taken captive, dominated, and raped by the deity. Men like

47. Ellis, *History,* 120 ("handsome stone house"); Allen, *Choicest Blessing,* 7 *("delight");* James [Allen], *Serious Advice to Delivered Ones from Sickness* (Boston, 1679), 3 ("Needful Season ... beauty"), 6 ("rational Agent"), 19 ("flower and sweetness"); Allen, *Neglect,* 4 ("sometimes useth"); Allen, *Man's Self-Reflection, Is the Special Means to Further His Recovery from His Apostasy from God* (Boston, 1699), 11 ("every side"), 17 ("reveals what is good").

Cotton understood spiritual pleasure through the metaphor of coerced sexual activity. This is because many white Christian men imagined that being raped was, ultimately, pleasurable. Dorcas would have approached that metaphor differently because she knew, better than those men and their white daughters, sisters, and wives, what it was like to be vulnerable to that power. Yet between Cotton's domination and Wigglesworth's buoyant doom, there exist other styles to describe human relations with the divine. Richard Mather, Dorcas's first minister, memorably explored that range. According to Mather biographer Robert Middlekauff, he tended to avoid the "rape of the soul" imagery so popular among colleagues like John Cotton, the first husband of Mather's second wife. Likewise, Allen's sermons were not typically interested in the feeling of being overwhelmed, enraptured, or dominated by spiritual powers. After Richard Mather's death, James Allen, rather than Increase Mather, might have seemed to be his closest spiritual inheritor.[48]

Happy remembering replaced passion in Allen's sermons. His ideas on happiness shaped his vision for relations between old and young, parents and children. His sermons represent children as opportunities for the elderly to think about the life of the love they shared. Like his colleagues, he was interested in generational obligation; he was not averse to teaching that the greater the gift, the greater the duty to recompense. But when he explained the model that filial relationships should emulate, he emphasized that the deity was interested in listening: "rejoyce, and have your heart engaged to God; as the Psalmist, Psal. 116.1. *I will love the Lord because he hath heard my voice, etc.*" At times Allen's deity could sound petulant, reminiscent of the aggrieved parent and bleeding judge: *"Is this thy kindness to thy Friend?"* he asks. But Allen's obligations instead took the form of friendship. Although at times Allen ceded to a conventional script representing young people as disappointments to their parents, he also insisted on specific reasons for educating children better. When he invoked the conventional "Counsel of *Solomon*. Prov. 22.6

48. Middlekauff, *The Mathers*, 73; Charles E. Hambrick-Stowe, *The Practice of Piety: Puritan Devotional Disciplines in Seventeenth-Century New England* (Williamsburg, Va., and Chapel Hill, N.C., 1982); Charles Lloyd Cohen, *God's Caress: The Psychology of Puritan Religious Experience* (Oxford, 1986); Amanda Porterfield, *Female Piety in Puritan New England: The Emergence of Religious Humanism* (Oxford, 1992); Jeffrey A. Hammond, *Sinful Self, Saintly Self: The Puritan Experience of Poetry* (Athens, Ga., 1993); Janice Knight, *Orthodoxies in Massachusetts: Rereading American Puritanism* (Cambridge, Mass., 1994); Michael McGiffert, ed., *God's Plot: Puritan Spirituality in Thomas Shepard's Cambridge,* 2d ed. (Amherst, Mass., 1994); Ivy Schweitzer, *The Work of Self-Representation: Lyric Poetry in Colonial New England* (Williamsburg, Va., and Chapel Hill, N.C., 1991), 1–10.

Train up a Child in the way he should go, and he will not depart from it when he is old," he made sure to remind readers why: "What old men love, they will remember in old age." For Allen, childrearing required thoughtfulness about a future when one's inheritors would occupy the place the parent was in now; it required always thinking about the love and happiness that children would be able to recall from their youth. By implication, that exhortation invited the elderly to turn away from the sufferings and sacrifices they had endured and toward the love and gratification they could recall. In Allen's sermons, generations were not fundamentally at odds. They were brought together by a shared pursuit of happiness and through acts of deliberate remembering that the elderly modeled.[49]

In those practices of recollection, sometimes strategic forgetting could be desirable. Forgoing, rather than preserving, one's own memories of wrongs meant accepting that one's own credits might occasionally be forgotten, too. Men like Mather excoriated that sort of disregard. In his Call from Heaven, for example, he cited the Ecclesiastical teacher to instruct Christians to "Remember now thy Creator in the dayes of thy youth"—addressing a caricature of youth presumed to have neglected their debts to their spiritual and material fathers. Allen's sermons began in a more modest place. They recognized that amnesia could sometimes be a blessing. Allen cited the more literary psalmist to model a disposition toward the divine—and toward others—that was remarkably less confident in its own authority to condemn others: "Lord remember not the sins of my Youth." Allen's ideal Christian does not forget his or her own sins but hopes that others, and the deity, will. Rarely in these sermons do elders appear in the trappings of triumphant, aggrieved piety. They spend little time invoking the ire of the wounded judge, eager to damn. Rather, Allen recommended that everyone, young and old, keep in mind their memories of imperfections, remember the presence of a past worth forgetting—that they once had been younger, sillier, more vain, often inconsiderate, and above all, ever-limited in their access to self-knowledge. Such a practice of remembering what one hoped others would forget could restore the balance sheet kept between generations.[50]

Forgetting need not mean leaving history behind. Political theorists of particularity, like Wendy Brown and Glen Sean Coulthard (Yellowknives

49. [Allen], Serious Advice, 2, 6 ("rejoyce"), 14 ("kindness"), 20; Allen, Self-Reflection, 11, 22 ("Counsel of Solomon").

50. Increase Mather, A Call from Heaven to the Present and Succeeding Generations (Boston, 1679), 95 ("Remember"); [Allen], Serious Advice, 12 ("remember not").

Dene), recognize the imperative of remembering, even of resentment. Brown, in her assessment of the attractions of resentful memory, observes that in a modernity defined by intimate experience of globality and by disturbed epistemological norms—a modernity that the seventeenth century shares with the twentieth of Brown's writing—it can be difficult for individuals to understand who they are without attaching to the memory of a prior injustice. Those attachments aren't easy to sever. For some, forgetting means further injury—for colonized subjects, "erased histories and historical invisibility are themselves . . . integral elements" of political harm. To advocate forgetting as the best solution for resentment can be "inappropriate if not cruel." And Coulthard has extended that insight. Drawing on Frantz Fanon, and from the standpoint of post-reconciliation settler Canada, Coulthard observes how forgetting, like Drew Lopenzina's unwitnessing, can be an instrument of colonial deracination and continued dispossession. Although Dorcas likely possessed many unpleasant memories, she didn't discard them entirely. To the degree that Dorcas's move to Boston sought to cultivate networks based on shared experience, the past continued to be a dynamic, conscious factor in shaping her actions. But Allen's sermons didn't straightforwardly advocate purging one's memory of unhappy recollections. One might infer that he advised practicing more satisfying ways of organizing past experiences and understanding them more clearly.[51]

Allen's sermons collectively suggest that the coveted status of divine favor manifested itself in the felicity of the stories that settlers told themselves during their earthly lives and in the ability to continue to revise them. As Dorcas looked ahead to the end of her life in a society tense with its expectations for its own youth, she was familiar with some of the most materially and ideo-logically powerful personalities in the English settlement. That familiarity offered substantial material to remember and to think over. Allen's sermons proposed distinct and dynamic strategies for organizing this material, new ways of understanding one's relationship to the past that didn't require indi-viduals to commit the rest of their lives to the story templates their fathers had bequeathed. It seems likely that Dorcas passed away before 1699, when Allen delivered his last extant sermon. But its central theme, and its reversal of conventional wisdom, shared the mild and reflective disposition of his earlier teaching. His last sermon affirmed that remembering and reflecting

51. Brown, *States of Injury,* 52–76, esp. 74; Glen Sean Coulthard, *Red Skin, White Masks: Rejecting the Colonial Politics of Recognition* (Minneapolis, 2014), 105–129; Drew Lopenzina, *Red Ink: Native Americans Picking up the Pen in the Colonial Period* (Albany, N.Y., 2012), 5–11.

were work and that such work was important in making good on the "spetial mark" that the deity reserved for his figurative children. For Allen, felicitous circumstances were not the precondition for acuity, insight, and committed thought. "A good memory," he claimed, was not the reservoir out of which an individual might draw the material for a "good Understanding." Rather, he argued, in a revision of what we think memory is, the reverse was true for the good Christian. Good memory was its offspring, its dependent: "Those that have the clearest understandings have the happiest memories."[52]

52. [Allen], *Serious Advice,* 6 ("spetial"); Allen, *Self-Reflection,* 21 ("good memory"), 22 ("understanding").

CHAPTER FIVE

Friendship, Fair and True

Sincerity Makes a Compromise with History

FRIENDSHIP, literature tells us, is a great deal of work. It requires prudence, compromise, self-abnegation, and emotional acuity. Because it has its origin beyond the conventions of the polis and the hearth, friendship also, exhaustingly, requires unrelenting sincerity—honesty to others and to oneself. This, at least, is how Ralph Waldo Emerson, one of the most eloquent theorists of friendship in American literary history, described it. He was fascinated with sincerity. Across many of his essays, he reflected on how real friendship—not its fake, illusory, or shallow substitutes—required sovereign mastery over the world's illusions as they encroached on the self. In 1841, for example, he wrote of the "days of sin" that persuade us, "foolishly . . . that we must court friends by compliance to the customs of society, to its dress, its breeding, and its estimates." All around him, he saw individuals sacrificing what was most true about themselves in order to be likable. Not he: "Only that soul can be my friend, which I encounter on the line of my own march, that soul to which I do not decline, and which does not decline to me." Like early moderns, Emerson thought of friendship as "sovereign amity." It was a meeting of unbendable personalities, unwaveringly erect: "Let him not cease," Emerson later commanded this phantom friend, not even "for an instant," he insisted, "to be himself." Friendship was a tall order, and Emerson liked it that way. He knew most people weren't up to the task. Sovereign amity was rare, and that thrilled him: "You demonstrate yourself, so as to put yourself out of the reach of false relations, and you draw to you the first-born of the world,—those rare pilgrims whereof one or two wander in nature at once." Emerson was blunt about the yield of labor in friendship's vineyard. The fulfilling solitude, the self-communion that friendship offered, exemplified sincerity's narrowing movement. The fruit of sincerity wasn't supposed to nullify isolation or triumph over it. Isolation was friendship's reward: "It is," he described friendship in "Spiritual Laws," a "sort of joyful solitude." Friendship, Emerson tells us, was a lot of work; moreover, it was lonely labor. Why in the world would anyone want this?[1]

If Emerson is right, if friendship is so rare and isolating, maybe the canon of friendship's true theorists really is quite small and "tightly knit." But friendship is extravagant to institutional life. This is its radiant heart. Accordingly, there may be just as many assessments of what friendship is as there are friends. Early American literary history has recovered some of these theories, but still more have eluded study, because many of those thoughtful friends would not write their theories down. Dorcas, the manumitted woman who chose, late in life, to move from Dorchester to Boston, lived in a society that cut her off from directly participating in the conventions of the polis and the hearth. For her, friendship's extravagant affiliation was a lifeline. Before, during, and after her enslavement, friendship made life worth living in conditions of extraordinary vulnerability. Some of these conditions she would have witnessed herself; others, she might have heard about through close companions. For Dorcas, friendship was necessary because of a near-total dispossession from a prior social world. Physical force was part of this dispossession, but not all of it. Many of Dorcas's kinspeople had confronted the horizon of a known world. Then they had been pushed beyond it. By the time they arrived at the Atlantic coast, African captives were "exhausted, emaciated, [and] injured from the traumas experienced thus far," and even if they had been able to escape coastal capture, they would not have been able to "easily disguise their condition" and avoid recapture had they tried to return to their inland homes. Alienation had

1. Ralph Waldo Emerson, "Spiritual Laws," in Douglas Crase, ed., *Essays: First and Second Series* (New York, 1991), 75–93, esp. 88 ("days of sin," "joyful solitude"); Emerson, "Friendship," ibid., 111–124, esp. 120 ("Let him not cease"), 123 ("You demonstrate"); Gregory Jusdanis, *A Tremendous Thing: Friendship from the "Iliad" to the Internet* (Ithaca, N.Y., 2014); A. C. Grayling, *Friendship* (New Haven, Conn., 2013); Jacques Derrida, *The Politics of Friendship,* trans. George Collins (New York, 1997); Laurie Shannon, *Sovereign Amity: Figures of Friendship in Shakespearean Contexts* (Chicago, 2002).

been incremental and therefore profound. A form of friendship, the relation of "shipmate," emerged among captives as an improvised answer to unprecedented dispossession.[2]

Unlike the word "friend," the word "shipmate" points insistently at its history; it refuses ignorance toward its own conditions of possibility. A little less directly, it also points to slavery's historical part in the emergence of the sovereignty that Emerson's friendship required. Sovereign individuality, Herman Bennett proposes, was one expression of the alienation characteristic of early modern Atlantic slavery. As European slavers engaged in trade with African polities, they developed a juridical category, the "individual," to describe a person who lacked the "protective shield of a culturally sanctioned corporate status" and was thereby exposed to captivity, alienation, and unrelenting vulnerability to harm. Individuality did not emerge in a bright flash. It took place across a series of removes. Because it was incremental, it was extremely difficult to undo or reverse. Dorcas and her friends would have known dearly what most white settlers have struggled to comprehend. Sovereign amity was a response to captivity and individuation, a slow and intensifying estrangement that white settlers innovated for themselves but tended not to see: captivity to the invisible but powerful expectations of responsible, individual personality—sincerity being, perhaps, the most intimate of these.[3]

Like the category of the shipmate, the friend was a stopgap, blunting the force of history. It wasn't, however, a solution. Friendship, early Americans saw, required what Lauren Berlant has described as the "cultivation of sel[f], will, desire, and inflated sense of poetic interiority." To this ideal, Berlant observes, "Only some people feel connected." These individuals did not. They knew they

2. Shannon, *Sovereign Amity*, 1 ("tightly knit"); Stephanie E. Smallwood, *Saltwater Slavery: A Middle Passage from Africa to American Diaspora* (Cambridge, Mass., 2007), 53 ("exhausted"); Abram C. Van Engen, *Sympathetic Puritans: Calvinist Fellow-Feeling in Early New England* (Oxford, 2015); Ivy Schweitzer, *Perfecting Friendship: Politics and Affiliation in Early American Literature* (Williamsburg, Va., and Chapel Hill, N.C., 2006); Caleb Crain, *American Sympathy: Men, Friendship, and Literature in the New Nation* (New Haven, Conn., 2001); Richard Godbeer, *The Overflowing of Friendship: Love between Men and the Creation of the American Republic* (Baltimore, 2009). See also the extraordinary collection of essays in Janet Moore Lindman, ed., *Histories of Friendship in Early America*, special issue of *Journal of Social History*, L (2017). For more historically expansive, theoretically oriented treatments of friendship, see Leela Gandhi, *Affective Communities: Anticolonial Thought, Fin-de-Siècle Radicalism, and the Politics of Friendship* (Durham, N.C., 2006); Gregg Lambert, *Philosophy after Friendship* (Minneapolis, 2017).

3. Herman Bennett, *African Kings and Black Slaves: Sovereignty and Dispossession in the Early Modern Atlantic* (Philadelphia, 2018), 57.

needed friendship, but they also knew that friendship directed them to understand personhood in an almost unbearably individuated fashion. Friendship required them to persuade others—and maybe, for the sake of convenience, themselves—that they possessed sincerity, that they possessed a commitment to personal truth through time. For reasons that varied according to their circumstances, that sort of sincerity wasn't available to them. Mary Rowlandson needed friends after she lost most of her family and neighborhood during the Indigenous revolt against settler Christianity and its transformation of the Algonquian world. Rowlandson knew that her relationships with the English left living would yoke her, intensely and unhappily, to the memory of those lost. She was grateful for her new friends but dissatisfied with the costs of maintaining them. Roger Williams, writing almost forty years earlier, explained one important condition of such dissatisfaction. For Williams, "friendship" named a relationship free from the risk of idolatry—the idols of English prejudice, English custom, and English church. But that commitment also required consistency through time; in turn, it foreclosed new forms of social relation and intensified his desire for necessarily few fellow zealots. Williams struggled to overcome this challenge. He might never have succeeded, as his unhappy recruitment as a counterinsurgent into that anti-Christian revolt suggested. The experience of James Quananopohit, also recruited into that war, offers some reasons why it might—just might—still be worthwhile to try. For Quananopohit, consistency of commitment to one side or another was probably impossible. The survival of his dearest relations, however, required him to try and perform it anyway. Friendship, for Quananopohit, named a provisional illusion that was useful in buying time—to negotiate, to enable others' flight, to live together a little bit longer. These individuals confronted high-stakes expectations that they *be* individuals, and sincere ones, too. They performed what they felt was necessary; but they all expressed deep weariness with the act. Sleep was one refuge from sincerity's demands. Yet sinking below the phenomenal world was less attractive, finally, for Anthony Thacher, barrel maker in Marblehead. Like Rowlandson, he lost nearly everything in a cataclysmic event. He also lived long enough to tell the tale and to voice, as well, his criticisms of the invisible, disastrous conditions that frontier friendship largely forgot. These isolatoes all felt the effects of their society's obsession with spiritual flourishing, biopoetically purchased. And they had the misfortune to find themselves very well positioned to count its costs.[4]

4. Lauren Berlant, *Cruel Optimism* (Durham, N.C., 2011), 157.

Mary Rowlandson became a celebrity in her time for the three months of captivity that she spent with the Pocassets. And she has become a literary celebrity in ours for the indeterminate length of time afterward during which she couldn't get a good night's sleep. *"I can remember the time,"* she wrote, *"when I used to sleep quietly without workings in my thoughts, whole nights together."* Sleep once offered the promise of thoughtlessness. For Rowlandson, oblivion promised an experience of wholeness, a numberless quantity of nights that "together," she recalled, added up to a period of unbroken, unconscious satisfaction. Though she was accompanied by her thoughts, they had not troubled her with their "work." "But now," she wrote, "it is other wayes with me." These other ways, Bryce Traister notes, speak powerfully to the present, where "few of us *cannot* understand the psychological extremis experienced in the condition of insomnia." Few critics, furthermore, dislike discovering a consciousness that longs for relief. Traister proposes that this is because Rowlandson's insomnia testifies to a psychoanalytically familiar sort of personality. In it, critics see a person shaped by experiences in ways that elude his or her full conscious comprehension. What Traister's critics have loved, however, Rowlandson loathed. Bearing that modern, psychoanalytically familiar personality was very unpleasant. The substance of her text's friendliness, its congeniality to modern readers and early modern ones, too, was a burden. Her most eloquent expressions of personhood claim, after all, that she wanted to turn her personality off and go to sleep, not stay up all night talking with such friends.[5]

5. Neal Salisbury, ed., *The Sovereignty and Goodness of God, by Mary Rowlandson, with Related Documents,* Bedford Series in History and Culture (Boston, 1997), 111 (hereafter cited as Rowlandson, *Sovereignty*); Bryce Traister, "Mary Rowlandson and the Invention of the Secular," *Early American Literature,* XLII (2007), 323–354, esp. 325. For evidence of the popularity of Rowlandson's insomnia, see Kathryn Zabelle Derounian, "Puritan Orthodoxy and the 'Survivor Syndrome' in Mary Rowlandson's Captivity Narrative," ibid., XXII (1987), 82–93, esp. 86–90; Tara Fitzpatrick, "The Figure of Captivity: The Cultural Work of the Puritan Captivity Narrative," *American Literary History,* III (1991), 1–26, esp. 11; Teresa Toulouse, "'My Own Credit': Strategies of (E)Valuation in Mary Rowlandson's Captivity Narrative," *American Literature,* LXIV (1992), 655–676, esp. 668; Susan Howe, *The Birth-Mark: Unsettling the Wilderness in American Literary History* (Middletown, Conn., 1993), 89–130, esp. 125; Lisa Logan, "Mary Rowlandson's Captivity and the 'Place' of the Woman Subject," *EAL,* XXVIII (1993), 255–277, esp. 273; Scott Michaelsen, "Narrative and Class in a Culture of Consumption: The Significance of Stories in Sarah Kemble Knight's 'Journal,'" *College Literature,* XXI (1994), 33–46, esp. 36; Peter Nicholls, "Unsettling the Wilderness: Susan Howe and American History," *Contemporary Literature,* XXVII (1996), 586–601, esp. 590; Dawn Henwood, "Mary Rowlandson and the Psalms: The Textuality of Survival," *EAL,* XXXII (1997), 169–186, esp. 175; Nan Goodman, "'Money Answers All Things': Rethinking Economic and Cultural

Rowlandson's narrative isn't simply about friends, though. It also attempts, with ambivalent success, it seems, to replace them. The story she wrote, titled alternately *The Soveraignty and Goodness of God* and *The Captivity and Restoration of Mrs. Mary White Rowlandson,* appeared in print in 1682, six years after she returned from captivity to English society, though she probably began drafting it closer to the events she narrated. Increase Mather, by then a leading figure of New England's print culture, was likely to have shepherded the text to publication, just as he had shepherded her back to the society they shared. Though Rowlandson lived in Lancaster, thirty-five miles west of Boston, she knew Mather through her husband, Joseph, Lancaster's minister, who had participated actively with Mather in discussions regarding the crisis in intergenerational continuity during the previous decade. During his wife's captivity, Joseph Rowlandson contacted Mather to try to secure her ransom. Joseph appeared next to her in the text, the author of a sermon appended to it—his final sermon, preached at Wethersfield in 1678, *The Possibility of God's Forsaking a People*. Mather might also be there on the page, too, in the preface attributed to the pseudonymous "Ter [or Per] Amicam." This combination proved extraordinarily popular. The text went through four printings in the first year of its publication, and, for some critics, inspired the modern novel of interiority. Her late-night loneliness seals her compelling representation of a personality. Though she had lost the companions of her old world (at least twice), she did, in fact, have friends by the time she wrote her story. But those friends tended, she suggested, to make her loneliness worse.[6]

Exchange in the Captivity Narrative of Mary Rowlandson," *ALH,* XXII (2010), 1–25, esp. 5; Suzanne Underwood Rhodes, "Mary Rowlandson's Removes," *Anglican Theological Review,* XCV (2013), 354–355; Wendy Anne Warren, *New England Bound: Slavery and Colonization in Early America* (New York, 2016), 202; Bridget Bennett, "The Crisis of Restoration: Mary Rowlandson's Lost Home," *EAL,* XLIX (2014), 327–356, esp. 348–349; Wai Chee Dimock, "Early American Literature as a Networked Field: Mary Rowlandson, Louise Erdrich, Sherman Alexie," ibid., L (2015), 103–124, esp. 117.

6. Goodman, "'Money Answers,'" *ALH,* XXII (2010), 8; Joseph Rowlandson, *The Possibility of God's Forsaking a People* (Boston, 1682); David L. Greene, "New Light on Mary Rowlandson," *EAL,* XX (1985), 24–38; Michael G. Hall, *The Last American Puritan: The Life of Increase Mather* (Middletown, Conn., 1988), 114–115; Kathryn Zabelle Derounian, "The Publication, Promotion, and Distribution of Mary Rowlandson's Indian Captivity Narrative in the Seventeenth Century," *EAL,* XXIII (1988), 239–261, esp. 239–241. On Ter Amicum's identity, see Teresa Toulouse, *The Captive's Position: Female Narrative, Male Identity, and Royal Authority in Colonial New England* (Philadelphia, 2007), 33–34. On the genre of the captivity narrative, see Kathryn Zabelle Derounian-Stodola, "The Indian Captivity Narratives of Mary Rowlandson and Olive Oatman: Continuity, Evolution, and Exploitation of a Literary Discourse," *Studies in*

Rowlandson, barred from sleep's deathlike thoughtlessness, cursed to weep while others slept, kept company with thoughts that worked. Late at night, and later at her desk, she reflected on what Theodor Adorno would archly call "the social produc[tion]" of loneliness. Loneliness shares at least one quality with sincerity, sentimentalism, and insomnia: they are all contingent experiences of historical conditions. It is not easy, therefore, to overcome. "To transcend collectively determined loneliness through . . . [one's] own decision and determination," Adorno proposed, "is not open to the individual." As Rowlandson lay supine, surrounded by sleeping Christians in Boston, she was not able to forget what Tara Fitzpatrick describes as the "isolation from her community" that had characterized her captivity. Boston life extended it. Rather than give up the task—an abdication that she was not likely to consider seriously—she used her solitary reflection to develop a clearer knowledge of what troubled her. By the end of her narrative, as the conclusion to her story brought her up to date with the present of her writing, Rowlandson proposed an insight on friendship with troubling implications. She depended on friendship, but it required her to pretend sincerely to be a person defined by an experience that she had to claim was her worst nightmare.[7]

Rowlandson's "redemption" required friendship. But redemption—what her title partially acknowledged in the word "restoration"—did not mean return to her old home at Lancaster. There was no more Lancaster. This was the consequence of the actions taken by an Algonquian coalition trying to restore balance to their homelands, attempting to reverse English property claims as far as it was possible. The town of Lancaster, in the report of one Boston diarist, had been "spoiled by the enemy." Destroyed along with it was Joseph Rowlandson's career and Mary Rowlandson's livelihood. As a minister, Joseph depended on congregational consent, attendance, and financial

Literary Imagination, XXVII, no. 1 (Spring 1994), 33–46; Pauline Turner Strong, *Captive Selves, Captivating Others: The Politics and Poetics of Colonial American Captivity Narratives* (Boulder, Colo., 1999); Lisa Voigt, *Writing Captivity in the Early Modern Atlantic: Circulations of Knowledge and Authority in the Iberian and English Imperial Worlds* (Williamsburg, Va., and Chapel Hill, N.C., 2009). On her unusual interiority, see Michelle Burnham, *Captivity and Sentiment: Cultural Exchange in American Literature, 1682–1861* (Hanover, N.H., 1997); Mitchell Robert Breitwieser, *American Puritanism and the Defense of Mourning: Religion, Grief, and Ethnology in Mary White Rowlandson's Captivity Narrative* (Madison, Wis., 1990). On the text as catalyst of the novel, see Nancy Armstrong and Leonard Tenenhouse, *The Imaginary Puritan: Literature, Intellectual Labor, and the Origin of Personal Life* (Berkeley, Calif., 1992), 196–216.

7. Theodor Adorno, "Reconciliation under Duress," *Aesthetics and Politics* (London, 1977), 151–176, esp. 165; Fitzpatrick, "Figure of Captivity," *ALH,* III (1991), 11.

support. All of that was gone, even beyond the thirty-seven people who had garrisoned in the Rowlandson household. As Algonquian protectors carried Mary Rowlandson from one remove to the next, she recalled longing for that lost home. She invoked the biblical psalmist's vengeful auto-exhortation not to forget her home and its spiritual community. Yet she knew, when she recalled that moment of self-conscious remembering, that although the abstract spiritual community of Christians still existed, her particular ties to that community—her extended family, her friends, neighbors, creditors, debtors, and petty rivals—no longer existed anywhere except her memory. New friends in Boston had to step in to replace those old networks. Unlike the prolonged removal from English norms and society after the raid, her return was abrupt. It was characterized by a great deal of self-consciousness. Rowlandson identified her new friends and thanked them for their help. She made sure readers knew that she understood how steeply and suddenly she was in their debt.[8]

Rowlandson's insomnia followed directly from her experience of owing—at least chronologically in the text and maybe thematically. Existential debt, as the colonial jeremiad claimed, was ineluctable to the human condition. Christian theology claimed that debt was universal, but occasionally evidence appeared that women, such as the furious ones at the Marblehead shore, bore that burden with less compensatory relief. Rowlandson had been one exemplary chronicler of that responsibility, but that was not the last of her reflections on unhappy owing. In a remarkable paragraph just above her description of her labored thinking, she recalled some unusual, very specific debts—not universal ones—and reenchanted them by describing them as debts that substantiated friendship. Consistently, she suffused her accounting with the vocabulary of sentiment. Some of these friends she knew well—like the Shepards at Charlestown, with whom she and Joseph stayed for almost three months after her return. "Others," however, "I knew not," she remarked, thinking possibly of those undifferentiated *"Boston Gentlemen,"* such as Hezekiah Usher, who had raised the twenty pounds she had told her captors she was worth. She knew the exact sum they raised to pay for her, but she insisted on pointing to their spiritual reasons for doing so: they were "tender-hearted Friends," they were "cordial *Friends,"* and, above all, they were "Christian

8. Rowlandson, *Sovereignty,* 108; Lisa Brooks, *Our Beloved Kin: A New History of King Philip's War* (New Haven, Conn., 2018), 155; *The Diaries of John Hull, Mint-Master and Treasurer of the Colony of Massachusetts Bay,* American Antiquarian Society, *Transactions,* III (Boston, 1857), 111–316, esp. 241; Bennett, "Crisis of Restoration," *EAL,* XLIX (2014), 327–356.

friends." She claimed, repeatedly, that she was indebted to friends; in doing so, she narratively eased her ineluctable financial dependence into less explicitly transactional relations.[9]

Rowlandson was in debt to friends for more than her restoration from captivity. She also owed them for any hope she had of re-creating a world of satisfyingly intimate relations. These friends also provided her with the financial resources to furnish her home, a gift that was supposed to keep on giving and enable her, in turn, to produce relations of obligations with others. "I thought it somewhat strange," she wrote of her new home in Boston, "to set up House-keeping with bare walls." Nevertheless, she knew what was required to make the strange homely again: "As *Solomon* says, *Mony answers all things.*" She knew how much furnishing cost, but she didn't care, she insisted, on the material furnishings, the chairs or tables that Anne Bradstreet had recollected fondly in her 1666 lament on foreclosed hospitality. Rather, Rowlandson reported, "in a little time we might look, and see the house furnished with love." She even owed her neighbors for the roof that covered her head and literally hung over those lovely furnishings. When she and Joseph moved from Charlestown to Boston, "*The* South Church . . . *hired an House for us.*" Boston's congregants, after paying for her redemption, paid her rent, too. Rowlandson recognized that she had long ago lost her power to determine whom she was indebted to and for how much. On one hand, debts rebuilt a network of affiliation and obligation. On the other hand, within a society where slavery was not a distant possibility, her weakness in controlling the rebuilding itself would have troubled her. Vigilant against seeming too indebted to one of colonial New England's craftiest postwar enslavers, she insisted, vigorously, that James Whitcomb, her landlord, was one of her dearest friends. Throughout, Rowlandson carried forward the accounting skills she exercised in recalling her captivity. She even counted how long her dependence lasted: *"about three quarters of a year."* "Friendship" was Rowlandson's name to mnemonically ease her unceasing, tirelessly increasing debts.[10]

9. Rowlandson, *Sovereignty*, 108, 111; Schweitzer, *Perfecting Friendship*, 73–102.

10. Rowlandson, *Sovereignty*, 111; Felicity Heal, *Hospitality in Early Modern England* (Oxford, 1990); Goodman, "'Money Answers,'" *ALH*, XXII (2010), 1–25; Breitwieser, *American Puritanism*, 125; Anne Bradstreet, "In silent night when rest I took," in Joseph R. McElrath, Jr., and Allan P. Robb, eds., *The Complete Works of Anne Bradstreet* (Boston, 1981), 236–237; Molly Farrell, "'Beyond My Skil': Mary Rowlandson's Counting," *EAL*, XLVII (2012), 59–87. Whitcomb's expenditures later that year included a sum of more than fourteen pounds paid to Richard Waldron for the purchase of thirteen Native captives, a purchase comparable in size to that of Samuel Mosely, one of the most aggressive and famously cruel leaders of the

Half a decade later, Rowlandson could see her best asset in assuaging that debt: herself. Or rather, it was a combination of individual experience and consequent self-knowledge that we call a personality and that friendship required her, sincerely, to perform. Experience, reflection, and sincere avowal made her attractive and interesting to her English neighbors and new friends. In this, she was unique. She had not been the only one to be taken captive or to return—although her allusion to Job's unlikely messenger, alone left to tell the tale, has the effect of making her seem the sole survivor. There had been at least twenty-three other captives from Lancaster. Few, however, wrote about their captivity, and few appear by name in other accounts of the war. By contrast, Rowlandson appears in virtually every seventeenth-century account of the war. Mather wrote of "the wonderful hand of providence, [who] wrought Salvation for *Mrs. Rowlandson* and returned her to *Boston*." Nathaniel Saltonstall, likely author of *The Present State of New-England,* began his final pamphlet by recalling "Mr. *Rowlandson,* whose Wife and Children they carried Captive." Even Daniel Gookin, who aspired to write about the neglected experience of the Praying Indians, recorded "the redemption of our captives, particularly Mrs. Rowlandson." Rowlandson was different. She was an exemplary wife of a well-connected minister. She was the daughter of the wealthiest landowner in Lancaster. For these reasons, she was uniquely, if somewhat randomly, positioned to fascinate English settlers as they consumed news about the war.[11]

If Rowlandson did not know her celebrity status while she bargained with her captors about redemption's cost, it would have been hard for her to remain

English military forces during King Philip's War. See Neal Salisbury, *Manitou and Providence: Indians, Europeans, and the Making of New England, 1500–1641* (Oxford, 1982), 145–146.

11. Increase Mather, *A Brief History of the Warr with the Indians in New England* (1676), in Richard Slotkin and James Folsom, eds., *So Dreadfull a Judgment: Puritan Responses to King Philip's War, 1676–1677* (Middletown, Conn., 1978), 55–206, esp. 117; N[athaniel] S[altonstall], *The Present State of New-England with Respect to the Indian War . . .* , in Samuel G. Drake, ed., *The Old Indian Chronicle: Being a Collection of Exceeding Rare Tracts* (Boston, 1867), 251; Daniel Gookin, *An Historical Account of the Doings and Sufferings of the Christian Indians in New England in the Years 1675, 1676, 1677,* American Antiquarian Society, *Transactions and Collections,* II (Camgbridge, 1836), 423–524, esp. 508; Kathryn Zabelle Derounian-Stodola, "The Captive as Celebrity," in Robert D. Habich, ed., *Lives out of Letters: Essays on American Literary Biography and Documentation, in Honor of Robert H. Hudspeth* (Vancouver, B.C., 2004), 93–113; Christopher Castiglia, *Bound and Determined: Captivity, Culture-Crossing, and White Womanhood from Mary Rowlandson to Patty Hearst* (Chicago, 1996). For an account that *does* name some of these captives, see Thomas Cobbet, "A Narrative of New England's Deliverances," *New England Historical and Genealogical Register,* VII (1853), 209–219, esp. 217–218.

ignorant of it after she returned to English society. As she and Joseph journeyed back to Boston, she learned, financially speaking, what her suffering had been worth. She learned exactly how much her fellow English were ready to pay for it. On the road east, she noted the demand among English towns for her husband's preaching. Rowlandson juxtaposed these speaking engagements with the money she knew she had to raise to buy back her remaining family members. Rumor had it her daughter's ransom had been valued at another twenty pounds, but the child had escaped, and the Providence settlers who found her returned her to Massachusetts. For her son, the "good People thereabouts" at Newbury raised a seven-pound ransom. And her sister's son "was redeemed for *four pounds,* which the Council gave orders for the payment of." Rowlandson noted, too, signs of recalcitrance toward giving English people what they wanted. Joseph, she recalled, was "not willing" to stay at Newbury despite their invitation to him to preach. Yet it wasn't an easy desire to deny. Rowlandson had become a celebrity because her life had been broken into parts, with some pieces reduced to dust. For her, more acutely than for anyone else, rehearsing the history of that breaking was a condition for restoring what was left. These were the demands of her new friends, sincere though they were: so ready to sympathize, to consume tearful narratives. As Emerson expected of his friend, Rowlandson's new friends required her never to cease, even for a moment, to be herself.[12]

Among her captors, Rowlandson had not been herself. She made sure to point this out to her readers. She recalled vividly moments when captivity's stresses transformed her beyond her own recognition. One reason for this self-estrangement was the difference of her new social context. Unlike the people of Ipswich, Rowley, Newbury, Salisbury, Portsmouth, and the other settlements she passed though during her return, her captors did not place very much spiritual value in her personality or in the distinctions—her status as a wife and daughter, a mother, an inheritor of property-owning status—that had shaped her social life among the English. Her captors cared that she protected them as collateral. Over time, they came to value her and reward her for skills that she considered conventional. She knew how to make garments, so they employed her to do so. During those winter months, she began (reluctantly, she emphasized) to participate in Algonquian life. She entangled herself in networks of production and trade, clothed their families, gathered provisions, ate around their fires, and slept—eagerly—in their residences. She witnessed, though only ever partially, her captors' preparations for martial conflict and

12. Rowlandson, *Sovereignty,* 109–110.

their celebrations of reunification with separated Pocasset and other allied bands, and even their mourning rituals, as in the death of Weetamoo's daughter only weeks after Rowlandson herself had lost her youngest daughter, Sarah. Losing former anchoring points for self-recognition, she gained a socially recognized function in her new, provisional world. She never professed to like it. But survival among her captors never required her to like it.[13]

Despite her sincere intentions to fortify herself against her enemy, she learned to apply English vocabulary to her new, closest neighbors. It wasn't instinctive. She recalled many instances of having to reassess these relationships and their constitutive parts because she couldn't take old social norms for granted. During her twelfth remove, for example, Rowlandson described the stresses of negotiating different social norms, particularly those of gender and rank, between two cultures. Among the English, her status as an elite woman entitled her to shelter, attention, and care. In captivity, she often had to ask for care—something she rarely would have done as the wife of the pastor of Lancaster. Sometimes she asked and did not receive. Other times, she did receive, as when an elderly man "bade me come to him" and, with his companion, "gave me some Ground nuts" and "also something to lay under my head." As a small group, they shared the warmth of a small fire during the late Dawnland winter, and Rowlandson benefited from Algonquian people's wintering expertise. "A good fire we had," she recalled. Eventually, she called Quinnapin (the husband of Weetamoo, the Pocasset leader who had strategized her captivity and who most regularly arranged for her shelter) "the best friend that I had" among her captors. As it was after her restoration, friendship was important for basic material support. In contrast with the Bostonians, her Algonquian captors did not require her, she saw in retrospect, to perform sincerity—to claim she knew the contents of a highly individuated, biographically inflected personality. It was true that the skills she used to participate in that community were unique to her, but when compared with her celebrity experience, the skills that distinguished her there were not acquired traumatically.[14]

Friendship, in restoration, meant an acute, unrelenting self-consciousness of social conventions—gender, class, and religious purpose—that she had

13. Jordan Stein, "Mary Rowlandson's Hunger and the Historiography of Sexuality," *American Literature*, LXXXI (2009), 469–495; Brooks, *Our Beloved Kin*, 245; Rowlandson, *Sovereignty*, 74–76, 78, 81–83, 85–87, 90, 91, 93, 95, 96, 101.

14. Rowlandson, *Sovereignty*, 86–87; Brooks, *Our Beloved Kin*, 253–298; Thomas M. Wickman, *Snowshoe Country: An Environmental and Cultural History of Winter in the Early American Northeast* (Cambridge, 2018); Breitwieser, *American Puritanism*, 131–188; Van Engen, *Sympathetic Puritans*, 192–198.

once taken for granted. It also meant a sharp memory of the losses that made self-consciousness necessary. All that self-consciousness: no wonder she longed for sleep. The effects of these losses were severe. If "identity is contingent upon [one's] position in relation to others," the catastrophe of Lancaster's destruction might have been responsible for the loss of an identity or a sense of self that, in turn, haunted her late into the night. Rowlandson's obsession with friendship's debts, however—what they were and how her friends made claims, even on her—suggests not so much that she lost her identity as she experienced it in unhappy abundance. Loss of community would certainly leave Rowlandson without formerly reliable social recognition. At the same time, it wouldn't dissolve the history that shaped her, the experiences and ensuing emotional responses that made her herself. Acute self-consciousness of history—this was the cost that Rowlandson paid for reintegration into English society's biopoetic utopia. Alone at night, she sorted through the biographical accumulation of harmonious experiences alongside internally dissonant ones. The individuality that English friendship required was not so much a noble commitment to what Emerson called "the line of my own march" as it was an unexpected, not exactly consensual continuation of alienating removes.[15]

Unlike Rowlandson, Roger Williams seemed to like being awake. More important, though, he liked to show off his ability to pretend he wasn't. In his *Key into the Language of America,* the genre-bending text for which he is most often remembered, he inverted Rowlandson's performance of insomnia. "Wearied with travell and discourse" with the Narragansetts, he wrote, "I lay down to rest." He had been conversing at length with his neighbors, comparing and contrasting his cosmology with theirs. Yet he suspected that the best, truest view of those differences would appear if he subtracted himself from the scene. He made a show to English readers of making a show to Narragansett companions of his self-subtraction in pretending to go to sleep. In between lying down to go to sleep and actually getting there, Williams believed he overcame what Emerson would call the polite "dissimulation" that got in the way of honest self-disclosure. Williams could now report what he overheard as if it were truer than what his interlocutors had said to him directly, achieving the fantasy of ethnographic authenticity that John Jackson, among others, has critiqued. Williams was especially interested in what they had to say about him because he believed that their esteem was useful, maybe necessary, to persuade them, his non-Christian neighbors, to understand themselves differently, to

15. Logan, "Mary Rowlandson's Captivity," *EAL,* XXVIII (2014), 266 ("identity"), 327–356; Emerson, "Spiritual Laws," in Crase, ed., *Essays,* 85 ("line of my own march").

recognize themselves as responsible individuals rather than "take all upon trust from our forefathers." Unhappily for Williams, the quality he sought to dissolve in his new friends was the quality he claimed was most congenial about them.[16]

Friendship, the *Key* inaugurally proposed, was one of the primary distinguishing qualities of the Narragansetts. It was a politically precious quality. Williams opened the *Key* by depicting the Narragansett people as fundamentally desirous of friends. They were, he claimed, "exceedingly delighted with" and eager to "resalute lovingly" any English person who addressed them thus: "What cheer *Netop?*" *Netop,* he clarified, was the Narragansett word for "friend." Of course, variations existed within his generalization. There were also variations within and across languages. Friendship wasn't one thing and one thing only. Better than most monolingual English people, Roger Williams knew that "words change, depending on their context." When he wrote that the Narragansetts liked to be addressed as "friend," he was basically describing their political congeniality and their capacity to relate to English people as allies rather than as enemies. These were ennobling qualities to English eyes, and an alliance between friendly sovereign entities was a relationship that had long fascinated and attracted English settlers, as Christopher Levett demonstrated when he wrote of his encounter with an Algonquian "queene" who extended hospitality to Levett and his companions as their political friends.[17]

Williams was careful to identify that specific sort of friendship later in his document. The Narragansett language had more than one word for "friend" and recognized more than one context in which to use it. In his twenty-ninth chapter, "Of Their Warre Etc.," Williams shared words and phrases like *Nowetompatimmin* ("We are friends"), *Wetompâchick* ("Friends"), *Nowepinnâchick* ("My companion in War or Associates"), and *Nowechusettímmin* ("We are Confederates"). Friendship overlapped with and introduced associated

16. Roger Williams, *A Key into the Language of America,* ed. Dawn Dove et al. (Yardley, Pa., 2019), 117; Emerson, "Friendship," in Crase, ed., *Essays,* 117; John Jackson, *Real Black: Adventures in Racial Sincerity* (Chicago, 2015).

17. Williams, *Key,* ed. Dove et al., 27; Nan Goodman, "Banishment, Jurisdiction, and Identity in Seventeenth-Century New England: The Case of Roger Williams," *EAL,* VII (2009), 109–139, esp. 137 ("words change"); Christopher Levett, *A Voyage into New England Begun in 1623, and Ended in 1624* (London, 1628), 11. See also Sarah Rivett, *Unscripted America: Indigenous Languages and the Origins of a Literary Nation* (Oxford, 2017); Schweitzer, *Perfecting Friendship,* 53–64; Lisa T. Brooks and Cassandra M. Brooks, "The Reciprocity Principle and Traditional Ecological Knowledge: Understanding the Significance of Indigenous Protest on the Presumpscot River," *International Journal of Critical Indigenous Studies,* III (2010), 11–28.

vocabulary for martial alliance and confederation. These words elaborated the many positive qualities of friendship that the *Oxford English Dictionary* leaves room for in its second, negative definition: "A person who is not hostile or an enemy." Friendship, in these usages, allowed English people more confidently to anticipate a "league" like the one John Winthrop and Williams had hoped to forge with the Narragansetts as they embarked in 1637 on the conflict that we now call the Pequot War. Williams knew English readers in the metropole would recognize friendship's political use. In case his local English readers missed it, he was explicit about that value. In a letter to Winthrop, governor of the Massachusetts Bay Colony, Williams described it directly, and he quantified it, too: "I probably conjecture" that the friendship of the Narragansett sachem, Miantonomo, "would appeare in attending of us with 500 men (in Case) ag[ain]st any forreigne Enemies." As it had for Rowlandson, friendship answered calculable material conditions, and then some. Here, friendly relations had the rhetorical effect of making English people seem more native to the territory, in contrast to future antagonists who they could say were alien, or "foreign," to it.[18]

For Williams, political convenience didn't exhaust friendship, at least not semantically. Narragansett friendship had emotional gratifications, too. When he introduced the Narragansetts as a people eager to be called friends, he made them appear to English readers as if they were collectively suffused by an affection that was horizontal, welcoming, and eager to reciprocate without reservations. He threw on their shoulders an exemplary, intuitive quality of fellow feeling that his banishers had idealized. Williams's *Key* championed the Narragansetts' superior capacity for what Jeffrey Glover calls "social cooperation," a concerted and successful effort to flourish collectively. In doing so, Williams rehearsed an old colonial trope wherein Europe fantasized that Native people across the globe were more naive and innately desirous, especially of European conquest. Friendship was the form of desire most appealing to English readers. Six years earlier, Thomas Morton had claimed that the Massachusetts, despite lacking Christianity and being "Infidels" to English religion, were nevertheless "most full of humanity" and "more friendly" than Plymouth's Christians. Forty-five years later, Aphra Behn would still be recycling that convention when she wrote about the Native people of formerly Dutch-occupied Surinam who "caress[ed]" English settlers "with all the brotherly and friendly affection in the world." It was not enough to be

---

18. Williams, *Key*, ed. Dove et al., 148, 151; *Oxford English Dictionary*, s.v. "friend"; Glenn Lafantasie, ed., *The Correspondence of Roger Williams* (Providence, R.I., 1988), 101, 131, 150.

liked, as Michael Wigglesworth had longed, only by those closest to oneself. English people wanted to be universally likable. As early as Sir Francis Drake's circumnavigations in the shadow of the Black Legend, English people were ready to travel all the way around the world to prove just how likable they were. Williams, too, craved such fantasy fondness. And he cherished it at least in part because he had found himself the object of intense dislike from his fellow English and depended on that hospitality and openness for survival.[19]

The relative openness and toleration of the Narragansetts was particularly meaningful for Williams because they, not the English, had the wintering skills necessary for survival. And this mattered to him because of his risky commitment to sincerity. Williams had refused to accept the Massachusetts Bay Colony's founding premise that a civic government could be an acceptable agent in cultivating a sincere theological community. In his dissent, Williams lobbied his colleagues like John Cotton to desist from practices, such as drawing the English crown's authority to claim land for a utopian theological endeavor, that he believed sullied the hoped-for purity of the colonial planters' project. He was relentless and, it seems, quite frustrating. For his commitments, the Massachusetts General Court banished him. They expelled him in winter, the three to five months of the year where fidelity to the line of one's own march was the riskiest. Yet although his fellow English people had exiled him based on intolerable differences of principle, Williams shared more with those other English than simply belief in an essential likability. Like his banishers—and even more intensely than they—Williams cared very deeply about being sincere and true to his beliefs. In his study of Christian doctrine and its application to worldly life, he stumbled on a paradox latent in that doctrine's application, a stumble that landed him beyond the pale of his fellow English people's care. Settler society dialectically bound communal identity with robust individualism; it was a community whose "religious energies" expressed themselves in "a deliberate effort to dichotomize and set apart." The best experience of

19. Jeffrey Glover, "Wunnaumwáyean: Roger Williams, English Credibility, and the Colonial Land Market," *EAL*, XL (2006), 429–453, esp. 444–445; Thomas Morton, *New English Canaan; or, New Canaan, Containing the Abstract of New England . . .* (1637), rpt. in Peter Force, coll., *Tracts and Other Papers, Relating Principally to the Origin, Settlement, and Progress of the Colonies in North America, from the Discovery of the Country to the Year 1776*, 4 vols. (Washington, D.C., 1838), II, no. 5, 15; Aphra Behn, *Oroonoko; or, The Royal Slave* (New York, 2004), 9; Louis Montrose, "The Work of Gender in the Discourse of Discovery," *Representations*, XXXIII (1991), 1–41; Annette Kolodny, *The Lay of the Land: Metaphor as Experience and History in American Life and Letters* (Chapel Hill, N.C., 1975), 10–25; Cassander L. Smith, *Black Africans in the British Imagination: English Narratives of the Early Atlantic World* (Baton Rouge, 2016), 59.

shared priorities, reform Protestantism claimed, was an introspective search for the ways in which the idol of social approval might distract an individual from the line of his own march toward realization of divine favor. That march, Williams and his fellow English Protestants knew, might lead one to theological conclusions that could risk alienating them. This would be an unhappy result, but it was always an abstract possibility.[20]

Thus the penalty of banishment suited the crime of the iconoclast. Cotton's claim that Williams had "banished himself" might have been severe, but it was not random. Banishment required that the iconoclast exercise his or her commitment to a conscientious, unaffiliated life without rest or reprieve. It was a tiresome requirement, especially because banishment from English society did not make Williams less English. Although he has been celebrated as a forerunner of church-state separation, a champion of Indigenous territorial sovereignty, he never renounced his fealty to English people or his national identification. He exercised his conscience for decades in his operations as a free agent—spying, translating, and liaising for the English in their contentious disputes with Narragansetts and Pequots, among other Algonquian polities. Both parties saw value in Williams's mediation. English people saw him as a "buffer" and an advantageous lever in local trade, mediation he had begun before his exile, as early as 1632, when he assisted in translating the Native conversions that *New England's First Fruits* documented. He also helped English settlers track down and return runaway Indigenous captives from the English homes that enslaved them in the years following the Pequot War. On the other hand, Narragansetts saw him as a crucial mediator in the arcane and esoteric legal language exercises in which English people coercively entangled their Indigenous neighbors. Navigating these competing expectations made Williams lonely. Friendship, an impersonal openness to strangers, might not have been semantically exhausted by political convenience, but living that friendship wore Williams out.[21]

20. Goodman, "Banishment," *EAL*, VII (2009), 114; Schweitzer, *Perfecting Friendship*, 28–40. For one of the clearest summaries of the reasons for Williams's banishment, see Jessica R. Stern, "*A Key* into the *Bloudy Tenent of Persecution:* Roger Williams, the Pequot War, and the Origins of Toleration in America," *EAL*, IX (2011), 576–616, esp. 584–585.

21. Goodman, "Banishment," *EAL*, VII (2009), 130; Christopher D. Felker, "Roger Williams's Uses of Legal Discourse: Testing Authority in Early New England," *New England Quarterly*, LXIII (1990), 624–648, esp. 632 ("buffer"); Stern, "*A Key* into the *Bloudy Tenent of Persecution,*" ibid., IX (2011), 576–616; Glover, "Wunnaumwáyean," *EAL*, XL (2006), 429–453, esp. 430, 435, 440; Anne G. Myles, "Dissent and the Frontier of Translation: Roger Williams's '*A Key into the Language of America,*'" in Robert Blair St. George, ed., *Possible Pasts: Becoming*

What alienated Williams continued to buffer him. The commitments wherewith he "banished himself" also kept him from fully replacing the social intimacies he lost. As much as Williams celebrated the welcome of Narragansett society, he also insisted on noting his fortification against deep and intimate relations within it. At the start of his chapter on "Religion, the Soule, Etc.," he declined to participate in the *Nickommo,* a "Feast or Dance," because of his deep personal convictions. The Nickommo was shared festivity, wherein individuals "actively join . . . as the spirit moves them." Its "strange gestures and actions," modeled by a *powwaw,* alerted Williams's vigilance. Patricia E. Rubertone explains: the Nickommo was a "ritual Southern New England Indians . . . held in times of general crisis or at other important turning points in their lives." The Nickommo prioritized circulation and distribution rather than accumulation, as Williams observed. It facilitated the circulation of vital goods and the permeation of individuals by collective affection, the sort that superseded, even nullified, the buffered self that Winthrop's "Modell" had cherished and dialectically upheld. The Nickommo was a binding convention of social life, drawing individuals together over and above the mastery of will that Williams thought his deity required him to maintain.[22]

Despite the wearisomeness of his commitments to conscience, Williams wanted to recruit his new neighbors to join him in his fantasy of immunity to excessive influence. In a 1637 letter to Winthrop, Williams shared an early theory about the dangers of these Indigenous dances, their capacity to undo the accreted habits of conscientious piety. They were a source of aggressively friendly affection—what today might more prosaically go by the name "peer pressure." In the autumn of 1637, Williams informed Winthrop about the status of Jaguante Tunkawatten (renamed Reprive), a Manissean man whom

Colonial in Early America (Ithaca, N.Y., 2000), 88–108, esp. 90; Margaret Ellen Newell, *Brethren by Nature: New England Indians, Colonists, and the Origins of American Slavery* (Ithaca, N.Y., 2015), 104; Brooks, *Our Beloved Kin,* 58–68; Martha C. Nussbaum, "Patriotism and Cosmopolitanism," in Garret W. Brown and David Held, eds., *The Cosmopolitanism Reader* (Malden, Mass., 2010), 155–162, esp. 161.

22. Williams, *Key,* ed. Dove et al., 109–112; Patricia E. Rubertone, "Monuments and Sexual Politics in New England Indian Country," in Barbara L. Boss and Eleanor Conlin Casella, eds., *An Archaeology of Colonialism: Intimate Encounters and Sexual Effects* (Cambridge, 2012), 232–251, esp. 235; Heather Miyano Kopelson, *Faithful Bodies: Performing Religion and Race in the Puritan Atlantic* (New York, 2014), 51–73; Alice Nash, "'Antic Deportments and Indian Postures': Embodiment in the Seventeenth-Century Anglo-Algonquian World," in Jane Moore Lindman and Michele Lise Tarter, eds., *A Centre of Wonders: The Body in Early America* (Ithaca, N.Y., 2001), 163–175.

Winthrop claimed as a servant and to whom he had granted a four-week leave to visit relations in his home on Block Island. Servitude among the English, Williams thought, weakened Indigenous relations, eroded the presumed sense of commonality among kin. Williams considered this a good thing. But that influence was vulnerable to counter-erosion. On his way to Block Island, Tunkawatten encountered Juanemo, a relative, who accused Tunkawatten of being "a Spie from Mr Govr"—that is, of deciding as an individual to shift his alliances elsewhere. After arriving at Block Island, however, Tunkawatten found the opportunity to renew these alliances, especially by participating in the Níckommo. These activities made Williams impatient: "[I] am bold to wish that he might now take his last fare well of his friends" and hurry in his return to Winthrop's household. There, English supervision prohibited impious collective activities and would, Winthrop believed, bring Indigenous people like Tunkawatten closer to individual salvation. Williams conceded that severing these ties was, for now, impossible, or at least inconvenient and inadvisable. Given that unlikelihood, Williams favored discretionary hospitality. Winthrop, Williams advised, ought "to give [Tunkawatten's friends] leave to visit him at Boston, for you can not believe how hard it is for him to escape much evil and especially uncleanenes while he is with them."[23]

Williams thought he saw these dangers with unusual clarity. His hyperbole "you cannot believe" presented him as possessing exceptional familiarity with the practices of the Narragansetts and with their consequences. If he had an exceptional vantage on their lives, however, he also had to make sure his life was sufficiently distinct from theirs. His *Key* occasionally did that distinguishing, buffering work. After listing the relevant vocabulary and phrases to describe these dances, Williams explained that his information was largely secondhand:

> I confess to have most of these their customes by their own Relation, for after once being in their Houses, and beholding what their Worship was, I durst never be an eye witnesse, Spectatuor, or looker on, least I should have been a partaker of Sathans Inventions and Worships, contrary to Ephes. 5. 14.

Though these ceremonies attracted many English spectators and even partakers, Williams was not like other English settlers. Here, as ever, Williams

23. Lafantasie, ed., *Correspondence of Roger Williams,* 127 ("am bold," "to give . . . leave"), 132 ("a Spie"); Newell, *Brethren by Nature,* 101–103.

followed "his 'tender conscience' wherever it guided him." And here, as often, he cited his conscience's biblical sources: a didactic epistle to the nascent church at Ephesus, an Ionian city in what is currently Turkey, written by Paul, the foundational Christian exegete, in which he instructed his readers in right relations with non-Christians: "Awake, thou that sleepest, and stand up from the dead, and Christ shall give thee light." Williams believed that wakefulness represented vigilance toward the ease with which one might slip into spiritual sleep's unthinking habit, too similar to death.[24]

For Williams, as for Wigglesworth, wakefulness represented a more masterful sensory experience of the world; Williams considered that wakefulness vital to maintaining a well-surveilled experience of friendship. Wakefulness also repudiated intimate, possibly uncontrollable relations with Narragansett people. Williams's citation of Paul's letter to his Ephesian coreligionists suggests that those potentially uncontrollable relationships preoccupied him the most. The sacred text warned readers against actions ("fornications and uncleanness, or covetousness, let it not be once named among you") and identities ("unclean person," "idolater"). Yet Williams's description of what he was most eager to fortify himself against did not prioritize these threats. Instead, he directed special attention toward threatening forms of relationships with others. He listed three overlapping ways to relate to someone else's actions—as a witness, a spectator, or a looker-on—and concluded with a fourth, more intimate and spiritually reprehensible relationship that followed from the first three: being a "partaker of Sathans Inventions and Worships." To prove that he was thorough in his buffering, Williams had to list all the ways he might fail in that fortification. In rehearsing the many ways he *might* have participated in those dances, Williams suggested that participation was something easy to desire—even if he denied desiring those relations himself.[25]

Given the closeness it cost him, Williams prided himself on his wakefulness. Resisting sleep, he narrated, had been a shortcut to friendly intimacy's unique knowledge. Deliberate wakefulness was also an emblem for what got in the way of that intimacy, why he felt the need to fake it in the first place. Beyond friendship, Williams longed to be a knowing master of his attachments. Thus, weary with travel, conversation, and the struggle to remain faithful to his individual conscience when the possibility of betraying it lurked around every corner (within any otherwise-welcoming home), Williams, at the end of

24. Williams, *Key*, ed. Dove et al., 112; Newell, *Brethren by Nature*, 72; Eph. 5:14 (Geneva); Stern, "A *Key* into the *Bloudy Tenent of Persecution*," *EAL*, IX (2011), 582.

25. Eph. 5:3–5 (Geneva).

his description of those perceived dangers, lay down to rest his easily offended eyes. Nevertheless, he was sure to narrate that he did not go to sleep so swiftly. In his committed wakefulness, he materialized the alienation that conscientious personhood required of exemplary English Christians. Sleep meant vulnerability, a renunciation of self-control, as his citation of the Pauline epistle reminded readers. Though his new friends welcomed him, he resisted friendship's volition-eroding qualities. If all of his friends, as the wisdom from our fathers has it, were jumping off bridges, he, most certainly, would not. He would not participate in practices inherited "on trust from [the] fathers," be they English fathers or Narragansett ones. Lying awake, having foregone what was required for intimate friendship, he consoled himself with knowledge he could use to trump those who had exiled him. He praised friendship yet insisted that he did not need it to achieve his own political and spiritual goals.[26]

The form of the *Key*, as idiosyncratic as the category of the friend, compensated for these losses. In his introduction, Williams proposed that he was writing a text with many values. Some weren't even immediately evident—it was a key that opened a box that contained many more keys. Primarily, he claimed, it would unlock conversations, maybe even intimacy between the English and the Narragansetts. He also proposed that it could generate intimacy within communities of English readers. Sensitive to the pieties of the eye, Williams drew on the emblem book as inspiration, presenting the *Key* to encourage Christian meditation through visual discipline. The *Key* also championed the power of the tongue and the ear, what happened in conversation with others. Williams suggested that "the Life of all Language is in the Pronunciation," and he anticipated that his close attention to diacritical notation would enhance the accuracy of the conversations he described and prescribed. It was not just through speaking, however, that his text shaped a future community of Christians; it was through listening, too. Williams hoped his readers would re-create the "implicite Dialogues" that his columns traced and begin to hear a conversation between the two parties, much as Williams himself had. Like Rowlandson, Williams knew how costly a commitment to sincerity could be. And he had palliatives that he claimed other Christians might benefit from, maybe even enjoy. Conscientious English readers could imagine themselves participating in a community of buffered eavesdroppers,

26. Ann Marie Plane, *Dreams and the Invisible World in Colonial New England: Indians, Colonists, and the Seventeenth Century* (Philadelphia, 2014).

insulated from gnawing desires for affection and able to avoid the risk of impiety as they were welcomed by a community of impersonal "friends."[27]

For settlers with troubled memories and troubled consciences, sleep promised a taste of what waking friendships lacked. Rowlandson cherished the possibility of impersonal communion; Williams, an escape from the burden of iconoclastic responsibility. By contrast, for James Quananopohit, Christian convert and Nipmuc scout, sleep was one of friendship's dearest purchases. In two testimonies recorded on January 24, 1675/76, after returning from a reconnaissance mission in Wampanoag country during some of the tensest weeks of King Philip's War, Quananopohit relayed to English strategists important information regarding the Algonquian alliance's plans. These plans included the February 10 raid on Lancaster that eventually did succeed in capturing Rowlandson and others. Quananopohit's mission had been a risk. Arriving among his estranged relations, he found himself greeted by mistrust. In the eyes of his non-Christian counterparts, his alliance with the English had constituted a rejection of the shared principles that they had received "on trust from our forefathers." Conversing with Tuckup William, Quananopohit learned, before anything else, that, along with "James Speen, Andrew, Pitimy, captain Hunter, Thomas Quanapu, and Peter Ephraim," he was on a list of people marked for death. Moreover, he wasn't just on the list; he was at the top of it. He was told, "I was one of the worst, and they would kill me . . . and bade me look to myself." Quananopohit did not have to look to himself, though. Friendship intervened. "Next morning I went to one-eyed John's [Monoco's] wigwam." There, he received a different welcome. "He said he was glad to see me; I had been his friend many years." As a result, "[he] said, nobody should meddle with me." Quananopohit went on to describe what that friendship secured him: "I lay in the sagamore's wigwan [sic]; and he charged his gun, and threatened any man that should offer me hurt." Because of his former friendship, he could sleep soundly at night. He used that friendship, in turn, to bring his relations closer to that security.[28]

27. Williams, *Key*, ed. Dove et al., 18, 25; John Teunissen and Evelyn J. Hinz, "Introduction," in Roger Williams, *A Key into the Language of America*, ed. Teunissen and Hinz (1643; rpt. Detroit, 1973), 13–69; Eric Wertheimer, "'To Spell out Each Other': Roger Williams, Perry Miller, and the Indian," *Arizona Quarterly*, L, no. 2 (Summer 1994), 1–18, esp. 8–10; Jonathan Beecher Field, "A Key for the Gate: Roger Williams, Parliament, and Providence," *NEQ*, LXXX (2007), 353–362.

28. [James Quananopohit,] "James Quanapaug's Information," *Massachusetts Historical Society, Collections,* 1st Ser., VI (Boston, 1799), 205–208, esp. 206.

Quananopohit's report models a form of friendship that shares certain qualities with Rowlandson's and Williams's. Yet it departs from theirs in significant ways. As it had done for Rowlandson, but more immediately, friendship meant support and protection to keep on living. In Rowlandson's case, this help was direct and positive. Benevolence from Christian friends saved her from destitution, starvation, and homelessness. For Quananopohit, friendship had a material yield, but in the negative: it saved him from the hostility of wartime's enmities. Quananopohit's friendship, like Williams's, acquired clarity in cultural, even martial conflict. For Williams, friendship foregrounded the responsibilities of dealing conscientiously and fairly between two antagonists. Friendship obliged Quananopohit similarly, but it burdened him with greater responsibility to perform sincerity between two expectant parties. When he returned to Cambridge, Quananopohit testified directly to the plans of the Wampanoag alliance; he also testified indirectly to the power of friendship and the vigor of shared feeling in mediating hostilities between nations.

The cultural differences that Quananopohit navigated were more complex than the ones Rowlandson and Williams confronted. Like them, he experienced sustained immersion in a different culture. But Christian conscience and the fidelity it demanded required greater renunciations. Quananopohit and his companion and fellow double agent, Job Kattenanit, professed to believe in the Christian doctrine that claimed, first, that humans were essentially imperfect; second, that a divine being could intervene and remedy that imperfection; third, that individual conscience was of paramount importance in effecting that intervention. This doctrine had consequences for any experience of friendship and intimate affiliation with others. It required its acolytes to be ready to leave behind their families and ancestors to follow the guidance of individual conscience, as Williams had done and as John Eliot had encouraged his converts to do when he founded Natick and the other Praying Towns. Eliot and his colleagues hoped that these towns, though external to the soul, would have effects on it, "educating" the desires of their inhabitants through biopolitical disciplines, especially self-surveillance. For men like Quananopohit and Kattenanit, the English dream of biopoetic fulfillment required significantly more self-conscious transformation through practices of bodily self-management. Those disciplines ran counter to the goals of protectors such as King Philip, Tuckup William, Monoco, and others, who sought to renew the principles of communal reciprocity that had guided their societies for centuries before the arrival of English settlers. As Algonquian leaders like Chickatawbut had noticed in the first years and decades of English settlement, biopoetic self-management and a networked vision of personhood were often at odds, but they were not mutually exclusive. Many Native converts, such as those at Natick and Noepe, strove to preserve their former ways of life by selectively taking up the theological innovations they found in Christian teachings. King Philip's War, a conflict that contemporary historians have reframed as a civil war among Algonquians in the region, however, suggests how difficult it was to sustain a balance between those priorities. Amid that tense context, Quananopohit's testimony distinguishes itself in its description of friendship. His friendships improvisationally departed from Christian models of individual conscience. They enabled individuals to evade Christianity's severe requirement of sincere, conscientious allegiance.[29]

Quananopohit and Kattenanit, interned at Deer Island after deportation from Hassanamesit, answered Daniel Gookin's solicitation to undertake an espionage mission among the enemies of the English assembled at Menimesit. Quananopohit, sometimes called James Rumney Marsh, was a relation of the sachem of Winisimet, though he had grown up with his mother at Natick. Kattenanit was the son of an eminent early convert at Natick, Naoas, who sent young Job as a child to Cambridge to be educated by white Christians at Roxbury. Kattenanit went to grammar school with his brother Wawaus, more frequently known as James Printer, who, after the war, helped print Rowlandson's captivity narrative. Kattenanit and Quananopohit's mission took almost four weeks. They left Cambridge on December 30, and both of James's testimonies are dated January 24, twenty-six days later. In addition to securing knowledge about the Wampanoag alliance's capabilities and strategies, Kattenanit and Quananopohit were instructed to assess whether the Praying Indians captive at Menimesit were sincere in their political allegiances. Had they indeed gone to Menimesit as captives, or had they gone as defectors? Where did their political friendships lie? Were their hearts in captivity or against it? Had they robustly exercised the "liberty of heart," so valorized by early modern friendship theorists, by rejecting the sympathies of relations? For these converts, sincerity had very high stakes. In the case of Philip's defeat, English people would consider reintegrating these captives into Christian society and use any evidence that the men like Kattenanit and Quananopohit brought back regarding their relations' sincerity—as well as

29. Kristina Bross, *Dry Bones and Indian Sermons: Praying Indians in Colonial America* (Ithaca, N.Y., 2004); Richard W. Cogley, *John Eliot's Mission to the Indians before King Philip's War* (Cambridge, Mass., 1999); Jean M. O'Brien, *Dispossession by Degrees: Indian Land and Identity in Natick, Massachusetts, 1650–1790* (Cambridge, 1997); Ann Laura Stoler, *Race and the Education of Desire: Foucault's "History of Sexuality" and the Colonial Order of Things* (Durham, N.C., 1995).

their own. As Gookin communicated it to these two agents, the errand was double-edged. It sought one piece of information and communicated another to those performing the errand. It conveyed English expectations to Kattenanit and Quananopohit: that they remain faithful to the community and the values that they had (English people presumed) chosen, and for which they had already sacrificed so much.[30]

For Kattenanit, at least, defection was quite plausible—his children were among the Menimesit captives, so both men had much to worry about on their journey. They had to remain faithful to men like Gookin and Eliot, on whose testimony of fidelity they depended. They had to avoid encounters with the unpredictable populist violence of white English settlers, as the previous chapter surveyed, and they faced a predicament similar to that of Tunkawatten. They had to persuade their Native relations that they were not what they truly were: spies. Gookin had anticipated this challenge and recommended at least one solution. In order to dissemble from their true roles, he told them to describe conditions at Deer Island as they actually were: "These spies were instructed to tell a fair, yet true story to the enemy." Here was the story and its truth: "They were some of the poor Natick Indians confined to Deer Island" (they weren't both immediately from Natick, but they had been confined at Deer Island) "where they had lived all this winter under great sufferings" (which they had) "and now these being gotten off, they were willing to come among their countrymen and find out their friends that had lived at Hassanamesit, and to understand the numbers, strength, unity, and estate of their countrymen, that were in hostility with the English." The story, Gookin observed, was "fair, yet true"—it was attractive first and honest second. It had the added convenience of a built-in exit strategy. Confessing frankly that they sought information, they could then ask for permission to return, so that "they might be the better able to advise their friends at Deer Island and elsewhere,

30. Gookin, *Historical Account of the Doings and Sufferings*, 486–487; Brooks, *Our Beloved Kin*, 82, 87–88, 147, 319–320; Alonzo Lewis, *The History of Lynn, Including Nahant* (Boston, 1844), 50; Samuel Drake, *History of Middlesex County, Massachusetts, Containing Carefully Prepared Histories of Every City and Town in the County* (Boston, 1880), II, 113–114. See also Cathy Rex, "Indians and Images: The Massachusetts Bay Colony Seal, James Printer, and the Anxiety of Colonial Identity," *American Quarterly*, LXIII (2011), 61–93, esp. 77–78, 85–87; Walter T. Meserve, "English Works of Seventeenth-Century Indians," ibid., VIII (1956), 264–276, esp. 266–268.

what course to steer, for the future." Gookin helped these men succeed as spies by telling them to pretend to be counterspies—by telling the truth, mostly.[31]

Quananopohit's testimonies suggest that Gookin's idea succeeded. The longer of the two testimonies that Quananopohit shared when he returned includes detailed information regarding the Algonquian alliance's plans. In his shorter testimony, Quananopohit abbreviated that information, describing instead how he acquired it. His account unfolds as a series of direct questions and answers between Monoco and Quananopohit, taking place within the safety that Monoco offered as a result of their friendship. "I asked" is often followed with "He said." If Monoco knew that Quananopohit was a spy, he did not behave as if he did. Or at least Quananopohit did not narrate Monoco's responses as if the latter knew, or even suspected, that Quananopohit would be reporting so much information back to English strategists. Quananopohit brought back detailed information regarding the Native alliance's plans, but he also, as the foundation for the trustworthiness of those plans, brought back evidence of a premise that English listeners would have cherished—that individual friendship, its sovereign amity, might overcome years of animosity and aggression, even transcend history.[32]

Quananopohit's narrative vindicated friendship's utility, but it also showcased subtle differences between English and Algonquian people's ideas of friendship. For Quananopohit and Monoco, friendship emerged from participation in upbuilding one's community of relations. It was less a matter of kin-jeopardizing conscience than a commitment to right relations that substantiated a self—a commitment and "utmost regard," as Lisa T. Brooks and Cassandra M. Brooks put it, for "individual responsibility to the community." Accordingly, friendship intertwined individual and history; it manifested itself in the possibility that a relationship existed between previous actions and a principle that could guide future ones. Quananopohit's friendships—and his enmities—built on long familiarity, unlike Williams's and Rowlandson's. Everyone at Menimesit seemed to know who Quananopohit was and what he'd done. He was at the top of their list of least liked because of actions that his estranged relations could recall. His presence on that list, Quananopohit knew, was warranted. He reported, according to Tuckup William, "They would kill me, because I went up with the army to Swanzey, where Pebe and one of Philip's counsellors were killed, and that I helped to cut off their heads." These

31. Gookin, *Historical Account of the Doings and Sufferings*, 487; Brooks, *Our Beloved Kin*, 246–252; Kopelson, *Faithful Bodies*, 183–184.

32. [Quananopohit], "James Quanapaug's Information," 206.

actions, Tuckup William suggested, were useful indexes of possible future acts and thus good indexes of the quality of friendship they might expect from Quananopohit.[33]

But the past could also protect Quananopohit. Retelling his mission to the English, he narrated Monoco's response to Tuckup William's charge. "He said he was glad to see me; I had been his friend many years, and had helped him kill Mohaugs; and said, nobody should meddle with me. I told him what was said to me. He said, if any body hurt me they should die." In addition to invoking friendly relations that had lasted for "many years," Monoco's story highlighted the same martial qualities as Tuckup William's. Before Quananopohit had fought against King Philip's alliance at Swansea, his martial expertise had been useful against the Nipmucs' enemies, the Mohawks. Friendship, at minimum, meant enmity toward a shared foe, similar to the "league" that Williams and Winthrop anticipated would fortify them against future, more foreign foreigners. Yet Quananopohit suggested a subtler contrast between the two assessments of his character. Friendship was a relationship less interested in decision making than in the postponement of certainty. Quananopohit narrated his confrontation with Tuckup William to English scribes. Then he narrated narrating it to Monoco ("I told him what was said to me"). His second narration invited Monoco to share counterevidence, Quananopohit's history of action against the Mohawks that demonstrated his commitment to the preservation of his Nipmuc people. The commitment neutralized, or at least diminished, direct antagonism toward Quananopohit after Swansea. Friendship valued committed action on behalf of a community rather than a static good or evil essence, or avowals of fealty, as English judgment tended to understand it. Monoco's protection and hospitality were a risk for him, but friendship found that risk worthy as it delayed definitive judgment.[34]

Quananopohit's previous actions helped Monoco to take that risk. Similarly, Quananopohit's actions at Menimesit renewed the basis of friendly relations. Monoco's vow to protect Quananopohit opened a door back into familiar social rituals: "Then," related Quananopohit, "came Matoonus his company and others, and went to dancing; we painted our faces and went to

33. Brooks and Brooks, "Reciprocity Principle," *International Journal of Critical Indigenous Studies*, III (2010), 14; [Quananopohit], "James Quanapaug's Information," 206; James Drake, *King Philip's War: Civil War in New England, 1675–1676* (Amherst, Mass., 1997), 173–186; Jill Lepore, *The Name of War: King Philip's War and the Origins of American Identity* (New York, 1998), 21–23.

34. [Quananopohit], "James Quanapaug's Information," 206; Cogley, *John Eliot's Mission*, 146–165.

dancing with them, and were very good friends. The dance continued two or three nights, after which they looked badly upon me again." Matoonus, on behalf of the Nipmucs he led, extended an invitation to Monoco and Quananopohit, and they prepared themselves according to the social customs they both knew. For Quananopohit, dances and decoration signified a return to Indigenous customs that English missionaries had tried vigorously to eradicate. Evangelists such as Eliot and Williams saw them as expressions of "evill and especially uncleanenes" that bound their participants into a community beyond the use of their rational faculties. Quananopohit insisted to his English auditors that, at the end of a period of dancing, which he refused to recollect specifically ("two or three days"), these friends "looked badly on me again." Having grown up according to English customs, he knew that those activities disappointed English people—still, he knew those activities and their constitutive gestures. It would have been deliberately acquired knowledge that, burdensomely, risked his esteem among English Christians. The dance, momentarily, unburdened him of the conflict between his past actions and what they portended for his future. As he told it, during the dance, he wasn't simply friends with Monoco, Matoonus, and their extended relations but "very good friends."[35]

Like the dreaming that Williams resisted, the dance renewed those friendships. And, as the narrative frame that ushered Quananopohit in and out of Native space, so did sleep. Slumber and dance sealed the successes of Gookin's "fair, yet true story." Quananopohit knew, on arrival, that he could sleep soundly when Monoco was protecting him. The motif of supine repose also concluded his narrative, when he explained to English listeners why he returned alone, without his companion. His listeners would have been eager to know whether Kattenanit had defected. According to Quananopohit, no. Or rather, not exactly. After the resistance leaders suggested that Quananopohit should be taken to Philip to prove that he was not a spy, Kattenanit and Quananopohit planned their escape—more specifically, Quananopohit's escape, since Kattenanit needed more time to secure the safety of his children. When Quananopohit described their defection from their pretended defection, he lingered on the scenes of departure: "Job and I consulted to go a hunting, and borrowed Sampson's gun, and wee found four deers, and killed them, and got into a swamp, and lay there all night. Next morning dressed our venison; then I came away, and left Job . . . We parted on Thursday last, about three o'clock in the morning." Some nights they spent together sleeping in the

35. [Quananopohit], "James Quanapaug's Information," 206.

swamps with which they had been long familiar. On the final night of their pretended hunting excursion, Quananopohit and Kattenanit woke up very early—as Rowlandson would have put it, "when all are fast about me, and no eye open." Yet unlike Rowlandson, Quananopohit and Kattenanit were awake, eyes open, together.[36]

For Quananopohit, nighttime could be a space of common repose and mindlessness. It could also be space of deliberation, full of purpose. Narrating those nights with his companion, one of the few people who shared his tense predicament as a liaison between enemies, Quananopohit communicated their purpose but also did so without naming any great emphasis on personality. He recalled his companionship with Kattenanit in passing details, such as the familiar work of hunting and dressing meat, adapting English instruments to preserve inherited modes of relating to their world and the beings that comprised it. Together they occupied the swamp, a site of common memory and placemaking. Together, he recalled, they settled down for the night. Yet the contrast between sleeping and waking was not so great here as it was for Williams and Rowlandson, or even for Quananopohit at Monoco's. There, sleep suspended the taxing work of self-consciousness—especially acute for a spy—but it also made one vulnerable. Here, Quananopohit did not indicate any difficulty getting to sleep. He did not indicate sleeping at all. Given the travel Quananopohit would have expected ahead of him, it's quite likely that he and Kattenanit actually did sleep. It's also quite likely that they talked. Nighttime intimacy with Monoco probably facilitated the information that James acquired and brought back to Cambridge. With Kattenanit, he likely discussed the stories they would each tell to men like Gookin and Eliot if and when they reunited in the settlements, and maybe also strategies that Kattenanit might take to secure his children's safety at Narragansett. They might have sung each other to sleep. According to the contours of friendship implied in Monoco's protection and in Matoonus's invitation, these men need not have communicated deep feelings for these scenes of rest and repose to constitute expressions of profound and restorative friendship.[37]

This friendship was very unlike early modern sovereign amity. Kattenanit and Quananopohit knew that every action and gesture they made and that

36. Ibid., 208; Rowlandson, *Sovereignty*, 111; Brooks, *Our Beloved Kin*, 246–252.

37. Rubertone, "Monuments," in Boss and Casella, eds., *An Archaeology of Colonialism*, 237, 246; Kathleen Joan Bragdon, *Native People of Southern New England, 1500–1650* (Norman, Okla., 1996), 105–106; and Dwight Heath, ed., *Mourt's Relation: A Journal of the Pilgrims at Plymouth* (Bedford, Mass., 1986), 67.

they narrated making would be performances, would risk insincerity, even before they enacted them. They knew how minutely they'd be examined for testaments of affiliation in one direction or another. They knew that they risked being considered false by virtually everyone they knew and how difficult it would be to be true to their own selves. Yet their knowledge of that difficulty might, in turn, explain one of the enduring puzzles of the entire episode: why it was that, despite the risks that Quananopohit and Kattenanit took to secure knowledge of the plan to raid Lancaster, all its English chroniclers described it as a surprise. According to Increase Mather, Lancaster had not been "Gerisoned as it might," but it could have been. According to the intelligence that Quananopohit brought back from Monoco, King Philip's alliance "intended to fall upon them [at Lancaster] in about twenty days time from Wednesday last." Quananopohit had delivered this information sixteen days before the actual raid on February 10. Still the English had not fortified.[38]

Quananopohit gave English people the intelligence they asked for. Yet English strategists, who cherished their skepticism and paranoia and who longed to second-guess the sincerity of others to be sure of their own righteousness, thought they had to extract that information from the narrative that bore it. And that narrative was full of reasons to doubt. Each description of friendship was one new reason. Matoonus, after all, had been remarkably open to Quananopohit and Kattenanit. Monoco, as well, had been voluble in answering Quananopohit's questions. If English people were skilled at anything, as the first chapter showed, it was speculating on the ways that those who were not like them might be plotting against them. The English strategists who received Quananopohit's news were not interpreting the events themselves, recorded directly from a hidden microphone. They were extracting that information from Quananopohit's thoughtful testimony of those events, and at every turn, his testimony offered reasons to doubt its integrity. Was it possible, English strategists would have wondered as they planned what to do next, that Monoco's answers weren't sincere, that they were counterintelligence sent by the enemy and conveyed under the guise of friendship? If that was their gamble, they were wrong—the attack on Lancaster came. But their suspicion might not have been misplaced. Quananopohit would have known English paranoia better than almost anyone—he would have known how high the bar was for men like him and Kattenanit to be accepted into the bright circle of honest, frank, biopoetic speech. He would have known how to make use of his

38. Mather, *A Brief History,* in Slotkin and Folsom, eds., *So Dreadfull a Judgment,* 64; [Quananopohit], "James Quanapaug's Information," 207.

his ffreind many years, & had helpt him till Mohauog, & saide, no
body should meddle with mee, & told him so was Peter wee Hees, if
any body should mee they should dye, & Ellen cam'd Matoonus his company & others, & went to danceing; wee painted Peter faces, & went to
danceing with them, & were very good freinds. This danceing continued two
or three nights, after which they looked badly upon mee again, I
lay in the Sagamores wigwam, & hee charged his gun, & threatned
any man that should offer mee hurt; & all those his wigwam were
of that mind, & sent a guard with mee to the place whence I came, &
I went to another Sachem, who told mee, no body should hurt mee, &
I askt one-eyed John, how many men hee lost, & hees, but two, & I
askt him how many hee lost up about Hatfield, & hees, hee lost one
in the fight with Capt. Beers, another in fight with Capt. Lathrop. Hee
hath about 30 men under him, I askt him how many Philip and
Northampton Indians lost, hee saide but two, & I askt him how much
I askt him how much amunition hee had, hee, 8½ a peck of powder,
& shewed mee it, hee saide hee had it from the soldiers that were
slain, some, & some from the ffort of Orania, they haudnt theire
Towne about twice so many women & Children as are persons upon
deere Island. Hees, hee expected helpe from the wampeeg & Mohauog, betwen this & planting time, the Mohauog say they will
not till the English, but they will till the Mohekins, the ffrench
men, that went up from Boston to Norwottuck, were with the Indians,
& shewed them some letters, & burnt some papers there, & bid them
they should not burn Mills nor meeting-houses, for there God was
worshipt; & told them that they would come by land, & assist them,
& would haue Connecticot River, & that ships would come from
ffrance & stop up the bays, & hinder English ships & soldiers
coming. And this Indian told mee, they would fall upon Lancast:
Groton, Malborough, Sudbury, & Meadfeild, & that the 1st thing they
would do should bee to cut down Lancaster bridge, so to hinder
theire flight, & assistance coming to them, & that they intended to
fall upon them in about 20 dayes time from wedensday last.
The Narragansetts sent up one English head to them by two of
theire men, & they shot at the Narragansets, told them they had
been freinds to the English, & that head was nothing. Afterward
they sent up two men more, with twelue scalps, then they received
them, & hung the scalps on trees, whilst I was there, another
messenger cam'd, brought nothing, but desired assistance, &
saide, they lost but 35 fighting men, & 300 old men, women, &
children, & hees, they had a great English Capt: among them
who had killed 5 English men, that Capt: Mosely was killed,

exclusion from that world of good-faith discourse. On his way to Menimesit, he probably reflected with great ambivalence on his position. At Menimesit, he probably learned more than he eventually told. Listening to Monoco and more broadly to the conversations of his estranged relations, including many that he chose not to narrate, Quananopohit might have come to understand the Algonquian alliance's reasons for the Lancaster raid as Lisa Brooks as recovered them: after the devastation and violence at the Great Swamp in December 1675, the alliance saw English captives as their best protection from the cruelty and vehemence of English militias, the fury that had become widespread—even normal—between 1637 and 1675. The counterintelligence that English strategists feared might have come, not from Monoco (at least not immediately), but from Quananopohit himself, counterintelligence that consisted not so much in content as context. He brought news of the truth of the planned raid, but he also communicated ample reasons to doubt it. In doing so, he would have been trying to ensure the safety of the Algonquian alliance and the children whose families he'd danced with for days.[39]

Quananopohit's friendships might not have been sincere. He might have been dissembling to his former relations or his English allies or both. True or untrue, his story took risks, and those risks suggest that he had motives that would be difficult to call "sincere" because Quananopohit's fealties were difficult to decide, even for himself. Perhaps it had all been true, transparently conveyed. If so, he would have been taking up the same instruments of English subterfuge they had offered him—a "fair, yet true story," if not a sincere one. Quananopohit's testimony hints that friendship's best expression might not be in the communication of true selfhood, fidelity to one's conscience, or even a clear sense of personal identity, inherited or adopted. Friendship, for Quananopohit, was a different sort of trust. It didn't try to transcend historical circumstances but instead to liaise between antagonists who wielded historical

FIGURE 8. Transcript of James Quanapaug's [Quananopohit] Information, Jan. 24, 1675 / 76 (recto). When James Quananopohit returned from Menimesit, Daniel Gookin recorded his testimony twice. Like the longer testimony, this shorter one features foreknowledge of the February raid on Lancaster (underlined, two-thirds down the page). This second page of the transcript, however, also features the friendship Quananopohit shared with Monoco and Matoonus—the former "his friend many years," as the page starts off—as well as the possibility that such friendship might have compromised the information itself. Ms. N–2196. Miscellaneous bound manuscripts collection, 1629–1908. Collection of the Massachusetts Historical Society

---

39. Brooks, *Our Beloved Kin*, 245.

forces that affected his life in ways he could not control. Friendship's dearest purchase might be a brief, shared experience of sleep so obvious and safe, one need not name that it took place at all.

Unlike Mary Rowlandson, Roger Williams, or James Quananopohit, Anthony Thacher was not interested in recollecting scenes of repose—desired, feigned, or tenuously achieved. In 1635, he survived a freak hurricane a few weeks after crossing the Atlantic uneventfully. The hurricane took from him almost all of his family, all of his possessions, and his dearest friend, Joseph Avery. He wrote it out for his brother Peter, forming a story that, after his own death, circulated widely among the settlements and even returned to England when Increase Mather included it in his 1685 *Essay for the Recording of Illustrious Providences*. The illustrious providence that caught Mather's attention wasn't simply Thacher's improbable survival. Rather, a strange detail nagged at Mather: Thacher recalled being able, mysteriously, to avoid the twin risks of supine or prone abjection. Somehow he managed not to fall "by the stroke of the wave flat on my face" while avoiding tumbling over onto his back, where he would be unable to cling to rocks, sand, or flotsam. Instead, he "stood bolt upright as if I had stood upon my feet but I felt no bottom nor had any footing to stand upon but the water." This was Mather's miracle, what he called providence. Thacher was grateful to his deity, but the memory of that miracle was also the cause for unhappy reflection. Alone in the water, he had managed to keep his head above the waves. And alone afterward, he reflected on what friendship could bring him, there on what he thought to be a stark colonial frontier. Within a month of the disaster, he already had found replacements for Avery, friends who supported him in his destitution. But, he wondered, was catastrophe, and its heightened alienation, necessary to vindicate friendship?[40]

Thacher didn't mean for his story to reach wide circulation, but it did anyway because Mather's *Providences* proved to be quite popular. Printed in Boston two years after Rowlandson's captivity narrative, it would go through at least three more editions, two in England, before Mather's death in 1723. As a preeminent example of that providence, Mather proposed not simply Thacher's inexplicable uprightness but that buoyancy's amazing duration—a detail of Thacher's story that Mather went to some lengths to ascertain. Mather copied long stretches of this narrative directly from Thacher's letter to his brother. Peter lived in England, but a copy of the letter seems to have remained in the colonies, perhaps with John Cotton, Increase Mather's father-in-law and

40. Anthony Thacher to Peter Thacher, September 1635, in Everett Emerson, ed., *Letters from New England* (Amherst, Mass., 1967), 168–174, esp. 171, 172.

a friend (at least eventually) to Thacher after his losses. Increase Mather was born in 1639, four years after his own father, Richard, had survived the same hurricane as he approached the American littoral. Like John Cotton, Richard Mather was also a minister, and through these professional networks, young Increase might have known Anthony Thacher in his childhood. He certainly knew about the storm. In Richard's autobiography, the elder Mather expressed his wish that their deity would "so imprint the memory of [the storm] in our hearts." The younger Mather was likely to have overheard his father and his father's colleagues and friends share their accounts of that memorable storm, perhaps to each other and almost certainly to their children.[41]

Mather had other sources for Thacher's account, however—sources that helped him fill in details that Thacher's confessional letter forgets. These details include the astonishingly long time that Thacher was able to stand, as if walking, within water—if not atop it. Thacher did not share that detail with his brother. He recalled being able to see his wife among the waves and then reaching shore: "Before I could get unto her she was gotten to the shore. When we were come to each other. . . ." As Mather copied this scene, though, he interrupted this sequence with a remarkably precise detail: how long Thatcher had been floating: "Before I could get unto her, she was gotten on to the shoare: I was in the water after I was washed from the Rock, before I came to the shoar a quarter of an hour at least. When we came to each other. . . ." Mather probably didn't invent this detail. He could have recalled it from the stories his elders told him as a child. Or he could have found it, or cross-referenced it, with information that Winthrop had preserved in the first of the three volumes that he kept to chronicle the same sorts of providences Mather had sought. These volumes circulated among the spiritual and political elite of the colony, and it's possible that Mather used them as a resource. Happily for Mather's research, Winthrop recalled the 1635 storm, recording the intensity as he experienced it from land and as others experienced it at sea: "In the same tempest a Barke of mr Allertons was cast away . . . none were saved but one mr th<a>cher and his wife, who were cast on shore, and preseved by a powder horne and bagge with a flinte." Winthrop described other jetsam, like the dead goat the couple cooked and ate on the beach, and noted that "the man was cast on shore when he had been (as he thought) ¼ of an howre

41. Richard Mather, "Journal," in Alexander Young, ed., *Chronicle of the First Planters of the Colony of Massachusetts Bay* (New York, 1846), 445–481, esp. 474; James Levernier, "Introduction," in Increase Mather, *An Essay for the Recording of Illustrious Providences*, ed. Levernier (Delmar, N.Y., 1977), v–xx.

beaten up and downe by the waves not being able to swimme one stroake." Like Mather, Winthrop wasn't present at the shipwreck or in the water with Thacher, yet he spoke confidently about this detail.[42]

Fifteen miraculous minutes were missing from Thacher's missive. One reason he might have skipped over them was that their miraculous quality didn't matter very much to him. For fifteen minutes, as the adrenaline left him and he began to succumb to the water's chill, he might have realized the enormity of the events that had just taken place, the intensity of the cataclysm that his later testimonies suggest. Like Mather, Winthrop probably didn't invent this detail, either. He wasn't present with Thacher at the wreck, but he was present at the September 1635 meeting of the General Court where Thacher testified to his experience. On the first of September, a little more than two weeks after the storm, Thacher presented himself to the colony's magistrates to confirm his status as the inheritor of the "goods and chattels" of Joseph Avery, fellow passenger on Isaac Allerton's ship, who had accompanied Thacher from England to America and from Ipswich to Marblehead. Thacher knew the piety of men like Winthrop and Mather well—Avery, his dear friend and, it seems, a familial relation to Thacher, had been a minister himself. Thacher would have known that details like the quarter-hour miracle would thrill them. But he also would have likely considered more immediate factors in his narration. In details such as the fifteen minutes of danger, clarified by the intervention of a divine hand, Thacher communicated his moment of absolute weakness. Through that moment shimmered a blinding ache that zealots such as Mather and Winthrop would happily interpret as the glare of God. Spiritually, those minutes supported the elders' belief that the deity had been with him, and materially, this supported the legitimacy of his petition. Nevertheless, emotionally, those fifteen minutes reminded Thacher that no one else had been with him. Those fifteen minutes were the most abandoned minutes of his life—and that abandonment still engulfed him.[43]

Momentarily reaching what Toni Morrison has called the "hem of life," Thacher might have longed to forget this providential moment. More

42. Mather, *Essay for the Recording of Illustrious Providences*, ed. Levernier, 1–14, esp. 10–11; Richard S. Dunn, James P. Savage, and Laetitia Yeandle, eds., *The Journal of John Winthrop, 1630–1649* (Cambridge, Mass., 1994), 152; Anthony Thacher to Peter Thacher, September 1635, in Emerson, ed., *Letters from New England*, 172; Katherine A. Grandjean, "New World Tempests: Environment, Scarcity, and the Coming of the Pequot War," *William and Mary Quarterly*, 3d Ser., LXVIII (2011), 75–100.

43. Nathaniel B. Shurtleff, ed., *Records of the Governor and Company of the Massachusetts Bay in New England, Printed by Order of the Legislature* (Boston, 1853–1854), I, 154, 191.

specifically, he might have longed to forget the gap between why men like Mather and Winthrop chose to care about that detail and why he had to. In his letter to Peter, little more than a month after the hurricane, Thacher emphasized the companionship that friendship with Avery had purchased. Take the dialogue Thacher recalled during the storm. When they realized the likelihood of their deaths, he remembered seeing himself through the eyes of his friend and the fear of abandonment that his friend had felt then. Avery "thought I would have fled from him and said unto me: 'O cousin, leave us not. Let us die together' and reached for this hand unto me." Thacher's response might have shocked Peter as he read it. Thacher chose to reach out in friendship to Avery rather than save his own son, Peter's namesake: "Then I letting go my son Peter's hand, [I] took him [Avery] by the hand and said to him, 'I purpose it not wither shall I go?'" Thatcher narrated his actions to vindicate the sincerity of his love: because of it, he would choose his friend first. He also claimed a textual precedent, invoking the biblical story of Ruth and Naomi. "Whither thou goest, I will go," Ruth had responded to Naomi after the death of her husband, Naomi's son, when they both faced destitution. Thacher's deep commitment to Avery appeared even earlier in his letter. They had arrived in New England earlier that year, and soon after, the church at Marblehead invited Avery to lead that congregation as their pastor. Initially, Avery had been "unwilling to go thither." Eventually, both he and Thacher were persuaded. Thacher explained to his brother that neighboring ministers had convinced them through taking advantage of their friendly commitments and pointing to the "benefit *we* might do" for the residents at Marblehead. Thus, "at length, *we* embraced it, and there consented to go." Thacher's profession was less elevated. He was a cooper, and though barrel making would have been a valuable skill on the colonial frontier, his expertise was less special to a town than the skills of a minister. And Marblehead was not looking for new coopers. As Thacher told it, the men were invited together, and they made the decision together. The colony's eminent ministers recognized their affiliation and saw value in preserving it.[44]

But before the shipwreck and resettlement, Thacher had narrated friendship explicitly. Friendship was the framework through which Thacher hoped his story to Peter would be read. "The story is thus," he began. "First there

44. Toni Morrison, *Song of Solomon* (New York, 1977), 18; Anthony Thacher to Peter Thacher, September 1635, in Emerson, ed., *Letters from New England*, 168, 170; Ruth 1:16 (Geneva). On homosocial and homoerotic uses of Christian stories of friendship, see Michael Warner, "New English Sodom," *American Literature*, LXIV (1992), 19–47.

was a league of perennial friendship solemnly made between my cousin Avary and myself made in Mr. Graves his ship"—the vessel that took them across the Atlantic before they tried to travel up the American littoral. In the belly of the ship, the two men vowed "never to forsake each other to the death but to be partakers of each other's misery or welfare as also the habitation in one place." Aware of what he would eventually narrate—the choice of Marblehead over Ipswich, Avery over young Peter—Thacher based his decisions on the compact of companionship in "misery" and in "welfare." A "league of perennial friendship" was a great responsibility, but one that early modern men knew well. The compact between Thacher and Avery expressed the fealty conventional to early modern friendship between men. Friendship, according to these expectations, was a socially meaningful set of commitments, often ceremoniously inaugurated—"solemnly," as Thacher described them. Those conventions explained Thacher's decisions and the rationale the magistrates used in distributing Avery's estate. Friendship was the reason "Mr. Cotton and most of the ministers in the patent" had addressed their arguments to both men. Friendship was also the grounds for Thacher to petition to inherit Avery's property after his death.[45]

Catastrophe vindicated Thacher's friendship. It mattered to him deeply as he began his new life in America, more deeply than he would have preferred. Friendship ensured that Thacher wouldn't go destitute after the hurricane, but he wasn't happy about the fulfillment of this provision. A shining bitterness glints in his letter to Peter. At its start, Thacher and Avery pursued friendship as a safeguard against the world's challenges. If sincerity had, over time, taken deep roots in response to settlement's many deracinations, friendship had been one strategy to mitigate these alienations in advance. But friendship would mean taking life-altering risks, such as moving to a new and remote settlement during storm season. As a strategy to mitigate the hazards of transatlantic removal, friendship had not failed. Assessing the consequences of the storm, Thacher remarked on the "spoil and loss of all our goods and provisions." Already, departure from England had required a reorientation toward "goods and provisions." Prospective settlers had to translate their earthly possessions into financial credit. Though Christian theology enjoined them to scorn the things of the world, it would not be easy to renounce these "materials of memory," the objects that had shaped their lives and loves. Thacher and Avery had done that and hoped their league would carry them across the Atlantic

45. Anthony Thacher to Peter Thacher, September 1635, in Emerson, ed., *Letters from New England,* 168; Alan Bray, *The Friend* (Chicago, 2003).

and into a future where those goods and provisions would be restored. The dearest possessions they had carried with them were now lost. And so was Avery. In his letter, Thacher described this loss as a "spoil"—a rank waste.[46]

Cold comfort was Avery's earthly treasure, as were the substitutes that Thacher found for Avery's companionship. Rescued from the waves, Thacher found his wife. Then the couple sat down on the shore to rest. Maybe one or both fell asleep. The memory of his wife's presence next to him assuaged his loneliness about as effectively as the slumber of Rowlandson's generous friends assuaged her insomnia. Under the cedar tree—or at least, a tree that evoked to Thacher the enduring stability of the cedar—Thacher slipped out of the past and into the present of his writing, to the "many such thoughts" that now "press down my heavy heart very much." His lack of friends in this part of the world bore him downward: "Now, having no friend to whom I can chiefly impart myself," he was lonely. Friendship meant material troth, but it also meant a distribution, or "imparting," of self. As Rowlandson had, Thacher lost his social world swiftly. He claimed to his brother that he was ready to move on, "learning to love new particulars." Nonetheless, the rhetorical effect of his claim was ambiguous. He began to catalog possible substitutes for his old friend and continued to survey an impressive reservoir of potential new friends: "Now having no friend to whom I can freely impart myself, Mr. Cotton is now my chiefest friend to whom I have free welcome and access, as also Mr. Mavericke, Mr. Warde, Mr. Ward, Mr. Hocker, Mr. Weles, Mr. Warhad, and Mr. Parker also Mr. Noyes, who use me friendly." These were the "diverse good people" that Winthrop noted had supported Thacher in the weeks that followed.[47]

Finding new particulars to love isn't easy, and almost all of Thacher's new English acquaintances struggled with this at some point during the early years of settlement. But it was specifically challenging for Thacher. For one, these particular men weren't new to him. According to his letter, he already knew several of them from before to his failed journey to Marblehead. "Mr. Cotton and most of the ministers in the patent" were the most important factor that led Thacher and Avery to board Allerton's unlucky ship in the first place. It was

46. Anthony Thacher to Peter Thacher, September 1635, in Emerson, ed., *Letters from New England*, 173; David Cressy, *Coming Over: Migration and Communication between England and New England in the Seventeenth Century* (Cambridge, 1987), 107–129.

47. Anthony Thacher to Peter Thacher, September 1635, in Emerson, ed., *Letters from New England*, 173; L. O. Frandenburg, "'Voice Memorial': Loss and Reparation in Chaucer's Poetry," *Exemplaria*, II (1990), 169–202, esp. 183 ("particulars"); Dunn, Savage, and Yeandle, eds., *Journal of John Winthrop*, 152.

John Cotton and the rest of the settlement's ministers, all Avery's colleagues, whose advice had led to this unhappy condition. In Thacher's letter, these men were supposed to be a substitute for his grief and loss. Not only were they not new to his grieving life, though; they were also his grief's indirect cause. If it seems too severe to suggest that Thacher listed them in order to propose, somewhat passive-aggressively, that they were responsible for his loss, their similarity to Avery as colleagues would have reminded Thacher of Avery, his death, and the reasons for it. Each one would have reminded him of the singularity of his once-leagued, now-lost friend.[48]

Thacher's turn to the list was not unique. In 1682, Mary Rowlandson longed to distribute her affections widely in the wake of catastrophic loss:

> *Our family being now gathered together (those of us that were living)*
> *the* South Church *in* Boston. . . . As *Solomon* says, *Mony answers*
> *all things,* and that we had through the benevolence of Christian-
> friends, some in this *Town,* and some in that, and others: And some
> from *England.* . . . The Lord so moved the hearts of these and those
> towards us, that we wanted neither food, nor raiment for our selves
> or ours, *Prov.* 18. 24. *There is a Friend which sticketh closer than a*
> *Brother.* And how many such Friends have we found, and now living
> amongst? And truly such a Friend have we found him to be unto us,
> in whose house we lived, *viz.* Mr. *James Whitcomb,* a Friend unto us
> near hand, and afar off.

Despite her skill in counting her enemies as well as the costs of her family's reunification, Rowlandson made a show of losing track of the friends she had among the English: "And how many such Friends we have found, and now living amongst!" As with Thacher, material assistance was friendship's substance. Friendship was their dearest hope of mitigating, if not transcending, bare exposure to material destitution. But neither survivor wanted it to be. Because Rowlandson's dependence was so intense and the friendship that eased it so clearly quantifiable, she emphasized friendship's qualitative, rather than quantitative, aspects—the house rented from New England's most prominent enslaver "furnished with love." Like Rowlandson, Thacher depended for survival on being able to claim friends. Each made sure, in the wake of disaster, to distribute his or her vulnerability widely rather than concentrate

48. Anthony Thacher to Peter Thacher, September 1635, in Emerson, ed., *Letters from New England,* 168.

their debts in a single source. Though confused, they weren't insincere. More clearly than most of their peers, and many of their readers since, they saw that friendship and the frankness it required might not be ultimately a matter of wanting but of needing.[49]

Above all, they saw that sincerity exhausted friendship, and they sought something different. Thacher's reflections show this best. Against future claims that sincere friendship consists of spiritual communion that transcends material life, Thacher and other early modern settler colonists saw that friendship was necessary, and not only materially. Two factors shaped this necessity. First, living on the frontier rendered these English-born settlers acutely vulnerable to the material world, an experience that heightened their longing for access to universally salient reason as a metric to organize their lives. This vulnerability made them cling to the possibility of a life organized in ways that promised regular, reliable, enduringly stable safety—the fantasy affordances of what Michel Foucault would call biopolitical discipline. Second, within what they thought to be more precarious circumstances, they tried to forge normalcy out of unprecedented volubility. They hoped that talking would bind them together, and therefore they championed sincerity through practices of self-disclosure—they tried, in other words, to preserve a biopoetic engagement with the self. Through volubility, they claimed, they'd triumph over vulnerability. Friendship was one way to experience triumph, but for these theorists, friendships that satisfied were the cost of triumphing. This was the paradox that Thacher faced when he recalled that he yearned for someone to whom he could "impart" himself. For these individuals, as for Pratt, Bradstreet, Dorcas, and Kanoonus and his companions, talking about the self wasn't simply what one did with a friend. Rowlandson, Williams, Quananopohit, and Thacher all saw sincere performances of selfhood, especially through talk, as one of the thorny conditions that made them wish for friendly companionship that *didn't* require talking, sincerity's signature activity. At life's hem, Thacher and his fellow early modern theorists of friendship could not forget the conditions that made them depend on friendship, and they couldn't experience their new friendships very far beyond that unhappy need.

These individuals are all dead, engulfed in the "deep anonymity of sleepers finally disburdened of the weight of bearing themselves." But the challenge of their shared dissatisfaction remains unanswered. Why has friendship been desirable? These vernacular philosophers of friendship show its appreciation

49. Rowlandson, *Sovereignty*, 111.

in value within severe historical circumstances: the erosion of a sustainable relationship with the nonhuman world, violent cultural conflict over the best methods to preserve that relationship, and, more quietly but just as disturbingly, an increasingly unavoidable responsibility for one's decisions on how to navigate that unsettled world. Biopolitical thinking—the fantasy of a clocklike, predictable life insulated from the sharp, psychic edge of that unsettlement—would, in the decades and centuries to follow, become one response to that obligation. And friendship promised a soothing balm to those cuts. Could it heal them? These individuals hoped so. But their words (their lists, their euphemisms, their allusions, their fair truths) suggest a bleaker picture. Eventually, words, rather than interlocutors, would come to offer that balmy hope. By the nineteenth century, Emerson claimed to have a simple answer for why he wanted friendship. Emerson cherished friendship for loosening his tongue and, mostly, his pen. "The scholar sits down to write," he observed, "and all his years of meditation do not furnish him with one good thought." Friendship saved eloquent old Emerson from aphasia. Yes, when "it is necessary to write a letter to a friend," then "forthwith, troops of gentle thoughts invest themselves on every hand with chosen words." Against what enemy? Emerson elsewhere offered clues. In his essay "Circles," he observed historical memory as volubility's enduring enemy: "See what I have overcome; see how cheerful I am; see how completely I have triumphed?" On the centuries-long "march of individualities toward liberal freedoms," Emerson's troops militate against the memory of modern friendship's artifice; they fight to preserve Emerson's desire to be the commander of "troops"—a necessarily plural noun—rather than an unremarkable participant in a happy society. Friendship, historians have persuasively shown, proves the power accrued by sincere, individual affection over the circumstances of history. Centuries later, it may still. But what have been that triumph's costs?[50]

50. Berlant, *Cruel Optimism,* 158 ("deep anonymity," "march of individualities"), 159; Emerson, "Friendship," in Crase, ed., *Essays,* 110; Emerson, "Circles," ibid., 173–184, esp. 178–179.

Miserable Comforts

A Dialectical Lyric

A NN NEEDHAM HETT didn't set out to be the most acute critic of sincerity in her neighborhood, colony, or continent, but she might have won that distinction in 1637. That was when she decided, then undertook, what she reasoned would be the most certain, efficient action to damn her soul. More than most of her neighbors, Hett noticed sincerity's costs. Its promises failed to redeem the taxations of its demands. She could not stop noticing the work it required of her, would continue to require of her for weeks, months, and years and would require of the people she might or might not have loved. Hett understood that, according to her neighbors' description of their deity, he was unlikely to transform her unhappy soul unless she was already working on that project herself rationally, systematically, and rigorously, with the best tools of self-management that humans had developed. Hett undertook that work of poeisis, of self-fashioning, diligently. It wasn't easy or happy, though. And she wanted her neighbors to know her difficulties, her discomforts, her doubts, as well as her response to them. Critics have mostly overlooked her insight. After centuries of stories that overfamiliarize readers with the scripts of personal responsibility, stories that vindicate its taxations, stories that end in happiness (or at least optimism about the path to happiness), Hett seems like an exception rather than the most obedient follower of the rules. It's easy to overlook the social sources of her failure and the history of deracination that sincerity required. That history was not exclusive to her people. Many early modern Europeans were eager to pursue projects of self-fashioning. But Hett's neighbors chose spiritual self-fashioning, a biopoetic fantasy, as their world-historical mantle. They have become a source of inspiration to a nation that "prides itself on being composed of immigrants," and their readiness to be pried retrospectively from a context of extraordinary deracination—a decontextualized example supposedly useful to console immigrants experiencing continued alienations—suggests that their world-historical ambitions were, to some degree, successful. They were not far off in hoping that their values would last much longer than their earthly bodies did. That project of surveillance and disciplined self-management might, as Sacvan Bercovitch noticed, sometimes feel like a war, but so much the better since it could thereby summon enthusiasm and vigor. Hett answered that summons with great seriousness, despite the "meanness and selfishness," if not cruelty, that, as some critics have observed, her neighbors' pursuit of sincerity tended to encourage. Her attempts to murder some of her family members cautions readers to come up with their own alternatives to the biopoetic happiness than those this American self would seem to require.[1]

If Hett's self-inquiries were morbid, they were also thorough, disorienting the sanguine tone of conventional early Americanist scholarship on interiority. Hett's decisive action invited witnesses to think in a more synthetic fashion about how settlers' language, their vocabulary and their narrative patterns— even their small talk and their attempts at consolation and cheer—bought individuals confidence in the rightness of their dreams for happiness. Those patterns presented Hett with something she knew she could desire reliably, but they also, she noticed, became obstacles to earthly flourishing. Those patterns guided her and her neighbors away from slower, more doubtful, yet consequently more thoughtful ways of experiencing neighbors who were like and unlike them. Optimistically confident of their sincerity, settlers became less sensitive to other modes of self-disclosure than discourse and other forms of self-relation than knowledge. They became worse at recognizing interior experiences. And then they became worse at recognizing the limits of their recognition. Hett felt this atrophy acutely. She might not have been able to explain what she felt because her neighbors, especially the loquacious men

---

1. Álvaro Enrigue, "Therapy: Therapy," in Brendan Riley, trans., *Hypothermia* (Champaign, Ill., 2013), 109 ("prides," "meanness"); Sacvan Bercovitch, *The Puritan Origins of the American Self* (New Haven, Conn., 1975).

like John Winthrop or John Davenport, were keen to claim that their methods for self-relation were the only game in town. They weren't, though. Some settlers, as the previous chapters have shown—individuals such as Anne Eaton, Phinehas Pratt, Anne Bradstreet, Michael Wigglesworth, and Daniel Gookin—intuited this. Their Indigenous and African neighbors noticed, too, and developed strategies for living within this strange but ascendant norm. Chickatawbut, the various Natick converts, Dorcas, and James Quananopohit all developed provisional, experimental strategies for pursuing happiness or, more often, alleviating unhappiness. Hett did not propose a clear programmatic alternative to the subjection she felt. But she went further than almost any of her peers in insisting that her society not forget or overlook what it demanded from her.

Hett probably didn't think of herself as a critic of sincerity, at least not explicitly. She seems not to have set out to criticize, far less resist or refuse, the privileged place that self-knowledge held in her world and the effects that it had on her happiness. More than anything, these norms alienated her. They did so in a subtle way, through a vocabulary that underestimated the strange but not illogical contours of her experience. She was almost certainly dissatisfied with her world's vocabulary, but some of the readily available terms in our vocabulary, such as "resistance" and "refusal," have the clumsy effect of obscuring a key feature of her frustration. Those two particular terms can vibrantly explain how individuals and communities may pursue desires and ambitions distinct from a colonial power's goals. Such words can describe the significance of an individual's actions, even the small ones, in contexts of strife and oppression with high stakes, when overt challenges are not always possible or wise. But Hett had a difficult time discerning where her society's aims ended and her own desires began. This is the challenge that "biopower" names. As if descending Pisgah, biopower often claims a glowing veil of biopoetic fulfillment, a promise of health and happiness in body and spirit. According to biopower as Michel Foucault theorized it, individual actions tend not to have clearly good or bad substance; rather, they're consistently dangerous. Confessional discourse, for example, and the rigors of self-scrutiny it required, could bring collective happiness closer. But it could also make the individuals who practiced it sadder, lonelier, and more estranged from their neighbors, especially when it was practiced in these unprecedented frontier contexts. Biopower, Foucault wanted readers to notice, was extremely difficult to refuse or resist because it often did help make progress in the happiness individuals experienced—or, at least, progress mitigating discomfort and suffering. Hett saw these practices of self-management make her neighbors happy, even as they failed her. And she wanted an explanation for that fail-ure. She wanted it so badly, she was willing to go to hell. She didn't have twentieth-century vocabulary for describing its power; she wasn't anywhere close to naming her subjection. Instead, she reflected with unrelenting rigor on the promises and liabilities of Calvinist predestination, both abstractly and as they appeared in her own life. And she expressed her conclusions in her actions. Those actions illuminate her society's dialectically tense reasoning from within. They illuminate faith's violent leap, a leap that takes desire—love—beyond what Søren Kierkegaard described as its naive, "lyric" stage. Her murderous pursuit of happiness pushes her society's commitment to responsible sincerity to a breaking point, to an internal "crisis" that the word "critique" etymologically invokes.[2]

Hett is a case study for the limits of sincerity as a technique of soul science, and she has been so since one of her earliest appearances in the documents of colonial settlement. Like Anne Eaton at New Haven, Ann Needham Hett and her unhappy soul interested the men in her orbit. Here, Hett provoked John Winthrop's curiosity, and he documented her frustration's progress. But even as she was a case study for Winthrop, she also troubled the obstinate optimism that he and his fellow soul scientists tried to make normal in the world they shared. Ann Needham left England in the earliest waves of English removal to Algonquian territory. Alone, without parents or husband, she joined the First Church at Boston within a year of arrival. Others who joined alongside her included John Winthrop's wife, Margaret, and future cultural ambassador John Eliot. She soon married a barrel maker, and within her first decade in the colony moved from Boston to Hingham, joining the church there. She had several children—Eliphalet, born in 1639; Mehetabell, born in 1648; Mary, born in 1649; and probably a fourth, a little older than Eliphalet, whose name has not been recorded. Beyond these very basic details, John Winthrop's recollection of her actions testify to a rich but tumultuous interior life. She seems to have experienced Calvinism with unusual distress. Predestination, as most historians of American religion will affirm, was an abstractly alarm-ing proposition. Most historians have thus been eager to temper the severity of that abstraction by showing all of the strategies that real people used to make that principle a positive, upbuilding feature of their lives rather than a

2. Wendy Brown, *Edgework: Critical Essays on Knowledge and Politics* (Princeton, N.J., 2005), 5 ("crisis," "critique"); Michel Foucault, *Discipline and Punish: The Birth of the Prison*, trans. Alan Sheridan (New York, 1977), 293–308; Søren Kierkegaard, *Fear and Trembling, a Dialectical Lyric*, ed. and trans. Walter Lowrie (Princeton, N.J., 1941).

consistently oppressive one. None of these strategies seem to have worked for Hett. She made great efforts to acquire certainty about the state of her soul, and this struggle for sincerity lasted some time. Eventually, she seems to have decided that the work sincerity required was too taxing, given her poor returns. She calculated that it was not worth the costs. Giving up hope, and doing so definitively, was spiritually easier than continuing to nurture it. After executing her plan to commit her crime against her deity and her society, she went to her neighbors to tell them that she had found freedom from that spiritual burden; then she explained how.[3]

Hett fascinated her neighbors. *O, abominable woman,* they gasped, *offscouring of society, what devil possessed thee?* But their attempts to make sense of her dissatisfaction, whether with the language of the satanic or the galenic, had the effects of pathologizing and thereby domesticating it, clipping the wings of the critique her actions posed to her community's utopian ideals. The first time she tried her hand at murder, in 1637, John Winthrop noted it in his *Journal*. Hett, Winthrop wrote, felt "trouble of mind about her spiritual estate," and that led to her "utter desperation." Winthrop noted that her neighbors had tried to help prevent that despair, but he also implied that their failure was her fault: "[She] could not endure to hear of any comfort." Five years later, she tried her hand at murder again. With precedent, this time, Winthrop felt more comfortable claiming psychological authority. Her personality and its defects were more important factors in explaining her actions than her own words. As he composed his second narration, between the subject and the verb, he inserted a detour to qualify her character: "A cooper's wife of Hingham, having been long in a sad melancholic distemper near to phrensy." For Winthrop, the best explanation for her actions was humoral imbalance. But he insisted that her excess of melancholy could be spiritually instructive: "Thus doth satan work by the advantage of our infirmities," he began his conclusion. Physical vulnerability had spiritual consequences. But he was optimistic about solutions. Knowledge of the spiritual enemy's tactics "should stir us up to cleave the more fast to Christ Jesus, and to walk the more humbly and watchfully in all our conversation." Everyone, in other words, should work harder than Hett in resisting Satan by resisting sadness. This was a convenient lesson, deduced in advance. And now, the "society of example," as Mitchell Robert

3. Richard D. Pierce, ed., *The Records of the First Church in Boston, 1630–1868,* Colonial Society of Massachusetts, *Publications,* XXXIX (Boston, 1961), 14, 284, 310, 316; Richard S. Dunn, James P. Savage, and Laetitia Yeandle, eds., *The Journal of John Winthrop, 1630–1649* (Cambridge Mass., 1994), 229–230, 391–392.

Breitwieser has described her world, had found a new example of that lesson to cherish. Winthrop was pleased to claim to know more about Hett than she knew about herself and to invite future readers to participate in that knowing, too. But Winthrop overlooked an unusual and possibly disturbing fact: Hett had already outpaced him in this regard. Hett confessed, frankly, that she did not know her spiritual status. More alarmingly, she confessed that she had lost the will to keep caring about achieving certainty of the *right* spiritual status. A weak spot in sincerity's system for confidence appeared: Hett had ceased to want what sincerity claimed to offer. She had ceased to want the distant, glowing good life and could now make pragmatic calculations regarding a less taxing course for what remained of her time among the living.[4]

Winthrop refused to be perplexed or frightened by Hett's actions. Modern critics follow suit. When they consider Hett's actions at all, they tend to find Winthrop's modern-sounding, protopsychiatric diagnosis satisfying, even though his explanation dismisses Hett's thoughts about her world and its idea of normalcy. A sense of normalcy was exactly what eluded Hett, and that lack made her world intolerable. It was especially unbearable because she seems once to have had real hope in its ideals and cherished something like optimism about attaining them. She had once held great expectations. But those hopes let her down. Some of Hett's weariness was probably a result of the heightened attention that simply staying alive on the frontier required, the stresses that men like William Bradford and Winthrop could barely comprehend but that other men, such as Edward Johnson, found most tolerable by making jokes about them, calling them "annoyances" and then pairing them off in rhyme. Some of Hett's weariness was a result of the burdensome solutions that colonial leaders proposed in order to overcome those stresses. Those solutions included directions to intensify attention to interior life, to perfect self-knowledge as a step toward more powerful "self-management." If Hett had wanted to communicate what frustrated her and wore her down, she would have had to contend with her neighbors' earnest enthusiasm to deny the endurance of these costs. She would have had to explain to her neighbors how their happiness—to put this book's argument most aggressively—depended on their "deceitful" and superlatively "wicked" hearts' telling them lies of omission that claimed, persuasively, to

4. Kierkegaard, *Fear and Trembling*, ed. and trans. Lowrie, 36 ("what devil"); Dunn, Savage, and Yeandle, eds., *Journal of John Winthrop*, 229–230 ("trouble of mind"), 391–392 ("A cooper's wife"); Mitchell Robert Breitwieser, *American Puritanism and the Defense of Mourning: Religion, Grief, and Ethnology in Mary White Rowlandson's Captivity Narrative* (Madison, Wis., 1990), 17.

be comprehensive, singular truths. These neighbors were caught up in the biopoetic dream of a soul liberated by practices of reflection and discourse, by its convictions of sincerity. Hett's deep dissatisfaction shows us the internal limits of that dream. She was unhappy with it from the perspective of a desirous believer. She had once been, and still was, committed to achieving sincerity, to discovering the truth about her soul and sharing that truth with others. And, ascending her own Moriah, she would pursue that goal where she thought her deity was leading her.[5]

Hett's critique of sincerity and its costs becomes clearer with each of the foregoing chapters' insights. First, Hett gave up on goodness, refusing the easy confusion between virtue and knowledge, especially self-knowledge. During her years of frontier life, Hett saw that the desire for goodness wasn't the same as, or even necessarily close to, goodness itself. And she saw, further, the costs of insisting on their proximity. Like Bradford, Hett was committed to collecting and synthesizing evidence of her deity's activity in the world around her. Unlike Bradford, however, in examining that evidence, she reckoned with the likelihood that her deity did not care about her all that much. In assessing this evidence, she was, her society told her, alone, left to her own mental strategies. On her own, Hett saw absence of evidence. She didn't immediately claim it was evidence of absence. But over time, that conclusion became less and less illogical. When she eventually did conclude that absence of signs of the deity's presence did mean personal abandonment, Hett achieved an insight that few others in her world seemed capable of reaching, especially since there were so many opportunities to evade it. In theory, Calvinism recognized that there would always be some excluded from the deity's favor. But in practice, it was often easier to suspend reflection on the possibility that you were one of the excluded by pointing to others who weren't like you, as Bradford had, and assigning them that role. Hett recognized that the deity's favor was random; it could not be reduced to human systems. It was just as likely that the unchosen

---

5. J. A. Leo Lemay, *"New England's Annoyances": America's First Folk Song* (Newark, N.J., 1985); Theodore Dwight Bozeman, *The Precisianist Strain: Disciplinary Religion and Antinomian Backlash in Puritanism to 1638* (Williamsburg, Va., and Chapel Hill, N.C., 2004), 107; Jeremiah 17:9 (Geneva) ("deceitful," "wicked"); Larry D. Eldridge, "'Crazy-Brained': Mental Illness in Colonial America," *Bulletin of the History of Medicine*, LXX (1996), 361–386; Laurel Thatcher Ulrich, "John Winthrop's City of Women," *Massachusetts Historical Review*, III (2001), 19–48; Kathleen Donegan, "'As Dying, Yet Behold, We Live': Catastrophe and Interiority in Bradford's *Of Plymouth Plantation*," *Early American Literature*, XXXVII (2002), 9–35; Ana Schwartz, "Annoyances, Tolerable and Intolerable," in Max Cavitch and Brian Connolly, eds., *Situation Critical: Critique and Early American Studies* (Durham, N.C., [forthcoming]).

perambulated in her neighborhood, attended her church, loitered on her street, ate in her household, slept in her bed, or even lived in her clothes. For a time, she wanted not to be among the excluded. She wanted to know herself to be good. But in her thoroughness, she refused to let the desire for goodness stand in for the object itself. For Hett, sincerity was only an instrument for piety, and it could always fail. It was not virtue itself.

If Hett began to suspect that her deity didn't care much about her, she seems not to have found evidence that her society cared much, either. Despite their avowed commitment to sympathy, to imagining the plight of another, as John Winthrop had proposed, they failed to persuade her that they were concerned about her soul. Her dissatisfaction and despair were not unheard-of. Despondency, after all, was part of the morphology of conversion. Settlers sought patterns in their deity's interventions that could offer consolations in the face of the prospect that, as James Allen observed, he might be "using sovereignty"—that is, not using any rule or principle at all—in selecting his earthly interventions. But such a pattern's potential encouragements could backfire, when thoughtlessly used, and have discouraging effects. Most of the pious who moved beyond despondency to peace might be tempted to universalize their accomplishment. True Emersonian victors, they would forget the intensity of what they suffered, the nagging and nearly overwhelming fear of facing a literal eternity of agony after the earthly chapter of their lives ended. That forgetting made it easier to be an unskillful, thoughtless witness of another person's suffering. From the happier side of that soul's dark night, someone who had eventually triumphed over it might be tempted to present their success as evidence of a very uncomforting, maybe even insulting, claim: that any experience of hopelessness Hett suffered was not all that bad. "I have heard many such things," Hett might have thought, recalling the biblical Job's suffering. "Miserable comforters are you all." Her neighbors would have been eager to extend their optimism to her, to believe that the stories they told about themselves would knit them together with her. In doing that, they diminished the gravity of what she felt. Years into her despair, Hett was tired of their optimism. She "could not endure" the words they shared to bring her "comfort," Winthrop wrote. And though he seems to have intended such a statement to describe Hett's mental state, an obstinate antisocial perversity, the description equally illuminates the intolerable quality of the words she received from her neighbors. Even if Hett agreed with Winthrop's diagnosis of mental weakness and permeability, such material affectability was part of the body that her deity had given her, and perhaps so was her susceptibility to humoral pessimism. Cursed thus, what comfort could confident sympathy, sincere but thoughtless, really be?[6]

And how much longer, she might have asked, would she have to keep trying to overcome the bad hand her deity had dealt her? This is a question that humans can't, of course, answer, the future being unceasingly full of surprises. But asking such a question can also communicate experience. Among its content is an intuition, maybe even a knowledge, of personal limits: *I may not have the strength to keep going.* Hett kept going for years. Her confessions of despair seemed to have spurred her neighbors to condescending attempts at comfort, implying that failure is the individual's fault and that the solution to that failure *(just keep trying)* is obvious. But despite these quiet humiliations, Hett kept at it. She kept trying and she kept asking. She seems to have wanted company. She wanted friends and neighbors, people who shared her commitments as well as the idiom that organized them into a life that felt worth living, at least for another few days or weeks. And even when she gave up on the hope of participation in the community of the chosen, she still wanted recognition from her neighbors. Like Wigglesworth, or Bradstreet, or the Natick converts, it was company that drew her on. After her attempted murder, she still found something attractive in the thought of communicating her motives to her neighbors. Immediately after her first attempt, in 1637, she "came into the house and said, now she was sure she should be damned." Five years later, she confessed at least some of what she knew about her motivation. She wanted to save her victim from their own miserable struggle with predestination and, furthermore, she wanted to be certain that "she had sinned against the Holy Ghost, and that she could [now] not repent of any sin." Hett was no Bartleby, no Eaton. She wanted her neighbors to know the truth that she had discovered about herself, even if it wasn't the happiest truth, even if it risked unhappy consequences. And she wanted her neighbors to care, to feel the effects of their failure, rather than leave her to bear that burden alone.[7]

After her second attempt to damn her soul definitively, the colony's magistrates decided to intervene. On September 6, 1642, the Massachusetts Court of Assistants convened for their quarterly meeting. Presiding and meting out punishments were "The Governor The Deputie Govr Mr. Dudley. Mr. Bellingham. Mr Saltonstall. Mr Stoughton. Mr Bradstreet. Mr Flint. Increase Nowell." There were eighteen cases; hers was the thirteenth. As she waited,

6. Job 16:2 (Geneva); Dunn, Savage, and Yeandle, eds., *Journal of John Winthrop*, 230.
7. Dunn, Savage, and Yeandle, eds., *Journal of John Winthrop*, 230, 392.

she listened to the court sentence John Woolridge to a fine of three pounds for "drunkenesse, and swearing"; John Lewis, a whipping for running away from the home where he was a servant; William Walcot, a whipping and imprisonment for "idleness, and abuse of his friends." She, for "attempting to droune hir child," received a sentence of whipping, too. And the magistrates went further. They thought it was best that she be "kept to hard labor." Not only hard labor, but unusual caloric austerity: she should be "kept to hard labor, and spare diet." Maybe this sentence distressed her. But she would have been accustomed to a life of labor. Her husband made barrels. She knew hard work well. She knew, on one hand, how the artifacts of human ingenuity could sometimes be useful in making the labor of living easier. On the other hand, she saw how acts of making shaped the human makers, too, how these technologies could intensify ambitions to produce more and to accumulate and store more earthly treasures. Her household's happiness depended on the power that this technology circulated. And her everyday labors supplemented that work. She maintained the household that prospered according to the success of her husband's barrels: she cooked, washed, sewed, mended, and rebuilt their material world. She was also responsible for reproducing the Hett lineage, for creating and nourishing the children whom men like Thomas Hett would have "craved" as a step along the path to personifying patriarchy and possessing the deitylike prerogative to judge other people's sincerity. From her childhood, Ann Needham had watched the mothers in her life carry such burdens. These women's labors included decades of gestating, lifting, hauling, shifting, and accommodating heavy, unwieldy little bodies and spiritually vulnerable souls.[8]

Hett's decision to damn her soul recruited her neighbors to feel, at least momentarily, what she had long felt. Her attempted infanticide surprised and horrified them and conveyed something of the despair that she knew, something of the brokenness of the biopolitical system of self-inquiry that wore her out. And she recruited them by recruiting her child into her unorthodox attempt to claim certainty. For Hett, the labor of staying alive and reproducing life into the future was unrelenting. It nagged in the form of little arms and legs that pulled and kicked, climbed on and pressed against her. She might have

8. "Records of the Court of Assistants, 1641–1644," in William H. Whitmore, ed., *The Colonial Laws of Massachusetts: Reprinted from the Edition of 1672, with the Supplements through 1686: Containing Also a Bibliographic Preface and Introduction, Treating of All the Printed Laws from 1649 to 1686; Together with the Body of Liberties of 1641, and the Records of the Court of Assistants, 1641–1644* (Boston, 1890), xxv–xliii, esp. xxxiv.

resented her children and the men whose hopes for spiritually and emotionally transcending the heavy material world depended on her bearing these burdens. But if she felt aggrieved, she thought about those obligations to her family and to her deity differently than most of her neighbors. Unlike Increase Mather's proposals in his relentless jeremiads, she did not insist that her children vindicate her hard work through working hard to be sincere on their own. Instead, she tried to interrupt the transmission of obligation. For her, the sincerity that searching out divine status required was an agonizing encumbrance, so maybe it would be better to prevent that agony from oppressing her own children. According to the reasoning of her contemporary, Wigglesworth, it might not be *so* bad to die an infant, to be sentenced to the "easiest room in Hell." It might be logical—and maybe even kind—to send her child to that fate, to "save it from misery," as she put it, rather than subject it to decades of mortal uncertainty that might lead them to a harsher room in the halls of damnation. Of course, it was a gamble. But for Hett, intellectual and spiritual misery were too heavy a cost. She decided to cash out early, for both her own sake and her child's. She had been brought to trial that September because four months earlier, in May 1642, she again tried to kill one of her children. This time, she tried to make sure she did it right. She had bungled the first throw—the toddler apparently crawled back out of the creek. So she hoisted the child again in her accustomed arms and "threw it in so far as it could not get out." Now, she hoped, this little soul would never have to worry about how best and most eloquently to invoke the conventional metaphor of drowning in their own magnificent vileness.[9]

Hett's sadness, finally, responded to the solipsism of her society's longing for individual confidence, her neighbors' myopia regarding the effects of their actions next to the eloquent, well-thought-out speeches they made about themselves. For a decade until that point, Hett had tried to put off her negative conclusion about her soul. Every day she got herself out of bed to face the energetically sincere world around her. Along with her neighbors, she knew it was her duty to rise and shine. Together, she and her friends would all go through the visible motions they thought characterized the superior spiritual beings they called "saints," activities of functional individuals in a smoothly moving world. But were they, Hett might have wondered, united in their skepticism toward the idolatry of appearances, especially their own

9. Michael Wigglesworth, "The Day of Doom," in Ronald Bosco, ed., *The Poems of Michael Wigglesworth* (Lanham, Md., 1989), 56, line 1444 ("easiest room"); Dunn, Savage, and Yeandle, eds., *Journal of John Winthrop*, 392 ("threw it in").

appearances? For Hett, this smoothly moving world could often feel like a dull nightmare of isolation. She saw her neighbors begin each morning freshly, as innocently as putting on a shirt laid out on the bed in advance. She listened to them talk at great length about their lives and then live them. In the churches they had built together, she listened to them narrate debilitating, overwhelming doubt. But she also saw them overcome that debilitation and doubt in their actions. She might have read her fellow con-gregant Anne Bradstreet's verses describing bodily infirmity and its spiritual value. But she likely also saw Bradstreet insisting to her children that they should never show off weakness and ugliness outside of her household's perimeter. She might have heard John Winthrop, whom she knew from Sunday meetings in Boston, hold forth about the power of fellow feeling in times of vulnerability and weakness, about the need to be like the Samari-tan neighbor and offer charity, even to the enemy. But she also might have witnessed the legal acrobatics he tried to develop in order to exclude some flesh-and-blood neighbors from that category and thereby find license to "deceive, beat, and otherwise damnify," as he would put it in 1643, "and not sin." She might have been present at John Underhill's very sophisticated and compelling public confession of shame, regret, and imperfection after being censured for trying to seduce their mutual neighbor, Jane Holmes. But she also witnessed his furious conviction that the imagined lustfulness of their Pequot neighbors justified his genocidal violence toward them. It was only three months after the violence he visited on the Pequots at Mystic, what he proudly called his "fury," that she had first decided her children might be safer in hell than in a world where her future famous neighbors claimed so tenaciously that they could never be certain of their chosenness yet where they also frequently acted as if they were. They seemed so certain that they strove to recruit others into a system of truth where cursedness was always an option. "Cursedness" could mean anything from finding oneself the object of enthusiastic exterminating violence to, less dramatically, not feeling the peace and confidence that everyone else claimed you would naturally, normally, eventually feel, even after more than ten years of unsuccessful trying. Friendship with these people required her not to think hard about her suspicions of cursedness. Day in, day out, as spring turned to summer, autumn to winter, as the sun rose earlier and earlier, then later again each morning, these friends offered her their optimism, their sincere, smiling comforts. Over time, however, Hett began to suspect that ignoring the likelihood of her cursedness and acting like the people who surrounded her, though it bought her companionship, also unwittingly told a lie about her spiritual status. These risks of insincerity grew as each day passed and she still felt sad.[10]

Modern readers don't need to befriend Hett. But her actions invite us to consider more thoughtfully whose perspective we are taking up—and whose we are neglecting—when we take any individual's claims to sincerity as authoritative. Historical narration, warns Allen Feldman, thinking of a different Protestant colonial context, can often find itself "collaborat[ing]" in the myths that rationalize violence when it overlooks the diffuse, subtle, and often thoughtless ways that power circulates. His word "collaborate" may frighten readers, putting them on their guard. Readers accustomed to easy access out of the realm of the political, skilled at "forgetting [and] repressing the political altogether," may find themselves disturbed by the possibility of such thoughtless collaboration. Such readers may protest by pointing to their own good intentions, what they claim to know about their own motivations and desires. This is sincerity's powerful legacy. It promises confidence that one's desires can thoroughly, consciously be known. It promises that those desires can extricate themselves from the historical tangle of forces that generate them, from the strategies that shape them, and from the material practices that inflect their execution and reception. Like eternal life, sincerity's promises are also a threat. Deracinated thus, intentions can appear to be the full, morally damning responsibility of the individual who claims them. Readers who wrestle with the fright of colonial collaboration may benefit from recognizing that this desire to escape personally from historical entanglement has an important precedent. Protestant settlers in Algonquian lands, on the banks and shoals of the world England knew, longed dearly to shuffle off such ties. Their strategies for doing so were very successful. Several decades of literary historians have helped; they, too, probably had good intentions. But forgetting sincerity's history—the history of those intentions—has meant repressing the heavy historical work sincerity required. Here, specifically, desires for sincerity, for a stable Manichean world, foreclosed recognition of how well the ideal of self-knowledge complemented a way of life that has been harmful in the long and not-so-long run—an "apocalypse," as Gerald Horne has named it. Settler colonialism, of course, isn't reducible to sincerity and

10. Dunn, Savage, and Yeandle, eds., *Journal of John Winthrop*, 264, 319, 448 ("deceive"); Joseph R. McElrath, Jr., and Allan P. Robb, eds., *The Complete Works of Anne Bradstreet* (Boston, 1981), 177–179; John Winthrop, "A Modell of Christian Charity," in *Winthrop Papers*, II, 1623–1630 (Cambridge, Mass., 1931), 282–295; Michael McGiffert, ed., *God's Plot: Puritan Spirituality in Thomas Shepard's Cambridge*, 2d ed. (Amherst, Mass., 1994), 172–177; John Underhill, *Newes from America; or, A New and Experimentall Discoverie of New England . . .* (London, 1638).

its illusion of triumph. But Eve Tuck and K. Wayne Yang, in their fascination with what they call settler colonial "innocence," have noticed that sincerity is a key instrument in making an individual's participation in harm recede from sight and significance. One consequence of this innocence is an impoverished understanding of life under colonial power and the various experimental responses by settler colonialism's early critics to that power's subtlety. That power included not simply proscriptions and suppressions but positive rules and norms. Both the negative and the productive aspects of colonial power expressed settlers' desires to include as many people as possible in the narrow vision of happiness they thought would vindicate their efforts. Some individuals responded to these rules with principled resistance and refusal. But often, responses consisted of attempts to feel less constricted and circumscribed, to minimize the costs of the good life. For Hett, this meant renouncing hopes for the good life itself.[11]

In their explicit, intense commitment to a fantasy of the good life, these settlers offer a glimpse into the mechanics of broader strategies of collective flourishing and the psychic disturbances to which those strategies responded. As they tried to secure a firm and quiet place to live, the English colonies in Algonquian territory during the seventeenth century were not unique; they did not invent a disposition that would be exported through time or across space. Zealous Protestants weren't the only ones trying to shuffle away. They were not exceptional relative to other English colonies, within or beyond the territorial limits of the United States that often draws them into the choreography of a mythic and redemptive origin story. Nor are they exceptional relative to European colonies around the globe. There were many frontiers, many strange, high-stakes, uncomfortable, violent encounters between Indigenous peoples and restless Christians who wanted to be good and who acted in harmful ways. Most agents of colonization, a practice that continues to perplex some of its eminent modern theorists, encountered epistemological disturbances, especially in the early decades of European empire's expansion, whether these colonial agents were the staying kind or not. Many of these agents were good at forgetting to write down any such disturbances, though; many were good at ignoring them, too. Useful in the project of ignoring them

11. Allen Feldman, *Formations of Violence: The Narrative of the Body and Terror in Northern Ireland* (Chicago, 1991), 2; Frederic Jameson, "Foreword," in Robert Fernández Retamar, *Caliban and Other Essays* (Minneapolis, 1989), vii ("forgetting"); Gerald Horne, *The Apocalypse of Settler Colonialism: The Roots of Slavery, White Supremacy and Capitalism in Seventeenth-Century North America and the Caribbean* (New York, 2018); Eve Tuck and K. Wayne Yang, "Decolonization Is Not a Metaphor," *Decolonization: Indigeneity, Education, Society,* I (2012), 1–40.

were the stories that these Christians told themselves. They knew, sincerely, that they desired goodness—usually moral, sometimes scientific, sometimes frankly nationalistic. Occasionally in the documentary archive appeared rival ideas of goodness. The English seventeenth century could famously claim a Roger Williams or a Thomas Morton. Other nations had theirs, too. In his 1546 *Confesionario,* a guide for fellow clergy on administering or suspending the deity's forgiveness among mortals, Bartolomé de Las Casas insisted, with significantly more force than almost any English writer, that with regard to colonization, claims to sincerity were often a sham. There was "no Spaniard in the Indies who may have acted in good faith" regarding the enslavement of the Indigenous population. There was "no one in the Indies who is invincibly ignorant." No Spanish person in the Western Hemisphere, he insisted, deserved a peaceful and quiet soul unless they began restitution for their violence. But in their attempts to preserve moral disturbance, these critics' rhetoric eventually found itself conscripted for mollifying effects, evidence of a nascent humanism that would allow these colonists' inheritors to believe optimistically that their ancestors, considered as a whole, had not accustomed themselves to "intellectually backward" and "unimaginative" mental habits and that, even though they tried to abandon it, they did not hail from a "depressed land."[12]

Optimists, Hett knew, are often miserable comforts. What makes them bad at comfort also makes them politically volatile, even violent: a disinclination to consider the entanglement between their desires for themselves and the historical circumstances that made those desires inimical, or at least "obstacles," as one celebrated critic has put it, "to your flourishing." The archive of these zealous, earnest settlers, of their eagerness to claim that those obstacles could be overcome is, with some distance, a symptom of disturbance that besieges the confidence of every document that Europeans produced in support of colonial endeavors. The many, many early modern arguments rationalizing colonial settlement suggest that European souls were not peaceful and quiet regarding the globe-transforming actions they undertook. Disquiet need not mean knowledge of guilt. It simply points to a disturbance that language can heighten or hide. Settler colonial ventures, the various hopes of living happily on other peoples' land, escalated the stakes of disturbance, but they

<hr>

12. On the continued challenges of defining a "colony," see David Thomas Orique, ed. and trans., *To Heaven or to Hell: Bartolomé de Las Casas's "Confesionario,"* Latin American Originals, no. 13 (University Park, Pa., 2018), 58 ("good faith"), 78 ("invincibly ignorant"); Cedric J. Robinson, *Black Marxism: The Making of the Black Radical Tradition* (Chapel Hill, N.C., 2000), 13 ("backward," "unimaginative," "depressed"); Ann Laura Stoler, *Duress: Imperial Durabilities in Our Times* (Durham, N.C., 2016).

didn't invent it. These pious settler colonies, rather, comprise a convenient window, opened wide, into the psychic life of Christian empire, an ideology disquieted by otherness and by the unhappy implications regarding the self that these encounters provoked. They show how dearly these restless people clung to the fantasy that their pursuits were not making their problems worse. This clinging isn't what's "cruel" about their optimism—or, at least, it's not the only thing that's cruel. Settlers learned to tell themselves stories about the reality and singularity of their attachments, came to believe the sincerity of those loves and desires. Those stories, first, made them eager to understand themselves as objects of cruelty without considering the consequences of those convictions for others, as Jodi Byrd has pointed out. Those consequences weren't simply indirect, the result of larger, always impersonal structures. Second, settlers' attachments to their stories about themselves drew them to directly and explicitly exercise cruelty toward others—what one early chronicler called, with uneasy triumph, "extremity." These sincere English people in Algonquian territory offer a valuable story about the quiet ascent of the dream of self-knowledge, about the loosening of multivalent obligations. Their lives, here and there, can show off the costs of making that self-knowledge the foundation for a good life that, they imagined with great and often harmful confidence, they wanted to share with you.[13]

It would be a stretch to say that no one was harmed in Hett's attempt to critique sincerity more concisely than I have. But no one died, at least. Not even Hett's soul. Her nameless infant lived. After her first attempt on its life, in 1637, some neighbors, "stepping presently forth, saved the child." And Hett eventually found spiritual recognition that mattered to her. On August 7, 1642, she was excommunicated from the visible church. But maybe the hard labor and spare diet had the intended effects. Or maybe the loneliness of being kicked out of the church was too great. Or maybe she finally got lucky, spiritually speaking. There were probably multiple conditions that changed her heart and mind. Whether Hett chose one story and presented it to herself as the true and singular cause for her transformation is not something we will ever know. A little over a year later, on July 23, 1643, she made a "pub-like poenitentiall acknowledgement" of her offenses against her society and was "restored againe to the Fellowship of the Church." Ten years later, she

13. Lauren Berlant, *Cruel Optimism* (Durham, N.C., 2011), 1 ("obstacles"); see also Jodi A. Byrd, *The Transit of Empire: Indigenous Critiques of Colonialism* (Minneapolis, 2011), 34–38; Ana Schwartz, "'Mercy as Well as Extremity': Forts, Fences, and Fellow Feeling in New England Settlement," *EAL*, LIV (2019), 343–379.

found a congregation more congenial to her intimacy with pessimism. She petitioned for "letters of Dismission" that would allow her to join the church at Malden, where the English settlements' most aggressively self-conscious theorist of repression had recently taken up post as minister. Her petition succeeded. Maybe his sensitivity would take her pessimism seriously. And maybe, in conversation with that minister, she eventually found a way to feel normal. This prospect may bring comfort to readers who feel a glimmer of recognition in reading about Hett's despair. But it may not. And maybe she never found happiness anyway. Maybe she just got better at pretending, at faking sincerity without any great hope of making it—but at least faking it in a less taxing fashion. She might not have ever succeeded in ignoring that, even as her friends and neighbors were knitting for themselves what they thought were tighter, happier social bonds, they were unwittingly fabricating what Lionel Trilling, in his assessment of authentic modernity, would call an "alienated social reality." Hett seems to have learned ways to make that reality's inconveniences tolerable. She learned what she could and could not sacrifice, and she learned, listening in the pews as if in an empty theater, how she would reason with her teachers and their sermons as a skeptical student. She would continue to attend her world's weddings and funerals and fasting days, having started, she thought, a new life elsewhere—yet looking forward to the day where she could sigh with relief that it was finished.[14]

14. Dunn, Savage, and Yeandle, eds., *Journal of John Winthrop*, 230 ("stepping"), 231, 391; Pierce, ed., *Records of the First Church*, 39 ("publike"), 54 ("letters"); Lionel Trilling, *Sincerity and Authenticity* (Cambridge, Mass., 1972), 171.

Index

Church: meetings, 2, 125, 129, 159, 190, 254; membership, 47, 159–160, 194–196. *See also individual churches and clergy*

Cliché, 30–31, 92, 174, 177, 182

Clocks, 92–93, 242

Close reading, 51, 67–68, 108, 251

Clothing, 81–82, 122–123, 189, 212

Coercion, 19, 37, 47, 92, 95, 161, 191, 193–194, 197–198, 218

Cogawesco (sagamore), 72

Collaboration, 14, 78, 80, *107*, 255

Collateral, 212

Colonization, 4, 16–12, 22, 44, 59, 66–67, 82, 92–93 n. 11, 95, 114, 172, 184–185, 193 n. 42, 200, 256–258. *See also* Settler colonialism

Common sense, 3, 40

Companionship: as object of desire, 127–128, 136–138, 140, 143, 195–196; sudden loss of, 148–152, 206–208, 237–239; unexpected, 213; abjured, 214; singular, 224, 228–230; dissatisfying, 239, 241, 254–255. *See also* Friendship

Competence, 91, 172

Conbitant (sachem), 117–118

Confession: as conventional genre for sincerity, 5–7, 27; analytical limits of, 19; as technique of revision, 27; as vehicle for shame, 47–48, 126–131, 133, 144–158; as reconnaissance strategy, 226; inarticulate skepticism toward, 254–258

Confidence: elusiveness of, 15–16, 84, 244–258; in psychic essence of settlement, 18–19, 20, 44–45; slow achievement of, 30, 154; hubristic, 30–33, 165, 253–254; regarding sources of harm, 53–79; regarding intentions, 123, 174; social erosion of, 189–190; and value of second-guessing, 199–201. *See also* Certainty

Consent, 41, 65, 143, 145, 167–169, 208, 237

Contact zones, 25

Contract, 94, 174; social, 63. *See also* Covenant

Conventions: as intellectual obstacle, 2, 19, 76, 114, 148, 188; as criteria for evaluation, 27; as passport to social participation, 38, 46, 129–134, 142, 147, 150–156, 202; literary, 56, 146, 154, 157, 177, 198; political caricature of, 63, 114; diplomatic, 73, 75; as symptom of political priorities, 90–95, 121, 173, 191

Conversion, 45, 123, 126, 133, 148, 149–151, 154–157, 159, 166 n. 6, 183, 192, 218; morphology of, 27, 250. *See also* Narrative: conversion

Corn, 72–73, 78, 101

Cotton, John, 19, 22, 33, 42–43, 197–198, 217–218, 238–240; *Spiritual Milk for Boston Babes*, 173, 177–178, 188

Coulthard, Glen Sean, 199–200

Covenant, 93, 174. *See also* Halfway Covenant

Craving, 8, 19, 174–176, 193–194, 217, 252

Creativity, 5, 25–26, 81, 120, 137, 146

Credit, 71, 171–179, 191, 199, 208, 238. *See also* Debt

Cruelty, 35, 59, 62, 66, 118, 145, 180–185, 187–188, 200, 233, 244, 257–258

Crusades, 140

Cunning, 41–43, 123

Curiosity, 8, 76–77, 246. *See also* Science

Cursedness, 130, 208, 250–255

Cushman, Robert, 151–152

Damnation, 165–169, 174, 178, 199, 243, 251–255. *See also* Hell

Dams. *See* Beavers; Hydroengineering

Data, 7, 17, 54–55, 190, 249. *See also* Evidence

Davenport, John, 1, 8–21, 26, 31–39, 45, 194–196, 245

Death: spiritual, 27, 130, 133, 163–167, 221, 258; and legal penalty, 63–65, 73–74, 223; heightened risk of, on colonial frontier, 68; fantasies of, 101; as consequence of epidemic, 120, 148–151; as catalyst for mourning, 148–151, 213, 237–238, 240; as

Death (*continued*)
  factor in evangelizing discipline, 155, 174,
  191; echoes of, in sleep, 208, 221, 240
Debt, 34, 71, 76, 122, 160–161, 169–172,
  176–180, 190–191, 193, 199, 209–211, 214,
  241. *See also* Credit
Deer Island, 184, 189, 225–226
Demographics, 8, 42, 119
Dent, Arthur, 130
Dependence, 45, 66, 84, 91, 96, 121, 131,
  172–175, 178, 210, 240–241
Deracination, 4, 24, 41, 97, 190, 192,
  200, 203–204, 238, 244, 255. *See also*
  Alienation
Descartes, René, 87–88, 95
Desire: as object of manipulation, 6, 10, 21,
  30, 38–41, 152, 193, 224; for knowledge, 8,
  76–77, 79; terrifying volatility of, 14–16,
  244; as proper to settler colonization,
  18–20, 245; epistemological ambiguity
  of, 21–22, 80–81, 84, 106–111, 147–158;
  for goodness, 33, 50–79, 86, 189–190,
  249–250, 255–257; for amnesia, 41, 199;
  for recognition, 47, 169–170, 184; for
  self-preservation, 55, 66; for revenge, 59,
  64, 72; for material gain, 61–62, 97–102,
  122; to punish, 78; bodily expression
  of, 87, 128–138, 141–142; forcefulness
  of, 89, 181, 256; as fantasized subjection to reason, 91–95, 128–138; for safe,
  affirmative companionship, 128, 137–138,
  215–222, 229–230, 239; domestic, 141, 145;
  to show off knowledge, 141, 153–156, 165;
  to consume the humiliation of others,
  142, 212; to be sheltered from humiliating exposure, 142–145, 155–156; to write
  poems, 143–144; to answer oppressive
  debt, 161–189; for parenthood, 174,
  194–195; to redeem unhappy suffering,
  191, 242. *See also* Craving
Despair, 97, 168, 247–259
Detail, 50–52, 67, 69, 110, 117, 137, 151, 155, 165,
  227, 234–237
Didelphiae. *See* Opossum
Dignity, 32, 150

Diplomacy, 48, 113, 121, 149–152
Discipline, 9, 11, 13, 25, 34, 36, 42, 45, 62,
  72–73, 78, 86, 92, 129, 152–153, 173–174,
  192, 222, 224, 241, 244
Diseases, 8, 109–110, 119, 131–132, 137, 148,
  197. *See also* Epidemics
Disenchantment, 93
Disgust, 139–142, 149, 154, 156
Dissatisfaction: with performances of truth,
  1–2, 5–6, 22, 45, 127; with repression's
  affordances, 34–37; with material
  circumstances, 60; with offspring, 170;
  with the process of intergenerational
  conscription, 182–189; with friends,
  205–214, 239–242; murderous, 247–258
Domesticity, 27–28, 127, 140–143, 145–146, 152
Dorcas (Boston congregant), 47, 159–163,
  170, 178, 190–200, 203–204, 241, 245
Dorchester (Mass.), 159–161, 179–180, 190,
  194–196, 203
Doubt, 41, 45, 48, 71, 120, 160, 231–233,
  243–244, 254. *See also* Certainty
Downing, Emmanuel, 193–194
Drake, Sir Francis, 57–62, 65, 77, 217
Drayton, Michael, 99
Dreams, 42, 108, 109–110, 131–133, 165, 229
Drowning: metaphorical, 133, 253; literal,
  234–236
Drunkenness, 252
DuBois, W. E. B., 25
Dudley, Thomas, 143, 146, 251
Due process, 63–64, 188
Duty. *See* Obligation

Early modernity: epistemological conditions of, 2–8, 25–26, 32, 43–44, 53, 56,
  129, 162; global ambitions during, 13–14,
  20–21, 57–58, 257; economic imagination
  in, 35, 88–94, 161, 168, 171; technology
  of, 56, 92, 98; and ideas of universality,
  61–62, 76, 105; scientific ideas of the
  body during, 84–87, 131–134; intimacy
  in, 138–139, 202, 206, 225, 230, 238; pious
  feelings in, 170, 181; Atlantic slavery in,
  203–204; self-fashioning during, 244

Lex talionis, 65

Liberalism, 41, 64, 123, 242

Lies, 22, 33, 65, 79, 248, 254. *See also* Honesty

Literary history. *See* Literary studies

Literary studies, 3–5, 35, 48, 54–55, 88, 95,
108 n. 27, 138, 140, 145–146, 196, 202–203,
206, 255

Locke, John, 92–93

Loins. *See* Genitals

Loneliness, 10, 41, 48, 126, 148, 166, 203,
207–208, 218, 236, 239, 258

Lopenzina, Drew, 40, 200

Lot's wife, 105–106. *See also* Emblems;
Sodom

Love: terrifying impermanence of, 15–16, 31,
33, 126, 199, 239, 243, 246, 258; of material
world, 61, 185; diplomatic professions
of, 70; exclusivity of, 124; desire to be
an object of, 128, 138, 149–158, 210, 241;
proof of, 237

Low Countries, 98, 120

Lukács, Georg, 4

Lynch mob, 188–189

Lyric, 145–146, 169

Machines, 9, 13, 62, 92–93

Madras, 1

Maio (Portuguese colony), 58

Malady, 128–131. *See also* Illness

Malden (Mass.), 38, 46, 128, 132, 259

Manamoick (sachem), 73–75

Manichean opposition, 9, 67–68, 255

Manomet (village), 73–74

Manumission, 159–160, 178, 192–193, 195. *See
also* Freedom

Marblehead, 187–188, 205, 209, 236–240

Ma-re Mount, 44, 57, 62, 64, 118

Martha's Vineyard. *See* Noepe

Marx, Karl, 41

Marxism, 55

Massachusetts (people), 45, 50, 60–61,
63–65, 70–72, 80, 83, 101–102, 113, 118–121,
216

Massachusetts Court of Assistants, 251–252

Massachusetts General Court, 217, 236

Master Bubble, 114–117

Mather, Cotton, 175

Mather, Increase, 47, 159–160, 162, 163,
171, 174–177, 179–180, 186, 188–190, 196,
198–199, 211, 231, 234–237, 253; *David
Serving His Generation,* 179; *A Brief
History of the Warr,* 188, 211; *A Call from
Heaven,* 199; as Ter [Per] Amicam, 207;
*An Essay for the Recording of Illustrious
Providences,* 234–236

Mather, Richard, 33, 169, 178–180, 194, 198; *A
Farewel Exhortation,* 170, 173–174, 178, 191

Matoonus (sachem), 228–233, 232

Mauss, Marcel, 161

Maverick, John (father of Samuel), 194, 239

Maverick, Samuel (son of John), 193–194

Mayhew, Thomas, 149, 166

Maypole, 62

Melancholy, 141, 247. *See also* Unhappiness

Melville, Herman, 95, 251

Memory: unverifiable contents of, 29;
unhappy contents of, 36, 133–134, 155,
169, 180, 205–209; of earlier colonial
contact, 59; sartorial preservation of,
81, 123, 139; of extinct megafauna, *104,*
105; strategic exercise of, 190–201, 230,
255–256; dissatisfaction with, 206–214,
234–242. *See also* Forgetting

Menimesit (settlement), 225–228, 233

Merchants, 96, 121–122

Mercy, 91, 118, 166, 184

Metaphor, 93–95, 131, 133–134, 198, 253. *See
also* Emblems

Mexico City, 98

Miantonomo (sachem), 216

Middle ground, 12, 26, 81–82

Mi'kmaqs, 102

Miller, Perry, 163, 169, 187

Mimicry, 27, 70, 102

Ministerial networks, 130–131, 157–158, 171,
207, 211, 235–240

Miracle, 234–236

Misery, 41, 58, 68, 131, 137, 150, 238, 250–251,
253, 257

Mitchell, Jonathan, 135–137, 178

Revenge, 58–59, 72–73, 187–188

Revision, 48, 143, 145, 151, 200–201

Reyner, Mary, 133

Rhyme, 55, 140, 146, 163–165, 248

Richardson, James, 183

Rome, 144

Roules, Robert, 187

Rowlandson, Joseph, 201–210, 212

Rowlandson, Mary, 15, 48, 185–187, 205–216, 222–227, 230, 234, 240

Rowlandson, Sarah (daughter of Mary), 213

Rowley (Mass.), 134, 212

Rubin, Gayle, 139

Rudeness, 125, 155–156. *See also* Insult

Ruth (biblical figure), 237

Sadism, 166

Sadness. *See* Unhappiness

Sainthood, 162, 186–188, 253

Salisbury (Mass.), 212

Saltonstall, Nathaniel, 182, 188–189, 211, 251

Santiago (Portuguese colony), 58

Satan, 130, 220–221, 247

Satisfaction, 2, 11, 18–19, 32–33, 43, 45, 49, 61, 64, 66, 72, 99, 136, 165, 171, 200, 241, 248. *See also* Pleasure

Savageau, Cheryl, 105–111

Schadenfreude, 66, 165

Science, 5–8, 27, 29, 87, 131, 140, 247; of the soul, 7, 27–29, 32, 36–37, 149, 157, 197, 246; fiction, 164

Screw (fastener), 11

Second Church (Boston), 159, 196

Seduction, 154, 254

Self, buffered, 31, 81, 87, 219–223, 242

Self-disclosure, 5–7, 9, 13, 27, 36, 45–49, 146–147, 160, 164, 214, 244

Self-disgust. *See* Self-loathing

Self-fashioning, 58, 123, 243–244

Self-interest, 62–66, 106

Self-knowledge: as socially mandatory, 5–10, 47, 160, 163, 245, 249, 255; desire for, 14–16, 248, 258; pursuit of, through language, 25–30; in service of repression, 38–41; difficulty of search for, 46, 79, 84,

166, 199; as unhappy norm, 48; frankness in, 129–137, 211

Self-loathing, 127–131, 149, 154, 156

Self-management, 9, 13, 38–39, 68, 94, 224, 243–245, 248

Self-opacity, 20, 26, 30, 83, 160, 172

Seneca (philosopher), 15

Sentimentalism, 88, 208

Separatists, 54–57, 60, 62, 73–75, 77 n. 32, 97, 117–118, 171

Sermons, 7, 39, 47–48, 88, 91–93, 131, 137, 170–181, 188, 190, 196–200, 207, 256

"Set on work" (phrase), 92

Settler colonialism, 6, 16–23, 26, 41–42, 127, 255–256

Sexuality, 10, 70 n. 22, 134–135, 150–152

Sexualized vocabulary, 31, 197–198

Shakespeare, William, 63

Shame, 113, 125–133, 139, 142–143, 147–158, 182, 254

Shepard, Thomas, 33, 39, 130–131, 154, 156

Shipmate, 203–204

Shipwreck, 48, 93, 234–239

Sill, Joanna, 130

Sill, John, 130

Singing, 230

Skepticism, 12, 36, 61, 231, 253, 259

Slavery, 16, 19, 23–24, 58–59, 95, 159–160, 192–196, 203–204, 210; metaphorical, 85, 178

Slave trade, 1, 59, 194, 203–204, 218

Sleep, 27–28, 131–132, 134–135, 205, 208, 214, 221, 223, 220–230, 234, 239, 242. *See also* Sleeplessness

Sleeplessness, 206, 208–209, 214, 222

Slime, 133

Smallpox, 148

Social contract, 63

Sodom, 150–151

Solidarity, 93–94

Solomon (biblical figure), 198–199, 210, 240

Sources, primary, 98, 165, 167, 221, 235

South Church. *See* Third Church (Boston)

Sovereignty and Goodness of God, The. See Rowlandson, Mary

Wetness, 94, 98, 120, 134, 138–139

Weymouth. *See* Wessagusset

Wheeler, Thomas, Jr., 188

Wheeler, Thomas, Sr., 188

Whitcomb, James, 210–211, 240

White, Richard, 12, 26, 81–82

Whitehead, Neil L., 67–69

Whiteness, 37, 142–144, 188, 193–195, 226

Whitman, Walt, 128

Wigglesworth, Michael: sleeplessness of, 27–28, 221; as theorist of repression, 38–40, 46–47, 245, 259; diary of, 38–39, 128–138; *The Day of Doom*, 39, 47, 162–170, 173, 253; post-college awkwardness of, 127–139, 217, 251; "In Solitude Good Company" ("Meat out of the Eater"), 137–138; as evasive confessor, 146–150, 153, 159; as theorist of obligation, 173–174, 177–179, 192, 197–198, 253

William, Tuckup, 223–224, 227–228

Williams, Roger, 26, 123, 166, 205, 214–224, 228–230, 241, 257; *A Key into the Language of America*, 81–82, 214–216, 219–223

Willows, George, 130

Winslow, Edward, 26, 73–77, 117–118, 122

Winter, 34, 134, 212–213, 217, 226; wintering, 119, 213, 217

Winthrop, John: *Journal*, 24, 62, 96–97, 101, 121, 154, 159, 194, 235–236, 239, 247–255, 258–259; as confident soul scientist, 33, 45, 245–251, 254; as theorist of property, 55; liaising with Chickatawbut, 81, 83–86, 111, 120–123; "A Modell of Christian Charity," 84–85, 88–95, 101, 121, 126, 219, 254; as theorist of class relations, 89–97, 101, 113, 131, 137; failures of, as theorist of intersubjectivity, 126; as connoisseur of sincerity, 154, 159; as correspondent with Williams, 216, 219–220, 228; as narrator of 1635 hurricane, 235–237, 239

Winthrop, Margaret, 246

Winthrop fleet, 62. *See also Arbella* (ship)

Witchcraft, 16, 24, 33

Wituwamat *(pniese)*, 118

Woburn (Mass.), 183, 188

Wolfe, Patrick, 18–19

Wollaston, Richard, 57

Wonder, 64, 101

Wonohaquaham (sachem), 101

Wood, William, 98–99, 102

Wuttinnaumatuk (Algonquian convert), 46, 125–127, 155

Wynter, Sylvia, 96

Yale University, 1

Zuider Zee, 120